Mysticism and Dissent

Mysticism and Dissent

*Religious Ideology and Social Protest
in the Sixteenth Century*

by Steven E. Ozment

New Haven and London, Yale University Press

1973

Designed by John O. C. McCrillis
and set in Baskerville type.
Printed in the United States of America by
The Colonial Press Inc., Clinton, Massachusetts.

Published in Great Britain, Europe, and Africa by
Yale University Press, Ltd., London.
Distributed in Canada by McGill-Queen's University
Press, Montreal; in Latin America by Kaiman & Polon,
Inc., New York City; in India by UBS Publishers'
Distributors Pvt., Ltd., Delhi; in Japan by John
Weatherhill, Inc., Tokyo.

To my wife
Elinor
and our children
Joel, Matthew, and Katherine

Contents

Preface

The subjects of this book are master theoreticians of dissent in the sixteenth century. They authored angry exposés of and idealistic alternatives to the religious establishments of Rome, Wittenberg, Zurich, and Geneva. Each had his own personal history of alienation within the particular system he came finally to oppose. Some even began as respected coworkers of the great reformers, the successful revolutionaries, as Müntzer with Luther and Castellio with Calvin. All were convinced in the end that the princes and priests of Christendom, even reformed Christendom, "serve only their bellies" and that the faith of their fathers had estranged men from their very souls. And all fell victim to their dissent: if not forced to face the sword or prison, which take the body, they were driven to exile, flight, or silence, which rack the mind.

Subsequent history has been kinder to them than their contemporaries were. Indeed, today they are praised as the truly modern men of a still medieval age, defenders of those truths most men would now hold to be self-evident. Marxist historians and theorists, especially, continue to embrace Thomas Müntzer as the first modern revolutionary. Although he cannot approximate the originality of Müntzer, Hans Hut has received high marks as his prudent "propagandist" within the circles of South German and Austrian Anabaptism. Hans Denck has long been considered the first to systematize that forward-looking "spiritual religion" which consolidates humanistic values and conceptions of man's nature and destiny. More than one authority has pronounced Sebastian Franck as on the whole the most advanced thinker in the sixteenth century. Not only liberal Protestants in the seventeenth century, but also the advocates of reason and tolerance in the Age of Enlightenment, counted Sebastian Castellio an ally. And when the origins of German Idealism are sought, the trail usually leads in the end to Valentin Weigel.

So modern—and yet so medieval. If one looks closely in historical context at the sources and logic of their arguments, one sees these "moderns" not only on the threshold of a brave new world, but under the Gothic arch of late medieval mysticism. Their key ideas and most trusted authorities are more often than not to be found within the mystical traditions of the late Middle Ages. And therein lies the origin of this book. Why do those who are considered so modern read mystical writings with such profit? Why do those specifically engaged in protest take up a literature so closely associated with retreat and meditation? Is there a natural alliance between the values of mystical experience and the concerns of those who feel estranged and persecuted? Is a mystical view of the world uniquely correlated, philosophically and historically, with dissent in the sixteenth century?

These are the larger questions that will preoccupy me in the pages ahead. Methodologically, I will take precautions to avoid falling into that quagmire of speculation and generality so often associated with the topic of mysticism. First, with an eye to the possibilities for dissent, I will permit four late medieval masters (Bonaventure, Meister Eckhart, Johannes Tauler, and Jean Gerson) to define mystical theology (chapter 1). Then I will examine the actual use of a major mystical writing common to sixteenth-century dissenters: the *Theologia Deutsch* (chapter 2). Given the historical orientation of these investigations, I will then proceed in individual intellectual biographies to study the development of dissent and the appropriation of mystical concepts at crucial points in the careers of our six magisterial dissenters.

Contemporary research in sixteenth-century dissent has spent much energy classifying nonconformists. The popular and authoritative typology of George H. Williams, for example, distinguishes, with intricate subdivisions, three major groups: Anabaptists, Spiritualists, and Rationalists. The recent German anthology of Heinold Fast concurs (although Fast adopts the description "Schwärmer" for those Williams would call "Revolutionary Spiritualists" and prefers the category "Antitrinitarians" to "Rationalists"). The present study does not aspire to be an exercise in typology. Happily, however, representatives of each of these major groups are among its major figures—only here they are considered in terms of their common adoption of mystical writings in protest against established Christendom. From this vantage point, the unity of dissent in the sixteenth century has been much more impressive than its argued variety.

In that period, as in every age of massive change, the powerful preyed upon the powerless. Rising prices, altered legal systems, shifting political alliances, and new centers of wealth upset the established social patterns, both high and low. Gerald Strauss's recent edition of documents illustrative of discontent in Germany on the eve of the Reformation gives rich and varied testimony to this. Although I have listened to the voices of protest and lamentation, a chronicle of social grievances is not the major purpose of the present study. The legitimacy of dissent in the sixteenth century is clear. I will seek to gauge its countervailing ideology, its reasoned response to a repressive Christendom.

This necessitates spending some time with theological arguments—and that necessitates a caveat. In many circles intellectual history is not in good repute. This unpopularity can be a special handicap for the Reformation historian, who must deal with ideas that are often very different from our own. In the sixteenth century, as perhaps in no other, religious ideology shaped history. After the "causes" and conditions of the Reformation have been recited, the important fact remains that the reformers to a man were theologians and their movements religious. Regardless of the underlying motives of those who embraced them, theological arguments and religious ideas had the force of law and, as such, remade the map of Europe in the sixteenth century.

Historians are not immune to the temptation to impose modern values and concerns upon the past. Like those tourists abroad who take snapshots of the great historical monuments and repair to hotels and restaurants that speak their language, historians can fail to meet the past on its own terms, mingling with the people and listening to their ideas and beliefs. That history which views men as only thinking minds and immortal souls without bodies and involvement in time must be protested. But that history which preys upon the past with grand "scientific" models and typologies, summarizing whole centuries with a handful of statistics, must also be reminded of its overweening modern bias. To challenge a popular maxim, the supreme object of the historian is not to measure and master the world but to understand it. When the task of the intellectual historian is surrendered, there is reason to fear that an objective understanding of the past, especially the premodern past, is threatened.

This study of course owes much to many. A Morse Fellowship from Yale University made possible a year of uninterrupted writing. Generous assistance was extended by the librarians of Yale,

Harvard, and the Hartford Seminary Foundation. George H. Vrooman, humanities bibliographer in Yale's Sterling Library, was particularly helpful in obtaining key primary and secondary sources. The patient ear of Roland H. Bainton permitted the testing of more than one wobbly idea. The official and personal support of my departmental chairmen, Howard R. Lamar and Julian N. Hartt, was encouraging. In this, as in all my work, I remain mindful of the skills imparted by my teacher, Heiko A. Oberman. And the book will put fewer readers to sleep because my colleague, R. Laurence Moore, has made me ashamed willfully to write an inelegant sentence. Finally, my wife and children, long since accustomed to the *rabies scholasticorum,* maintained their usual high level of tolerance and understanding.

S.E.O.

Branford, Connecticut
July, 1972

List of Abbreviations

AGPh	*Archiv für Geschichte der Philosophie*
ARG	*Archiv für Reformationsgeschichte*
HThR	*Harvard Theological Review*
LW	*Luther's Works*
MQR	*Mennonite Quarterly Review*
WA	*D. Martin Luthers Werke: Kritische Gesamtausgabe*
ZbKG	*Zeitschrift für bayerische Kirchengeschichte*
ZKG	*Zeitschrift für Kirchengeschichte*
ZRGG	*Zeitschrift für Religions- und Geistesgeschichte*
ZThK	*Zeitschrift für Theologie und Kirche*

1

Introduction: Mystical Theology
as a Dissent Ideology

It was surely no accident that magisterial dissenters in the sixteenth century were intimately conversant with medieval mystical writings. These writings would furnish refuge and weaponry to nonconformists in any age. Whether in the form of mystical theologies (i.e. theoretical treatments of the values and methods of mystical experience) or as the personal confessions and sermons of practiced mystics,[1] they set forth what can fairly be called the latent revolutionary possibilities of the Christian religion. For whether the product of a great orthodox churchman like St. Bonaventure or of a brilliant alleged heretic like Meister Eckhart, medieval mysticism was a refined challenge, always in theory if not in daily practice, to the regular, normative way of religious salvation. It fed

1. On this distinction between mystical theology and practiced mysticism, cf. Walter Dress, *Die Theologie Gersons: Eine Untersuchung zur Verbindung von Nominalismus und Mystik im Spätmittelalter* (Gütersloh, 1931), p. 49; Conrad Gröber, *Der Mystiker Heinrich Seuse: Die Geschichte seines Lebens* (Freiburg i.B., 1941), pp. 218–19; and H. A. Oberman, "Simul Gemitus et Raptus: Luther und die Mystik," *Kirche, Mystik, Heiligung und das Natürliche bei Luther: Vorträge des III. Internationalen Kongresses für Lutherforschung* (Göttingen, 1968), pp. 21 ff. Mystical literature in the late Middle Ages ranges from the deeply philosophical to the very folksy. A collection assembled to illustrate this variety (distinguishing eight forms of mystical literature) is *Texte aus der Deutschen Mystik des 14. und 15. Jahrhundert,* ed. Adolf Spamer (Jena, 1912). In English we have the two collections by Elmer O'Brien, *Varieties of Mystic Experience* (New York, 1964), and Ray Petry, *Late Medieval Mysticism* (Philadelphia, 1957). Standard treatments which focus on the more philosophical forms of mysticism are Joseph Bernhart, *Die philosophische Mystik des Mittelalters von ihren antiken Ursprüngen bis zur Renaissance* (Munich, 1922) and Martin Grabmann, *Mittelalterliches Geistesleben: Abhandlungen zur Geschichte der Scholastik und Mystik* I–III (Munich, 1926–36). Standard works stressing the practical end of the spectrum are Herbert Grundmann, *Religiöse Bewegungen im Mittelalter* (Darmstadt, 1935; 2d ed., 1961) and J. Leclerq, F. Vandenbroucke, and L. Bouyer, *La spiritualité du Moyen Âge* (Paris, 1961; English: London, 1968). Especially pertinent is Grundmann's "Die geschichtliche Grundlagen der deutschen Mystik" in *Altdeutsche und altniederländische Mystik,* ed. Kurt Ruh (Darmstadt, 1964), 72–99.

on the de facto possibility of the exceptional, on God's freedom to communicate immediately with men, to speak more conclusively in the depths of the individual heart than through all the official writings and ceremonies of even the most holy institution. It offered its successful practitioners a certitude and perfection which a doubting and imperfect world does not even pretend to make possible. Man could, for a moment, become again like Adam before the Fall, or, according to the more ambitious mystical thinkers, he could know that very "godness in God" which he was before his creation.

In late medieval theology a distinction was made between the absolute and the ordained powers of God: the *potentia Dei absoluta* and the *potentia Dei ordinata*. The latter was a catch-phrase for the whole of God's de facto decisions from the Creation to man's redemption. It represented "what is" rather than what theoretically could have been in the history of salvation; in accordance with his "absolute power," God could have chosen otherwise than he in fact did. In the practical terms of medieval religious life and theological debate, however, the *potentia Dei ordinata* was simply the church with her orthodox doctrines and sacraments, which embodied God's "revealed will." And the *potentia Dei absoluta* was that sphere of divine freedom above and beyond this chosen system of salvation. Concretely, the former represented the "establishment"; the latter the permanent possibility of historical novelty.

Mysticism in the late Middle Ages can be called a commonsense science of a presently active *potentia Dei absoluta*.[2] Objectively, its most basic building block is the biblical witness to God's sovereign freedom to operate beyond what he himself has established as normative. In the late Middle Ages one did not have to be a learned theologian to know that God had spoken more authoritatively through persecuted prophets, ragged ascetics, and even a braying ass than through the religious authorities who lay claim to his truth. He was a God who dwelt more intimately among those who deny the world in body and in spirit than among those who attempt to run it from the pulpit and by the sword.

2. I elaborate on this description of mysticism in the larger context of late medieval intellectual and religious history in my forthcoming article, "Mysticism, Nominalism, and Dissent: A *Forschungsbericht* in Search of a Thesis," in *The Pursuit of Holiness in the Late Middle Ages and Renaissance* (Proceedings of the Conference on Late Medieval and Renaissance Religion, University of Michigan, Ann Arbor, April 1972), ed. Charles Trinkaus and H. A. Oberman (Leiden, 1973).

Subjectively, mysticism rests on an anthropological base uniquely structured to transcend the limitations of the normal, mechanical processes of sense perception, reason, and volition. The subjective base of mystical experience might also be called a *potentia absoluta* —a *potentia hominis absoluta*. In the technical language of the medieval theologian, this base is an inalienable and irrepressible "spark of the will and reason" (*synteresis voluntatis et rationis*) or "ground of the soul" (*Seelengrund*)—an indestructible orientation to God, which one can speak of simply as the direction of the heart or the testimony of conscience. Its sights are set on experiences well beyond the normal expectations of the common *viator*. It is a receptacle for more intimate communications from God than those which the eyes and ears behold in the sermons, sacraments, ceremonies, and writings of the church.

Before venturing into historical details, it is instructive to hear a modern authority, who, far from speculating on the revolutionary possibilities, offers the following pregnant definition of "traditional mystical theology."

> Beyond these kinds of knowledge [viz. natural knowledge of God through the process of reasoning—natural theology—and revealed knowledge of God through Holy Scripture—dogmatic and speculative theology] there is a third by which God and the truths of Christianity can not only be believed and acted upon but can in varying degrees be directly known and experienced. . . . This knowledge, this experience, which is never entirely separable from an equally immediate and experimental union with God by love, has three main characteristics. [1] It is recognized by the person concerned as something utterly different from and more real and adequate than all his previous knowledge and love of God. [2] It is experienced as something at once immanent and received, something moving and filling the powers of the mind and soul. It is felt as taking place at a deeper level of the personality and soul than that on which the normal processes of thought and will take place, and the mystic is aware, both in himself and in others, of the soul, its qualities and of the divine presence and action within it, as something wholly distinct from the reasoning mind with its powers. [3] Finally, this experience is wholly incommunicable, save as a bare statement . . . but it brings absolute certainty to the mind

of the recipient. This is the traditional mystical theology, the mystical knowledge of God, in its purest form.[3]

In a classical statement of the options open to the medieval theologian, Bonaventure, the *magister* of Franciscan mysticism and spirituality, set forth three possible theologies: *"symbolic,* by which we deal correctly with sensible things, *proper,* by which we deal correctly with intelligible things, and *mystical,* by which we are taken up into mind-transcending ecstasies." [4] This division was later repeated in Jean Gerson's magisterial synthetic work, *De mystica theologia* (1402). Gerson points out that "mystical theology draws its doctrine from experiences within the hearts of devout souls, just as the other two theologies proceed from extrinsic effects." [5] What nature is to the symbolic theologian and historical documents to the scholastic theologian, the recorded "experiences within the hearts of devout souls" are to the mystical theologian, i.e. they are his authoritative "text."

For both Bonaventure and Gerson (and that includes Franciscan and so-called nominalistic mysticism),[6] mystical experience is be-

3. David Knowles, *The English Mystical Tradition* (New York, 1961), 2–3; cf. Evelyn Underhill *Mysticism: A Study in the Nature and Development of man's Spiritual Consciousness,* 12th ed. (New York, 1961), pp. 23–24, 415 ff. These historically informed definitions compare well with those standard definitions of mysticism and mystical theology which focus exclusively on universal philosophical characteristics. Cf. W. R. Inge, *Christian Mysticism* (Bampton Lectures, 1899), esp. appendices A and B; Cuthbert Butler, *Western Mysticism,* 2d ed. (London, 1966), pp. 4–5; Rudolf Otto, *Mysticism East and West* (New York, 1932); and, more recently, W. H. Auden's introduction to *The Protestant Mystics,* ed. Anne Fremantle (New York, 1965), pp. 13–38. For historically minded, typological definitions, which appreciate the peculiarities of divergent mystical traditions in the late Middle Ages, see especially the collection of articles in Ruh, *Altdeutsche und altniederländische Mystik.*

4. "Per symbolicam recte utamur sensibilibus, per propriam recte utamur intelligibilibus, per mysticam rapiamur ad supermentales excessus." *Itinerarium mentis in Deum,* ed. J. Kaup (Munich, 1961), chap. 1, sect. 7, p. 62. For an elaboration of the meaning of symbolic theology, see ibid., pp. 172–74, n. 15.

5. "Theologia mistica innititur ad sui doctrinam experientiis habitis ad intra in cordibus animorum devotorum, sicut alia duplex theologia ex hiis procedit, que extrinsecus operantur." *De mystica theologia speculativa* in *Ioannis Carlerii de Gerson: De mystica theologia,* ed. André Combes (Lugano, 1958), *cons.* 2, 8.4 ff. Combes has also authored the standard work on Gerson's mystical theology, *La théologie mystique de Gerson: Profil de son evolution,* vols. 1–2 (Rome, 1963–64).

6. Heiko A. Oberman, *The Harvest of Medieval Theology* (Cambridge, Mass., 1963), pp. 323 ff. Oberman's definition of "nominalistic mysticism" is well within the bounds of what traditional scholarship has generally characterized as Cistercian and/or Franciscan mysticism. Cf. Aimé Forest, "Das Erlebnis des consensus volunta-

yond normal sense perception and rational reflection. A St. Francis may build a theology on the manifestation of God's glory in the world round about him, and the scholastic theologian may construct his system from a scientific analysis of creeds, Scripture, and *Sentences* commentaries. The mystical theologian, however, must attempt to articulate mind-transcending ecstasies which erupt from the depths of the soul. He must systematize the recorded experiences which have occurred in the history and tradition of the heart.

Hence, mystical theology focused attention upon a unique anthropological base, a structure within the soul of man capable of transcending the limitations of the senses and reason. Bonaventure and Gerson described this structure as a *synteresis voluntatis*—a spark of the will. It is the highest affective power, a "virginal part of the soul," a "natural stimulus to good," the "highest point of the heart and mind" (*apex mentis*).[7] As it is the function of the senses to collect data and the function of reason to organize and abstract from the perceptions of the senses, so it is the function of the *synteresis* to promote the experience of ecstatic love, that transcendental "wisdom of God hidden in mystery, which is mystical theology." [8] As the residue of man's prefallen and even precreated purity, the *synteresis* is a special anthropological base for the achievement of mystical experience, the unique locus for God's mystical birth in the soul.

---

tis beim hl. Bernhard," *Bernhard von Clairvaux: Mönch und Mystiker,* ed. Joseph Lortz (Wiesbaden, 1955), pp. 120–27; Kurt Ruh, "Zur Grundlegung einer Geschichte der Franziskanischen Mystik" in *Altdeutsche und altniederländische Mystik,* pp. 240–74, and *Bonaventura Deutsch: Ein Beitrag zur deutschen Franziskaner-Mystik und Scholastik* (Bern, 1956); Joseph Bernhart, *Bernhardische und Eckhartische Mystik in ihren Beziehungen und Gegensätzen* (Kempton, 1912), esp. p. 156; and Stanislaus Grünewald, *Franziskanische Mystik: Versuch zu einer Darstellung mit besonderer Berücksichtigung des hl. Bonaventura* (Munich, 1932), esp. pp. 121 ff.

7. Gerson, *De mystica theologia speculativa, cons.* 14, 34.24–35.31. Cf. Bonaventure, II *Sent.,* d. 39, a. 2, q. 1–3. On the definition and history of the *synteresis* concept, see Heinrich Appel, *Die Lehre der Scholastiker von der Syntheresis* (Rostock, 1891), and "Die Syntheresis in der mittelalterlichen Mystik," *ZKG* 13 (1892): 535 ff.; F. Nitzsch, "Der gegenwärtige Stand der Streitfrage über die Synteresis," *ZKG* 19 (1898): 1–14; H. Kunisch, *Das Wort "Grund" in der Sprache der deutschen Mystik des 14. und 15. Jahrhundert* (Osnabrück, 1929); H. Wilms, "Das Seelenfünklein in der deutschen Mystik," *Zeitschrift für Aszese und Mystik* 12 (1937): 157–66; Hans Hof, *Scintilla Animae* (Lund, 1952), esp. pp. 161 ff.; W. Frei, "Was ist das Seelenfünklein beim Meister Eckhart?", *Theologische Zeitschrift* 14 (1958): 89–100; and Endre von Ivánka, *Plato Christianus* (Einsiedeln, 1964), pp. 315–51.

8. *De mystica theologia speculativa, cons.* 27, 69.33 ff.

The three theologies can be paralleled with the traditional threefold anthropology or psychology. Symbolic theology is the study of created things and their perfections as signs and indications of God and divine perfection. Scholastic theology is the learned study of the sacred and traditional writings of the church. Both are activities which draw on the full range of man's sensory, rational, and volitional powers. When the sphere of mystical experience is entered, however, one must have recourse to the activity of the highest cognitive and affective powers of the soul: pure intelligence and the spark of the will.

	The Soul	
	Cognitive Powers	Affective Powers
Symbolic and scholastic theology:	Sensibility Reason	Sensual appetite Will
Mystical theology:	Pure intelligence	*Synteresis*[9]

The mystical thinker spies and builds upon a unique correlation. Just as there are biblically attested exceptions to God's normal self-mediation through the priestly-sacramental system of the church, so there are psychological structures within the human soul which transcend the limitations of the soul's normal sensory, reasoning, and volitional processes. Just as God has retained—as a sovereign deity must—an area of freedom above and beyond his covenantal commitments to the church, so the soul knows—as an immortal being must—an area of freedom above and beyond its necessary and chosen responses to the visible world. It is this "supra" dimension, this superabundant structural freedom of God and of the soul, which makes mystical experience and theology both possible and necessary.

What we have seen with Bonaventure and Gerson is not a peculiarity of this tradition of mysticism alone. The situation is even more pronounced in the so-called German Dominican mys-

9. See my *Homo Spiritualis: A Comparative Study of the Anthropology of Johannes Tauler, Jean Gerson and Martin Luther* (Leiden, 1969), p. 70. Bonaventure parallels the six stages of the mind's ascent to God with progression through the six powers of the soul: "Iuxta igitur sex gradus ascensionis in Deum sex sunt gradus potentiarum animae per quos ascendimus ab imis ad summa, ab exterioribus ad intima, a temporalibus conscendimus ad aeterna, scilicet sensus, imaginatio, ratio, intellectus, intelligentia et apex mentis seu synderesis scintilla." *Itinerarium mentis in Deum*, I, 6, p. 58 f.

ticism of Meister Eckhart and Johannes Tauler. In a sermon on
Luke 14 : 16–17—the story of the man who prepared a great feast
and sent his servant to invite his friends—Eckhart presents the
following analysis. The man who extends the invitation is of
course God, and the feast is union and fellowship with God. But
who is the servant designated to bring the two parties together?
Eckhart's answer ascribes—could one say usurps?—the clerical
function to the special anthropological resource of mystical theology:

> This man sent out his servant. Now St. Gregory says that
> the preachers are this servant. From another point of view
> one could say that the angels are this servant. But there is a
> third possibility. It seems to me that this servant is the spark
> of the soul [*daz vünkelin der sele*], which is created by God
> and inserted [into the soul] as a light from above. It is an
> image of divine nature, constantly opposed to everything that
> is not of God. But it is not a *power* of the soul, as several
> teachers suggest. It is constantly inclined to what is good;
> even in hell it is directed to what is good. The teachers say
> that it is of such a nature that it struggles incessantly [toward
> God]. It is called a *synteresis,* and that designates both a
> connection [with God] and an aversion [from all that is not
> God]. It has two activities. The one is bitter combat against
> every impurity. The other is constant attraction to what is
> good. That attraction is directly built into the soul and re-
> mains even in those who are in hell.[10]

Tauler points out that nothing whatsoever in heaven or on
earth can satisfy the "spark of the soul" except God himself.

> The soul has a spark, a ground in itself, whose thirst God,
> even though he can do all things, cannot quench with any-
> thing except himself. He could give it the spirit of the forms
> of everything he has ever created in heaven and on earth,
> and it would still not be sufficient to satisfy it.[11]

10. *Meister Eckhart: Die deutschen Werke,* ed. Joseph Quint, vol. 1 (Stuttgart,
1958), 331.13 ff. Cf. *Daz Buoch der götlichen Tröstunge* in Franz Pfeiffer, *Deutsche
Mystiker des 14. Jahrhunderts,* vol. 2, *Meister Eckhart* (Leipzig, 1857), 420.31–40
(English translation in R. B. Blakney, *Meister Eckhart* (New York, 1941), 44–45).
11. *Die Predigten Taulers,* ed. Ferdinand Vetter (Berlin, 1910), 137.1–5.

Like Bonaventure and Gerson, the German mystics located the mystical enterprise within an extraordinary structure and function of the soul. This structure was set apart subjectively from the soul's normal sensory, reasoning, and volitional functions, and objectively its desire could be satisfied only by the direct presence of God. The following diagram summarizes the situation.

The Soul

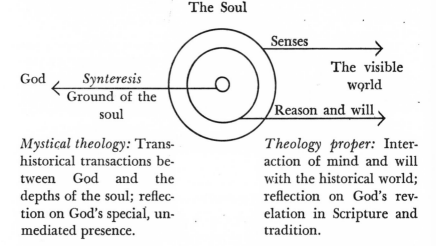

Mystical theology: Transhistorical transactions between God and the depths of the soul; reflection on God's special, unmediated presence.

Theology proper: Interaction of mind and will with the historical world; reflection on God's revelation in Scripture and tradition.

Both in terms of its objective orientation and its subjective power the mystical enterprise is peculiar, departing the ordinary way to religious truth and salvation for a more direct and intimate communion with God. It reaches further than the normal psychological functions of the soul can grasp and demands more than the normal institutional structures of the church can give. In the most literal sense of the words, the mystical enterprise is transrational and transinstitutional. And because it is such, it bears a potential *anti*-intellectual and *anti*-institutional stance, which can be adopted for the critical purposes of dissent, reform, and even revolution.

Even the most traditional, church-supporting form of mystical theology carries a patent potential anti-intellectualism. Gerson, for example, summarizes a long tradition when he maintains that mystical theology, the way of love, is absolutely superior to scholastic theology, a way traversed only by those with a university education. Not only is mystical theology the "most perfect knowledge possible," but it is also a knowledge in which even "young girls

and simpletons" can excel.[12] Indeed, the latter can be much closer
to the ultimate truth of life than those with technical knowledge
sufficient to move mountains.

Gerson, of course, did not intend this remark in any revolutionary anti-intellectual or anti-institutional sense. He uttered a biblical truism—the "anti-intellectualism" of New Testament Christianity, one might say—and he uttered it as a professor and
chancellor of the University of Paris. The remark, in fact, was
part and parcel of his program to reform what he considered to be
an excessively cerebral theological faculty within the university.
He desired to overcome the errant head by subjecting it to the
inerrant heart—the *synteresis voluntatis*.[13] For him, mystical theology was a potent weapon within the church to be taken up when
the essence of Christian truth, which is love and union with God,
became lost in the penultimate pursuits of speculative theologians
and the boring routine of insensate clerics. Still, within this constructive context, mystical theology remained a sharp rebuke of
the intellectual establishment of the church, and it bore obvious
possibilities for dissent and revolution when taken up by one less
concerned than Gerson was simply to patch and darn the given
institutions of society.

It is an ironic commentary on Gerson's peculiar concept of
mystical theology and a telling judgment on certain developments
in late medieval spirituality on the eve of the Reformation[14] that
Gerson himself came under attack in the mid-fifteenth century for
allegedly *overintellectualizing* mystical theology. His attacker was
the Dionysian purist, Vincent of Aggsbach (d. 1460), prior of a

12. Gerson, *De mystica theologia speculativa*, cons. 30, 78.33–34.

13. See my article, "The University and the Church: Patterns of Reform in Jean
Gerson," *Medievalia et Humanistica* n.s. 1 (1970): 111–26. Nicholas of Cusa is
another classic example of mystical theology in the service of conservative reform;
the "supra" dimension of mysticism does not become militantly "contra." Paul
Sigmund summarizes the profound influence on Cusa's thought of Pseudo-Dionysius,
Raymond Lull, Meister Eckhart, and Jean Gerson. *Nicholas of Cusa and Medieval
Political Thought* (Cambridge, Mass., 1963), pp. 44–63.

14. Piety on the eve of the Reformation was strikingly naive and practical, averse
to refined theological abstractions and distinctions. Cf. Bernd Moeller, "Frömmigkeit
im Deutschland um 1500," *ARG* 56 (1965): 5–30 (English translation in *The Refor-
mation in Medieval Perspective*, ed. S. E. Ozment [Chicago, 1971]); Gundolf
Gieraths, "Johannes Tauler und die Frömmigkeitshaltung des 15. Jahrhunderts" in
Johannes Tauler: Ein Deutscher Mystiker, Gedenkschrift zum 600. Todestag, ed.
E. M. Filthaut (Essen, 1961), pp. 422–34, esp. pp. 426–27; Maria A. Lücker, *Meister
Eckhart und die Devotio moderna* (Leiden, 1950); R. R. Post, *The Modern Devotion:
Confrontation with Reformation and Humanism* (Leiden, 1968), esp. p. 320.

Carthusian monastery and, like the mature Gerson, a devoted conciliar reformer.[15] After a close rereading of Gerson's mystical writings in the last days of 1452, Vincent concluded that Gerson
fundamentally contradicted the true nature of mystical experience.
In the forty-third consideration of his *De mystica theologia* of 1402,
Gerson had defined mystical theology as an "experiential knowledge of God received through the union of spiritual affection with
him," and identified it with prayer or the "highest mental and
intellectual affection" (*affectus mentalis aut intellectualis su-
premus*).[16] For Vincent, this was to forfeit outright the sine qua
non of true (Dionysian) mystical theology, viz. absolute ignorance.
One must rise up to God without concomitant knowledge of him:
"ignote vel inscium consurgere oportet, id est sine cogitatione concomitante." [17] Zeroing in on Gerson's forty-third consideration,
Vincent retorted: "If mystical theology can be called prayer, it is
not as an intellectual and attentive prayer but as transintellectual
[*superintellectualis*] prayer." The peak of human affection enters
the holy of holies only as it has left understanding outside ("intellectu . . . foris relicto").[18] Hence the dismissal of Gerson and
the praise of the way of ignorance:

> In the practice of mystical theology, to ascend in ignorance,
> i.e. without concomitant knowing [*cogitatio*], is the unique
> and definitive foundation of this art. It is from this foundation
> that Doctor Gerson departs, and by thus contradicting the
> expositors of Dionysius, the practitioners (of the art of mysti-
> cal theology), and even himself, he makes it clear that his

15. Committed to the decrees and programs of Constance and Basel, Vincent
watched with much dismay the resurgence of papal power and the rise of more
moderate curial reform programs such as that of Nicholas of Cusa. He attacked
Cusa's views on mystical theology along lines similar to those followed against
Gerson. E. Vansteenberghe, *Autour de la docte ignorance: Une controverse sur la
théologie mystique au XVe siècle* (Münster, 1915), p. 26.

16. *De mystica theologia speculativa, cons.* 43, 118.31 f. (English translation in
*Jean Gerson: Selections from A Deo exivit, Contra curiositatem studentium and
De mystica theologia speculativa*, ed. and trans. S. E. Ozment [Leiden, 1969], pp.
64–67).

17. *Tractatus cuiusdam Carthusiensis de mystica theologia* in Vansteenberghe,
Autour de la docte ignorance, pp. 189–201, 190. Influenced by Hugh of Palma,
Vincent intensifies this position by prohibiting also "previa cogitatio": "omnino
affirmat (Hugo de Palma) consurgere oportere sine cogitatione concomitante, addens
etiam quod omnino nec cogitatio previa requiratur." Ibid., p. 191.

18. Ibid., p. 197.

is not the mystical theology of Dionysius, but one of his own devising, in which one does not rise up [to God] in ignorance.[19]

Potential anti-intellectual and anti-institutional stances are more apparent features of German mysticism. When Eckhart praises the *synteresis*, he cites St. Augustine in support of the conviction that "this spark has more truth within it than everything man can learn." [20] The possible revolutionary impact of Eckhart's teaching on the "corda simplicium" was repeatedly cited in the documents pertaining to the posthumous censure of his teaching.[21] What would result if the masses were convinced that there is more truth in their commonsense instincts than in the universities of Christendom? How can men embrace the routine of the church after they have been in the very mind of God?

A recent study has convincingly shown how, beneath the historical and sacramental relation between God and man transacted by the church, Eckhart constructed a more fundamental natural and involuntary (*non voluntate, sed naturaliter*) arrangement played out in the depths of the individual soul.[22] A "natural covenant" of more basic soteriological significance than God's historical covenants can also be extrapolated from the writings

19. Ibid., p. 192. Vincent concedes that "contemplation" is an ascent with concomitant knowledge, and he obviously thinks that Gerson has confused contemplation with mystical theology. Ibid., p. 200. The parallel with Bonaventure, who permits only an *affective transitus* at the peak of mystical experience, is striking. *Itinerarium mentis in Deum*, VII, 4, p. 150: "In hoc autem transitu, si sit perfectus, oportet quod relinquantur omnes intellectuales operationes, et apex affectus totus transferatur et transformetur in Deum."

20. *Meister Eckhart: Die deutschen Werke*, 1 : 336.1–2.

21. Josef Koch, "Meister Eckharts Weiterwirken im Deutsch-Niederländischen Raum im 14. und 15. Jahrhundert" in *La mystique Rhénane. Colloque de Strasbourg 16–19 Mai 1961* (Paris, 1963), pp. 133–56, esp. pp. 136, 152–54. See also the bull of condemnation *In agro dominico* (March 27, 1329) in Denzinger, *Enchiridion symbolorum* 32d ed. (Freiburg i.B., 1963), §950–80, pp. 290 ff.

22. Schizuteru Ueda, "Ueber den Sprachgebrauch Meister Eckharts: 'Gott Muss . . .' Ein Beispiel für die Gedankengänge der spekulativen Mystik" in *Glaube, Geist, Geschichte: Festschrift für Ernst Benz*, ed. G. Mueller and W. Zeller (Leiden, 1967), pp. 266–77, esp. pp. 267–68, 271. In connection with Ueda's study, Thomas Müntzer's translation of Psalm 117 : 5 ("De tribulatione invocavi Dominum et exaudivit me in latitudine Dominus") in the liturgical office is striking: "Mit solcher weise rief ich an den herren in meiner trübsal, *do gab ich im raum er kunt es nicht lassen, er muste mich erhören*" (emphasis mine). Cited by Felicitas Dobratz, *Der Einfluss der deutschen Mystik auf Thomas Müntzer und Hans Denck* (Münster/Westfalen, 1960), p. 29. Cf. *infra*, p. 83.

of Tauler.[23] For Eckhart and Tauler, religious institutions had worth only to the extent to which they subserved the retreat into the depths of the soul. Institutions existed, so to speak, to be used against institutions.

The mystical way of salvation is paradigmatic of the operative value judgments. According to Eckhart and Tauler, true self-realization entails the suspension of normal rational and volitional activities, a shutting down of the regular processes of the soul. The latter are immobilized (*Gelassenheit*) and cut off from the external world (*Abgeschiedenheit*). For a moment, the soul surrenders its accustomed routine (*Entleerung*) and takes refuge in its self-sufficient inner ground. With the collapse of the normal activities of the soul follows as surely as the night the day the irrelevance of everything the visible world has to offer, whether it be of good or of ill. One is above popes and kings, beyond sacraments and laws, immune to worldly praise and condemnation.[24] Even if the experience (or the theory) does not issue in dissent, reform, or revolutionary activity, it uniquely drives home the ideological prerequisite for such, viz. an understanding of the penultimate character of all worldly power and authority. In the mystical traditions, quietism is no less negative a judgment on established power than violent revolution. Mystical salvation is the discovery of the final power and authority of the Self within one's own self.[25]

Medieval mystical writings uniquely contain the raw material of dissent, and the thinkers we are now going to meet were most

23. *Homo Spiritualis*, pp. 13–26, esp. pp. 25–26. Also instructive is the recent article by Martin Greschat, "Der Bundesgedanke in der Theologie des späten Mittelalters," *ZKG* 1 (1970): 44–63. Cf. David C. Steinmetz, *Misericordia Dei: The Theology of Johannes von Staupitz in Its Late Medieval Setting* (Leiden, 1968), pp. 160 ff.

24. In regard to Tauler and Müntzer, H.-J. Goertz makes the pregnant summary: "Die 'innere Ordnung' wird zu einer 'ewigen Ordnung.' . . . Da Gott den Menschen innerhalb der 'inneren Ordnung' anspricht und seine Stimme allein innerhalb derselben zu vernehmen ist, kann sein Wort . . . sich nicht ein für allemal in einem historischen Dokument niederschlagen, es muss vielmehr, die Geschichte ständig durchbrechend, das Tempus 'kegenwertiger ceyt' annehmen . . . Vor Gott gibt es keine Geschichte und keine kirchliche Tradition." *Innere und äussere Ordnung in der Theologie Thomas Müntzers* (Leiden, 1967), pp. 67–68.

25. For concrete examples of mystical thinking informing revolutionary activity in seventeenth-century England, see Rufus M. Jones, *Mysticism and Democracy in the English Commonwealth* (Cambridge, Mass., 1932), esp. pp. 115 ff. On the other hand, Dionysian mysticism, with its strong sense of established hierarchy, could be enlisted to promote a very conservative "descending" view of political authority. Cf. Sigmund, *Nicholas of Cusa and Medieval Political Thought*, p. 64.

adept at exploiting it. Familiar with both the Cistercian-Franciscan and the German Dominican traditions, their favorite mystical writing proved to be a syncretic tract by an anonymous late fourteenth-century German author, which bore the title its first publisher, Martin Luther, gave it: *Eyn Theologia Deutsch,* the *German Theology.*

2

A Common Mystical Writing:
The *Theologia Deutsch*

In 1892, the late Tübingen philosopher and church historian, Alfred Hegler, argued that the basic source for what he then described as the "radical reform movements," the "radical tributaries," or the "left wing" of the Reformation was medieval mysticism. The "radicals" from Thomas Müntzer to the Antitrinitarians (Socinians), he maintained, were inaccurately portrayed as those who simply exaggerated Protestant ideas. Rather,

> they turn back to medieval ideas. . . . For what has most determined the theories of the radicals in a positive way is mystical soteriology in the form it received in German mysticism during the fourteenth and fifteenth centuries. Tauler and the *Theologia Deutsch* have been primarily influential, although for many Staupitz was nearer at hand.[1]

Before his death in 1902 Hegler was able to probe his thesis only in regard to Sebastian Franck. Since then monographs have appeared to suggest the extent of mystical influence on such magisterial dissenters as Thomas Müntzer, Hans Denck, and

1. Alfred Hegler, *Geist und Schrift bei Sebastian Franck: Eine Studie zur Geschichte des Spiritualismus in der Reformationszeit* (Freiburg i.B., 1892), p. 13. Cf. Goertz, who considers the Dominican mysticism of Tauler and the *Theologia Deutsch* to be the "Interpretament für die nebenreformatorische Theologie und Frömmigkeit." *Innere und Aeussere Ordnung in der Theologie Thomas Müntzers*, pp. 9–10, cf. p. 12. Hans Maier summarized the matter thus: "die Ideen dieser älteren deutschen Mystik, wie sie besonders im Kreise der Eckhart, Tauler und der Gottesfreunde ihr spezifisches Gepräge erhalten haben, gehen durch alle Gruppen der radikalen Reformer hindurch: Der politische Revolutionär Thomas Müntzer, die Taüfer und die spiritualistische Gruppe stehen hier in einer Linie." *Der mystische Spiritualismus Valentin Weigels* (Gütersloh, 1926), pp. 16–17. Karl Holl had earlier opposed Troeltsch's sharp separation of Anabaptism and mysticism, maintaining: "Es gibt kein Täufertum, das sich nicht auf eine wenn auch noch so einfache Mystik stütze." "Luther und die Schwärmer," *Gesammelte Aufsätze*, vol. 1, 7th ed. (Tübingen, 1948), p. 424, n. 1.

Valentin Weigel.[2] A comprehensive synthetic work on the relation between medieval mysticism and dissent in the sixteenth century has not yet appeared. The best test case for such a study would no doubt be that omnipresent little treatise mentioned above by Hegler, the *Theologia Deutsch*. The historian of the sixteenth century cannot regard the popularity of this work as simply a routine occurrence in the history of Christian spirituality. Beginning with Luther, who edited it in 1516 and 1518, this treatise by a still unknown German author[3] has functioned more as a declaration of dissent than as a guide to peaceful meditation and ethical sanctification. Those who edited, praised, and read it were those who had parted ways with the ecclesiastical establishment(s) of the sixteenth century. It was, for example, a basic and widely used document for Anabaptist theology and ethics.[4] A leader of the peasants' revolt in Thuringia, Thomas Müntzer, possessed a copy; and the more modest vicar of Orlamünde,

2. In addition to the works by Dobratz, Goertz, and Maier, which have already been cited, the following are especially to be noted: M. M. Smirin, *Die Volksreformation des Thomas Münzer und der grosse Bauernkrieg*, 2d ed. (Berlin, 1956), pp. 207–71; Martin Schmidt, "Das Selbstbewusstsein Thomas Müntzers und sein Verhältnis zu Luther. Ein Beitrag zu der Frage: War Thomas Müntzer Mystiker?", *Theologia Viatorum* 6 (1954/58): 25–41; Winfried Zeller, "Meister Eckhart bei Valentin Weigel: Eine Untersuchung zur Frage der Bedeutung Meister Eckharts für die mystische Renaissance des sechzehnten Jahrhunderts," ZKG 62 (1938): 309–55. A popular synthetic sketch with an eye to the modern world is Heinrich Bornkamm, *Mystik, Spiritualismus und die Anfänge des Pietismus im Luthertum* (Giessen, 1926). A modest prospectus is offered more recently by Jan J. Kiwiet, "Die *Theologia Deutsch* und ihre Bedeutung während der Zeit der Reformation," *Mennonitische Geschichtsblätter* 15 (1958): 29–35.

3. Cf. K. Wessendorft, "Ist der Verfasser der 'Theologia Deutsch' gefunden?", *Evangelische Theologie* 16 (1956): 188–92. Discussed by Georg Baring, "Neues von der 'Theologia Deutsch,' und ihrer weltweiten Bedeutung," *ARG* 48 (1957): 1–11, 7. Hubert Schiel, "Heinrich von Bergen oder Johannes de Francfordia als Verfasser der 'Theologia Deutsch,'" *Archiv für mittelrheinische Kirchengeschichte* 22 (1970): 85–92.

4. Cf. G. H. Williams, "Popularized German Mysticism as a Factor in the Rise of Anabaptist Communism," in *Glaube, Geist, Geschichte: Festschrift für Ernst Benz* (Leiden, 1967), pp. 290–312, esp. pp. 294–95. The magisterial Anabaptist, Pilgram Marbeck, quotes from chapters 1, 2, 14 (Mandel = 16 Pfeiffer), 34, 42, 45, and 50, with especially heavy citation from chapter 14, which deals with the old and the new man, *Pilgram Marbecks Antwort auf Kaspar Schwenckfelds Beurteilung des Buches der Bundesbezeugung von 1542*, ed. J. Loserth (Wien, 1929), pp. 213 ff., 266 ff. On possible Eckhartian influence on Marbeck, cf. William Klassen, *Covenant and Community: The Life, Writings and Hermeneutics of Pilgram Marbeck* (Grand Rapids, Mich., 1969), pp. 184–85.

Andreas Bodenstein von Karlstadt, employed it with high praise.[5] The syncretic radical Louis Haetzer made an expurgated (i.e. de-Lutherized) edition for use in circles opposed to the German theology of Luther. Hans Denck, friend and colleague of Haetzer,[6] wrote a series of theological propositions which Haetzer appended to his edition as a summarizing commentary. Sebastian Franck, the most uncompromising spiritualist of the sixteenth century, authored an extensive Latin paraphrase of it.[7] Sebastian Castellio, eloquent advocate of religious toleration against the Calvinists, translated it into Latin and French. Valentin Weigel, whose posthumously published works attacked the very foundations of Lutheran orthodoxy, made it the model for his first writings. It is further distinguished by the fact that John Calvin condemned it as the poison of the Devil,[8] and Pope Paul V placed

5. See Müntzer's book list in *Thomas Müntzer. Schriften und Briefe. Kritische Gesamtausgabe,* ed. Günther Franz (and Paul Kirn) (Gütersloh, 1968) [hereafter cited as Franz], p. 558. On Karlstadt, see Hermann Barge, *Andreas Bodenstein von Karlstadt* (Leipzig, 1905), 2 : 25–26, and Gordon Rupp, *Patterns of Reformation* (Philadelphia, 1969), pp. 116 ff.

6. The influence of Müntzer on Denck is assessed by Georg Baring, "Hans Denck und Thomas Müntzer in Nürnberg 1524," *ARG* 50 (1959): 145–81. See below, p. 118.

7. A. von Grolman has pointed out the strong influence of the *German Theology* on Franck's *Paradoxa.* "Das Wissen um das Verhältnismässige in der Paradoxie des Seins: Studie zur teutschen theologie des Sebastian Franck," *Blätter für Deutsche Philosophie* 2 (1928): 57–72.

8. Hermann Oncken, "Aus den letzten Jahren Sebastian Francks," *Monatshefte der Comenius-Gesellschaft* 11 (1902): 86–101, 88. When this judgment was made, the Latin and French translations of Castellio had injected the *German Theology* into the French Reformation. Two years earlier, in a letter to Heinrich Bullinger (July, 1557), Calvin's colleague William Farel initially adjudged the pseudonymous Latin edition of Castellio to have sprung from the circle of the radical Anabaptist David Joris (d. 1556), and lamented it as "delirium anabaptisticum." Discussed by Alfred Hegler, *Sebastian Francks lateinische Paraphrase der Deutschen Theologie und seine holländisch erhaltenen Traktate* (Tübingen, 1901; hereafter cited as Hegler 1901), pp. 15–16. According to Ludwig Keller, Luther had already begun to turn against the *German Theology* in 1521–25, regarding it as a source of "Schwärmerei." "Die Gottesfreunde, die 'Deutsche Theologie' und die Rosenkreuzer," *Monatshefte der Comenius Gesellschaft* 11 (1902): 145–57, 146–47. Cf. also Keller's *Die Reformation und die älteren Reformparteien* (Leipzig, 1885), p. 472, where Luther is credited with an approving preface to Johannes Kimeus's 1537 attack on the ideas of the *German Theology.* Flacius, however, listed it in the *Catalogus testium veritatis* (1562), thereby bestowing the blessing of Lutheran orthodoxy. Noteworthy in this regard is Schwenckfeld's complaint of Luther's turnabout on Tauler: "Luther hat am ersten Taulerum commendiert, jetzt veracht er ihn." Cited by Gottfried Maron, *Individualismus und Gemeinschaft bei Caspar von Schwenckfeld* (Stuttgart, 1961), p. 102.

it on the Index of Forbidden Books where, somewhat ironically, it still remains even today.[9]

It will be the task of the present chapter to sketch the major evaluations of the *German Theology* from Martin Luther to Valentin Weigel. We will see that this treatise, as mystical writings generally, was not simply taken up as an antischolastic tract by those who desired to exalt right living over right thinking. Its significance cannot be adequately assessed within the hackneyed theological problem of justification versus sanctification. Rather, it was championed by those who found the normal historical media of religious truth (specifically, Scripture and tradition) monopolized by a repressive Christendom, and whose very survival depended in the final analysis upon a persuasively competing alternative concept of God's revealed plan for man. The *German Theology* subserved the need to reinterpret the *potentia Dei ordinata,* to redefine the ecclesiopolitical "establishment." The explanation of its popularity in the sixteenth century most clearly emerges in the context of the struggle involved in this redefinition of religious authority.

LUTHER'S PREFACES OF 1516 AND 1518

Until very recent times only one MS of the *German Theology* was available to scholars—that from a Cistercian cloister at Bronnbach near Wertheim on the Tauber, which bore the copy date of September 27, 1497. Apart from the Bronnbach MS, only one other access to the *German Theology* existed—the Luther editions of 1516 (containing nineteen chapters) and of 1518 (containing the entire treatise). Recent discoveries have shown that, contrary to suspicions about the objectivity of a theologian with a reformation afoot, Luther's editions are absolutely correct and unmarred by any self-serving interpolations.[10] That Luther should edit the

---

9. See *Index librorum prohibitorum Vatikan* (Rome, 1948), p. 462. The *decretum* of November 13, 1612, extends not only to the 1557 Latin edition of Castellio but further to "libellum inscriptum Theologia Germanica quocumque idiomate . . . impressum," a fact that has raised questions about modern Catholic editions. See Georg Baring, *Bibliographie der Ausgaben der 'Theologia Deutsch' (1516–1961): Ein Beitrag zur Luther Bibliographie* (Baden-Baden, 1963) [hereafter cited as **Baring** 1963], pp. 6–7.

10. The debates over the *German Theology* are discussed by Eberhard Teufel, "Die 'Deutsche Theologie' und Sebastian Franck im Lichte der neueren Forschung: I, Die 'Deutsche Theologie,'" *Theologische Rundschau* 11 (1939): 304–15, with a

German Theology with maximum exactitude in 1516 and 1518 is hardly surprising when one takes his situation during this period into account. As we shall see, he had very good reasons for being as faithful to the original as possible.

Luther's prefaces to the *German Theology* set forth the basic themes that appear again and again in subsequent prefaces and

---

convenient summary chart, pp. 314–15; and Georg Baring, "Die französischen Ausgaben der 'Theologia Deutsch,'" *Theologische Zeitschrift* 16 (1960) (hereafter cited as Baring 1960) 176–94. Since the three texts varied considerably in length— the Luther 1516 being the shortest and the Bronnbach MS containing some 230 lines more than the Luther 1518—the question was whether Luther was condensing in his complete edition or whether the copier of the Bronnbach MS was inflating. Roman Catholic scholars tended to put more trust in the scholarship of a Cistercian monk than in that of the Reformer. In defense of the Bronnbach MS, Jules Paquier bluntly stated: "In 1516, and still more in 1518, Luther was incapable of treating a text with scientific impartiality." Baring 1960, p. 191.

An early defender of the Luther editions was Heinrich Hermelink, who found in the Bronnbach MS not only stylistic changes but also consistent efforts to weaken Neoplatonic and to strengthen Aristotelian (scholastic) terminology. It was a conscious alteration for theological and pedagogical purposes. The Luther editions (especially the 1516), by contrast, while probably not based on the original, were based on less inflated versions than the Bronnbach MS. "Text und Gedankengang der Theologia Deutsch," in *Aus Deutschlands kirchlicher Vergangenheit: Festschrift zum 70. Geburtstage von Theodor Brieger* (Leipzig, 1912), pp. 1–19, esp. pp. 9–10, 12–13.

The debate was carried further by Karl Müller, Gottfried Siedel, and Edward Schroeder. Müller considered the Luther 1518 edition merely an incomplete version of the Bronnbach MS and criticized modern Protestant editions based on it. Teufel, "Die 'Deutsche Theologie,'" pp. 305–06, 307. Siedel agreed with Müller on the Catholic orthodoxy of the *German Theology*, placing it in the tradition of Dominican mysticism. But he considered the Bronnbach MS an arbitrary reworking of the original, an attempt "to make the *German Theology* more monastic than it really was." "Nochmals zum Text der 'Theologia Deutsch,'" *ZKG* 55 (1936): 308; Teufel, pp. 307–09. Schroeder, a Germanist with no theological stake in the matter, pointed the debate toward its final resolution when, on the basis of strict text-critical considerations, he declared the 230 additional lines of the Bronnbach MS to be interpolations and the 1518 edition of Luther to be closer to the original. Teufel, pp. 312–13.

The victory of the Luther texts was sealed by the dual discoveries of Max Pahncke and Kurt Ruh. Ruh discovered a Munich MS of the *German Theology* that conformed to the Luther 1518 edition. Pahncke came upon a complete copy of the *German Theology* in Dessau, dated 1477. This copy fully conformed to the Luther texts; the latter, Pahncke wrote, were "faithful and unchanged copies of their originals, which had not been prejudiced by (Luther's) theological concerns but reproduced with the philological trustworthiness characteristic of the spirit of the young humanism of that age." "Zur handschriftlichen Ueberlieferung des 'Frankfurters,'" *Zeitschrift für deutsches Altertum und deutsche Literatur* 89 (1959): 275–80, 276; Kurt Ruh, "Eine neue Handschrift des 'Frankfurters,'" in ibid., 280–87, esp. p. 286.

commentaries throughout the sixteenth century. But while these basic themes remain much the same, their assessment varies considerably. Differing theological predilections and concepts of reform quite naturally make a common point of departure no assurance of a common point of destination. Also, with variations in the particular historical theater of dissent come variations in the tactical use of the *German Theology*.

By comparison with the preface to the 1518 complete edition, Luther's recommendation in the preface to the December 1516 incomplete edition seems almost perfunctory. He writes:

> This little book warns all who would read and understand it, especially those who are rationally gifted and clever, that they not, on first encounter, hasten past it with too swift a judgment because it seems unlearned in some of the words it uses and fails to speak the accustomed pastoral and scholarly language. For it does not drift on the surface like foam on water but is issued forth from the depths of the Jordan by a true Israelite whose name is known to God and those to whom God reveals it. That is why this little book is now found without a name and title. Were one to surmise an author, what we find here is almost in the style of the illumined Doctor Tauler of the Dominican Order. Now as always, as the Apostle Paul says in 1 Cor. 1[: 23], what is true and solid teaching of the Holy Scripture must either make fools of men or become itself foolish. We preach Christ who is foolishness to the heathen, but the wisdom of God to the saints.[11]

By June of 1518, when Luther had readied the entire treatise for publication, the historical situation had changed profoundly. Behind him lay the *Disputation Against Scholastic Theology* (September, 1517), with theses directed not only against propositions drawn from Duns Scotus, William of Ockham, Peter d'Ailly, and Gabriel Biel, but also against propositions supported by "all scholastics." Furthermore, Luther had dispatched his ninety-five theses against indulgences (ca. October 31, 1517) and had written the theological and philosophical theses for the Heidelberg Disputation (April, 1518). Unlike the relatively obscure *Doctor scripturae* who had authored the 1516 preface, the Luther of

11. *WA* 1 : 153.

1518 was the leader of a national reform movement and was under examination by both political and ecclesiastical enemies.

In the 1516 preface Luther begs tolerance for the author's literary style. The 1518 preface embellishes this motif, stressing what had long since become basic in Luther's theology: God speaks only in and through the weak, declaring his glory *ex ore infantium*.[12] Then follows a new emphasis in the 1518 preface, which is fully understandable given the new historical situation in the summer of 1518. The *German Theology*, Luther now argues, is not only in line with the Bible and St. Augustine, but it is also a perfect anticipation of the Wittenberg theology. Luther comes down hard on this point on two occasions when he insists that, far from being innovative, Wittenberg theology is but a recapitulation of a "German theology" which can claim the best biblical and traditional lineage.

> I now for the first time became aware of the fact that a few of us highly educated Wittenberg theologians speak disgracefully, as though we want to undertake new things, as though there had been no people previously or elsewhere [who had undertaken these things]. Indeed, there have been others. . . .[13]
>
> Let anyone who wishes read this little book, and then let him say whether theology is original with us or ancient, for this book is not new.[14]

Luther concluded his preface of 1518 with slightly chauvinistic praise for German theologians, and the language he chose forbode the use to which the *German Theology* would be put in future ventures into dissent. Where books in the Latin, Greek, and Hebrew tongues have failed to lead the German people to God, Luther declares, a book in the German tongue has succeeded.[15] This statement, it is important to emphasize, was made in the context of a sustained effort *to blunt the charge of innovation*. There is the implicit suggestion, however, that a noncanonical writing from the late Middle Ages can more effectively lead people to God than the Latin, Greek, and Hebrew Scriptures. In a dif-

12. *WA* 1 : 378 (= *LW* 31 : 75).
13. *WA* 1 : 378–79 (= *LW* 31 : 75–76).
14. *WA* 1 : 379 (= *LW* 31 : 76). Cf. Heinrich Boehmer, *Martin Luther: Road to Reformation,* 3d ed. (New York, 1960), p. 343.
15. *WA* 1 : 379 (= *LW* 31 : 76).

ferent historical setting, such a view of the *German Theology* could function to reverse Luther's purpose in 1518. As we shall see, the *German Theology* can become a powerful witness *for,* rather than a strong defense *against,* innovation.

Our concern to underscore the importance of the *German Theology* for Luther's budding Reformation should not obscure his genuine agreement with various of its themes. He had no manifest tactical purpose in mind when he published nineteen chapters of it in 1516. Apparently he simply found much in it with which he agreed. Of the themes in the *German Theology* which, it could be argued persuasively, conform to Luther's own theological predilections in the formative years 1513–17, the following can be mentioned.[16] There is the emphasis on the "bitterness" of the true Christian life for a selfish human nature and for reason, which shun the way of suffering.[17] There is criticism of that "spiritual pride" which would dispense with Scripture and doctrine altogether.[18] The *German Theology* elaborates this point against the Free Spirits, who think that man can be "like God," i.e. live self-sufficiently above suffering and conscience, and hence

16. In listing these motifs I am not concerned to argue that Luther and the *German Theology* mean the same thing by them; I wish to say only that Luther could find in them material congenial to his own theological predilections at that time. The recent study by Jared Wicks shows (albeit one-sidedly) just how enthusiastically Luther could embrace these common motifs of medieval spirituality in the formative years 1513–17: "Luther found Tauler and *Eyn theologia deutsch* . . . thoroughly congenial to his own aims and way of thought." *Man Yearning for Grace: Luther's Early Spiritual Teaching* (Washington, D.C., 1968), p. 152 and passim. Erwin Iserloh goes so far as to argue that Luther even supports an "ontologische Umwandlung" in the tradition of German mysticism. "Luther und (die Mystik" in *Kirche, Mystik, Heiligung und das Natürliche bei Luther,* pp. 60–83, 83. Iserloh here fails, as Luther's contemporaries did not, to take account of the consequences of the crucial fact that such transformation is "fide" for Luther. Cf. my "Homo Viator: Luther and Late Medieval Theology," *HThR* 62 (1969): 275–87.

17. *Theologia Deutsch,* ed. Hermann Mandel (Leipzig, 1908), chap. 18, p. 40, lines 10–26. Cf. chap. 38, pp. 71–72, where nature is discussed as "das falsch liecht." A more systematic comparison of Luther's reflection in a later period with the *German Theology* is Wilhelm Thimme, "Die 'Deutsche Theologie' und Luthers 'Freiheit eines Christenmenschen.' Ein Vergleich," *ZThK* 3 (1932): 193 ff.

18. "Syder nu disse reiche geistliche hoffart dunckt, sie durff nit geschrifft noch lere und des gleich, so werdent da alle weis, ordnung und gesetz und gebot der heyligen kirchen und die sacrament zu nichte geachtet und auch zu einem spott und auch all menschen, die mit disser ordnung umbgend und davon haltent." *Theologia Deutsch,* chap. 23, p. 48. 13–17.

beyond ethical rules and institutional regulations.[19] There is the description of the perfect man as one who is free from the fear of hell and the selfish desire for an eternal reward;[20] and an effort to bring the whole man into the religious life is made by emphasizing the importance of both love and knowledge.[21] Finally, there are the various motifs which stress humility and self-denial, such as the description of the perfect man as always groaning over the persistence of sin,[22] willing to suffer even eternal damnation if that be God's will,[23] and always striving to suppress his selfishness by the hard way of the cross.[24]

On the other hand, there are motifs in the *German Theology* regarding mystical anthropology and speculation on man's union with God, which are not easily adjusted to Luther's thought in this period. It is doubtful, for example, that the demand for the annihilation not only of selfishness but also of "creatureliness" and "createdness" [25] would find an affirmative response from the young

19. "Wan als man spricht: Got ist durftloss und bedarff keines dinges, frey, müssig, ledig und uber all ding und der gleich (das alles war ist) und ist unbeweglich und nympt sich nichtz an und ist on gewissen, und was er tüt, das ist wol getan: 'Sieh, allso wil ich auch sein,' spricht das falsch liecht. 'Wann so man got gleicher ist, so viel pesser ist man, und darumb wil ich got gleich sein und wil auch got sein und bey gott sitzen, und sein ym gleich,' recht als lucifer der teüfel tet." "Auch spricht dis falsch liecht, es sey uber gewissen und conscientz komen, und was es thut, das sy alles wol getan. Ja es ward gesprochen von eym falschen freyen geist, der yn disser yrrung was: ertotete er zehen menschen, es wer ym als klein gewissen, als ob er ein hund ertötet. Kurtzlich, dis falsch betrogen liecht fleucht alles, daz der natur wider und swer ist." Ibid., chap. 38, 72. 16–23; 74. 9–15. Cf. 73. 10–15.

20. Ibid., chap. 10, 23. 13–16.

21. Ibid., chap. 39, 78. 1–16.

22. Ibid., chap. 35, 67. 17–21. This is not exactly Luther's description of faithful people as "semper clamantes" [cf. *WA* 4, 374.36 ff.], since the sin over which one groans is not necessarily one's own but that which will exist until God is all in all. Still it is a theme Luther can adopt and adapt to his own theology.

23. Ibid., chap. 11, 25. 12–19.

24. Ibid., chap. 52, pp. 96–97.

25. "Nu wenn dass volkommen kumpt, so versmecht man das geteilte. Wen kumpt es aber? Ich sprich: wenn es, als ferre als muglich ist, bekant und enpfunden und geschmeckt wirt yn der seel. . . . Wan yn wilcher creatur dis volkommen bekant werden soll, da muss creaturlicheyt, geschaffenheit, icheyt, selbheyt, verlören werden unde tzu nichte. Dis meint das wort sant Pauls 'wen das volkommen kumpt, das ist: wenn es bekant wirt, so wirt das geteilt, das ist: creaturlicheyt, geschaffenheyt, icheyt, selbheyt, meinheit, alles verschmecht und fur nichtz nit gehalten.'" Ibid., chap. 1, pp. 8–9.

Luther. There are reasons to believe, however, that this demand does not find a consistently affirmative response even within the *German Theology*. In a restatement of what must be removed in preparation for union with God, mention is made only of Adam's "ich und sein mich und sein myr und sein mein"—not of his creatureliness and createdness.[26] Also, the *German Theology* can place creatureliness on a par with "multiplicity," in contradistinction to that unity which God is. Hence to remove creatureliness and createdness can mean simply to overcome involvement in the fleeting world of the "many." [27] This interpretation is more congenial to the Cistercian and Franciscan mystical traditions, where Adamic conformity of will with God—perfect createdness—is the unitive ideal in this life. In the German tradition represented by Eckhart and Tauler, and on which the *German Theology* draws in its first chapter, the goal sought is precreated oneness—a return to the soul's existence in the divine essence prior to its creation.[28] It is a significant commentary on the syncretic character of the *German Theology* that both traditions find representation. We also see why very diverse, even categorically opposed, thinkers have considered it an ally to their cause. Its elasticity makes it a truly ecumenical document.

A second motif not easily reconciled with the theology of the young Luther is the quest for a "deification" (*vergottung*) and "union" (*vereynigung*) in which man's will is "dissolved" and "destroyed" entirely and God's will put in its place.[29] Here also, however, one finds alternative statements, which again move in the direction of Cistercian and Franciscan spirituality. The forfeiture of one's own individuality (*eigen*) and self (*selbheit*) and the concomitant acquisition of divine nature are presented in lan-

---

26. Ibid., chap. 2, pp. 10–11.

27. Cf. ibid., chap. 9, p. 21.

28. See Eckhart, *Daz Buoch der götlichen Tröstunge* in Pfeiffer, *Deutsche Mystiker des 14. Jahrhunderts*, 2 : 430 (English translation in Blakney, *Meister Eckhart*, pp. 55–56). For Tauler see my *Homo Spiritualis*, pp. 14 ff., 35 ff. Cf. note 29 below.

29. "'Was ist nu die einigung?' Nit anders dan das man lautterlichen und einfelticlichen und gentzlichen yn der warheit einfeltig sey mit dem einfeltigen, ewigen willen gottes oder auch zumal on willen sey und der geschaffen wille geflossen sey yn den ewigen willen und daryn versmeltzet sey und zunichte worden, also das der ewig will alleyn daselbst wolle, thun und lass." *Theologia Deutsch*, chap. 25, 53. 10–17.

guage suggesting volitional conformity (or unselfish love of God)
—intense piety—rather than an ontological transformation.[30]

Thirdly, Luther would not sympathize with an anthropology
that endows man with a soteriologically significant "eye" that can
look into eternity[31]—a sister metaphor to the mystical "ground of
the soul," which is elsewhere employed by the *German Theology*.[32]
Closely connected with this anthropology is the call for man to do
the best that is in him if he hopes to achieve union with God.[33]
Even in the subtle mystical form of passive resignation—a "doing"
which is a "doing nothing"—this is still allied to that semi-Pelagian
facere quod in se est, which Luther overcame theologically in his
first lectures on the Psalms (1513–16) and attacked explicitly in
writings against the nominalists in 1516–17.[34]

In summary, we could say that, of the three areas of mystical
theology—(1) ontology and anthropology, (2) the steps to salvation,
and (3) the union with God—Luther is interested primarily in
what the *German Theology* has to say about the second and he
shies away from the conclusions drawn in the first and third areas.
This is consistent not only with his prefatorial comments, but also
with the evolution of his thought in the formative years 1513–17.[35]
In subsequent prefaces and commentaries on the *German Theology*

---

30. "Auch sol man mercken, das das ein, da gott und mensch vereyniget sind, an
sich selber und an all und alles ledig steet und ist, das ist gottes halben und nit
des menschen oder der creaturen halben. Wann gotz eigen ist on diss und das und
on selbheyt und icheit und dem es gleich stee und sey. Aber creaturen und naturen
eygen ist, das sie sich selber und das yr und dis und das hie und da suchet und
wil yn allem dem, das sie tut oder lasset. Wan nu die creature oder der mensch sein
eigen und sein selbheit und sich verleusst und aussget, da get got ein mit seim
eigen, das ist mit seyner selbheyt." Ibid., chap. 22, 46. 17–27. Cf. ibid., 93. 12–15.
See also the definition of the new man in terms of "gehorsam," chap. 14, pp. 32–33.
On Bernard and Eckhart, cf. Bernhart, *Bernhardische und Eckhartische Mystik in
ihren Beziehungen und Gegensätzen,* p. 51. On Bonaventure and Eckhart, cf. Kurt
Ruh, *Altdeutsche und altniederländische Mystik,* p. 264. On Bernard, Tauler, and
Gerson, see my *Homo Spiritualis,* 34 ff., 55 ff., 72 ff.

31. *Theologia Deutsch,* chap. 7, 17. 18–20.

32. Ibid., chap. 21, 44. 20.

33. "Wer aber den ernst und lieb und begird nit hat, der sucht auch nit, so
findet er auch nit und bleibet unbereit und kumpt nymer zu dem end." Ibid.,
chap. 20, 44. 6–8. Cf. 53. 16–54. 26.

34. *Homo Spiritualis,* pp. 159 ff.

35. In addition to my *Homo Spiritualis,* cf. especially Bernd Moeller, "Tauler
und Luther" in *La mystique Rhénane,* pp. 157 ff., and H. A. Oberman, "Simul
gemitus et raptus: Luther und die Mystik" in *Kirche, Mystik, Heiligung und das
Natürliche bei Luther,* pp. 20–59.

a reverse tendency can be observed. The mystical way to salvation will certainly be embraced, but it is the presuppositions of mystical anthropology and reflection on man's union with God in this life that will be of primary interest to those who dissent from the gospel according to Rome, Wittenberg, Zurich, and Geneva.

THE 1528 WORMS EDITION

In Worms in 1528 an edition of the *German Theology* appeared, which, although based solidly on the 1518 Luther edition, bore the deceptive subtitle, "Recently with great effort corrected and improved." Although the editor of the work is not mentioned on the title page, it is relatively certain that this responsibility belongs to Louis Haetzer (d. 1528), a friend and colleague of Hans Denck (d. 1527).[36] It was Denck who aroused Haetzer's interest in mystical theology and put him in touch with the *German Theology*. The Haetzer edition, intended to supplant the editions of Luther among those who found Wittenberg as errant as Rome, went through six versions in the sixteenth century and served as the basis for Sebastian Franck's extensive Latin paraphrase (1541–42) and, indirectly, for Sebastian Castellio's polished Latin translation of 1557.[37]

Peter Schoeffer, friend and publisher to Haetzer and Denck, authored the brief preface to the Worms edition of the *German Theology*. His words not only elaborate the boast of the subtitle to have improved upon the Luther editions, but also adumbrate motifs dear to the dissenting heart—especially the primacy of the personal experience of the Holy Spirit for clear and full understanding of religious truth.

> This exceedingly precious little book was sent to me by a servant of God that I might publish it anew in service to all who believe in Christ. I am especially pleased to serve the faithful in this way. For I could see [already when I received

36. J. E. Gerhard Goeters, *Ludwig Haetzer (ca. 1500 bis 1529): Spiritualist und Antitrinitarier. Eine Randfigur der frühen Täuferbewegung* (Gütersloh, 1957), pp. 133–34; Baring (1963), pp. 46–47; *Hans Denck. Schriften*, vol. 1, *Quellen und Forschungen zur Reformationsgeschichte* (Gütersloh, 1955) 24 : 40.

37. Georg Baring, "Ludwig Haetzers Bearbeitung der *Theologia Deutsch* Worms 1528: Ihr Druck und ihre Handschrift von 1529, ihre Nachwirkung und ihr Verhältnis zu Luthers Ausgabe von 1518," *ZKG* 70 (1959): 218–30, 229; Goeters, *Ludwig Haetrer*, p. 136.

it] that over against previously published copies [i.e. the
Luther editions] this copy was proofread in a fresh and
comprehensive way and carefully corrected with special
diligence and labor. Indeed, it is now so improved that it is
no surprise that many previously considered this little book
dark, coarse, and incomprehensible, whereas in itself it is
fully understandable and in no way confusing. For the Spirit
of God (who reveals the witness [of this book]) neither speaks
nor testifies in a dark and confused way. God is rightly to be
praised for so generously giving through his power refresh-
ment and new life to the souls of the thirsty in these last days
in such gifts [as this little book]. God desires to reveal to us
this and every other witness of truth by means of the key of
David [i.e. the Holy Spirit] through Jesus Christ. Amen.[38]

Comparison of the Worms text with that of the 1518 Wittenberg edition has yielded significant, although hardly as radical,
variations as the subtitle and preface of the Worms edition might
lead one to suspect. Apart from numerous stylistic changes, Haetzer
has on three occasions taken the liberty of bringing the *German
Theology* materially into line with his own theological convictions.

First, at the beginning of the sixth chapter of the *German
Theology,* the honorific title "Meister" is dropped from "Meister
Boethius." Parallel to this is the removal of the "Sanctus" from
"Sanctus Paulus." [39] The deletion of these honorific titles has been
interpreted as indicative of the biblicistic attitude adopted by
Anabaptists following Matthew 23 : 8–10,[40] which warns against
calling others and/or being called "teacher," "father," or "master."
While there is no doubt truth in this explanation, it seems equally
plausible, especially in light of Haetzer's low-profile Biblicism in
1527–28 (cf. below), that such deletions also serve to undercut
present academic and ecclesiastical establishments that derive and
defend their authority from a tradition of masters and saints.

A second material adjustment of the Wittenberg text occurs in
the opening words of the second chapter. The Wittenberg edition

38. Reprinted in Ludwig Keller, *Monatshefte der Comenius Gesellschaft* 11 (1902):
148–49.
39. Baring, *ZKG* 70 (1959): 226–27.
40. Ibid., p. 226.

reads: "Scripture, faith, and truth say. . . ." The Worms edition has amended this order to read: "Truth, faith, and Scripture say. . . ." [41] This change concurs with the common insistence among many of those who dissent from Wittenberg as well as from Rome that Scripture is a "witness" to and not the truth itself. Only as the latter is known in personal experience does the former become meaningful. Haetzer's colleague, Hans Denck, summarized this matter in the following way. If someone gave you a letter in which you were promised many good things, yet you did not know personally whether the author of the letter really was a pious and rich man, you would be foolish to trust the letter. Should you discover, however, that he really is pious and rich and will keep his word, then you can freely entrust yourself to him, quite regardless of his letter. Theologically applied: "For one who is not in God's household, the letter [i.e. Scripture] is of no use; one who is in his household knows how trustworthy the Lord is without the letter." [42]

A final alteration of the Wittenberg text is noted in the prayer that concludes the *German Theology*. In the Wittenberg edition the prayer reads: "May he [sc. Jesus Christ] help us who has surrendered his will to his heavenly Father and who lives and reigns in heaven with God the Father in the unity of the Holy Spirit eternally in perfect trinity [*dryvaltigkeit*]." The Worms edition has given this prayer what seems to be a distinctively theocentric and perhaps even antitrinitarian twist: "May God help us through him who has surrendered his will to his heavenly father and who lives and reigns in heaven with God the Father in the unity of the Holy Spirit eternally in perfect threeness [*dreiheit*]." [43]

In addition to these changes the Worms edition has deleted Luther's preface and replaced it with the introductory comments of Peter Schoeffer. It has also taken a still more important step in the assessment of the *German Theology*. It has appended a hereto-

41. Ibid.

42. *Vom Gesetz Gottes* (1526) in *Hans Denck. Schriften,* (Gütersloh, 1956), 2 : 61. 6–20. This theme is also consistent with Haetzer's conviction, amply documented against the "Schriftgelehrten" of Wittenberg in the preface to his 1527 German translation of selected Apocrypha writings, that the key to truth is the presence of the Spirit in the depths of the soul. *Baruch der Prophet. Die Histori Susannah. Die Histori Bel zu Babel* (Worms, 1528). See below, pp. 110–12.

43. Baring, ZKG 70 (1959): 227; Goeters, *Ludwig Haetzer,* 134–35.

fore unseen postscript to the *German Theology*, viz. the *Hauptreden* of Hans Denck.

THE *Hauptreden* OF HANS DENCK

Attached to the 1528 Worms edition of the *German Theology*, and continuing as an appendix to subsequent editions based on the Worms edition even into the twentieth century,[44] was a series of knotty statements written by Hans Denck and bearing the title: "Several Propositions [*Hauptreden*] by which every sincere student of Christ can test and search what should be known about true and essential union with the one and highest Good." It is problematic whether the *Hauptreden* can be taken as a conscious interpretation of the *German Theology* or whether they simply form what was considered a congenial addition to it. It is certainly clear that they do not constitute a literal summary of it, although they are, as one scholar puts it, "written in the spirit of the *German Theology*." [45] Still, whether as Denck's systematic deduction of the essence of the *German Theology* or as an independent statement of the theological truths he held to be self-evident, it is obvious that the *Hauptreden* would not have been appended to the Haetzer edition had no strong affinity with the *German Theology* been considered present. Hence we may include the *Hauptreden* among the major evaluations of the *German Theology* in the sixteenth century.

In highly abstract language—requiring the reader's patience— the *Hauptreden* set forth a theology of surprisingly simple piety. In the first series of propositions Denck explains that God is one and the source of all unity. When two come together, he points out, discord is possible. They need only disagree with one another (*uneyns in willen werden*), and we see the advent of dissension. For the cause of all disunity, wherever it occurs, is dissimilarity of wills (*ungleiche der willen*). God, being one and desiring unity, is unalterably opposed to all that is "two." He created everything with an eye to unity, not only for the sake of order, but also to give his creation no cause to will contrary to himself and therefore to

---

44. *Hans Denck, Schriften*, 1 : 40 ff.

45. Cf. Goeters, p. 135. In regard to the terminological and thematic importance of the *Theologia Deutsch* for Denck's own thought, the editor of his works concludes: "Alle seine Schriften sind von ihr durchdrungen." Walter Fellmann, "Der theologische Gehalt der Schriften Dencks" in *Die Leibhaftigkeit des Wortes: Festgabe für Adolf Köberle zum 60. Geburtstag*, ed. O. Michel and U. Mann (Hamburg, 1958), pp. 157–65, 159.

suffer the ruinous consequences which fallen man now knows.[46]

Denck brings forth two propositions that state this simple soteriological formula—salvation is unity of will with God—in terms of the epistemological axiom of medieval thought from which it is ultimately derived: like is known only by and through like. Unity can be grasped and known only by and through the One, even in what stands in opposition to the One.[47] In other words, one must be overcome by and conformed to his opposite before he can know his opposite; the sinner must be purified if he is to know God.

These, then, are the fundamental points. God is one and opposed to the discord and dissension that result from man's willing contrary to his will. If the unity that overcomes discord and dissension is to be achieved, it will only be through him who is One. Ideally this should, and ultimately it must, occur through personal experience. Denck, however, faces the dilemma known to every mystical theologian who would seek to reach the heart through the head. He must assume the ambivalent role of teaching about something that is, by his own conviction, truly known only in direct experience. Thus, he tells us that, although the One is known in the highest way only as he gives himself to personal experience, it will be necessary to "make the Best an object" so that others may learn of him.[48]

This One, we now learn, was and is "the being and 'Is' of all creatures" (*aller creaturen wesen und Ist*), especially of that creature which Adam was prior to his Fall. Further, the One undertakes nothing without the creature, although the creature is not permitted to reciprocate by coauthoring the activities of the One. This inclusion yet exclusion of the creature from the activities of the One is expressive of the omnipotence, mercy, and infinite goodness of the One whom men call the "Lord of all." [49]

Denck now brings forth propositions on creaturely freedom and sin, topics investigated two years earlier in a biting treatise against Luther.[50] God, he points out, has so created that the

46. *Etliche Hauptreden* in *Hans Denck. Schriften*, 2 : 111. 13–26.

47. Ibid., 111, 27–29.

48. Ibid., 111. 30–31.

49. Ibid., 112. 1–6.

50. *Was geredt sey, das die schrifft sagt, Gott thue und mache guts und böses* (1526) in *Hans Denck. Schriften*, 2 : 27 ff. Translated in *Spiritual and Anabaptist Writers*, ed. G. H. Williams and A. M. Mergal (Philadelphia, 1957), pp. 88 ff.

creature remains free for ever greater knowledge. This was done so that what was eternally free and remains free now need not live from and suffer the disadvantages of creatureliness. What better way can the creature freely understand and distinguish itself, Denck asks, than in that which is its opposite, viz. the uncreated One? The creature which is and should remain free and yet turns into itself and chooses what is its own, opposes him who has created and made it free. This, Denck concludes, is the meaning of sin.[51]

At this point Denck brings forth the fundamental tenet of mystical anthropology and makes it the cornerstone of his soteriology: there is a "seed" or "image" of God indestructibly present within every man. Hatred of sin arises in what is opposed to sin, in that which one truly calls "the seed of God or the image of God [*der Som Gottes oder Gottes bildnuss*], which craves freedom incessantly." This seed or image, we learn further, "remains, 'Is' and must abide as long as God, in whom it is, is and abides; for it comes from the One and cannot be forced eternally away from the One." [52] In order that this seed or image may return to its origin, the One is prepared to welcome back everything that has been separated from him. The return of the latter can occur only through "something" which, while "like" that which is separated, still remains distinct and innocent of every defection from unity. This "something" should and must (to the extent that it is of the One) undertake to glorify unity in the highest so that the freedom which has never been lost may be revitalized.[53]

Thus far Denck has associated this "something," which is "like" yet distinct from all that is alienated from God, with the seed or image of God in every man. What he has referred to as a lower case "it" and "something" is now, however, presented as a higher case "Something," and it is spoken of not as an omnipresent anthropological structure but as a particular historical example of perfect return to God. "It (Jesus Christ of Nazareth)" had taught and practiced, possessed and used, the freest of wills. And, as he himself pointed out, this will was not his own but that of the One from whom he received it. Still this will is rightly in his power and not to be taken from him, lest he lack the perfection requisite to glorify freedom in the highest. The most perfect thing

51. *Etliche Hauptreden,* 112. 7–14.
52. Ibid., 112. 15–18.
53. Ibid., 112. 19–25.

about Jesus, Denck concludes, is this absolutely perfect union with God's will. It is a union in which he claimed nothing as his own; and thereby he was, is, and remains in the One.[54]

In a concluding series of propositions Denck reemphasizes the reality of freedom—what he calls now "das Frei"—and the individual's responsibility to grasp it. Freedom is still present and must not be lost. For if and when it is lost there is not only great insult to God, from whom it comes and to whom it belongs, but also the ominous fact that if the divine gift of freedom can perish, nothing else can hope to fare any better. If this freedom is now to be taken up and implemented, it must be done according to the example of the highest fulfillment of duty (ostensibly Jesus Christ). It must happen according to the way and the will of one who was never divided in himself. In practical terms that means that one must strive throughout one's life to turn away from all that is divided and to that which is unity. Exhorts Denck: "he who chooses to do it can do it; let him who doubts it only try it." [55]

The concluding proposition summarizes the challenge to each individual in terms of that "abandon" known to the mystics of the Middle Ages as "resignation" (*Gelassenheit*). He who does his best in obedience to the seed of God within and in imitation of the life of Jesus without may achieve that self-surrender which is "Christ" and thereby claim that power which is of the Father.

> [Freedom] can and must be established solely through the abandonment [*verlierung*] of everything that is opposed to unity. Such abandonment is resignation in resignation [*gelassenheyt in gelassenheyt*], complete surrender, a perfect voluntary sacrifice. In sum, that is Christ, the true son of God, the firstborn among the brothers, who can claim everything that is in the power of the Father, and who is the true and only means by which one can, should and must come to the Father. It is for this reason that the Father sent him forth.[56]

Finally, it is important to note that Denck has put his propositions beyond critical discussion by adding a censure for those who will not acquiesce in the teaching of the Holy Spirit as set forth

54. Ibid., 112. 26–113.3.
55. Ibid., 113. 4–13.
56. Ibid., 113. 14–19. See below, pp. 39–45, 201, where Sebastian Castellio summarizes the teaching of the *German Theology* in terms of power.

in the *Hauptreden*. By making the Spirit the key to true understanding in this as in all matters of religious truth, alternative conclusions from even the most eminent historical authorities need
not be seriously entertained. The postscript to the *Hauptreden*
states:

> He who cannot come to grips with these statements lacks the
> witness of the Spirit, whose instruction he refuses and will not
> have. Let him who understands them judge, [remembering
> that it is] the Spirit of God [who] judges all things. If anyone
> finds error or shortcoming in that, it is his own fault. For he
> is unwilling to correct his own defection. . . . Someone has
> said: It is sagacity to know that the greatest foolishness (so
> to speak) of the Holy Spirit is wiser than the greatest wisdom
> of the whole world.[57]

SEBASTIAN FRANCK'S LATIN PARAPHRASE

Given his declaration that the Christian church fell with the
death of the original apostles and his dismissal of the magisterial
church fathers (Ambrose, Augustine, Jerome, and Gregory) as
"apes of the apostles and antichrists," [58] it might seem strange to
find Sebastian Franck busy constructing an authoritative historical
tradition of religious truth from the writings of late medieval
mystics during the last years of his life. Yet that is precisely the
meaning of his Latin paraphrase of the *German Theology*, written
in 1541–42. This elaborate paraphrase runs to some 550 manuscript pages, about one-third of which is Franck's inflation beyond
the original.[59]

In the preface to the paraphrase[60] Franck presents detailed
comments on the significance of this treatise and, in effect, summarizes through it what he considers true theology in every age
to be. The opening paragraph reports the traditional assessment
of this work—an assessment which has flowered considerably since
the prefaces of Luther witnessed its excellence—and Franck's
immediate reason for putting it in Latin form.

57. Ibid., 113. 20–26.

58. *A Letter to John Campanus* (1531) in *Spiritual and Anabaptist Writers*, pp.
150–51.

59. Hegler 1901, pp. 29 ff., 44 ff.; Baring, *ARG* 49 (1957): 3.

60. The full preface is transcribed in Hegler 1901, pp. 20–29.

This celebrated theological handbook the Germans know by the name of a certain member of the Teutonic Order, and it is popularly called the "German Theology." Many of the most preeminent men—men whose taste is refined and judgment exact—value this little book as a sheer star and what they call a "white stone." [61] Some attribute to it first rank after the Bible, and others prefer it to the whole of scholastic theology. Still others elevate to the very heavens this little book, which is as devout as it is brief and contains an epitome, indeed the very kernel and the most succinct summary possible, of the whole of theology. It is thought to have been written years ago by a certain German theologian with the most intense illumination. His age was as Thebes defiled by error, with abomination resident even in the holy place. In comparison with the infirmity of his age, which was darkened by so many and such great clouds of ignorance, and the weakness of this age of ours, it can certainly be called a light to the world, truly a miracle of nature, a rose among thorns, and a Lot in the midst of Sodom. For those periods when the Spirit is withdrawn, this little book sets before one not only extraordinary erudition and the [instruction of the] divine Spirit, in which it is neither excelled nor equaled, but also certain profound mysteries and hidden things of the Spirit and truly sincere, genuine transworldly theology. Because in such periods some cannot go to the original source,[62] it is resolved now to put it into Latin so that those who read this language [*Latini*] may have for themselves what even the Greeks and Hebrews might well beg and borrow from the Germans.[63]

Franck formulates a more personal assessment of the *German Theology* as he characterizes it as a divine communication equal to what God has given his church through the Hebrews, Greeks, and Latins.

---

61. "Albo calculo." Cf. Rev. 2 : 17: "calculus candidus." This can carry the connotation of a standard for judgment and also, if interpreted along the lines of Rev. 2 : 17, a sign of the last age.

62. Hermann Oncken argues that the paraphrase was not written for a learned audience, but for "Leser, die den oberdeutschen Dialekt Francks und der Deutschen Theologie nicht verstanden." *Monatshefte der Comenius-Gesellschaft* 11 (1902), pp. 96–97.

63. Hegler 1901, p. 21.

Although this theology is called "German," may I be struck
dead if it is not the same as true, genuine transworldly
philosophy. For it is nothing else than that very theology
which, by divine decree [*divinitus*], has descended upon us
from heaven. As my own assessment of it, for whatever it may
be worth, I would with your indulgence, join many of the
most preeminent men to declare freely of it the following.
Apart from the Bible and with no author of religious writings
excepted, I have read nothing more excellent in any of the
many books of either the modern authorities or the ancient
masters and fathers of the primitive church. Although others
may have been affected otherwise, I am still confident that I
speak not simply out of affection but from careful judgment
and in agreement with many others who judge keenly and
honestly, when I say this. The Germans, having once been
raised up in hope, are even more uplifted [to learn] that that
highest Good which is God now as always has been a god of
the Germans, a God who in this one German theologian (as
in those lights to the world, Thomas à Kempis and Johannes
Tauler, whom I mention in passing) imparted as much to his
church as has ever been communicated to it by any theologian
from the ranks of the Hebrews, Latins, or Greeks. Because of
this fact and with experience as our mistress and with the
very reality of which we speak crying out and teaching us,
let us learn that theology, the science of piety, and all faith in
and understanding of truth are not only in those languages
[Hebrew, Latin, and Greek]. Indeed, the righteousness of the
heart is bound to no language and to the lips of no people,
since the word of God is not bound, howsoever much it is
tied to the one who speaks it.[64]

The *German Theology*, like Thomas à Kempis and Johannes
Tauler, demonstrates for Franck that God's word is absolutely
free to speak with full authority wherever and whenever it chooses.
The *German Theology* is certainly not a canonical writing, nor
is it among the magisterial documents of ecclesiastical tradition.
Still, through it, God gives as much to his church as through the
canonical and traditional authorities. There is a logical conclusion
to be drawn here, and Franck does not hesitate to draw it, as he

64. Ibid., p. 24.

turns to censure those who discredit the author of the *German Theology* because he is ignorant of scholarly languages.[65]

In the following passage Franck releases religious life, as medieval man had known it, from all traditional moorings. In late medieval theological terminology, he appears to be proposing nothing less than that the direct, absolute power of God is the normative ordained power of God:

> Faith, an innocent and guiltless life, simple charity without sanctimony, the fulfillment of [God's] command which flows from a pure heart, a good conscience and an unfeigned faith, self-knowledge not paled by guilt, in brief, the very science of piety, the understanding of the mysteries of God, the knowledge of Christ, the attainment of salvation, that divine theology and transworldly philosophy which the Spirit of God gives to many and, finally, the whole glory, knowledge and majesty of the New Testament—these are not tied to tongues nor bound to any language, observance, knowledge, or rule. Rather they are pressed into the tablets of the heart . . . by the finger of the living God.[66]

Every medieval theologian would have agreed that God, considered in his absolute sovereignty, was free to work independently of all secondary causes and traditional means of self-communication (i.e. churches, priests, and sacraments). Normally (*regulariter*), however, God works through his ecclesiastical system, and, unless one thinks he is a liar, one ought to be prepared to meet him within these established structures. For Franck, however, the normal has become the exception. The divine freedom to work independently of all secondary causes and traditional means of self-communication is no longer viewed as a rarely exercised option; it is the normal, de facto form in which God has and always will communicate his holy gifts. Neither pope, council, church, nor holy book is the immediate locus of divine truth.

---

65. "Linguarum ignarus pure Germanus fuit." Ibid., p. 25. For a parallel with Francis of Assisi, whose simplicity was no bar to beholding the highest truth, cf. Kurt Ruh, *Altdeutsche und altniederländische mystik*, pp. 259–60. The anti-intellectualistic consequences of this line of argumentation are clearly highlighted in Franck's statement (which he borrowed from Erasmus), "Docti perversi quo doctior eo perversior." Hegler 1901, p. 25.

66. Ibid., p. 25.

Rather, "the whole glory, knowledge, and majesty of the New Testament" is written on the "tablets of the heart."

A concluding summary of the *German Theology*, which Franck sets forth as he brings his paraphrase to a close, points back to this statement in the preface. Here Franck notes the opposition of *Scripture* to Scripture-and-tradition religion. The written Book advocates the "living Book"; the Bible cedes authority to the free Spirit of God:

> Theology is more a matter of experience than of knowledge, and the secret of all theology is therefore more a matter of rebirth than something which can be communicated by any words. But it is possible for theology to be foreshadowed and entered [so to speak] from a distance in a kind of crude way, viz. through the pen of Scripture. Hence in the fifth and sixth chapters of Hebrews [esp. Heb. 5 : 12–14] and the fourth chapter of 1 Corinthians, Paul calls Scripture the milk of infants and the basic nourishment of one who is a beginner in the words of God. [It is to be used] until, as adults and those advanced in Christ, we can turn our backs on everything external, understanding no one and knowing nothing according to the flesh, but being already carried over into the Spirit, we have the Holy Spirit as the living Book of God, and are instructed of God by the one true teacher of the godly. . . . The solid food of the perfect does not come from Scripture. It is the mind of Christ, who sends forth the Spirit of Scripture. Here the very finger of God is the true teacher of the faithful, their living Bible and their open book. Hence, God the Spirit is called the teacher and Rabbi of his own (Matt. 23)—not Scripture. For Scripture is only a witness or testimony to truth for those who are taught by the Spirit, and it is this only insofar as it is understood in the Spirit according to the mind of Christ (John 5[: 29]).[67]

With the displacement of traditional loci of authority—pope, council, tradition, the Bible—the practical experience of the individual assumes the role of critical judgment. Institutional structures give way to anthropological or psychological structures ("heart" or "conscience") as the loci of the power and authority of the Holy Spirit.

67. Ibid., pp. 72–73.

This displacement comes to the fore in especially striking form in Franck's preface as he escalates his polemic against the learned. Scriptural and classical citations and allusions are piled up to form a full-fledged theology of humility. According to Scripture, as well as to experience, it is to the *humiles* and *parvuli,* not to the intellectually and linguistically gifted, that God speaks; it is through his Spirit, not through the university curriculum, that he communicates his truth.

> Nowhere is it said [in the Bible] that the Lord reveals his mysteries to those before all others who are most advanced in many languages and in the sciences and who think themselves a light to the world and the leaders of the blind. Nor is it anywhere said that God reveals his mysteries through their many sciences, languages, and philosophy. Rather Scripture testifies that it is to the little ones that God gives understanding and that it is the Holy Spirit who teaches all truth, applies all healing balm and admonishes all of us. He it is who writes the necessary things in the tablets of our heart with his skilled finger. And to whom do these tablets belong? To those big "mountains" [i.e. the learned]? No! Then to whom? Listen to Isaiah who responds by saying: "the Lord teaches his knowledge to those who are weaned and taken from the breast." (Isa. 28 : 9) David sings out in Psalm 25: "With righteousness he leads the humble in the way they should go, and he teaches the afflicted his way . . ." (Ps. 25 : 9).[68]

In the final analysis, then, it is only personal experience and suffering, not the most accomplished intellectual disciplines, which form the truest "media" of divine teaching. It is indicative of the intensity of Franck's rejection of the intellectual establishment of the sixteenth century that he here instances Raymond Lull, perhaps the most obfuscating of the late medieval *mystici,*[69] in his chastisement of the learned.

> The means by which God teaches is Christ, i.e. the word of the Father, his cross, and the word of the cross. We find it repeated so often in the New Testament: "through Christ,"

---

68. Ibid., p. 27.

69. Cf. Jean Gerson's censure of Lull in his second lecture *Contra curiositatem studentium* (1402), *Jean Gerson, Oeuvres complètes,* ed. P. Glorieux (Paris, 1962), 3 : 245, "habet [Lullus] enim terminos a nullo doctore usitatos."

i.e. through the cross and the word of the cross. David testifies to it in Ps. 18: "your discipline taught me" [cf. Ps. 18 : 8]. Elsewhere we read that "trial gives one understanding; what does one who has not been tried know?" [Eccles. 24 : 10–11] "Reprove me," says the voice of Truth through Solomon [Prov. 1 : 23], "and I will bring forth my Spirit and show you my words." To that one can add Rom. 5[: 4]: "suffering begets trial, knowledge, and experience." [70] Nowhere does one read that God teaches us about himself through the sophistic art of [Raymond] Lull, through rhetoric, dialectic, many languages, commentaries, decrees, Summas, or through the great heroes and amazing gods of the world. Hence you ought not immediately cast our author aside because he is anonymous or because he is not gifted with many languages or because he strove more for simplicity than elegance. I might rightly wish for many similar books and authors in the church of Christ. [71]

Franck closes his preface to the *German Theology* by urging on every man the right and duty to judge in the Spirit about religious truth. Citing the recorded errancy and fraud of traditional religious authorities, Franck sees in the testimony of the individual human spirit, guided directly by God's Spirit, the more dependable witness to truth.

Read everything with judgment, for the spiritual man is judged by no one but judges all things fully in the Spirit [1 Cor. 2 : 15]. Follow the counsel of Paul (1 Thess. 5), and do not quench the Spirit or spurn the prophecy of any man no matter how slight and insignificant he may seem. We read that God even spoke once through an ass. [72] On the other hand,

70. Cf. the Vulgate: "Patientia autem probationem, probatio vero spem." This passage was central in Castellio's assessment of the *German Theology*. Oncken points out that Castellio not only wrote his 1556 Latin translation in Basel, where fourteen years earlier Franck had made his Paraphrase, but also cited liberally from the works of Franck in his *De haereticis an sint persequendi*. Also, Oncken finds parallels between the two prefaces to the respective editions, which suggest that, if not explicitly dependent on Franck's Paraphrase, Castellio at least knew of it. *Monatshefte der Comenius-Gesellschaft* 11 (1902), p. 91.

71. Hegler 1901, p. 28.

72. The example of Balaam's ass had also been used by Luther in his 1520 *Open Letter to the Christian Nobility of the German Nation*: "Balaam's ass also was wiser than the prophet himself. If God then spoke by an ass against a prophet, why should He not be able even now to speak by a righteous man against the pope?" *Three Treatises: Martin Luther* (Philadelphia, 1960), p. 23. Cf. below, pp. 69, 147, 185, n. 66.

the oracle of Apollo often spoke falsely, prophets and patriarchs have at times been found wanting and overcome by
ignorance, and it is stated fact that the mighty gods, when
left to themselves, were commonly quite mad and even sheer
deceivers.[73]

SEBASTIAN CASTELLIO AND THE *German Theology*

Prior to the publication of his Latin and French translations of
the *German Theology*, Sebastian Castellio was vigorously challenged by his friend Nikolaus Zurkinden (Zerchintes) (d. 1588) to
defend its contents. Zurkinden was Bernese *Staatssekretär* during
the period of ecclesiastical conflict between Bern and Calvin's
Geneva. A close acquaintance of Calvin's, he nonetheless rejected
his views on predestination and stood with Castellio against Calvin's execution of Michael Servetus in 1553.[74] In his correspondence with Castellio on the nature of the *German Theology* in
1556–57, however, Zurkinden assumed the role of a staunchly conservative critic of departures from orthodoxy.

Their relationship was sufficiently intimate that Zurkinden
could request from Castellio advice on how best to prepare for
death. It was a subject that engaged Castellio fully in 1556. In a
letter to Zurkinden on October 21 of that year, Castellio explains,
with all the seriousness and simplicity of a medieval preacher,
that the chance to live well and as a Christian is extended to us in
this life, and he who fails to grasp it will in the future hear behind
closed doors the sad voice of the Bridegroom saying, "I knew you
not." Then follows a theme that was to become central in the
preface to Castellio's Basel 1557 Latin translation of the *German
Theology:* Christian faith is the possibility of "omnipotence" here
and now on earth.

> We prepare ourselves, my Zurkinden, to become new crea-
> tures—new men created according to God. And, just as prior
> to this creation we extended our members as servants of
> unrighteousness, so afterwards we will stretch them forth as

---

73. Hegler 1901, p. 28. Cf. Hegler, *Geist und Schrift bei Sebastian Franck*.

74. Basic for Zurkinden's relationship with Castellio are the two volumes of
Ferdinand Buisson, *Sébastien Castellion: sa vie et son oeuvre (1515–1563). Etude
sur les origines du protestantisme libéral français*, 2 vols. (Paris, 1892) [hereafter
cited as Buisson]. On Zurkinden and Calvin, cf. C. Guggisberg, "Jean Calvin und
Nikolaus Zurkinden; Glaubensautorität und Gewissensfreiheit," *Zwingliana* 6 (1937):
374–409.

servants of righteousness. And this we can do if we will henceforth believe in the omnipotent Son of the omnipotent God, Jesus Christ, who, when he lived on earth . . . made those who believed in him omnipotent, for all things are possible for one who believes. But our faith, alas, is so weak. We do not truly believe that all power, even on earth, is given to the one who believes. Hence small powers follow small faith.[75]

On the heels of this statement Castellio announces the dispatch of the *German Theology*. Zurkinden had apparently requested a copy after learning earlier of Castellio's intention to translate and publish it. Castellio explains that it is necessary to send the German copy since his "Lugdunum" translation is not yet available.[76] The letter concludes with a brief assessment and recommendation of the *German Theology*:

> Although the book is obscure, it is written with great spirit [*magno spiritu*] and ought to be read often. Here you will find how man can, while living, die—which is the true preparation for death.[77]

Zurkinden, having had the opportunity to read the *German Theology* in his native tongue, responded to Castellio on November 4, 1556. In a brief introductory paragraph he announces that, while he found much that he liked, Castellio should look again at certain problematical passages. Then Zurkinden proceeds to raise critical questions about chapters 7, 8, 11, 14, 19, 22, 29, 31, 34, 38, and 39. He found ridiculous fantasy, error, hyperbole, crudity, inconsistency, sophistry, and possible madness at various junctures in the book. And he summarizes his reaction as a whole by maintaining that the book has nothing positive to say about Christian life which was not more purely and clearly taught by Christ and the Apostles. He even questions Luther's ever having supported it—

75. Buisson, 2 : 382. The correspondence is collected in Buisson, 2 : 381–92.

76. The reference to "Lugdunum" (Lyon or Leiden) is somewhat confusing. The first Castellio edition to appear was the Basel 1557 Latin translation (with Johannes Oporinus) under the pseudonym Joannes Theophilus. Castellio's French translation appeared without name in an Antwerp 1558 edition (with Christoph Plantin). A Lyon 1559 French translation (with Alexander Marsilius) is listed by Baring, yet he refers this to a 1569 Leiden or Lyon edition. Baring 1963, pp. 59–60, 64, 66, 68.

77. Buisson, 2 : 383.

the preface, he concludes, must be a "pseudo-Lutheran preface" —[78] and he warns Castellio not to associate his name with it in his forthcoming translation.[79]

Castellio, obviously taken aback by Zurkinden's frontal assault on the *German Theology*, wrote a defense of it on November 11, 1556. It opens with what will become the leitmotiv of his last work, the *De Arte dubitandi* of 1563: in matters of religious truth, doubt and measured judgment are of absolute necessity. He admits that while he had not, as Zurkinden surmised in his letter, torn into the *German Theology* with an eye to testing every part, Zurkinden's rash assessment has not now convinced him of its shortcomings. He forthrightly confesses the obscurity of the book and even the fact that it contains some things he does not understand. Still, he feels that he has understood a number of things which have escaped Zurkinden. If, Castellio warns, we are going to be rash in our judgment even of sacred writings, then our ignorance may very well lead us to condemn what ought to be praised.

Castellio then brings forth some examples which, for him, illustrate the difficulty into which the rash judgment of religious matters can lead. Who, he asks, could today disseminate the opening words of the sixth chapter of Hebrews, where one is admonished to "leave the elementary doctrines of Christ and go on to maturity," or Christ's words that those who believe in him will do even greater works than he himself did—without being accused of blasphemy? And what of Paul's statement that he was not sent to baptize, when nevertheless the Apostles were commanded to baptize? Who would not call that false had Paul himself not written it?

> You say that these are matters which must be correctly interpreted. I agree, and the Spirit of God agrees too. But I say further that the same equitable conduct [*aequitas*] [which we extend to sacred writings] be also extended to the judgment of the works of others, even those which are not of great authority. If I may say so, you ought in your assessment [of

---

78. The fact that the Luther preface is mentioned confirms that Castellio sent Zurkinden a copy of the Frankfurt/M 1246 (1546) Cyriacus Jacob edition, which was distinguished by the fact that it combined the Luther preface of 1518 with the Worms 1528 text and the *Hauptreden* of Denck. Baring 1963, pp. 55–56. It was the basis for Castellio's Basel 1557 Latin translation.

79. Buisson, 2 : 385.

a writing] to bring forward one or two passages by which doubt can be cast upon your own judgment of it.[80]

Castellio follows this censure with a defense of the authenticity of Luther's preface and, citing Tauler, the sound character of the age in which the *German Theology* was written.[81] He then takes up the particular points of criticism made by Zurkinden. At the beginning of the letter he had pointed out that Zurkinden's criticism was so extensive that to answer it fully would require a book rather than a letter. Forced to be selective in his rebuttal, it is a telling judgment on Castellio's assessment of the *German Theology* that he was especially eager to set aside Zurkinden's criticism of the nineteenth chapter of this work, in which the following paradox is stated. Only the man who has experienced God's light knows and can truly speak about it. Yet, since this experience is fundamentally incommunicable by words, he cannot enlighten one who is inexperienced.[82] Zurkinden considered this insistence upon the exclusiveness of experience as teacher to stand in contradiction to Scripture and the accounts left us by the truly pious.[83]

Castellio counters his criticism by maintaining that the nineteenth chapter of the *German Theology* says nothing other than what Christ said to Nicodemus:

"What happens within the reborn man is like the wind; he can sense it, but he cannot express it in words." [John 3 : 8] You can teach no one what the wind is, although you might say a great deal about it, and the same is true for the man who is born of God. He who does not understand what it means is one not yet reborn, and he who is not reborn is one who cannot understand it.[84]

The importance of this point for Castellio is indicated by the further fact that he returns to a defense of chapter 19 toward the conclusion of his letter, this time quoting the *German Theology:* "Whoever wants to know it [i.e. the new birth], let him wait till it happens." [85] To this is added the gloss: "The flesh cannot judge

80. Ibid., p. 387.
81. Ibid.
82. *Theologia Deutsch,* chap. 19, p. 41.
83. Buisson, 2 : 384.
84. Ibid., p. 387.
85. Ibid., p. 388; *Theologia Deutsch,* chap. 19, p. 41.

the Spirit, no matter how many writings it masters, for the letter kills and the Spirit makes alive." [86] The primacy and authority of experience is thus maintained.

Zurkinden had also taken issue with the distinction made in the twenty-ninth chapter of the *German Theology* between God as "Godhead" (*gotheit*) and as "God" (*got*)—the former referring to God hidden in himself and beyond any human description, the latter to God in his revelation and various incarnations.[87] By pointing to a God who is, so to speak, beyond the revealed God, this distinction, so basic to German mysticism,[88] makes possible an appeal to an authority higher than that to which established Christendom in any age pays homage. In religious matters the depths are never fully plumbed by what is revealed.

For Zurkinden this distinction is sheer sophistry and not to be preferred to the more wholesome teaching of Paul in Romans 1 and Colossians 3. Equally abrasive, Zurkinden adds, is the fact that the *German Theology* teaches that God loves himself not "as God," but rather "as the [highest] Good" [89]—a distinction which is intended to emphasize that God knows and loves himself as the ultimate, and not as any possible penultimate, reality (as a revealed God could conceivably be). For Zurkinden, that God is or could be anything but the very highest Good is a deluded suggestion.[90]

Castellio replies to both criticisms with an apparently sarcastic dismissal of what he considers rash, dogmatic quibbling. "And what next, my Zurkinden? Even Christians cannot make it so that there is neither male nor female, and yet in Christ there is neither male nor female nor any reason for sexes." [91]

The points of Castellio's defense of the *German Theology*—

---

86. Buisson, 2 : 388.

87. Ibid., p. 384; *Theologia Deutsch,* chap. 29, p. 58.

88. See Ueda, "Ueber den Sprachgebrauch Meister Eckharts," in *Glaube, Geist, Geschichte,* pp. 266–77. Cf. Weigel, below, p. 52.

89. *Theologia Deutsch,* chap. 30, p. 61.

90. Buisson, 2:384.

91. Ibid., p. 388. Castellio, in conclusion, agrees with Zurkinden that he should disassociate his name from the forthcoming publication of the *German Theology.* In the Basel 1557 Latin translation the pseudonym Joannes Theophilus appears, while the 1558 Antwerp French translation bears no name, real or pseudonymic, on the title page. Zurkinden could be credited with the pseudonym on the Basel edition as well as with the absence of name altogether on the Antwerp edition. Cf., however, Baring 1960, p. 176.

the primacy of experience, the necessity of doubt, and God's transcendence of his revelation—are not accidentally selected. Indeed, each is mutually presupposed and supported by the other. The primacy of experience and the necessity of doubt in matters concerning religious truth find their objective correlate in the affirmation of a sovereign Godhead behind the revealed God. And the affirmation of a God beyond God finds its subjective correlate in the anticipation of fully new experiences and suspicion of final dogmatic conclusions.

After the correspondence with Zurkinden, Castellio's preface to the *German Theology* is almost anticlimactic. It does, however, elaborate a correlation between faith and power which was only touched upon in this correspondence. The preface points immediately to the practical character of the *German Theology:* "He who wishes to read the book [simply] for knowledge and not to put into practice what is contained in it, will read it in vain." [92] The subject of the book, we are told, is man's return to his previous state of righteousness by the conversion of his will to God. As in the *Hauptreden* of Denck,[93] Castellio highlights "abandonment" of one's own will and subjugation to its "opposite":

> The theme and subject [of the *German Theology*] is the new man or new creature, for it tells us how man can be revived from sin and returned to the God from whom he has wandered. We recognize that this cannot be realized without a true and holy theology [to show us the way]. Since man fell by his own will, he can rectify his situation and return to his previous state [of righteousness] only if he abandons [*délaisse*] his own will and follows the will of God. For the remedies of things are always through their opposites, and the will of man is the opposite of the will of God.[94]

92. *La théologie germanique: chapîtres choisis,* intro. Sebastian Castellio and trans. Pierre Poiret, ed. Marius Valkhoff (Haarlem, 1960), p. 5. Valkhoff repeats Castellio's 1558 French preface, which is a literal translation of the Latin preface of the preceding year. Baring 1963, pp. 149–50; Baring 1960, p. 179.

93. Since the Basel 1557 Latin and, in turn, the 1558 Antwerp French translations were based on the 1546 Frankfurt/M edition, which in turn goes back to the 1528 Worms edition, Castellio, of course, had Denck's *Hauptreden,* which he appends to his own editions and by which he was no doubt influenced. Hence the parallels in terminology. Cf. *Hans Denck. Schriften,* 1 : 45; Baring 1963, p. 60.

94. *La théologie germanique,* p. 6.

The agent of return Castellio summarizes as "living faith"—a faith, he tells us, that "lives by works and effects." [95] This faith not only appropriates the (objective) remission of sins by the merit of Christ but, further, transforms members previously engaged in unrighteousness into "ministers of righteousness." [96]

Having properly covered the traditional ground, Castellio gives this faith his own peculiar slant, and one made all the more understandable when we bear in mind that he is under siege by the Calvinists. It is a faith which is best defined in terms of power. "Faith produces virtue [*vertu*], that is, the force and power to make what we believe become reality." [97] True believers receive the "force and courage" to fulfill the commandments.[98] With words deceptively reminiscent of Luther's "Wer glaubst, hast" and anticipatory of developments in the *De Arte dubitandi*, Castellio summarizes:

> A man is as strong as he believes—*Autant que l'homme a de Foy, autant a il de vertu.* Moreover, this strength produces knowledge [*science*]. For true knowledge consists of experience in the sense that he who has had the power to do something knows once and for all and for certain what he can do.[99]

Valentin Weigel and German Mysticism: The Earliest Writings

In 1571 Weigel wrote a *Short Account and Introduction to the German Theology, or How one should read this little book in the most rewarding way so that an understanding of the fundamental truth of Holy Scripture can be reached.* Before he dedicated this treatise to it, however, the *German Theology*, like German mysticism generally, had already begun to function in his thought in a highly formative way. In his works of the preceding year (1570)— *On the Conversion of Man* and *On Poverty of Spirit or True*

95. "J'entends la Foy, non pas celle qui est morte, laquelle ne se doit point appeler non plus Foy que l'homme doit estre appelé Homme quand il est mort. Mais j'entends ceste Foy vive par oeuvres et effects." Ibid., p. 7.

96. Ibid., p. 8.

97. Ibid.

98. Ibid.

99. Ibid., p. 9. Joshua and Caleb are cited as examples of two who had such faith and strength. Compare Müntzer's predilection for Gideon as the true knight of faith. Franz, 237, ll. 15 ff. Cf. below, pp. 81–82.

Resignation—Weigel made heavy use not only of the *German Theology* but also of the sermons of Eckhart and Tauler. Since the *Short Account and Introduction to the German Theology* continues positions set forth in these earlier works, we will be better informed in our effort to assess it if we tarry awhile with the latter.

The ostensible occasion for the treatise *On the Conversion of Man* is the contemporary synergistic controversy, which had divided Lutheran theologians since 1555.[100] Weigel, however, is more interested in the topic than in the controversy over it. He develops the issue in the language of mystical rather than scholastic theology, ceding to the *German Theology* the task of authoritative definition.

He speaks first of the necessity of every man's "deification"—not as sinful Adam attempted it but as the obedient Christ exemplified it.[101]

> Let Adam now be "as God" and also be God, but not through the counsel of the Serpent. Rather let Adam be God through the counsel of the seed of woman [Gen. 3 : 15], [i.e.] by grace. All that God is by nature let man now be by grace. Now as Adam, having perished in himself, was taken up by God and born from God as the Son of God, for God [as the *German Theology* says] "was incarnate in him and Adam was deified —for God was then himself man and Adam was no more— so must my, yours, and every man's fall and sin be repaired," or removed through repentance or conversion until the last day.[102]

This "becoming God," this existentialized incarnation, as it were, is what Weigel has in mind when he speaks more traditionally about "new birth," "new man," "conversion," "true obedience," or "repentance."

> God comes and assumes man, renews him, rules in him and in this way becomes man; for he assumes the entire man.

100. Cf. Reinhold Seeberg, *Text-Book of the History of Doctrines,* trans. C. E. Hay (Grand Rapids, Mich., 1968), 2:367 ff.

101. "Wenn kein Buch noch Lehrer inn der Weldt wehre und hetten wir nur das Exempel Christi, so wehre es uns zur Weissheit und Seeligkeit Genug." *Von der Bekehrung des Menschen* in *Valentin Weigel. Sämtliche Schriften,* ed. W.-E. Peuckert and W. Zeller (Stuttgart-Bad Cannstatt, 1966), 3 : 15.

102. Ibid., pp. 13–14; cf. *Theologia Deutsch,* chap. 3, ll. 10–29.

Hence man becomes God's son, not by nature but by grace, and that is what we mean by the new birth, the new man, conversion, true obedience, doing repentance.[103]

Weigel not only permits the *German Theology* to define his topic, he further cedes to its authority on the particular point at issue in the synergistic controversy. We are informed that the problem of whether or not man can cooperate with God in the new birth is debated by "false theologians" who have written great books in vain. For the answer is short and simple: on the one hand, man does not receive the new birth because of his powers and cooperation; on the other hand, God does not grant one who withholds his power and cooperation the new birth. As the *German Theology* has it:

> God does not want it to happen without man, and man does not want it to happen without God. Hence God neither wishes nor may [grant the new birth] without man, and man neither wishes nor may [attain the new birth] without God.[104]

In the logic of German mysticism, man cooperates in the attainment of his salvation by simply freely doing nothing (i.e. *Gelassenheit*).[105] Weigel dismisses the synergistic controversy with a mystically influenced reciprocity of divine and human activity—a reciprocity, we will shortly see, which springs from the most basic presuppositions of his theological thinking. His last words on the issue are:

> Man must bring forth sheer passivity, resignation, a surrendered will, a dying to self, and hold himself still. For as soon as man goes out of himself with his own will, just so soon does God enter with his will.[106]

It is not only in regard to the synergistic controversy that Weigel finds contemporary theologians victimized by false assumptions about the new birth. Equal confusion, he tells us, is evidenced by

103. *Von der Bekehrung des Menschen*, pp. 14–15. See Weigel's discussion of the "heavenly flesh" of Christ and his "bodily" presence in believers, below, pp. 299 ff.

104. Ibid., p. 16, citing *Theologia Deutsch*, chap. 3, 11. 15–21.

105. Cf. *Theologia Deutsch*, chap. 25, 53. 18 ff.; chap. 3, 12. 1–7: "kan ich oder mag oder soll nichtz nit der zu thun, sunder eynn ploss lautter leiden."

106. *Von der Bekehrung des Menschen*, pp. 18–19. On Tauler, cf. *Homo Spiritualis*, pp. 30 ff.; on Eckhart, Ueda, "Ueber den Sprachgebrauch Meister Eckharts," in *Glaube, Geist, Geschichte*, pp. 268, 271.

the teaching that the new birth is connected in a substantive way with the sacrament of baptism. This is an especially important series of comments in this early work of Weigel's, since it is at this juncture that he ventures to make explicit some fundamental assumptions in his own religious thought.

Weigel's basic (and hardly original) position is that baptism with physical water is simply a prefiguring of baptism with inward, heavenly water—the renewal and purification of the Holy Spirit.[107] The latter, the new birth, owes absolutely nothing to any powers intrinsic either to the priest or to the water; only to the free and sovereign Spirit of God, which lights where it wills, is man indebted.[108] In a passage reminiscent of Thomas Müntzer's exclamation against Luther that without the Spirit no man can speak authoritatively about God even if he has eaten a hundred Bibles,[109] Weigel proclaims:

> The Holy Spirit is bound neither to water, priest, nor time, for what is born of the Spirit is and remains Spirit [John 3 : 6] and is in no man's power and certainly not in water. . . . The Holy Spirit is present to man without the baptism of water. Hence rebirth certainly occurs without water and man is saved without water, assuming only that he believes [*so er nur glaubet*]. On the other hand, if a man receives the baptism of water from the priest but has neither faith nor a new birth within in the Spirit, surely he must remain damned in his baptism with water. For without exception he who does not believe in Christ is already damned [cf. Mark 16 : 16] even if he were baptized a hundred times by the priest.[110]

Weigel has, in effect, released the new birth from its traditional mooring in priestly activity and sacramental power and made it a reciprocal act between the individual and his God. New birth is an affair of each soul, contingent only on the presence of God's omnipresent spirit.

---

107. *Von der Bekehrung des Menschen*, p. 21.

108. Ibid., pp. 24–25.

109. Franz, p. 251: "wilcher mensch dieses [the inner Word in the depths of the soul] nit gewar und empfindtlich worden ist durch das lebendige gezceugnis Gottis, Roma. 8[: 2], der weiss von Gotte nichts gründtlich zu sagen, wenn er gleich hunderttausent biblien hett gefressen."

110. *Von der Bekehrung des Menschen*, pp. 27–28.

The external witness does not save; only the inward new birth through the Holy Spirit or faith does that. He who has this new birth within, be he husband or wife, young or old, Jew or heathen, Christian or Turk, is already saved, even if he is not physically baptized with water.[111]

On the surface Weigel's argument is a commonsensical and biblically supportable placement of the free, living spirit of God over against the mechanical performance of an external act, baptism with water. If, however, the external institutional sacramental act is taken as representing not only centuries of tradition but also the way in which, whether interpreted covenantally or as a literal, physical medium, God has, in his very revelation, authorized the communication of spiritual goods to men, then the displacement of priestly mediation and sacramental efficacy has far-ranging consequences for the definition of religious life. If the sacramental act is not authoritatively representative of the means God has freely and faithfully chosen to communicate his grace, then what will be the definitive temporal locus of divine power? Where will the habitation of the Spirit now be found? If not in institutions, external rituals, tradition, and books—in short, in historical symbols—then where?

The answer to this question is approached as Weigel brings together the results of his criticism of contemporary theological preoccupations. His comments on the synergistic controversy ended with the establishment of a reciprocity of divine and human activity in the new birth. His comments on the role of priestly mediation and sacramental efficacy ended with a witness to religious universalism. Weigel now unites this reciprocity and universalism as he comments critically on still another contemporary theological preoccupation—the doctrine of Original Sin. In so doing, he makes manifest the presuppositions behind his belief in the reciprocity of divine and human activity and the equidistance of the Spirit from every soul. A transition is made from history to ontology as anthropological structures replace institutional structures as the authoritative locus of the spirit of God.

Every man is blessed by his own faith and every man is damned by his own unbelief. As soon as the child lives in

111. Ibid., p. 31.

the body of the mother, it has body, soul, and spirit, and when it is born into the world it has body, soul, and spirit.[112] Through the light of this spirit it believes in Christ. This faith is the new birth, which the Holy Spirit effects in children. And that is the true baptism about which Christ speaks, when he says, "whoever believes and is baptized will be saved" [Mark 16 : 16]. Such baptism or new birth is not only in the children of Christians but in the children of Jews, heathen, and all peoples. I am, of course, not able to give my child the new birth of the Spirit of God through my own faith. And, conversely, I am not able through my unbelief to take the new birth or heaven away from my child. The child will not bear the sin of the parents, but each will die and be damned only for his own sin.[113]

Divine favor is thus democratized absolutely, but at the price of fully dehistoricizing the traditional *media salutis*. The means of grace and the authoritative channels of divine power are not connected in an exclusive or even necessary way with any external structures. Not a historical institution but an anthropological structure—the spirit with which every child is born—is the definitive locus of divine Spirit.

For as the sun shines on the good and the evil, a thousand times more does the Spirit of God illumine each man equally. From the light of the Spirit is every child born anew, baptized, made faithful, and saved.[114]

As each child enters manhood he approaches the time of decision and must now choose between Spirit and flesh. He reaches the stage when reciprocal action must occur. He may keep and increase, or he may reject and lose the Spirit and the sanctification he has received, so to speak, from the womb.

As the child becomes a man and reaches the age of reason, he finds himself in the middle. If he lives according to the

112. For an apparently identical anthropological schema, see Balthasar Hubmaier, *Von der Freiheit des Willens* (1527) in *Balthasar Hubmaier. Schriften*, ed. G. Westin and T. Bergsten, *Quellen und Forschungen zur Reformationsgeschichte* (Gütersloh, 1962), 29 : 382 (English translation in *Spiritual and Anabaptist Writers*, pp. 112–35).
113. *Von der Bekehrung des Menschen*, pp. 32–33.
114. Ibid., pp. 33–34.

spirit, he remains in God's grace. If he lives according to the flesh, he falls away from [spiritual] baptism.[115]

For Weigel, it is important to point out, this is considered to be true *biblical* theology—the very arrangement set forth in the New Testament as God's plan for his people in this life.[116] It is the "true inward covenant" to which the priest with his external and visible ceremonies—his historical covenantal activities—must direct his congregation if priestly mediation is to have any merit. For it is this inner covenant, the covenant whose terms are transacted in the depths of the soul, which is the decisive ingredient in religious life. It has become for Weigel, as for Sebastian Franck, the true *potentia Dei ordinata,* the only religious "establishment."

> The priest baptizes the little child with water not as a forgiveness of sins, but as a memorial and indication that we men are led through external visible ceremonies to the true inward covenant [which testifies] that we are children of God and seals it with the Spirit of God [Eph. 1 : 13]. This is the true rebirth and baptism through which all the faithful are saved.[117]

Weigel's second treatise, *On True Poverty of Spirit or Passive Resignation,* does not advance new thoughts beyond the treatise *On the Conversion of Man.* It does, however, bring forth material from German mysticism, especially the sermons of Meister Eckhart, which significantly supplements Weigel's views on the "true inward covenant." The third chapter quotes extensively from Eckhart's sermon on Matthew 5 : 3 ("Blessed are the poor in spirit for theirs is the kingdom of heaven"), including the following pregnant statement, which I would interpret as indicative of the kind of mystical ontology that bulwarks Weigel's location of the saving work of the Spirit in anthropological rather than institutional structures.

> "In this poverty [writes Eckhart] man pursues the eternal being which he has been, which he now is, and in which he shall live eternally." Hence man should neither have nor wish for "any place where God may work. As long as man

115. Ibid., p. 34.
116. Ibid., p. 39.
117. Ibid., p. 42.

clings to a place, he clings to distinction. Hence I pray God t
set me free from God and hence [free for] that absolutel
purified Being which is above God and above distinction.[11]
I was once [in that purified being]; there I thought an
willed myself to be this man [that I am]. Hence I am th
creator of both my eternal and my temporal being. I am bor
into a temporal being, but because of my eternal birth I ca
never die. According to my eternal birth, I have always beer
am now, and shall always be. My temporal being shall pas
away and come to nought, for it is meant only for a tim
and must pass with time. All things were brought forth i
my birth. I was the cause of myself and of all things. Indeec
had I so wished, I and all things would not yet be. Were
not, God would not be." [119]

Later in this same treatise, Weigel brings together thought
from the *German Theology* and Paracelsus to argue that the ir
ward renewal which true resignation effects as it returns man t
his "inward being" can extend the life of the body for severa
hundred years. This passage, somewhat astonishing on first reac
ing, is expressive of a very traditional understanding of the ir
terconnection between the renewal of the soul and the sanctifica
tion of the body.[120] But in Weigel's case it is much more than tha
It is also a striking testimony to the saving power latent in th
depths of man's soul.

True resignation is a dying and forgetting of oneself. Whei
one is dead to the whole of creation, then God lives [in one
eternally. As often as you die, so often do you receive a nev
life. That is the art of living long, viz. that one assemble al
the powers of the soul into the inward being [of the soul]
hold oneself perfectly still, and forget oneself and everythin;
in the world. In this dying, man receives a new strength an
is always younger. Through this kind of inward renewal th

118. See the distinction between God as "gotheit" and as "got" in the Germa
Theology debated by Castellio and Zurkinden, above, p. 43.

119. *Von waarer Armut des Geistes oder gelassener Gelassenheit* in *Valenti
Weigel: Sämtliche Schriften*, 3 : 66–67. For citation, see Pfeiffer, *Deutsche Mystike
des 14. Jahrhunderts*, vol. 2, sermon no. 87, 283. 39–284. 10.

120. Cf. Gerson, *De mystica theologia speculativa*, cons. 41, 111. 106 ff. (Englis
translation in *Jean Gerson: Selections*, pp. 57–58).

outward body can be maintained for several hundred years, as happened in Adam and Methuselah.[121]

It is not surprising when, toward the end of the treatise, Weigel argues that a necessary reciprocity exists between poverty of spirit or resignation and God's acceptance. "God and man are united," Weigel tells us, "through such resignation. And just as little as God can deny his own life and being, just so little can he damn the one who is poor in spirit and truly passive." [122] This reciprocity between human resignation and divine acceptance makes manifest in act the community of being which man has with God at the deepest level of his soul. It is in terms of such community of being and reciprocity of action that Weigel exalts the "true inward covenant."

When Weigel wrote his *Short Account and Introduction to the German Theology* in 1571, he did so as one already fully conversant with the ontology of German mysticism. The fact that statements from Tauler, Eckhart, and Sebastian Franck appear in explication of the *German Theology* is sufficient testimony to the extent of his reading in German mystical writings.

Weigel's most succinct summary of the contents of the *German Theology* came in a comment on the opening words of the treatise which quote 1 Corinthians 13 : 10: "When the perfect is come, the imperfect will pass away." It is significant, if coincidental, that this biblical verse was also of fundamental importance for Joachim of Fiore (d. 1202).[123] Weigel and the *German Theology,* unlike Joachim, give the verse an exclusively anthropological rather than institutional interpretation. Joachim expected the papal church to be transformed (around 1260) by a new, monastically modeled societal form.[124] Since for Weigel religious

---

121. *Von waarer Armut des Geistes,* pp. 81–82, with references to relevant statements in the *German Theology* and the writings of Paracelsus.

122. Ibid., p. 86.

123. Morton Bloomfield, "Joachim of Flora: A Critical Survey of His Canon, Teachings, Sources, Biography and Influence," *Traditio* 13 (1957): 264.

124. Most pertinent is the recent study by Marjorie Reeves, *The Influence of Prophecy in the Later Middle Ages: A Study in Joachimism* (Oxford, 1969), esp. pp. 129 ff., 135 ff. Cf. Ernst Benz, *Ecclesia Spiritualis: Kirchenidee und Geschichtstheologie der franziskanischen Reformation* (Stuttgart, 1934), pp. 10–21 and passim; Georg Müller, "Jugendrevolte und Linksopposition im Hochmittelalter," *ZRGG* 22 (1970): 113–30. See Weigel's views on the "new Jerusalem," below, pp. 228 ff.

institutions are, in theory if not in his own practice, nonessential
to religious perfection, the perfection which is to come and which
is the subject matter of the *German Theology* is God's ruling
presence in the soul of the individual rather than in a democratized
church of the Spirit.

> The sum and contents not only of this first chapter [of the
> *German Theology*][125] but indeed of practically the entire
> little book are stated in the words of Paul: "When the perfect
> is known, one despises what is imperfect" (1 Cor. 13 : 10).
> That is, when the kingdom of God comes upon me, and I
> find and experience in myself the very God who is the truly
> perfect good, I hate everything that is partial or imperfect,
> i.e. I deny myself.[126]

Another earlier summary of the *German Theology* states this
theme in highly traditional terms. What is especially interesting
here, however, is Weigel's brisk reduction of the message of the
German Theology and of the prophets, Christ, and the Apostles
to the first three chapters of the book of Genesis. The teaching
of the Old and New Testament is boiled down to the *Gelassenheit*
theme of German mysticism.

> Not only this little book which we now have before us—the
> *Theologia Germanica*—but, indeed, the first three chapters
> of Genesis and, therefore, the entire prophetic and apostolic
> Scriptures—for the prophets, Christ, and the Apostles do
> nothing else than present and clarify the first three chapters
> of the book of creation, which are themselves a brief summary
> of the whole of natural and supernatural knowledge or
> wisdom—not only, I say, this beautiful little book but the
> entire Holy Scripture drives, excites, and admonishes us in
> this one thing: that Adam die in us and Christ arise and live
> in us, i.e. that the natural sinful man be sacrificed, killed,
> eradicated, and brought to nought so that Christ may find a
> place to work, live, rule, and reign, and hence become and

125. Weigel's *Short Account and Introduction* deals directly only with the first
chapter of the *German Theology,* but is paradigmatic of the teaching of the entire
treatise.

126. *Kurtzer Bericht und Anleitung zur Teutschen Theologey/nemblich: Wie
man fructbarlich solches Büchlein lesen soll/auff dass man hiemit zum gründtlichen
Verstandt der Heiligen Schrifft kommen möge,* in *Valentin Weigel, Sämtliche
Schriften,* 3 : 117. Cf. *Theologia Deutsch,* chap. 1, 7. 1 ff.; 9. 8 ff.

remain everything in us. For the more one dies to oneself and becomes nothing, the more God arises, lives, and rules in one.[127]

When religious life is focused exclusively on changes within the soul of the individual, consequences result, first of all, in the definition of religious authority. The shift from institutional to anthropological structures, under way in Weigel from his earliest writings, entails a shift in the horizon of religious authority from historically mediated and interpreted tradition to experiences interior to the individual soul. Institutional criteria of authority —the traditional and present judgments of duly appointed *experti* —fall by the side, or else the experts now become those who deny the necessity of experts! There is a Scripture against Scripture and a tradition against tradition.

Weigel has prepared the way for such an affirmation in the writings preceding this treatise. Now he makes it fully explicit. Neither the Bible nor the *German Theology* bears an intrinsically clear and authoritative mandate. What each means is not to be extrapolated by reading and discussion but received by direct divine communication. The "pure eye" of the soul must make the authoritative assessment.

> It is not sufficient to have, read, and take at face value useful and good books—not even the Bible. One must have an absolutely pure eye[128] if one is to take up and read divine writings. There are many who are so deluded as to think the Bible an open book which anyone who picks it up can read. But the Bible is a book closed with seven seals, which no one can open save he who has the key of David. The same is true of this little book called the *Theologia Germanica*, which, like the Bible, also requires a pure heart in order to be understood. Truly, we all have equal access to Scripture on earth, but God keeps its understanding with himself in heaven.[129]

127. *Kurtzer Bericht und Anleitung zur Teutschen Theologey*, p. 94.
128. Cf. *Theologia Deutsch*, chap. 7, p. 17.
129. *Kurtzer Bericht und Anleitung zur Teutschen Theologey*, pp. 91–92. Compare Sebastian Franck's comment on the fall of the church after the death of the Apostles: "I believe that the outward church of Christ, including all its gifts and sacraments, because of the breaking in and laying waste by Antichrist right after the death of the apostles, went up into heaven and lies concealed in the Spirit and in truth." *A Letter to John Campanus*, in *Anabaptist and Spiritual Writers*, p. 149.

The traditional objective correlates of religious life are finally internalized absolutely.

> We theologians should have learned well from Christ that paradise, heaven, the Kingdom of God, God the Father, and Christ are neither to be sought nor found outside ourselves. For the Kingdom of God is bound to no persons, time, place or location, or to outward appearances or ceremonies. Let not the simple-minded think that in eternity we will see the Godhead outside ourselves first here, then there. No, we will behold God in ourselves and see him face to face [as One] in no way outside ourselves. In this world each believer bears everything in himself [*ein jeder Glaubiger tregt alles bei sich selber*]. And just as little as the Kingdom of God, which is God himself, is bound to a place [in this present life], just so little, indeed, still less, will the Kingdom of God in that future life be bound to specific places.[130]

Seven years after writing the *Short Account and Introduction to the German Theology*, Weigel recorded in the twenty-fourth chapter of his book, *The Golden Grasp (Der güldene Griff)*, a highly personal statement of his own conversion. It was an appropriate book in which to record his conversion. The "golden grasp" of the title is Weigel's metaphorical description of certain knowledge in the midst of surrounding error and uncertainty.[131] The conversion account has a special significance as a conclusion to our consideration of prefaces and commentaries on the *German Theology* in the sixteenth century. In a very real sense, the transition Weigel makes is the transition made by the sixteenth century.

Before he came to true faith and concentrated on pleasing God rather than men, as he puts it, Weigel tells us that he was often very troubled over this or that article of belief. He desired a sure

---

130. *Kurtzer Bericht und Anleitung zur Teutschen Theologey*, pp. 105–06.

131. Heinz Längin saw in this treatise Weigel's anticipation of Kant. "Grundlinien der Erkenntnislehre Valentin Weigels," *Archiv für Geschichte der Philosophie* 41 (1932), esp. p. 439. Längin also put great weight on the *Methodus ad omne genus Scientiarum* in executing his project. The *Methodus*, however, is of questionable authenticity at a work of Weigel. Israel, from whom Längin got this primary source, places it under "auf Weigel fussende Schriften." A. Israel, *M. Valentin Weigels Leben und Schriften* (Zschopau, 1888), pp. 131 ff. W. Zeller's critical study of Weigel's writings does not even mention it. *Die Schriften Valentin Weigels. Eine literarkritische Untersuchung* (Berlin, 1940).

foundation and read many theological books in the hope of secur-
ing it. But his displeasure and uncertainty only increased with the
number of books he read. Surveying past and present theological
argumentation and religious persecution, Weigel summarizes his
trek to true faith as follows.

I saw and pondered our lamentable and pitiable darkness
—the fumbling, stumbling, and bungling of men. I found
so many different sects and beliefs only among those who
craved certainty and believed they had found a refuge in Holy
Scripture. I beheld what an errant and confusing thing our
Babylonian tower was. When the first man spoke of faith, the
second wanted works. And if the second asked about the
fruits [of faith], the first [accused him] of having only a
feigned faith. The third maintained that sacraments were
necessary for faith and salvation. The fourth asserted that
faith must be received through the sacraments. The fifth
countered that if faith does not precede, the sacraments are
without power and of no use. And the sixth said: only true
faith in Jesus Christ justifies and saves and absolutely nothing else is of any significance. For saying this he was rebuked
as an enthusiast [*Schwärmer*] and sacramentarian.

I then looked at how the one gave the other over to the
temporal power to have him imprisoned and tormented because of [his beliefs about] original sin, free will, and the
person of Christ. Such skirmishing for heaven, and nobody
truly wanted it! It continues still today in the year 1578, and
there seems to be no end to it.

Now as I was uncertain and hard-pressed for an answer, I
cried out to God with a sincere and fervent heart: "O God
and Truth, to you I complain! How can we wander about so
wretchedly in darkness? It is just as if someone baited the
blind to struggle and fight with each other in darkness, for
now one just as easily as not happens upon his best friend and
slays him as an enemy. Enlighten me, O Lord, so that I, as
others, may be saved from this desert of darkness."

As I so cried and prayed to the Lord, grace fell upon me
from above. For to me was your face made manifest, and it
gave me joy and enlightened my heart so that I could see and
judge all things with greater truth and clarity than all the

teachers and their books in the whole world could teach me.
For out of this Book were all the books written from the beginning of the world, and this Book is in me and in every
man, in the great and the small, the young and the old, the
learned and the simple. Yet only a few, indeed, only a very
few can read this Book. Many of the very learned who thirst
after it suppress and deny it in themselves, cling to dead
letters and to what is outside themselves, and hence forsake
the Book of Life which is written by the finger of God into
the hearts of all men. But I thank you, O Lord, you who are
the strength of my life and the light of my understanding, that
you make me more learned than all my teachers and book-
writers, for you show me the true Book in my heart, through
which I can read Holy Scripture which is given to me as a
witness. For I look upon Holy Scripture according to the
nature and Spirit [*Wesen und Geist*] which is in myself, and
not in accordance with the shadows and dead letters which
are outside myself. If I turn within to you, in myself I will
discover and confess that the faith which is united [with God]
is the guiding principle and the epistle [*die Richtschnur und
der Brief*] which is to be read and in accordance with which
all sects and spirits are to be judged.[132]

In July, 1524, in an attack on Thomas Müntzer and his radical
followers, Luther boasted in a letter to the princes of Saxony:
"God's grace has assured me beyond any doubt that I am more
learned in Scripture than all the sophists and papists." [133] It was
an appropriate claim for Luther to make. He had executed his
Reformation theologically by going to Holy Scripture and, on the
basis of what he read there, recasting the *potentia Dei ordinata* as
medieval Christendom had defined it. He argued that a self-
interpreting Scripture and not pope, council, or tradition was the
definitive locus of authority in the church; that salvation was by
faith alone in Christ alone, not by sacramentally infused and
ethically formed love; that baptism and the Eucharist were the
only sacraments of the church; and that worldly vocation and
marriage, not the monastery, formed the arena of Christian per-

132. *Der güldene Griff/Das ist: alle Dinge ohne Irrthum zu erkennen/vielen
Hochgelehrten unbekannt/und doch allen Menschen notwendig zu wissen*, in
Theologia Weigelii (Frankfurt, 1699), pp. H 4 a–H 5 b.
133. *WA*, 15 : 216. 4–5.

fection. It was a lesson in dissent and reform not to be forgotten in the sixteenth century.

Together with Luther's claim to mastery over Holy Scripture, nonconformists faced the equally forceful assertions of authority over the historical media of truth from Rome. In the 1520s the traditional routes to ultimate authority in religious life, and hence to historical legitimization of particular religious beliefs and practices, were monopolized by the uncompromising claims of Rome and Wittenberg (to which those of Zurich and Geneva were soon to be added). If members of the various dissenting bodies in the sixteenth century were to navigate successfully between what was to them the Scylla of Rome and the Charybdis of Wittenberg, Zurich, and Geneva, it was imperative that they speak with authority which could compete with the claims of established Christendom. Everything ultimately hinged on a successful demonstration of the insufficiency of a religion based on the authority of Scripture and tradition—even a Scripture interpreted by a theologian so proficient as Luther and a tradition defended by an institution so ancient as Rome. The search was on for a Scripture to speak against Scripture and a tradition to stand against tradition.

The writings of medieval mysticism were not appropriated primarily in order to promote a concern for ethical sanctification allegedly absent in the Reformation;[134] rather, they were taken over in order to ensure historical survival. The dissenters' ethical critique of the priests of Christendom was part and parcel of an effort to redefine the nature of religious truth and authority. What nonconformists needed most was not good works but a theological justification. Mystical anthropology and reflection on man's union with God made possible direct communication with that Power and Authority to whom pope, council, tradition, and holy book must necessarily cede. Mystical theology, with abundant scriptural proofs, promoted the view that the individual heart and conscience, not traditional institutional structures or historical writings, was the immediate locus of this Power and Authority.

---

134. Cf. G. H. Williams, "Popularized German Mysticism as a Factor in the Rise of Anabaptist Communism," in *Glaube, Geist, Geschichte*, p. 294, and "Sanctification in the Testimony of Several So-Called Schwärmer," in *Kirche, Mystik, Heiligung und das Natürliche bei Luther*, pp. 194–211, 197. Cf. also H. J. Hillerbrand, "Anabaptism and the Reformation: Another Look," *Church History* 29 (1960): 404–23.

The conclusion that stands out in evaluations of the *German Theology* in prefaces and related commentaries following Luther's, is the declaration of the priority—if not sovereignty—of individual experience and insight in religious matters. If, as many argue, this declaration is a major point of transition from medieval to modern intellectual history, it is a transition made more in alliance with than in opposition to at least one major tradition of the Middle Ages; for its driving wedge is the ontology of late medieval mystical theology.

3

Thomas Müntzer

Prior to one of his frequent absences from Zwickau, Johann Sylvius Egranus (d. 1535), pastor of the Marienkirche, invited Thomas Müntzer to be his temporary replacement. Egranus, a humanist sympathizer of Luther's who would later break with the Reformation on the same issues as Erasmus,[1] had apparently received Luther's endorsement of Müntzer during the Leipzig disputation. With an appointment as interim pastor of the Marienkirche till Michaelmas, the youthful Müntzer arrived in Zwickau to begin his official career in May, 1520.[2]

Serious friction existed in the city between Egranus and an aggressive colony of Franciscans. Already the Franciscans had brought official charges of heresy against Egranus. Müntzer hardly contributed to the pacification of the situation when, in his first sermons, he attacked the Franciscans with such malice that a formal protest was made by high officials in the bishophric of Naumberg ("he goes too far and is too coarse in his sermons"). The Franciscans and their leader, Father Tiburtius of Weissenfels, so forcefully countered the new pastor of the Marienkirche that,

---

1. On Egranus see Hubert Kirchner, *Johann Sylvius Egranus* (Berlin, 1961).
2. Paul Wappler, *Thomas Müntzer in Zwickau und die 'Zwickauer Propheten,'* (1908; 2d ed., Gütersloh, 1966), pp. 19–20. For recent biographical data on Müntzer prior to 1520, see Adolar Zumkeller, "Thomas Müntzer—Augustiner?," *Augustiniana* 9 (1959): 380–85, and Erwin Iserloh, "Zur Gestalt und Biographie Thomas Müntzers," *Trierer Theologische Zeitschrift* 71 (1962): 248–53. Both expand on H. Goebke, "Neue Forschungen über Thomas Müntzer bis zum Jahre 1520: Seine Abstammung und die Wurzeln seiner religiösen, politischen und sozialen Ziele," *Harz-Zeitschrift* 9 (1957): 1–30. S. Bräuer summarizes the unanimously negative scholarly reaction to Goebke's early dating of Müntzer's birth (1468 rather than 1489/90). "Zu Müntzers Geburtsjahr," *Luther-Jahrbuch* 36 (1969): 80–83.

by mid-July, Müntzer felt forced to appeal to Luther for counsel and support.[3]

The appeal, which runs deep and is most sincere,[4] concludes with a summary of Franciscan teaching in Zwickau, which Müntzer says will cause Luther's ears to "tingle." Müntzer's view of their agreement against a common enemy is instructive, not only as a measure of his early commitment to Lutheran doctrine, but also as a foreshadowing of his future course. The false teaching of the Franciscans is summarized as follows:

1. That Christ died once and does not now die in us, nor is his sacrament present with us as a consolation, nor is his example something for us to imitate. We go to mass in order to avoid suffering in this world.

2. The new evangelists [sc. the Lutherans] preach only the gospel, but in the worst way. For they contradict human laws which are strictly to be observed. There are many things which must be added to the gospel.

3. One is not to live continuously according to the gospel.

4. Were poverty truly evangelical, it would not permit kings dominion over the riches of the world.

5. If an example of faith is to be given by the renunciation of riches by pastors and members of religious orders, so that in word and deed they show their flock the way, then even princes and kings should observe a poverty so great that they own nothing and become mendicants.

6. It is not a precept of the gospel when it is written: "If anyone strikes you on the right cheek, offer him your left." Rather, that is an allegation of heretics who wish to persecute the church without interference from the secular arm.

7. Predestination is an imaginary thing and ought not be founded on faith, as if through faith we could be certain of our status. Rather ought it to be founded in works, from which people should never be turned.

8. Eternal beatitude cannot be called the rule of faith which

3. Wappler, *Thomas Müntzer in Zwickau*, pp. 21–23.

4. "Tu mihi in domino Iesu patrocinium es. Rogo, ne porrigas aures tuas obloquentibus me. Non credas hiis, qui me dixerunt inconstantem, mordacem et sexcentis nominibus aliis [me] dehonestarunt." Franz, 358.18 ff.

is already within us; rather eternal beatitude is something present only in our future home. Here we are most uncertain about our beatitude.[5]

Each of these propositions could, as it stands, summon Lutheran opposition. Müntzer, however, seems especially to dwell, in at least four propositions (1, 3, 7, and 8), on one central concern, viz. that religious faith possess something living, effective, personal, and final already in this life. Franciscan teaching negates the existential benefits of faith. In different historical contexts and in gradually intensified forms, Müntzer later turned this bona fide Lutheran concern against Luther himself during the bitter polemics of 1524.[6] In the fall of 1520, he turned it not only against the Franciscans but also against his immediate benefactor, Egranus.

Egranus, by right and by desire of the city fathers of Zwickau, was to return to the Marienkirche in October. Müntzer, by split decision of the city council, was accordingly moved to the lesser position of the Katharinenkirche. No doubt some enmity was created by the city's clear preference of Egranus,[7] who, to his surprise and dismay, returned to find that his interim replacement had become his most hostile adversary. Some indication of Müntzer's aggressiveness is present in Johann Agricola's letter of November 2, in which he pleads with Müntzer "not to act and plot hatefully in the open against Egranus." [8]

By mid-December Egranus felt driven to request and receive another leave of absence from the Marienkirche, this time in the

5. Ibid., 359.8 ff.

6. In this sense I agree with Annemarie Lohmann's assessment of this letter: "Inhaltlich gründet sich Müntzer in dem ganzen Brief durchweg aufs Luthertum, und Luther wird um diese Zeit kaum an irgendeiner Stelle Anstoss genommen haben. Dennoch sind auch in dieser Hinsicht schon Ansätze spürbar, an denen Müntzers spätere Glaubenslehre aufquellen konnte." *Zur geistigen Entwicklung Müntzers* (Leipzig/Berlin, 1931), p. 13. Müntzer, of course, was not in the future to be distinguished for his defense of the *sensus literalis* of Scripture (proposition 2), absolute Christian pacifism (proposition 6), or predestination (proposition 7).

7. Wappler, p. 27.

8. Franz, 362.6–7. A second letter of remonstrance is written before April, 1521. Ibid., p. 368. In a letter of instruction on a marital matter to the mayor of Neustadt (January 17, 1521), Müntzer is clearly defensive about his ministry, which had been under attack from one quarter or another since his first weeks in Zwickau. He takes up the words of Luke 4 : 18–19 (which we shall see again)—"The Spirit of the Lord is upon me"—in order to insist that he is a priest sent by God for exactly the same purpose that Christ was sent to men, viz, to give solace to weakened consciences. Ibid., 366.6–7.

form of appointment as preacher in neighboring Joachimsthal. On February 16, 1521, he wrote a letter to Müntzer, which skillfully confines his outrage within the boundaries of sarcasm. Pointing out that Müntzer has attacked him from the pulpit as recently as a week before and has "long desired to crucify" him, Egranus pledges not to return evil for evil, but to suffer patiently for God's truth. The letter ends with the trenchant comment: "I have written in German [rather than Latin] for a reason: I detect that your spirit despises learning and all letters." [9]

Assuming that jealousy is an insufficient explanation, why did Müntzer turn against Egranus? Müntzer scholars have tended to see the catalyst if not the crucible for the "radicalization" of Müntzer in the leader of the so-called Zwickau prophets, Nicholas Storch. According to Philip Melanchthon, who housed Storch's colleague Michael Stübner during the prophets' visit to Wittenberg, Storch and his followers "preach marvelous things about themselves—that they are sent to teach by the clear voice of God, have intimate conversations with God, see into the future, etc." [10] According to a second contemporary report of Agricola, Storch maintained that "it is fitting for us, having put Christ and the gospel aside, to hear the voice of God the Father in our hearts," and that "no one is worthy of God except he who, in a vision, has seen God with the eyes, heard him with the ears, and sensed him with the heart." [11] In the useful though late (and Lutheran) history of Marcus Wagner (Erfurt, 1597),[12] there are reports, not only of Storch's support of polygamy, communism ("das alles gemyn seyn soll"), revolt against established political authority, and denial of infant sin and baptism, but also his insistence that the direct presence of the Spirit and not the spoken, institutional "word" of the church is God's singular means of grace.

> Where the Spirit is not present, word and noise, sound and voice, can do absolutely nothing. My voice may travel forth

9. Ibid., 368.2–3.

10. In a letter to Frederick the Wise (December 28, 1521), cited by Wappler, p. 46, n. 193. According to Wappler, the prophets divided their labor tactically, Storch visiting the workers of Wittenberg, and Stübner concentrating on the professors of the University. Ibid., p. 64.

11. Cited in ibid., p. 68, n. 193.

12. *Einfeltiger Bericht Wie durch Nicolaum Storcken die Auffruh in Thüringen und umbligenden Revir angefangen sey worden etc.* It seems striking that in the year 1597 anyone, even a Lutheran propagandist, could make Storch the author of the peasants' revolt in Thüringia.

as the gong of a clock, but nothing comes in return. The Spirit, however, is busy, living, active. Hence it is not right that one directs you to wooden and stone churches, and that every Sunday and on workdays you must obediently appear under the threat of the ban and hear their word. It is not God's word, but pure noise and fuss. Don't you believe that God has another word and that he will reveal it to you through the Spirit? Should God let himself be bound to the creature? He does not do that. He is *liberrimum agens*. He does what he wishes. Hence the external, audible word, which the priests bring forward, is not God's word but their own. Listen daily to how God himself spoke with Adam in paradise, direct from heaven, how he appeared to Moses in a bush, and how he conversed with Elijah.[13]

This insistence that God's direct sovereign power is his only authoritative covenantal power is a revolutionary notion which Müntzer, in more sophisticated form, will later advance. That Storch showed him the way to it, however, is a hotly contested issue in Müntzer scholarship. Paul Wappler and Eric Gritsch see a rapid and total capitulation of Müntzer to Storch's extreme spiritualism during the Zwickau period.[14] Annemarie Lohmann is more cautious,[15] and Gordon Rupp is suspicious of the influence of Storch altogether.[16] The Marxist historian Max Steinmetz makes

13. The document is reproduced in Wappler, pp. 81 ff., 85–86.

14. Writes Wappler: "Die aus Böhmen mit heimgebrachten religiösen Ansichten Storchs fanden nun allmählich bei Müntzer immer grösseren Anklang, ja Storchs geradezu überraschende Belesenheit in der Bibel und seine staunenswerte Gewandtheit in der Auslegung der einzelnen Schriftstellen durch andere erfüllten ihn mit solcher Bewunderung, dass er nicht anstand, öffentlich von der Kanzel herab zu erklären, Storch sei 'fuer alle Priester erhaben, als der Eynige, der so bass wisse die Bibliam, und Hoch erkannt im geyst.' " *Thomas Müntzer in Zwickau*, p. 30. Wappler sees the capitulation to Storch as a natural course from Müntzer's study of Tauler. Ibid., p. 29. Eric Gritsch sees the matter thus: "Like the weaver-prophet [Storch], Müntzer proclaimed that one must feel with certainty the powerful presence of the Holy Spirit in the soul; that the authority of the Bible is spiritual rather than literal; that the Holy Spirit revealed itself not only in apostolic times, but also in the present age; that inner conversion experience has greater authority than rational theological knowledge; and that the uneducated layman stands closer to God than the scholar." *Reformer Without a Church: The Life and Thought of Thomas Müntzer 1488 [?]—1525* (Philadelphia, 1967), p. 36.

15. Lohmann, *Zur geistigen Entwicklung Müntzers*, pp. 15–16, where Wappler's analysis is disputed.

16. Rupp insists that Lohmann, who is much more careful in this matter than Wappler and Gritsch, still exaggerates when she makes "Storchismus" a special

a strong case that the Storchian background and influence on Müntzer is largely a legend created by Philip Melanchthon,[17] and he agrees with the (pre-1531) Luther that Müntzer was very much his own man vis-à-vis Storch.[18] It is certainly not unreasonable to suppose that Müntzer knew and was attracted to the ideas of Storch, but probably more because they corresponded to his own direction of theological growth than because they provided him with a radically new orientation. Storch was a helpful coincidence.

This conclusion is supported by Müntzer's twenty-four "Propositiones probi viri d. Egrani," a critical statement of the teaching of Egranus which Müntzer put together, probably in early 1521, as the final indictment in their embittered feud. These propositions are similar in polemical method and in overriding theological concern to the critical summary of Franciscan teaching which Müntzer had sent to tingle Luther's ears. Against the Franciscans Müntzer had urged a living, effective, personal faith. Now Egranus, precisely like the Franciscans earlier, is depicted as the champion of an easy, inexperienced, externally officiated Christianity. If,

---

phase of Müntzer's development. "Thomas Müntzer: Prophet of Radical Christianity," *Bulletin of the John Rylands Library* 48 (1966): 475. Rupp has later maintained that it is "far more likely that Müntzer led rather than was led by, these men [i.e. the Zwickau prophets]." *Patterns of Reformation*, p. 167.

17 Melanchthon is also accused of creating the legend of Luther's nailing ninety-five theses on the door of Castle Church. See the persuasive study of Erwin Iserloh, *The Theses Were Not Posted: Luther Between Reform and Reformation* (Boston, 1968).

18. "Philipp Melanchthon über Thomas Müntzer und Nikolaus Storch: Beiträge zur Auffassung der Volksreformation in der Geschichtsschreibung des 16. Jahrhunderts," in *Philipp Melanchthon: Humanist, Reformator, Praeceptor Germaniae* (Berlin, 1963), pp. 160 ff. Steinmetz summarizes his thesis succinctly: "Luther hatte Storch wohl 1522 in seinen Briefen mehrfach genannt; aber für ihn war Müntzer in jeder Hinsicht der Bedeutendere und Gefährlichere. Während er von Storch kaum noch spricht, kämpft er mit aller Leidenschaft gegen den incarnatus diabolus von Allstedt und Mühlhausen. In Melanchthons Erinnerung rückt Storch an erste Stelle: Müntzer wird sein Schüler und Mitarbeiter. . . . Luthers Einschätzung ist offenkundig weit richtiger, sachlich zutreffender." Ibid., p. 171. Steinmetz's article, it might be added, is a Marxist version of the kind of "exposé" of sixteenth-century Lutheran historiography which we in the West have come to know in such authors as H. S. Bender, "The Zwickau Prophets, Thomas Müntzer and the Anabaptists," *MQR* 27 (1953): 3–16; R. Friedmann, "Thomas Müntzer's Relation to Anabaptism," *MQR* 31 (1957): 75–87; and, more recently, John S. Oyer, *Lutheran Reformers Against Anabaptists: Luther, Melanchthon and Menius and the Anabaptists of Central Germany* (The Hague, 1964). Steinmetz, in fact, praises Friedmann's criticism of the *Histori Thome Müntzers, des anfengers der Döringischen uffrur* (1525), which is attributed to Melanchthon.

in the following selected propositions, parallels with Storchian spiritualism can be discerned,[19] still more clearly can we see the steady maturation of Müntzer's earlier concern for a sincerely impassioned faith. According to Müntzer, Egranus defends the following false propositions.

2. Christ did not come into the world to teach us patiently to bear our sufferings and so to follow in his steps; rather he died so that we might be more secure and know no bitterness.

5. The passion of Christ was not bitter. . . . Nor can man's death be bitter, for it is a sweet dissolution of soul and body.

6. The remission of sins occurs without any penalty; for contrition of the heart suffices, and even thieves can perform that. . . .

6.[20] Penalties are not to be sought; it suffices that man know himself by [the normal exercise of] his own powers. The temptations of faith are rightly rejected. . . . They are surely the contrived fantasies of human affections.

7. There is no experience of faith in the world, save that which is received from books. Hence neither the laity nor the uneducated, although sufficiently tried, can judge matters of faith. Rather every [such] judgment awaits [those who, although] most inexperienced, wear the priest's fillet.

13. The seventh chapter of Romans says nothing about the two men [who struggle in us], as the Martinians [i.e. Lutherans] dream; it concerns the Jews and does not pertain to us.

14. The eighth chapter of Romans says that we are completely free from the law. Hence we rightly reject the ten commandments of the law. We have knowledge of sin without them through the gospel. . . .

15. The fear of God ought not to enter into the hearts of men, for the New Testament says nothing about it, and perfect love casts out fear.

21. Only the Apostles had the Holy Spirit. It was not neces-

19. See Lohmann's assessment, *Zur geistigen Entwicklung Müntzers*, pp. 15–17.
20. The MS lists two proposition 6's.

sary for other men because the church was sufficiently
established by the labors of the Apostles.

22. No man has had the Holy Spirit for a thousand years no
is the church ruled by it.[21]

Müntzer had already laid the groundwork for his later attack
on Luther in the indictments of the Zwickau Franciscans and
Egranus. Ironically, these fateful indictments were put forth by
one who, in early 1521, considered himself a true if tormented ally
of Luther.

THE ALLIANCE SHATTERS

By mid-April, 1521, Müntzer was forced to flee Zwickau, and
he made his way to Prague.[22] Partially because he was accepted as
a follower of Luther (who, at the Diets of Leipzig and Worms, had
given the impression that all true Christians were Hussites),[23] and
partially because his teaching had genuine points of contact with
radical Hussite theology, Müntzer found a welcomed and initially
welcoming audience in Bohemia. His journey evidently brought
charges that he was seeking to build an independent power base
there;[24] for on June 15, 1521, he wrote an intensely personal letter
of self-defense to Nicholas Hausmann, Luther's friend in Zwickau
insisting: "Know that I have visited Bohemia, not for my own
glory, not because of a desire for riches, but in the hope of my

21. Franz, pp. 513–15. In a letter to Hausmann (June 15, 1521), Müntzer (who
describes himself as "servus electorum Dei") takes Hausmann to task for remaining
silent in the face of the "blasphemous Egranus," who now teaches that "the church
has had the Holy Spirit only during the time of the Apostles." Franz, 372. 16–17
According to Wappler, this was one of two critical statements Egranus made against
Müntzer after his transferal to Joachimsthal. The other was that he would not
believe Müntzer and Storch unless he saw and heard them perform miracles before
his very eyes. *Thomas Müntzer in Zwickau*, pp. 35 ff. The latter condition is one
Luther also later makes for accepting Müntzer's departure from "die ordenliche
weisz." "Ein Sendbrief an Burgermeister, Rat und ganze Gemeine der Stadt Mühl
hausen" (August 21, 1524), *WA* 15 : 240. 3 ff.

22. This was the first of at least two visits. Müntzer had returned in June, 1521
but was back again in Prague in late July, as is evident from the July 31, 1521
letter of Hans Sommerschuh to Müntzer "iczundt zu Prag." Franz, 275. 24–25.

23. Cf. J. Pelikan, "Luther's Attitude Toward John Huss," *Concordia Theologica
Monthly* 19 (1948): 747–63.

24. Gritsch speculates that Müntzer "had hopes of becoming the 'Martin Luther
of Bohemia.'" *Reformer Without a Church*, p. 50.

future death. I wish these things so that the mystery of the cross which I preach cannot be eradicated." [25]

It was during a second, extended visit to Prague that Müntzer drafted the so-called *Prague Manifesto* of November, 1521.[26] Although it is not explicitly critical of Luther, it has been justifiably considered the first direct statement by Müntzer of a theological position which could not but collide with Reformation theology.[27] The *Manifesto* declared that, upon the death of the followers of the original Apostles, the church had become and had since remained an unfaithful whore.[28] It further accused the clergy of having "stolen Scripture out of the Bible" and of alienating the people from the living word which God had inscribed in the hearts of men.[29] In order to downgrade established authority, Müntzer adopted what proved to be a stock model for dissent in the sixteenth century,[30] the prophet Balaam who knew less about God's will than his own ass:

> They do not, as does the hen, gather their children together to keep them warm. They do not share the good nature of God's word (which lives in all elect men) with the heart, as a mother gives milk to her child. Rather they deal in the manner of Balaam [*Balams weyse*], i.e. they have the bare letter [of Scripture] in their mouth, but their hearts are well over a hundred thousand miles away.[31]

Against this situation Müntzer maintained that "revelation" from God qualified the clergy to preach, and he pointed in conclusion to a "new church" of the elect, to replace the "pfaffen und

25. Franz, 372. 25–30.

26. There were three versions of the *Manifesto*—a shorter and longer German and a Latin translation of the longer German version for the intellectuals. The Latin version is translated in Rupp, *Patterns of Reformation*, pp. 175–78.

27. Cf. Lohmann, *Zur geistigen Entwicklung Müntzers*, pp. 22–24, and Gritsch, *Reformer Without a Church*, pp. 56–60.

28. Franz, 497. 2–7. See also on this point Müntzer's later *Fürstenpredigt*, translated in *Spiritual and Anabaptist Writers*, p. 51. The same motif appears in Sebastian Franck's *Letter to John Campanus*. Cf. below, pp. 145–46. The general theme of the "fall of the Church" in Anabaptist literature is treated by F. H. Littell, *The Origins of Sectarian Protestantism: A Study of the Anabaptist View of the Church*, 3d ed. (New York, 1964), pp. 46–78.

29. Franz, 492. 1–15.

30. On Balaam's ass as a model for dissent, cf. pp. 38, 147, 185, n. 66.

31. Franz, 492. 31–493. 2.

affen" who then claimed to constitute the church.[32] The *Mani-festo* was understandably interpreted as a covert threat to the social order of Prague, and Müntzer found it wise to be on his way once again.

Four months after the *Prague Manifesto*, Müntzer penned a letter to Melanchthon in which the first explicit indictment of the Reformation was made. This letter of March 27, 1522, is significant not only because of its criticism of Luther but also because it employs Joachite motifs and imagery to buttress the long-standing demand for an impassioned and experienced faith. Further, it is evidence of the consistency of Müntzer's intellectual growth. For in it, exactly as with the Franciscans, Egranus, and the Roman "pfaffen und affen," he accuses the Reformation itself of silencing God's word and making an easy compromise with the world; Luther too is imperfect. After initial praise for the way "your theology" has impeded Rome,[33] Müntzer feels forced to protest:

> But in this I reprove you, that, while you worship a muted Lord [*os domini mutum adoretis*], not knowing because of your ignorance whether the elect or the reprobate are to be increased, you reject altogether the future church in which knowledge of the Lord will emerge most fully.[34] That error of yours, dearest friend, comes totally from ignorance of the living word. Look at the Scriptures. . . . "Not by bread alone does man live, but by every word which comes from the mouth of God." [Deut. 8 : 3, et al.] Behold that the word proceeds from the mouth of God and not from books. A witness to the true word does indeed come from books. But if God's word does not arise in the heart, the word of man damns the deceitful scribes who have stolen the holy oracles. Jer. 23[: 30].[35]

32. Ibid., 493. 14–17; 494. 10–18.

33. Repeated later by Müntzer. Franz, 381.28–29.

34. "Domini scientia orietur plenissime." "Plentitudo intellectus" is a mark of the Age of the Spirit for Joachim. See Benz, *Ecclesia Spiritualis,* pp. 10–12. Note, however, how utterly biblical this can be for both Joachim and Müntzer. In a defense of his purpose, Müntzer wrote an unknown recipient: "Nihil aliud spiro nisi eternam Dei voluntatem, qua replendi omnes amici domini in omni sapientia et intellectu spiritus, Coll. I [9]." Franz, 382. 12–14.

35. Franz, 380. 6–14.

Luther is further accused of dangerous hesitation and com
promise with the world:

> Our dearest Martin acts ignorantly because he does not want
> to offend the little ones—the very "little ones" who are al-
> ready like the cursed children of a hundred years [Isa. 65 : 20].
> Indeed, the persecution of Christians is *already* in the public
> places, and I don't know why you think it is something still
> to be expected. Dear brother, rise up for the time has come!
> Do not hesitate for Summer is at the door.[36] Do not seek the
> favor of your princes, for if you do you will behold your own
> destruction.[37]

Joachite motifs notwithstanding, Müntzer later insisted, and
I think quite correctly, that those who attributed his teaching to
Joachim and mocked it as an "eternal gospel" erred; for, while
respecting Joachim, he read only his commentary on Jeremiah,[38]
and he took his own teaching from "much higher" sources, viz.
the very words of God.[39] Certain Joachite motifs and images, like

36. Summer is a Joachite image for the third age. Benz, *Ecclesia Spiritualis*, pp.
10–12.

37. Franz, 381. 20–26. On Müntzer's criticism of Luther's Reformation as a halfway
house, too timid to draw the full sociopolitical consequences which would break
with the past, see Manfred Bensing, *Thomas Müntzer und der Thüringer Aufstand
1525* (Berlin, 1966), pp. 16–17.

38. This is a pseudo-Joachite work printed three times in the sixteenth century
(Venice, 1516, 1525; and Cologne, 1577). Bloomfield, *Traditio* 13 (1957): 251. M. M.
Smirin argues that Müntzer knew Joachim's *Concordia novi ac veteris testamenti*
and even employed it in the *Fürstenpredigt*: "Es unterliegt keinem Zweifel, dass
Müntzer sich in seiner Predigt vor den Fürsten, in der er vom 2. Kapitel Daniel
ausging, auf das fünfte Buch der 'Concordia' Joachims stützte." "Thomas Müntzer
und die Lehre des Joachim von Fiore," *Sinn und Form* 4 (1952): 69–143, 134.

39. "Bey mir ist das gezeugnis abatis Joachim gross. Ich hab in alleine uber
Jeremiam gelesen. Aber meine leer ist hoch droben, ich nym sie von im nicht an,
sundern vom ausreden Gotis, wie ich dan zur zeit mit aller schrift der biblien
beweisen wil." Franz, 398. 15–18. This confession is appended to the treatise *Von
dem getichten Glauben* (December 2, 1523) as a letter to Hans Zeiss. Smirin, who
wants to depict Müntzer as the modern and Joachim as the typically medieval man,
distinguishes them at three points: (1) Müntzer does not wait passively for the
inevitable, but acts concretely to implement the new order; (2) for Müntzer, the
plentitudo intellectus is pragmatic judgment, not an otherworldly mystical experience; and (3) Müntzer is engaged in present history and manmade revolution.
This, in Smirin's view, is what Müntzer means when he says "meine leer ist hoch
droben." *Sinn und Form* 4 (1952): 121–22, 137. Bloomfield, however, has argued
persuasively that Joachim himself "is not a mystic unless we wish to use the

certain emphases in Lutheran theology, Storchian spiritualism, Taborite ideology and, above all, medieval mystical theology, understandably served to articulate Müntzer's biblically derived concern for an impassioned and experienced faith. The escalation of this concern intensified Müntzer's criticism: from the Franciscans of Zwickau to the reformers of Wittenberg faith was compromised. And with the intensification of his criticism came a radicalization of the remedies Müntzer was prepared to apply to the situation: he was finally to recommend and lead an Old Testament style cleansing by slaughter.[40] But throughout, his sources—past and contemporary—were more ideological aids for the justification of his quite literal commitment to the human perfection and total intimacy with God about which the Bible speaks, than they were a new, imported content.

This is forcefully stated in a letter Müntzer wrote to Luther after his wandering had ceased. In April, 1523, Müntzer settled in Allstedt as pastor of the Johanniskirche. On July 9 of the same year, he wrote Luther a careful account of his teaching on the subject of "revelations," defending himself against those who had spread the word that his "head is filled with demons." [41] Luther had sharply rejected the authority of present revelations in favor of the traditional means of clerical authorization at the hands of men. Criticizing the claims of the Zwickau prophets, he had earlier urged Melanchthon to find out "whether they can prove their calling [*vocatio*]," and maintained that he "definitely did not want the 'prophets' to be accepted [in Wittenberg] if they can only state that they were called by mere revelation [*nuda revelatione*]." [42]

---

word very loosely. He was concerned with the kingdom of God in history." *Traditio* 13 (1957): 261. Goertz, in distinction from Smirin, considers the apocalyptic strain quite secondary to the mystical (Tauler) in Müntzer. *Innere und Aeussere Ordnung in der Theologie Thomas Müntzers*, pp. 146, 148. Gerhard Zschäbitz, on the other hand, following Walter Nigg, *Das Buch der Ketzer* (1949), maintains that chiliasm, both as a religious and a sociopolitical expectation of the purification of mankind, was the center of Müntzer's thought and the entire Anabaptist movement. *Zur mitteldeutschen Wiedertäuferbewegung nach dem grossen Bauernkrieg* (Berlin, 1958), p. 39. Rupp has recently agreed with Goertz that mysticism is more important than apocalyptic in the formation of Müntzer's thought. *Patterns of Reformation*, p. 277, n. 2. Cf. below, n. 109.

40. See *infra*, pp. 77–78.

41. Already in September, 1522, Müntzer had received word (from Johann Buschmann) that he was under attack by "Martinians." Franz, 386.5–6.

42. *Luthers Werke im Auswahl* 6 : 92 (= *LW* 48 : 366).

In his letter of July 9, Müntzer avoided direct criticism of the Zwickau prophets, while cautiously not challenging Luther's negative assessment of them.[43] Assuming that Müntzer was not pulling his theological punches in order to curry Luther's favor,[44] the following statement on the subject of revelations is an intense expression, cast in the language of the Psalms that had meant so much to the young Luther, of the experienced faith Müntzer had demanded since the beginning of his career. If there is a fault in it, it is not an identifiable medieval heresy, but unabashed biblical literalism.

> The personal acknowledgment of the divine will, by which we are filled through Christ with infallible spiritual wisdom and understanding, is the knowledge of God, as the Apostle teaches the Colossians [Col. 1 : 9–10], which is to be received by all men. We are taught by the mouth of the living God, and thereby know with complete certainty [*certissime*] that the teaching of Christ is not fashioned for us by man, but extended to us without deception by the living God.[45] For Christ himself wants us to be able to judge his teaching [*vult nos habere iuditium doctrinae suae*]. . . . He says in John 7[: 17]: "If anyone is committed to God's will, he will know whether the teaching is from God or from myself." No mortal knows the teaching [of God] or whether Christ is a liar or one who tells the truth, unless his will is conformed to the crucified, and he has first suffered the surging and beating of his waters [Ps. 93 : 3–4], which everywhere overwhelm the soul of the elect. The storm causes many to sink, but then with effort [the elect] is pulled out, and, crying with a parched throat [Ps. 69 : 4], he can hope against hope [Rom. 4 : 18] and petition a single will on the day of visitation after the long

43. "Hic non tam arrogans sum, quim [sic] superiori testimonio tuo et corrigi et doceri volo, ut simul ingrediamur charitatis viam. De Marco [Stübner] et Nicolao [Storch] obiicis; quales sint, ipsi videant, Gallatas 2. Contremisco in divinis iudiciis. Quid tibi loquuti sint vel quid egerint, ignoro." Franz, 391. 19–24.

44. Cf. Lohmann, who maintains: "Noch bis 1523 hat Müntzer ernsthaft die Hoffnung gehegt, Luther zu sich herüberzuziehen." *Zur geistigen Entwicklung Müntzers*, p. 23.

45. Müntzer maintains that "one who is supported by such great certitude of divine revelation distinguishes the work of God from that of evil spirits." Franz, 391. 1–3. Hence Müntzer's readiness to distinguish here and now the elect from the reprobate. Cf. below, p. 93.

wait. Then his feet are made steadfast on the rock [Ps. 40 : 3] and, wondrously from afar, the Lord appears, and the testimonies of God are made credible.[46]

Between July, 1523 and July, 1524, Müntzer's alienation from Saxon Christendom became complete. His immediate and most persistent irritant was Count Ernst of Mansfeld, who in September, 1523, forbade his people to frequent what he called Müntzer's "heretical mass and preaching." [47] Müntzer, in return, accused the count of "wanting to be more feared than God," and concluded with the warning: "If you try to suppress me with the fist, I will deal a hundred thousand times as angrily with you as Luther with the pope." [48] On October 4, 1523, with appropriate apocalyptic warnings, Müntzer petitioned the judgment and defense of Frederick the Wise against the charges and coercive activities of the Count of Mansfeld.

In his December, 1523, treatises, *On Feigned Faith* (*Von dem getichten Glauben*) and the *Protestation odder Empietung Thome Müntzer*, Müntzer's judgment on the Lutherans generally had become as bleak as that upon the local political authorities. He now maintained that the Lutherans overcame the "werkheiligen" only "so that they could poison the world more thoroughly with a feigned faith than the others had done with their stupid works." [49] These two writings, it is important to note, were read by Conrad Grebel and his radical followers in Zürich, who had recently broken with Ulrich Zwingli over the nature and pace of the Swiss Reformation. The Swiss radicals, in quest of new allies, were

---

46. Franz, 390. 8–24. In a letter to Christoph Meinhard (Dec. 11, 1523), Müntzer stressed that Scripture must become true in the individual believer—a heightened version of Luther's *pro nobis* theme. "Nymant muge salig werden, er erdulde dan, das Got dye gantze schrift yn yhm warmache, Mattei 5 [18]." "Dye gancze schrift muss yn ydern menschen wahr werden, nach eyns yeder mass, eh er salig werdt." Ibid., 399. 1–2, 22–23. Those who would hasten to contrast Luther and Müntzer in terms of letter versus Spirit—who has not fallen into that trap?—should meditate on Müntzer's own assurances to Luther: "Ego non suscipio vel extases vel visiones, nisi deus me coegerit, immo susceptas non credo, nisi videro opus. . . . Crede nihil me loquuturum, nisi quod clarissimo et germano textu commonstrare potero." Franz, 391. 8–9, 26–27.

47. Müntzer to Ernst von Mansfeld (Sept. 22, 1523), Franz, 394. 1–2.

48. Ibid., 394. 18, 31–32.

49. Letter to Hans Zeiss (Dec. 2, 1523), appended to *Von dem getichten Glauben*, Franz, 398. 1 ff. I will deal in greater detail with these two writings in the context of my analysis of Müntzer's *Ausgetrückte Emplössung*.

so impressed by Müntzer's writings that they wrote to him as a "faithful proclaimer of the gospel" and a "beloved brother." Even after learning later of Müntzer's indifference to the issue of adult baptism and his support of armed resistance against the princes, Grebel and six of his colleagues could still conclude a second letter to Müntzer with the closing signature: "your brothers and seven new young Müntzers against Luther." [50]

The events that would drive Müntzer from Allstedt and into open revolt in Mühlhausen were soon set in motion by the destruction of a chapel in neighboring Mallerbach. The chapel, which belonged to the Cistercian nunnery at Naundorf, had long been an object of Müntzer's preaching, and on March 24, 1524, it was burned to the ground. The nuns of Naundorf quickly protested to the Elector. On May 9, the city fathers of Allstedt appeared in Weimar, where they received Duke John's directive to apprehend and punish the guilty parties. On June 7, the city responded to the order in a letter very probably drafted by Müntzer himself. The letter defended the Christian correctness of razing an idolatrous chapel—and therein foreshadowed Müntzer's defense of the Christian use of the sword against the ungodly in the *Sermon Before the Princes (Fürstenpredigt)* of July 13[51]—and admonished Duke John with biblical instruction in this matter:

> We beg for God's sake that your grace will, as a praiseworthy Christian prince, observe and take to heart what God our creator himself tells the devout Moses (Exod. 23 : 1): "You shall not defend the godless." Since the entire world is now aware that monks and nuns are idolatrous, how can they reasonably be defended by devout Christian princes? We want to do everything with body and goods which is reason-

50. Franz, pp. 437 ff., 446–47. English translations in *Spiritual and Anabaptist Writers*, pp. 71 ff. The first letter is dated September 5, 1524. Mennonite historiography stresses the character of these letters as "feelers" and Grebel's critical stance against Müntzer's theological views. See Bender, *MQR* 27 (1953): 3–16 and Friedmann, *MQR* 31 (1957): 75–87. On the crucial issues in the Swiss Reformation between Zwingli and his radical critics, see especially John H. Yoder, "The Turning Point in the Zwinglian Reformation," *MQR* 32 (1958): 128–40, and Robert C. Walton's critical rejoinder, "Was There a Turning Point of the Zwinglian Reformation?," *MQR* 42 (1968): 45–56. Yoder has recently replied to Walton (with a title that indicates Walton's victory), "The Evolution of the Zwinglian Reformation," *MQR* 43 (1969): 95–122. Walton's larger study should also be consulted: *Zwingli's Theocracy* (Toronto, 1967).

51. *Spiritual and Anabaptist Writers*, pp. 66–70.

ably requested of us for your grace and our praiseworthy
Elector. But that we should permit the Devil to be worshiped
at Mallerbach . . . is something we will no more do than
we would become servants of the Turk.[52]

The letter clearly indicates that the people of Allstedt were,
at least for the present, prepared to stand firmly behind their
pugnacious pastor. This in part explains the hesitation of the
Saxon princes to move decisively against Müntzer. But beyond
this show of force by the people of Allstedt, the hesitation of the
princes was also encouraged by apparently sincere doubts about
what constituted true religious faith. Elector Frederick remained
externally cooperative with the old faith and tried his best to face
the new religious disputes with a posture of neutrality. His brother
and coruler, Duke John, was already decisively against the old
faith, but he remained flexible about the particulars of the new
faith.[53] The Elector had said that, if God wills it, "the common
man shall rule." And Duke John, who was also buffeted with
radical ideas by his own court preacher in Weimar,[54] could, with
princely humility, honestly conclude: "God has made me a prince
so that I can ride many horses; but if he does not want me to
remain a prince, I will gladly ride four or even two. If he chooses
to protect me, no one can overcome me; if he does not, I can also
live as a simple man." [55] Only the electoral heir, Crown Prince
John Frederick, was unshakeably in Luther's camp.

This indecisiveness understandably irritated Luther.[56] In late
June or early July, 1524, he admonished the princes for being "all
too good and soft" [57] and, with an apparent reminder of the
episode at Mallerbach, dismissed Müntzer with the words: "I de-

52. Franz, 405. 37–406. 9.

53. Carl Hinrichs, *Luther und Müntzer: Ihre Auseinandersetzung über Obrigkeit und Widerstandsrecht* (Berlin, 1952), p. 32.

54. Cited in ibid., pp. 30–31.

55. Cited in ibid., pp. 83–84; 8.

56. No doubt Luther's irritation was further complicated by the fact that he had defended princely prerogatives challenged by Müntzer and his followers. He had strictly forbidden revolution against established authority in his 1522 *Eine treue Vermahnung zu allen Christen, sich zu hüten vor Aufruhr und Empörung*, made clear the divine sanction of worldly government in his 1523 treatise *Von weltlicher Obrigkeit*, and defended a moderate degree of profiteering in his 1524 treatise *Von Kaufshandlung und Wucher*.

57. "Ein Brief an die Fürsten zu Sachsen von dem aufrührischen Geist," *WA* 15 : 211. 15–16 (= *LW* 40 : 50). Cf. also Hinrichs, *Luther und Müntzer*, pp. 143 ff.

tect no other fruit of this spirit of Allstedt, save that he wants to fight with the fist and break wood and stone. Love, peace, patience, goodness, and long-suffering are so far not demonstrated." [58]

Luther's irritation notwithstanding, the princes granted a hearing, and Müntzer seized upon it as his golden opportunity to convert the princes of Saxony to his own concept of reformation. On July 13, in the presence of Duke John, Crown Prince John Frederick, Dr. Gregor Brück (chancellor of electoral Saxony), Dr. Hans von Grefendorf (electoral counselor), and the higher officials of Allstedt, Müntzer delivered his famous *Fürstenpredigt*—an exposition of the second chapter of the book of Daniel. His major point was as simple as it was brash: just as King Nebuchadnezzar found that the Spirit-guided prophet Daniel could interpret his dreams and define the present course of history better than all his wise men, so the princes of Saxony should realize that Müntzer could better define and direct a godly transformation of the world with Saxon sword [59] than "Brother Fattened Swine" (Luther), who mocked the spirit of Christ and denied God's present revelations.[60]

Although later Lutheran propagandists depicted Müntzer as being conscious of a miserable failure as soon as the sermon ended, no document exists to confirm the immediate reaction of his select audience.[61] That a negative verdict was indeed anticipated by Müntzer is strongly suggested by a letter he wrote to Duke John some hours after the sermon was preached. In the letter he declared his intention to continue to censure Christendom in sermons and books regardless of the orders issued by the princes. "I censure senseless Christendom to its foundations, for I know my responsibility to the advent of my faith. If you still permit my books to circulate, I accept it gladly; if not, I commend the matter to the will of God." [62]

Around July 15, Müntzer wrote to the persecuted Christians of Sangerhausen that a cleansing slaughter was needed, since both

---

58. *WA* 15 : 217. 10 ff (= *LW* 40 : 56).

59. Hinrichs summarizes well: "Müntzer will die Revolution, nicht die Evolution 'ohne Hand,' wie sie Luther und die Seinen predigen. Das Kurfürstentum Sachsen ist der Hort des Neuen, Müntzer will es zum Zentrum der revolutionären Bewegung für ganz Deutschland machen." *Luther und Müntzer*, p. 63.

60. *Spiritual and Anabaptist Writers*, pp. 61, 54. The sermon as a whole is thoroughly analyzed by Hinrichs, *Luther und Müntzer*, pp. 5–76.

61. Ibid., pp. 76, 64.

62. Franz, 407. 23–27.

the ecclesiastical and political orders were corrupted beyond hope. His words suggest a bitterly disappointed man:

> I tell you truly that the time has come for bloodshed [*ein blutvorgyssen*] to fall upon this impenitent world for its unbelief. . . . Why do you want to let yourselves be led around by your noses any longer? One knows full well and can prove it with Scripture that lords and princes as they now present themselves are not Christians. Your priests and monks pray to the Devil, and there are ever fewer Christians. All your preachers are hypocrites and worshipers of man. Why do you want to hope [in them] any longer? [63]

On July 22 he wrote the castellan Hans Zeiss:

> I tell you that one must take powerful note of the new movement of the present world. The old approaches will simply no longer do, for it is [now] nothing but slime, as the prophet says: "All the wicked of the earth will drink the dregs of the cup of anger which is not emptied." [Ps. 75 : 9] Those who have thirsted for blood will drink blood.[64]

"Obrigkeit" is now interchangeable with "Teufel." [65] The local regents act not only against Christian faith but also against "their natural right" (*yhr naturliche recht*) and must, therefore, be "strangled as dogs." [66] Zeiss is advised to depend no longer on the old custom of appealing to higher offices, since they too have absolutely no regard for the Christian faith.[67] This point is further elaborated in a second letter of July 25, where Müntzer points out that "our princes are silent and completely motionless," while the godless regents destroy the peace of the land. One can no longer appeal to the princes; their "negligence" has destroyed the "fear and respect" of the people.[68] The common man, Müntzer con-

63. Ibid., 414. 7 ff.

64. Ibid., 419. 20–25.

65. Ibid., 412. 36 ff.

66. Ibid., 417. 11–13.

67. Ibid., 417. 22–25, with the conclusion: "Do hat yhr gewalt auch eyn ende, sye wyrt in kurzer zeyt dem gemeinen volk gegeben werden." He insists, however, that it is "far from me" to arouse the wrath of the common man against "frume amptleut." Still, it is absolutely clear that he no more trusts the higher offices of the princes than he does the local tyrants who manage Sangerhausen.

68. Ibid., 421. 22–24; 422. 1–2, 6.

cludes, has but one alternative. He must follow the natural law of self-defense and make a discreet, protective covenant with rulers who are truly pious. This is to be undertaken as a tradition sanctioned emergency measure, in the hope of so terrifying the godless rulers that they will sheath their swords.[69]

THE *Special Exposé of False Faith*
THE RELOCATION OF AUTHORITY

Müntzer had made his impressive but abortive bid for political support from the princes of Saxony. He would not be the new Daniel who interprets the signs of the times to these rulers. The house-prophet Luther had retained their ear and even consolidated princely favor. Müntzer knew all too well that his days were numbered, as Saxon sword and pulpit made ready to rid the land of the "rebellious spirit of Allstedt."

If Müntzer could not be a new Daniel to the princes of Saxony, could he perhaps be a new John to the peasantry of Thuringia? That was the revolutionary proposition he now entertained with grand prophetic defiance in a work drafted between the delivery of the *Sermon to the Princes* (July 13) and early August, 1524, and entitled: *A Special Exposé of False Faith, drawn forth from the witness of Luke's gospel and set before the unfaithful world in order to remind weak, pitiable Christendom of its error.* The text for this masterpiece of dissent lay in the revealing words of Ezekiel 8 : 7–10:

> And God brought me to the door of the court; and when I looked, behold, there was a hole in the wall. Then he said to me, "Son of man, dig in the wall;" and when I dug in the wall, lo, there was a door. And he said to me, "Go in, and see the vile abominations that they are committing here."

69. "Es muss eyn beschydner bund gemacht werden yn solcher gestalt, das sich der gemeine man mit frummen amptleuten vorbinde alleyne umbs evangelion willen." Franz, 422. 24–26. "Ehr [der bund] sol alleine eyn bedrauen [Drohung] seyn der gotlosen, das sye still halten myt yrem wuten." Ibid., 422. 37 ff.; cf. 422. 10–20. "Es ist de bund nicht anderst den eyne nothwere, welche nymant geweygert wyrt nach dem naturlichen ortheil aller vornunftigen menschen." Ibid., 423. 5–7. As these citations show, the matter is much more intricate than simply "relativizing" or rendering "objectless" obedience to rulers, as Goertz argues in reference to the *Fürstenpredigt* and the *Ausgetrückte Emplössung. Innere und Aeussere Ordnung in der Theologie Thomas Müntzers*, p. 139.

So I went in and saw; and there, portrayed upon the wall round about, were all kinds of creeping things, and loathsome beasts, and all the idols of the house of Israel.

Already in the first line of the preface mention is made of Luther's betrayal—his "schmachbücher"—and the consequent necessity to counter with the true, definitive account of the secrets and judgments of God.[70] Müntzer explains his refusal to debate with Luther privately[71] by reference to Christ's refusal to enter into private disputations with the pharisees. Those who are willing to obey God already know that his teaching is from God (John 7 : 17) and understand that he would say nothing in private that has not already been said in public (John 18 : 19 ff.).[72] Then the biting censure, which joins the issue of the treatise, is added:

Our learned ones [*gelerten*] would like to bring the witness of the Spirit of Jesus into the university. But they will fail completely. For they have not taught in order that the common man, through their teaching, might be brought up to their level. No, they want to sit alone in judgment on faith with their stolen Scripture. They have no faith whatsoever, whether before God or before men. Everyone can see how they seek goods and honors. Listen, common man! You must teach yourself if you are to avoid further deception! The Spirit of Christ himself, who to our learned ones is a mockingbird of doom, is present to help you. Amen.[73]

70. Franz, 268. 1–14. Müntzer's reference to "schmachbücher" concerns primarily Luther's *Brief an die Fürsten zu Sachsen.* Cf. above, pp. 76–77.

71. Luther's first instruction to the princes of Saxony was that one "lasse die geister auff einander platzen und treffen." *WA* 15 : 219. 1–2; 213. 19 ff.

72. Franz, 269. 32 ff. Already in the *Protestation oder Empietung* (December, 1523) Müntzer refused ever to argue his teaching "auff einem Winckel," ostensibly meaning a private session with Luther in Wittenberg. Franz, 239. 29–240. 4. Cf. Hinrichs, *Luther und Müntzer*, p. 97.

73. Franz, 270. 7 ff. Who is Müntzer's "common man?" Socioeconomic profiles of Anabaptists in this period stress the preponderance of small craftsmen and especially the agrarian peasant class. Initially, as was also the case in medieval heresies, members of the upper classes and the well-educated were not only attracted but could even assume positions of highest leadership (Conrad Grebel, for example). As the speedy alliance between imperial and city law and established theology drove nonconformity from the urban centers and towns, a lower-class constituency understandably resulted. Cf. Paul Peachey, "Social Background and Social Philosophy of the Swiss Anabaptists, 1525–1540," *MQR* 28 (1954): 102–27; Claus-Peter Clasen, "The Sociology of Swabian Anabaptism," *Church History* 32 (1963): 150–80;

The treatise proper opens with the witness of the first chapter of Luke to the rarity and difficulty of true faith. Müntzer is eager here to strike at the heart of what may in fact be his own carica-ture[74] of Luther's doctrine of justification by faith alone. The ex-amples of Zachariah (who must struggle to believe that his aged, barren wife will bear him a son) and Mary (who must adjust to the information that she will, without marital assistance, conceive not only a child but even the son of God) are set forth by Müntzer to ridicule the sheer faith of Luther.[75] Faith must be formed in the face of the absurd and the impossible, in the presence of what, to reason, seems to be madness.

Zachariah and Mary did not attain their faith in the rosy way believed today by this insane world. They did not one day say: "Yes, I will simply believe [*schlecht glauben*][76] that God will make it all right." With such an easy advent [of faith] this drunken world concocts a faith more deadly than that of Turks, heathens, and Jews. Mary and Zachariah were frozen in the fear of God until the faith of a mustard seed [77] over-

"Medieval Heresies in the Reformation," *Church History* 32 (1963): 392–414; and *Die Wiedertäufer im Herzogtum Württemberg und in benachbarten Herrschaften* (Stuttgart, 1965), 118–144, 155; and Robert Stupperich, *Das Münsterische Täufertum: Ergebnisse und Probleme der neueren Forschung* (Münster/Westf., 1958), pp. 18–19. On the sociology of medieval heresies, see Grundmann, *Religiöse Bewegungen im Mittelalter*, pp. 157–69.

74. Cf. Gordon Rupp, "Word and Spirit in the First Years of the Reformation," *ARG* 49 (1958): 13–26, 25; Thomas Nipperdey, "Theologie und Revolution bei Thomas Müntzer," *ARG* 54 (1963): 145–81, 167: "Er sieht in Luther . . . den Entwurf der Wortorthodoxie." Martin Schmidt argues that Müntzer's "mystical Spiritualism" forced this misreading of Luther. *Theologia viatorum* 6 (1954–58): 41, n. 59.

75. Earlier in *Von dem getichten Glauben* (December, 1523), Müntzer censures those who would "storm heaven with a promise," and stresses the biblical witness to the difficulty of true faith: "all vether, die patriarchen, propheten und sunderlich die aposteln gantz schwerlich zum glauben kommen seint." Franz, 220. 19–25; 220. 2–4; cf. 223. 12 ff. Repeated caricatures of establishment Christendom via the *sola fide* are set forth in the *Protestation oder Empietung*. "Ach, wan nicht mehr gepuert dann gleuben, ey wie leichts wiltu dartzu kommen! Es sagt weitter: Ja, ane zweyffel, du bist von christlichen eltern geporn, du hast nye kein mal getzweyffelt, du wilt auch feste stehn. Ja, ja, ich bin ein guter christ. Ach, kan ich so leichtlich selig werden?" Franz, 236. 15–18; cf. 227. 15 ff.

76. "Schlicht Glaube an" is Ernst Bizer's definition of Luther's mature concept of faith. *Fides ex auditu. Eine Untersuchung über die Entdeckung der Gerechtigkeit Gottes durch Martin Luther* (Neukirchen, 1961), p. 42.

77. For exposition of this faith, cf. *Von dem getichten Glauben,* Franz, 224. 24–30.

came their unbelief. Theirs was a faith attained only through great fear and trembling.[78]

Fear of God is a central concept in Müntzer's effort to undermine the authority of established religion. He sees it as the sine qua non of God's presence and hence of religious truth, and develops it quite literally along the lines of the *Entleerung* or *Gelassenheit* motif of German mysticism.[79] The crux of the matter is that only true fear of God creates a place where the Holy Spirit can reside and operate. "He who believes easily has a shallow heart; but fear of God creates a place for the Holy Spirit." [80] In his exposition of the eighteenth Psalm for Christoph Meinhard in Eisleben, Müntzer explained that, where there is no experienced reception of Christ "through the spirit of the fear of God in the heart," there can be no meaningful reception of him through the words of the preacher in the ear.[81] After his forced expulsion from Halle, he wrote an unknown follower that the experience was salutary *"Anfechtung,* clearing out the depths of the soul so that it can be more and more illumined." [82] Through "pure fear of God," the Spirit penetrates into the "depths of the soul" (*abgrund der seelen*), unmasks and absolutely uproots false faith; it is an exposé of the person.[83]

> The power of the Highest, as Luke's gospel shows from beginning to end, expels completely all feigned faith, all secret unbelief; for such is uncovered through the arrival and penetration [*anthün oder durchgang*] [of the Spirit] into the

78. Franz, 272. 1 ff. Moses, Jacob, and Gideon are further heroes of faith for Müntzer. See Franz, 273. 11–12, 15 ff.

79. In the expanded German version of the *Prague Manifesto,* "fear of God" and salutary "lehrmachung" are explicitly connected: "Auch dye heilsamen anfechtunge und nutzbarlichen abegrundt des fursehen gemutes in seiner lehrmachung haben sie [i.e. gar vihel menschen] nicht kunt endecken. . . . Wen der geist der forcht Gots hat dyeselbigen nicht besessen." Franz, 496. 1–4. In *Von dem getichten Glauben,* the "empty soul" is the locus for the "living word": "last uns die heiligen biblien dartzu nützen, do sie zu geschaffen ist, zu tödten . . . und nicht lebendig zu machen wie das lebendige wort, das eine lere sele hört." Franz, 220. 22–25.

80. Franz, 273. 30 ff.

81. Franz, 204. 19–23. This is then extrapolated in the mystical imagery of a return to one's origin via "langweyl" (or *Gelassenheit*), sadness and suffering unknown to the Lutherans. Ibid., 403. 23 ff.

82. Franz, 387. 21–22 (March 19, 1523).

83. Note in this regard Müntzer's description of John the Baptist as the ideal preacher. Franz, 306. 28 ff.

depths of the soul. Paul says, "Clothe yourselves in Christ" [Rom. 13 : 14], and, when that is done, false faith can have absolutely no place. But he who has not experienced this transition [*durchgang*] knows absolutely nothing about faith.[84]

Müntzer can state this in terms of a simple proportion and reciprocity reminiscent of Tauler: no fear, no grace (and, by implication, no power and authority):

God cannot give grace to one who . . . does not fear him from the depths of his heart. . . . We cannot be saved by the hand of our enemies, and the heartfelt mercy of God cannot enlighten our inconceivable darkness so long as the fear of God does not empty us [*nicht leer macht*] so that we can receive unending wisdom.[85]

Indeed, God is in bondage to the heart of one who truly fears him.

Through fear the Spirit of God is so fully revealed that the heart is softened completely and made capable of receiving the gifts of God. God cannot despise a repentant and humbled heart; he must listen to it [*er müss es erhören*], so sweet is the incense which rises from it.[86]

Müntzer does not hesitate to draw the polemical conclusions. First and most fundamental, this idea shifts the locus of final religious authority and challenges those who would claim exclusive authority on the basis of Scripture and tradition. Authority does not reside within a theological circle of learned *doctores*, but rather within the "holy temple," directly authorized by and responsible to God, which each and every man is.

Every man should look closely at himself and see in his own life how he himself is a holy temple—1 Cor. 3[: 16–17: "Do you not know that you are God's temple and that God's Spirit dwells in you?"] and 1 Cor. 6[: 19: "Do you not know that your body is a temple of the Holy Spirit within you,

---

84. Ibid., 274. 5 ff. There is no possibility of a Lutheran "simul iustus et peccator" here, as Müntzer makes clear by adding Luke 5 : 36: "No one tears a piece from a new garment and puts it on an old garment."

85. Franz, 286. 8 ff.; cf. 292. 1 ff. On Tauler, see my *Homo Spiritualis*, pp. 30 ff.

86. Franz, 292. 1 ff.

which you have from God?"]—a temple authorized by and responsible to God from eternity [*Gott züstendig von ewigkeit*]. Every man should further understand that the Holy Spirit is present as his schoolmaster in faith and be attentive to the Spirit's workings—John 14[: 26], John 16[: 13]. And, finally, let every man know that this very same temple, which he himself is, is laid waste beyond measure by the ignorant clergy.[87]

The devastation of the people's "temple" by the clergy is engineered by the twin theological concepts of the religious establishment: the doctrines that Scripture is the sole authority in the church (*sola scriptura*) and that saving faith comes through hearing the Scripture preached (*fides ex auditu*). These are skillfully crafted tools for the exploitation of the poor and the aggrandizement of the powerful.

> The learned theologians [*schrifftgelerten*] turn their thin little tongues and softly say: "Search the Scriptures, for you believe, you must let yourself believe, that there you will receive salvation" [cf. John 5 : 20]. And so the poor needy people are more thoroughly deceived than any words can say. With all their works and words, the learned theologians have seen to it that the poor man may not learn to read because of his preoccupation with making a living. And they preach unashamedly that the poor man should submit to the skinning and fleecing which the tyrants have prepared for him. When will the poor man learn to read the Scripture? Oh, but my dear Thomas, you speak as a madman [*du schwermest*]. Theologians should read the beautiful books and peasants should listen to them, for faith comes through hearing. Oh yes, there the theologians have found a fine trick.[88]

87. Ibid., 292. 33 ff. Already in the shorter German version of the *Prague Manifesto* we find the argument: "Sant Pawel screibt . . . [2 Cor. 3 : 3] das dye herzen der menschen sein das papyr adder pergemen, do Got myt seynem finger seynen unvorrucklichn willn unde ewyge weysheyt nit mit tinten inscreybt, welche scryfft kan eye itzlicher mensche lesen, so er andrst aufgethane vornunfft hatt." Franz, 492. 5–9. In a letter to Jeori (undated, but in the critical period of late July/early August, 1524), Müntzer fumes against the "pigs" who cannot tolerate "the invisible writer, who does not write with ink or other material, but with the stylus of his Spirit in the depths of the soul, where one recognizes that he is a son of God and that Christ is the highest among the sons of God. For what all the elect are by grace, Christ is by divine nature." Franz, 425. 20–24.

88. Franz, 275. 17 ff.

The masses, Müntzer recognizes, are not noted for critical acumen. They have always been taught that their clergy were learned and hence fully authoritative, and it is this assumption which has permitted the priests and theologians to keep them in a godless state.

> The people have always assumed and think still today that the clergy are authorities in the faith because they have read so many great and beautiful books. Hence the poor common man marvels: "Such impressive men with their red and brown berets! Should they not know what is right and wrong?" But in truth the people (because they do want to be Christians) have judged stupidly, although Christ has emphatically warned that the false servants of God must be recognized and distinguished from the true servants, Matthew 7[: 15]. But no one attends to anything but creaturely goods. Hence each tarries outside the temple and cannot enter his heart because of his great unbelief, which he cannot even recognize because he is so busy trying to earn a living. The Holy Spirit laments that very fact in Jeremiah [Lam. 2 : 12]. But when the people have given themselves up so completely and for so long to the clergy and the theologians, the Holy Spirit becomes [for them] a mute idol and knows less about God than an oaken block or a flintstone. What Psalm 30[31 : 18] says is true: "The lips of the deceitful grow dumb." [89]

Müntzer accuses the clergy and the theologians of being "Bible thieves." [90] They are like the pharisees of old who were so preoccupied with "Scripture alone," ignoring the "spirit of Scripture," that they completely misevaluated Christ.

> The stupid, blustering, insane pharisees thought in their fleshly brains that Jesus could in no way be the Christ because he was reared in Galilee. They held to the Scripture without the spirit of Scripture, just as the godless are accustomed to do today.[91]

---

89. Ibid., 293. 17 ff.

90. Already in the *Prague Manifesto* Müntzer criticizes the "cursed pfaffen" who speak of "sheer Scripture, which they have stolen out of the Bible as murderers and thieves." Franz, 491. 15–492. 2.

91. Franz, 315. 15 ff.

Had these Bible thieves not loved Scripture only for their belly's sake, they could have known through Daniel [2 : 44; 12 : 1 ff.] the time of Christ's birth, visited through Micah [5 : 1–2] the place of his birth, and learned through Isaiah [7 : 14 ff., 9 : 6 ff., 11 : 1] and others the procession of our Saviour.[92]

The obvious fact of their exploitation does not cause Müntzer to view the peasantry romantically as passive innocents, however. Indeed, he comes now to feel that their own stupidity and selfishness have contributed substantially to the desolate state of Christendom.[93]

All men are to blame that the whole Christian community worships a mute God. For where did this start if not in every peasant's desire to have a priest in order to insure prosperity throughout his life? A true priesthood is unwanted, and the world supports it only reluctantly. Indeed, it is now the custom to behead true priests. Such a good office is bitter gall for the world. One must speak truly. We men are much cruder in relation to the nobility of our souls than irrational animals; for we have absolutely no understanding for anything but the profiteering and malicious deceits of this world. When something is said of God, the reaction brings the proverb of Solomon to mind: "He who preaches for a long time to a fool hears at the end of his sermon: 'Uh, what was that?' " [Prov. 23 : 9].[94]

Müntzer finally takes Scripture completely out of the hands of the scholars and theologians by arguing (1) that their unbelief and immoral lives disqualify any claim to authority and (2) that Scripture itself stands firmly against a religious life based on Scripture alone.

92. Ibid., 316. 4 ff.

93. Criticism of the common man appears in sharp form first in the *Special Exposé*, although shortcomings were pointed out already in the *Fürstenpredigt*. The strong criticism in the *Special Exposé* no doubt results in part from Müntzer's growing awareness that the people are as likely to betray as to aid him after the abortive *Fürstenpredigt*. Cf. Hinrichs, *Luther und Müntzer*, pp. 52, 72, and Müntzer's bitter letter of censure to the people of Allstedt on August 15, 1524. Two versions in Franz, pp. 432 ff., and pp. 434 ff.

94. Franz, 295. 16 ff.

Shortly before he speaks to the pious people, Christ tells the learned theologians: "My word is not with you" [John 5 : 38]. And why? Because [their] unbelief gives absolutely no room to the true roots of sincere faith.[95]

Let them preach what they want; they still seek their belly, and to sustain it they gladly accept golden gulden with great devotion. They hardly have need of one-hundreth of what they take, and yet they would still be our evangelists. For this reason their teaching has no power [*hat ire lere auch keyn krafft*], Matthew 7[: 29]. Their teaching sets absolutely nothing free except the freedom of the flesh. So they poison the Holy Spirit with the Holy Scripture.[96]

But even if their lives were exemplary, the learned would still be false teachers, for the doctrines of sola scriptura and fides ex auditu verbi fundamentally distort the biblical message for Müntzer. Scripture, as will be echoed by every sixteenth-century dissenter, gives only a witness and not the very experience of faith. It *describes* the truly faithful, but does not create true faith. In the following passage the biblical citations support direct, unmediated communion between God and man. It is significant that two of the citations invoke a covenant concept—not the covenant expressed historically in churches and priests, but that which God has written in the hearts of men (Jer. 31 : 33–34) and made known to those who truly fear him (Ps. 25 : 14).

The Son of God has said that Scripture gives a witness [to faith]. The learned theologians say that it gives faith itself. O no, my dear friends. . . . The truth that has been so long suppressed and so long asleep must now come boldly to the light of day, and to such an extent that, should a Christian among the poor masses say that he has learned the Christian faith from God himself, he is not to be believed (as we are now prepared to do) unless, in his report, he agrees with what Scripture says is the way all the elect should be taught by God [viz. as set forth in] John 6[: 45], Isaiah 54[: 11 ff.], Jeremiah 31[: 33–34], Job 35[: 10–11], Psalms 17[18 : 29], 24[25 : 14], 33[34 : 12–23], 70[71 : 17], 93[94 : 10],

95. Ibid., 276. 12–13.
96. Ibid., 306. 8 ff. Cf. Denck, *Schriften* 2: 35. 12–13.

and many other passages of Scripture, each of which emphasizes that one must be taught by God alone.[97]

Immediately on the heels of this statement, Müntzer, pointing to the sole sufficiency of the inward covenant of the heart, maintains: "If one had throughout his entire life neither heard nor seen the Bible, he could still have a sincere Christian faith through the true teaching of the Spirit [*lere des geystes*], as all those have had who, without any books, have written the Holy Scripture." [98] This directly experienced faith is the *truly objective and certain faith:* "He [who so experiences the Spirit] is absolutely certain [*auff höchst versichert*] that he has received such faith from God, who does not deceive, and has not taken it from the pious fantasies [*abgekunterfeyten*] of the Devil or of his own nature." [99] Contrary to those who seek faith in Scripture and blindly accept tradition,

we have the opposite example of Mary, Zachariah, Abraham, Joseph, Moses, and all the patriarchs who, having received the incitement of the Holy Spirit, stood fast in the depths of their hearts and refused absolutely to be turned by the counsel of the fearful and incompetent godless.[100]

It is along these lines that Müntzer's concept of the "order of God" (*ordnung gottes*) is to be interpreted. Contrary to recent analyses, it is probably not indicative of a sophisticated "natural theology." [101] Rather, it is more a statement of what Müntzer considers to be the *biblically revealed* definition of God's true covenant with men. In the *Prague Manifesto,* for example, he laments the way established Christendom ignores this order: "I have not heard even the slightest mention by any of the learned of the order of God established in all creatures." The larger German version of the *Manifesto* somewhat sharpens the lament: "I have

97. Franz, 276. 34 ff.

98. Ibid., 277. 25 ff. Cf. Denck, *Schriften* 2: 106. 13–14: "Also mag eyn mensch, der von Gott erwelet ist, on predig und geschrifft selig werden."

99. Franz, 278. 1 ff.

100. Ibid., 280. 9 ff.

101. Gordon Rupp views this concept as a "natural theology" along the lines of the *theologia naturalis* of Raymond of Sabunde. "Thomas Müntzer, Hans Hut and the 'Gospel of all Creatures,'" *Bulletin of the John Rylands Library* 43 (1961): 492–519, esp. 492–98. Walter Klaassen recognizes the connections of the concept with medieval mysticism. "Hans Hut and Thomas Müntzer," *The Baptist Quarterly* 19 (1962): 213 ff.

heard not a whisper about the orders [*ordennünge*] (established in God and in all creatures) from any donkey-farting Doctor." [102] Of course no learned (establishment) theologian will call attention to this higher "order"; for him the primary covenantal arrangement is that made visible in the traditional offices of the church. In the treatise *On Feigned Faith,* Müntzer depicts the "order of God" as a kind of omnipresent teaching ordinance, which can instruct those sufficiently sensitive to perceive it in the true nature of God and man. "Moses," he points out, "might still have taken God for a devil, had he not recognized the cunning of the creature and the purity of God in accordance with the order established in God and creatures." [103] And, in his letter to Jeori, he maintains that a "serious, suffering, diligent man, who does not believe in God just because the entire world believes this or that," learns how to live his life from "the order established in himself and all creatures." [104]

In the *Special Exposé,* fully consistent with the development of his earlier thought, Müntzer constructs a correlation between the Holy Spirit and the depths of the heart as God's true, biblically witnessed covenant with man. This arrangement is placed in firm opposition to the (Lutheran) Scripture-hearing correlation as the definitive objective and subjective correlate of true faith. It is not the preacher speaking to the ears but the Spirit of God working within the heart that makes true believers. Müntzer has adroitly used Scripture against Scripture to place Scripture on his side. He has put together a clearly defensible and, for him, fully authoritative *potentia Dei ordinata,* which undercuts and finally rejects altogether the arrangement sanctioned by established Christendom.

THE ART OF GOD

A second major section of the *Special Exposé* discusses the *Magnificat* (Luke 1 : 46–55)—Mary's praise of God's uncanny exaltation of the lowly and humiliation of the proud and mighty. We must bear in mind that Müntzer has just argued for the

---

102. Franz, 491. 11 ff., 496. 9 ff.

103. Franz, 219. 23–26. Cf. Castellio's interpretation of *ratio,* below, pp. 193 ff.

104. Franz, 425. 29–36. This statement is in the general context of an intense statement of the necessity of "armut des geysts" and retreat from the world. See especially ibid., 426. 5 ff.

relocation of authority from the Scripture-hearing correlation of Luther to what is for him a more basic, biblically backed Spirit-heart arrangement. The *Magnificat* now becomes the occasion for a practical application of this relocation of authority. It gives Müntzer the opportunity to talk "power-politics."

He tells us that his is a gospel of God's ability to accomplish not only the unexpected but even the impossible. This is why it so threatens the established powers: it upsets the accustomed status quo. The influence of mystical theology, both in concept and in terminology, is truly striking as Müntzer opens the discussion.

> The angel said to the Mother of God: "With God nothing is impossible" [Luke 1 : 37]. Why did the angel say that, my dear friends? Truly, because what God was going to do [through Mary] was, to human nature, a completely impossible, inconceivable, and unheard of thing[105]—1 Cor. 2[: 9], Isa. 64[: 4]. The same is true for what must be experienced by all of us in the advent of faith, viz. that we fleshly, earthly men are to be gods through the incarnation of Christ and so, with Christ, students of God [*Gotes schüler*], taught directly by God, and deified [*vergottet*], yes, even transformed completely into God [*gantz und gar verwandelt*], so that earthly life is ruled from heaven, Philippians 3[: 20] . . . And why is it that Brother Soft-Life and Father Step-Lightly [i.e. Luther] is so enraged [by this gospel]? [Because of what] Job 28[: 15 ff. says: "It cannot be gotten for gold . . ."]. He thinks he can continue to follow his desires, maintain his pomp and riches, and still have a worthy faith, even though the Son of God has censured the learned theologians with the clear words: "How can you believe when you continue to seek your own honor?" John 5[: 44].[106]

These words are not only for the learned theologians. Müntzer is every bit as negative about "the art of Herod," or present worldly government, as he is about its priests. Princes have absolutely no constructive social purpose; their "gantzes hantwerck" is as hangmen and jailers, those who only suppress blatant evil.[107]

---

105. Cf. Franz, 286. 37 ff.; 287. 18 ff.

106. Ibid., 281. 14 ff.; 282. 8 ff.

107. On the novelty of Müntzer's negative interpretation of Romans 13 (especially in contradistinction from Luther), cf. Hinrichs, *Luther und Müntzer,* pp. 112–13.

God has cast down the powerful because they presumed to rule over and master Christian faith, while never even thinking about its advent. They wanted no one to be prepared for it so that they alone would be judge over all people, they alone the highest power, they alone feared, prayed to and honored by all people. And this they have expected while slandering the gospel in the most horrible manner yet devised. Therein is the true art of Herod, the true nature of worldly government, made clear, as prophesied by the holy Samuel [1 Sam. 8 : 5 ff.] and most truly and clearly by Hosea: "God has given lords and princes to the world in his anger, and he will do away with them again in his wrath" [Hos. 13 : 11].[108]

Applied to society, the theology of the heart becomes a truly revolutionary ideology.[109] Müntzer finds it understandable that reason hastens to render his gospel harmless by dismissing it as sheer madness (*schwermerey*): the world is terrified by the de facto possibility of the impossible.

O my dearest brother, of what else does this gospel remind us than that faith and all that is involved in its creation force

108. Franz, 284. 17 ff.
109. There is much commentary on this relationship. Thomas Nipperdey interprets the transition from the individual to the social level as the consequence of Müntzer's identification of *justificatio* and *sanctificatio;* this identification makes "the Christification of the world" (*Verchristlichung der Welt*) a necessary goal, and collapses equality before God into the equality of social rights and privileges. *ARG* 54 (1963): 170–73, 176. While more subtle and aware of the mystical motifs, Goertz makes essentially the same point when he argues that, for Müntzer, the battle fought psychologically in the "inner order" of the soul must also be fought physically in the "outer order" of sociopolitical power. *Innere und Aeussere Ordnung in der Theologie Thomas Müntzers*, pp. 133–36, 145. Lohmann argues that Müntzer's mysticism, in contradistinction to Tauler's, drives him "Jenseits" only so that he can more effectively operate "Diesseits." *Zur geistigen Entwicklung Müntzers*, pp. 31–32, 37–38. Dobratz, on the other hand, works with a highly oversimplified view of medieval mysticism and stumbles over this transition in Müntzer's thought, when he maintains that Denck's "individualism," vis à vis Müntzer's involvement in social revolution, places Denck closer to mysticism than Müntzer. *Der Einfluss der deutschen Mystik auf Thomas Müntzer und Hans Denck*, p. 107. Smirin argues along similar lines that Müntzer's revolutionary ideology and world-view are "only formally" connected with mystical notions, *Sinn und Form* (1952), p. 143. The "revisionist" work of Manfred Bensing, on the other hand, can see medieval mysticism as a servant of Marxism: overcoming the "creaturely" and "returning to God" are concepts that embrace sociopolitical as well as individual-religious alienation. *Thomas Müntzer und der Thüringer Aufstand 1525*, pp. 48, 53. Cf. above, n. 39.

us to face the impossible? The weaklings never dare dream it
will actually come to pass. The whole insane, fantastic world
sets forth on a false, glossy path [of faith] and tells us with
a little forked tongue: "Let us preach the gospel, fear God,
and also honor our foolish regents, even though they oppose
every request for justice and ignore the Word of God. For
God's sake let us in every matter be obedient to the good
Junkers." O, welcome, you defender of the godless! How very,
very fine it must be to serve with praise two lords who oppose
one another. . . . O, how skillful has our clever reason
learned to be! How she shines and decorates her hypocrisy in
the most stately manner with the love of neighbor! But it
is absolutely impossible in our time, much more so than at
any time since the beginning of perverted government, that
the world tolerate the blow. Countless people think [such
talk] is utter madness [*mechtig gross schwermerey*]. They cannot judge otherwise, for they think it impossible that such
a thing could begin and succeed, that the godless could indeed
be knocked from the seat of power and the poor and wretched
raised up [Luke 1 : 51–52]. So they do not want to hear Mary,
although she is their most beloved matron.[110]

With a certain eloquence Müntzer concludes that it is the very
nature of the world to take greatest offense at what would most
improve it.

The world's most perverse habit is to be most offended by
what would better it. That, dear friends, is the wisdom of
the cross with which God greets his elect. One is not supposed
to become angry at the world when he looks around and
nowhere finds anything good. Yet the world is angered by
the efforts of the best good and calls it a "devilish ghost." [111]

Hence, what is most possible for God and what, for Müntzer,
defines his very nature, namely, the ability to remove the mighty
from their thrones of power and to exalt the lowly, is the most
impossible thing for the "bedeviled" world [112] and its learned
theologians to believe. They postpone a definite encounter with

110. Franz, 288. 6 ff.
111. Ibid., 317. 6 ff.
112. "Das verteufeln hebt sich nu auffs höchst." Ibid., 311. 21–22.

evil until the end of time and history. For Müntzer, a definitive separation of the righteous and the unrighteous can and should occur here and now. Eschatology becomes just another skillful way for establishment theologians to suppress the truth.

> The world and its learned theologians, who have never known trial, think that nothing is so impossible as the exaltation of the lowly and their separation from the unrighteous. And that is [their] true, hard, and entire obstacle. They refuse to give any place to the thirteenth chapter of Matthew, which speaks of the separation of the godless from the elect [vv. 47–50]. There they have rather imagined, visualizing an old-fashioned scale, that the angels should come with long spears on the day of judgment and then separate the righteous from the unrighteous. Why, they might just as well thumb their noses at the Holy Spirit. They say unashamedly that God may reveal his judgment to no one.[113]

Against these "neütrales," these "neutral ones," [114] Müntzer maintains that a definitive statement of God's judgment is possible now, just as in biblical times, by those who possess God's spirit. Sinners though they may be, the elect, unlike the godless, know in their consciences where God's law is inscribed, exactly what sin and evil are.[115] What the world needs most is a "new John" to proclaim this eternal law.

THE NEW JOHN

The third and final section of the *Special Exposé* issues a call for just such a "new John"—a spiritual leader who, by pointing anew to the old truth, will expose and invalidate the claims of the godless.

> If Christendom is to be made right, the profiteering scoundrels must be removed and made dog servants, for they can hardly claim to serve the Christian church as prelates. The poor common folk must learn again to sigh for the Spirit, Rom. 8[:14–21], to pray and wait for a new John, a new preacher, who overflows with grace and who has learned his

113. Ibid., 289. 19 ff.
114. Ibid., 290. 7 ff.
115. Ibid., 291. 5 ff.

faith through the trial of unbelief. For he must know the mind of an archunbeliever and understand that faith is a match for the industry of lust, Eph. 4[: 7–8], Psalm 67 [68 : 19].[116]

But the new John is not only tough and shrewd, experienced in the ways of the world as well as in the truth of God. He is also the perfect model of the true priesthood of God. In contradistinction to the clergy who set only the flesh free, poison the Spirit with purloined Scripture, and prevent the people from entering their hearts,

> John is a very different kind of preacher, a witnessing angel of Christ, an example for every true preacher. He deserves universal praise. Not for merit but because of the earnestness of his unstinting sobriety he suppressed his lust and stripped the powers of his soul so that the depths of the spirit could be seen in them. For it is there [in the depths of the spirit] that the Holy Spirit must speak, Psalm 84 [85 : 8 ff.]. In just such laying bare [of his soul] must a preacher be forced from his very youth to suppress his own will. For this reason John was already consecrated in the womb of his mother to be a model for all preachers [Luke 1 : 15–17].[117]

The basic task of the new John is evident in the mystical terminology of this passage. He must awaken men to the depths of their spirits, wherein the Spirit of God continues to speak. This consists, to Müntzer's mind, of the difficult if not impossible task of convincing men that God's revelation is an ongoing process, by no means ended.[118] The difficulty lies in the fact that the people have been indoctrinated by their clergy to believe that God has already spoken once and for all. And, of course, if revelation is over and God's truth sealed for eternity in a book Luther interprets better than anyone else, then Müntzer hardly has a case to make. It is in this context that one understands Müntzer's incessant demand for an *experienced* faith; it is basically a defense of continuing revelations of God's will. The issue of present authority over God's truth is absolutely fundamental.

116. Ibid., 296. 21 ff.
117. Ibid., 306. 28 ff.
118. Cf. Franz, 297. 8 ff. This was the major point of the *Fürstenpredigt*.

Almost all say: "Ey, we find satisfaction in Scripture and do not want to believe in any revelation; God speaks no more." What do you think would have happened if these people had lived in the time of the prophets? Would they have believed the prophets or rather struck them dead? They are even blind to Holy Scripture, for they do not want to see and hear the powerful emphasis there that one should and must be taught by God alone.[119]

In the face of such obstinacy, the rectification of Christendom cannot but be a painful cleansing process. "It cannot be otherwise," Müntzer concludes, "for man must be forced to destroy his stolen and feigned Christian faith through great suffering of the heart, painful sorrow, and irrepressible wonder" [120] (the last no doubt the reaction to the consequent discovery of new, personally experienced revelations of God).

As Müntzer carries the themes of the new John and ongoing revelation to their logical conclusion, the criteria of authority lose their traditional institutional linkage and become most difficult to measure objectively. We are told that true preachers are in no way qualified for their office by the number of books they have read. "Even though he may have read all the books there are, no one can fulfill this office if he does not first have the certainty of his faith, as those who have written the Scripture had. Otherwise it is all thieves' talk and a battle of words." [121] Neither learning nor ordination suffices; personal persuasion and moral excellence are finally the overriding criteria.

The shameless defense of godless, accursed, false preachers by wicked archhypocrites who want to be better than God no longer goes. They say: "Be he good or evil, a priest may still dispense God's sacrament and preach the true word." These perverted defenders of the godless . . . are obviously hardened against the clear, lucid twenty-third chapter of Exodus where God says: "I am not honored among the godless and you shall not adorn their cause." And they are still more crudely in contradiction with the forty-ninth psalm where the ordination [*verordnung*] of the servant of God and his

119. Franz, 297. 32 ff.
120. Ibid., 298. 28 ff.; cf. 300. 14 ff.
121. Ibid., 307. 20 ff.

word is discussed, and God says to the godless preacher: "Who has appointed you to preach my righteousness, you who take my declared covenant upon your lips and yet have hated my discipline?" [Ps. 50 : 16–17]. He would say to this man: "Will you preach my dear crucified Son to the world for the sake of your belly, and not know how one must be conformed to him? Rom. 8[: 29]. You have not yet learned the craft, and still you would be a schoolmaster to others?" [122]

The concluding words of the *Special Exposé* bring everything together in a focused statement on God's plan for man's salvation in this life, as Müntzer now understands it. The first chapter of Luke's gospel, the text of the *Special Exposé,* is connected with Romans 4 : 13: "The promise to Abraham and his descendents that they should inherit the world did not come through the law but through the righteousness of faith." Müntzer describes this as a statement of "the holy covenant which God swore to Abraham and every one of us." [123] Its conjunction now with the first chapter of Luke means that the ground rules for God's dealing with men according to the Abrahamic or new covenant are those set forth in the first chapter of Luke's gospel, i.e. the direct, unmediated way of the Spirit's communion with Mary, Zachariah, and Elisabeth.[124]

> The sum of this first chapter [of Luke's gospel] is the strengthening of the spirit [which we receive] in faith. It says nothing else than that the omnipotent God, our dear Lord, wants to give us the very highest Christian faith through the incarnation of Christ, so that, through the overshadowing of the Holy Spirit, we may be conformed to his suffering and life. Against this teaching the world sins bitterly and mocks it in the coarsest way. For this reason the Spirit is given only to the poor in spirit (who recognize their unbelief). This concluding word is confirmed by the entire first chapter, and especially the wonderful songs of praise by Mary and Zachariah [Luke 1 : 46 ff., 67 ff.]. They clearly tell of the heartfelt mercy [of God] which will be received through the spirit of

---

122. Ibid., 307. 29 ff.

123. Ibid., 319. 8–9.

124. Cf. ibid., 299. 9 ff.: "Gott verachtet die grossen hansen . . . und nam auff zü seynem dienst die kleynen, als Mariam, Zachariam und Elisabeth."

the fear of God. And that is to keep the holy covenant, which God swore to Abraham and to all of us, Rom. 4[: 13], and to serve him in the holiness and righteousness which will truly be valid before him. He who does not truly fear God cannot be renewed from day to day in the knowledge of God.[125]

Müntzer, of course, did not survive his dissent. He was executed on May 27, 1525, twelve days after his followers were massacred in the disastrous battle of Frankenhausen. Though few would praise—much less repeat—his revolutionary tactics, he, more than any other, is the *magister* of sixteenth-century dissent. To a significant degree, his basic sources, logic, and rhetoric are echoed whenever protest is made against established Christendom. Differences in party affiliations and doctrinal tenets notwithstanding, few subsequent dissenters escaped his example. And of the various epithets subsequent dissenters had to bear—among them, heavenly prophet, *Schwärmer,* enthusiast, Anabaptist, spiritualist, sacramentarian, Schwenckfeldian, Osiandrian—"Müntzerite" rarely failed to find its place at the top of the list.

125. Ibid., 318. 22 ff.

4

Hans Hut

THE PATIENT REVOLUTIONARY

Either while in flight from Allstedt to Mühlhausen in early August, or during a subsequent retreat from Mühlhausen in late September, 1524,[1] Thomas Müntzer stopped in the little town of Bibra near Memmingen. There he spent a night and a day in the house of a friend, to whom he delivered for publication the original, unabridged version of his *Special Exposé*.[2] This friend was the bookbuyer and binder, Hans Hut,[3] who forms the immediate link, both historically and intellectually, between Müntzer and the Anabaptist movement in South Germany and Austria.[4]

Hut's intellectual pilgrimage, as we can reconstruct it primarily from the lengthy records of his trial (September–December, 1527), began routinely enough. In the summer of 1524, during one of

1. Franz, p. 265.

2. A carefully abridged version was delivered to the censor earlier during Müntzer's hearing at Weimar on August 1. It is reproduced in parallel with the original by Franz. The unabridged version of the *Special Exposé* was subsequently published in Nürnberg by Johann Hergot.

3. The visit is later recounted by Hut during his interrogation in Augsburg. He insisted to his judges that he had no business with Müntzer during the visit, save to receive "a little book on the first chapter of Luke." From the trial documents collected by Christian Meyer, "Zur Geschichte der Wiedertäufer in Oberschwaben, I: Die Anfänge des Wiedertäuferthums in Augsburg," *Zeitschrift des historischen Vereins für Schwaben und Neuburg* (Augsburg, 1874) 1 [hereafter cited as Meyer]: 243. On Hut's varied occupation background, see ibid., p. 223.

4. A recent biographical effort treats Hut as a "cofounder [with Balthasar Hubmaier (who baptized Hans Denck) and Hans Denck (who baptized Hut)] of the South German Anabaptist movement," and maintains that he "baptized more converts, founded more new congregations, and commissioned more Anabaptist apostles than any other early leader in South Germany." Herbert Klassen, "The Life and Teachings of Hans Hut," *MQR* 33 (1959): 171–205, 267–304; 174, 205. Klassen, concerned to keep the radical Müntzer at arm's length from genuine Anabaptism (cf. ibid., pp. 270–79), concedes that it is "conceivable that they (Hut and Müntzer) were friends." Ibid., p. 268.

his frequent journeys to Wittenberg, he conversed with a miller, a tailor, and a clothmaker. These men shared with him a belief in arguments against infant baptism which would finally lead to his own rebaptism two years later at the hands of Hans Denck.[5] But the immediate consequence of this conversation was Hut's adamant refusal to permit the baptism of his newborn infant son.[6] By sixteenth-century logic, to challenge the propriety of infant baptism was to question the authority of the church that administered it and, in turn, to challenge the society with which the church was fused. Hence adult rebaptism, which rejected the baptism received as a child, was legally "blasphemous." The guilty party could either be fined, sent on a pilgrimage, beaten, exiled, have his tongue removed or split, or put to death.[7]

Hut's refusal to baptize his child led to his exile from Bibra in the autumn of 1524. Thereafter, he wandered from Wittenberg to Erfurt and Nürnberg. In the spring of 1525 he found himself in the town of Frankenhausen, where a revolt was taking shape under Müntzer's leadership.[8] There Hut witnessed Müntzer's fiery sermon on the eve of the great battle with the princes (May 13)[9] and survived the battle an eager prophet of Müntzer's revolutionary gospel. He confessed that he returned to Bibra and preached that the time had come for the people to rise up and wrest power from the princes.[10]

5. Meyer, pp. 223, 245.

6. George H. Williams makes the curious comment that Hut refused to baptize his child "under Denck's influence." *The Radical Reformation* (London, 1962), p. 78. Since Hut's contacts with Denck appear not to have begun in earnest until the fall of 1524, it is questionable that Denck exercized such influence on Hut at this time.

7. For the technical definitions of blasphemy, heresy, and revolution, which formed the basic legal grounds for persecuting Anabaptists, see Horst W. Schraepler, *Die rechtliche Behandlung der Täufer in der deutschen Schweiz, Südwestdeutschland und Hessen 1525–1618* (Tübingen, 1957), pp. 17–27.

8. Meyer, pp. 239, 241.

9. See the vivid account, which concludes with Hut's confession of beholding with the assembled crowd the miraculous appearance of the rainbow—the sign of the covenant—at the conclusion of Müntzer's sermon. Meyer, p. 241; translated in Klassen, *MQR* 33 (1959): 268.

10. Meyer, p. 241. Also Thomas Spiegel of Ostheim and the brothers Viet and Martin Weischenfelder of Uetzing single out Hut as the "haubtman oder furer" of Anabaptist teachings and revolutionary activities in their regions, and further associate him with Müntzer. They were interrogated in early 1527. Trial documents collected in Paul Wappler, *Die Täuferbewegung in Thüringen von 1526–1584. Beiträge zur neueren Geschichte Thüringens* (Jena, 1913) [hereafter cited as Wappler 1913], 2: 234, 237–41.

Hut, however, was soon to temper his revolutionary activity. He reported to his judges that, approximately one year after the episode in Frankenhausen, he visited Königsberg. There he preached to a group of about ten men in an effort to clarify certain biblical passages from which seditious conclusions were apparently being drawn. Hut cites the eschatological statements in Matthew 24; the conflation of Luke 22 : 36 and Luke 3 : 11 (already popular in *Flugschriften*), with the result, "He who has two coats should sell one and buy a sword"; John 18 : 10, where Jesus tells Peter to sheath his sword after hacking off the ear of the high priest's slave; Matthew 10 : 34, where Jesus declares that he came, not to bring peace but a sword; Psalm 149 : 5–9, where two-edged swords are delivered into the hands of the faithful to exercise judgment on kings and nobles; and, finally, Jeremiah 48 : 10, which curses the man who withholds the sword from God's work. Hut told his judges that he pointed out to his hearers how misinterpretations of these passages had earlier led the peasants to act unjustly, "seeking their own in place of God's honor." [11]

Assuming that Hut's story was not his own concoction to mollify his judges[12] (who, despite his protests, considered him to the end a bona fide Müntzerite),[13] it indicates not so much a renunciation as a tactical reformulation of his revolutionary beliefs. Within the space of a year, Hut shifted from outspoken agitation for a present, prophetically led revolution to an expectant awaiting of God's explicit inauguration of Armageddon. "A Christian may certainly have a sword," he went on to tell his audience in Königsberg, "but he must keep it sheathed until God tells him to draw it." [14]

11. Meyer, p. 241. On the conflation of Luke 22 : 36 and Luke 3 : 11, see Reinhard Schwarz, "Luthers Erscheinen auf dem Wormser Reichstag in der Sicht Thomas Müntzers," in *Der Reichstag zu Worms von 1521: Reichspolitik und Luthersache,* ed. Fritz Reuter (Worms, 1971), pp. 208–21; 220, n. 46.

12. Hut consistently protested that he was no revolutionary. The trial records of October 5, 1527 report: "er wiss von kainer andern zukunft Christi, dann wie es die heilig geschrifft anzaig, so werde kain leiblich, sonnder ain gaistlich reich werden"; "er halt, das under den christen gesatzte oberkait sein sollen und das aller gewalt von got sei"; "er wiss von kainem anschlag, der wider die oberkait gemacht sei, hab auch der kainen helffen machen (so wiss er vom schwertt Gedeonis nicht zu sagen)." Meyer, pp. 230–31; cf. also the records of September 16, 1527, esp. Hut's responses to articles 59, 63, 82. Ibid., pp. 227–29.

13. Meyer, pp. 244, 249, 251; Wappler 1913, pp. 246–47.

14. Meyer, p. 242. On the impact of Hut's chiliasm, cf. Clasen, *Die Wiedertäufer im Herzogtum Württenberg,* 69 ff.

The inference seems to be that at God's unmistakable signal, not on the word of a charismatic prophet like Müntzer, the powerful will be knocked from their thrones by the swords of the righteous.[15] No doubt this moderating shift, which makes revolutionary activity an eventual eschatological rather than an immediate political undertaking, was influenced by Hut's perception of the recent fate of prophetic revolutionaries and those they had (mis)led. But it was also influenced by his contact with the more moderate Anabaptists of Augsburg, whose leader, Hans Denck, rebaptized Hut on May 26, 1526, during the latter's first visit to the city.[16]

Despite his friendship with Denck and his acceptance by the Anabaptist community in Augsburg, Hut remained in the eyes of important Anabaptist leaders an intruder within their camp. This was made instructively clear by his confrontation with the Anabaptist leader Balthasar Hubmaier in the so-called Nikolsberg debate of May, 1527. This encounter ended with Hut's temporary imprisonment by the counts of Lichtenstein, who supported Hubmaier's interpretation of the gospel.[17] In the court records of November 4, 1527, Hut recalls the following theses, which Hubmaier had composed for the debate as apparent critical summaries of Hut's teaching:

1. That Christ was not God's Son.
2. That Christ was merely a prophet.
3. That Mary had more sons (after Christ).
4. That the angels should have become man with Christ.
5. That when a man is possessed by a good angel he can do

---

15. Ibid. This interpretation finds confirmation in the report of Sebastian Franck: "Allein in Joanne Hutten etwan/yren Vorsteher ist ein büchstabischer eifer gwesen/ der hat auss Mose und den Propheten genummen/und gemeint/sy werden wie Israel als Gottes kinder/die gottlosen aussreiten müssen/*aber nit ehe/dann sy Gott darzu fordere und anschicke.*" *Chronica* (1531), p. cccci a. Franck adds that everyone condemns this position. I do not see the justification for viewing this shift as pacifistic Anabaptism. Cf. Klassen, *MQR* 33 (1959): 279. It could just as appropriately be described as "patient Müntzerism."

16. Wappler 1913, p. 28: "Seitdem traten die sozialrevolutionären Ideen Müntzers bei Hut immer mehr zurück." Cf. Klassen, *MQR* 33 (1959): 282.

17. Wilhelm Neuser portrays Hut as taking a position between unconditional sufferance of the *Obrigkeit*, argued by Widemann, and the moderate assertion of social responsibility advocated by Hubmaier. In practice, however, Neuser thinks Hut was much closer to Widemann than to Hubmaier. *Hans Hut. Leben und Wirken bis zum Nikolsburger Religionsgespräch* ([Excerpt from larger Bonn dissertation] Berlin, 1913), pp. 32–34. Cf. Williams, *Radical Reformation*, pp. 225–26.

only good, and when possessed by a bad angel only evil.

6. That Hut and his followers put stock in visions and dreams.

7. That Hut and his followers maintain a specific time for the last day.[18]

8. That with Scripture one receives lies as well as the truth.

9. That Christians wish to rule the world.

10. That no prince or power in this world has accepted or recognized the truth.

11. That power should be taken from the government and given to Christians.[19]

It is obvious from propositions 9–11 that Hubmaier considered Hut a full-fledged revolutionary. Hut, however, insists that only two of these propositions, 6 and 8, accurately represent his teaching. He could not deny the sixth proposition, he tells his judges, because

> dreams and visions are neither wholly to be accepted nor wholly to be rejected, for the omnipotent God [*got der all-mechtig*] has revealed many things to his elect through visions and dreams, and he has promised in another chapter of John's gospel that he would in the last days pour out his Spirit upon all flesh, so that your young will see visions and your old have dreams and prophesy.[20]

This very same appeal beyond the normal historical media of divine truth to God's absolute power also underlies Hut's embracing of the eighth article. "One may receive lies as well as the truth when one deals with Scripture, for the pope has drawn both to his side in [his teaching on] the forgiveness of sins and the in-

18. This issue comes to the fore in the so-called Martyr's Synod in Augsburg in August, 1527. According to a later confession (August, 1530) of one Marx Mayr of Altenerlangen, some sixty people gathered in Augsburg under the leadership of Hut and Denck. "Hut said that in three and one-half years sin would be punished and the government eradicated, although he did not indicate through whom. The gathering was not able to agree because of this article, since several could not believe that such punishment and destruction would occur in three and one-half years." Wappler 1913, p. 323.

19. Meyer, p. 232. It is indicative of the thoroughness of their disagreement that Hut twice maintained that Hubmaier acted "aus zorn und neid." Ibid., pp. 235–36.

20. Ibid., p. 232. Hut goes on to distinguish these "prophetic dreams and visions" from those that come "from the flesh" and "from the Devil" (ibid.). He also insists that he, like every true preacher of God's word, is a "prophet" (ibid., p. 237).

dulgence; hence, it belongs only to God to forgive sins." [21] The historical means of grace is penultimate and corruptible; allegiance can be given only to more final authority.

The Gospel behind the Gospel

There are two authentic tracts from Hut's hand, both written in 1527. The first is entitled *On the Mystery of Baptism* and the second is called *A Christian Instruction on How Divine Scripture Should Be Compared and Judged*.[22] Influenced both in terminology and argument by Müntzer[23] and Denck,[24] these critical writings present the full repertoire of dissent.

The tract *On the Mystery of Baptism* opens with a powerful blast at the "masters and teachers of Scripture." In Hut's view these authorities discern the meaning neither of the Bible nor of the present course of history, an indictment reminiscent of Müntzer's *Sermon Before the Princes*.

Since we have now reached the last and most dangerous period of this world, we can with open eyes see and recognize

21. Ibid., p. 233.

22. *Von dem geheimnus der tauf, baide des zaichens und des wesens, ein anfang eines rechten warhaftigen christlichen lebens, Joan. 5; Ein christlicher underricht, wie göttliche geschrift vergleicht und geurtailt solle werden* in Lydia Müller, *Glaubenszeugnisse oberdeutschen Taufgesinnter* (Leipzig, 1938) [hereafter cited as Müller], 1: 12–28, 28–37. Müller dates the former ca. 1527. Rupp's challenge of Hut's authorship (in favor of Müntzer) has not taken hold, *Bulletin of the John Rylands Library* 43 (1961): 498 ff. Reprinted in *Patterns of Reformation*, pp. 325 ff. Cf. Zschäbitz, *Zur mitteldeutschen Wiedertäuferbewegung nach dem grossen Bauernkrieg*, p. 28, n. 20.

23. Together with Rupp, Grete Mecenseffy stresses Hut's dependence on Müntzer. "Die Herkunft des oberösterreichischen Täufertums," *ARG* 47 (1956): 252–59, esp. p. 257. Friedmann inflates Hut's marginal independence from Müntzer in his reply to Mecenseffy. *MQR* 31 (1957): 75–87. Herbert Klassen depicts the mature Hut as a pacifistic reformer, absolutely independent of the "mystical," "individualistic," and "revolutionary" Müntzer. *MQR* 33 (1959): 270–79. Walter Klaassen, on the other hand, correctly sees substantive influence of Müntzer on the mature Hut in (1) the theme of the gospel of all creatures, (2) the secondary role of Holy Scripture, and (3) the development of a *theologia crucis*. *The Baptist Quarterly* 19 (1962): 209–27.

24. In *A Christian Instruction on How Scripture Should be Compared and Judged*, Hut repeats the bulk of Denck's 40 "gegenschrifften" or, as they are formally entitled, the treatise *Wer die Wahrheit wahrlich lieb hat* (1526). Denck's treatise occasioned the critical response of the Lutheran pastor of Eltersdorf and later Nürnberg, Andreas Althamer: *Dialloge, hoc est Conciliatio locorum scripturae, qui prima facie inter se pugnare videntur* (1527). The first scholarly work of Denck's admirer, Sebastian Franck, was ironically a German translation of this treatise.

how everything the prophets, patriarchs, and apostles in the
beginning prophesied and proclaimed would happen now
takes hold and is brought to pass. . . . But of all this the
entire world (God be merciful!) has absolutely no understanding, especially those who are the teachers of others. Although they would be the masters and teachers of Scripture,
they understand and know less of it than apes. Sevenfold is
Scripture sealed to them, and they refuse to suffer so that
God, whom they oppose as an enemy, might open it for them,
as Paul says. Hence everything they teach and read comes out
upside down and bears a false judgment, the true meaning
being absolutely hidden and concealed from them. Hence the
poor man who listens to them is seduced, deceived, and led
astray into every kind of harmful and corrupting mischief.
. . . No worldly, pleasure-seeking, learned theologian . . .
can know the judgment of the Lord. They are confused in
themselves and in all the things they do, and lead rich and
poor alike astray with their fancy words. . . . They preach
for money and have their belly, not you [their parishioners]
in mind. . . . Their teaching, as one hears, is of nothing but
faith [*nichts anders den glaub*].[25] They go no further and
tell us how one should come to faith. And so they keep the
world in fear. But where the order of divine mystery [*die
ordnung götlicher gehaimnus*] is not rightly maintained,
there one finds nothing but sheer error and this cannot stand.
. . . Therefore, my dearest brothers in the Lord, you must
learn for yourselves the true meaning of God's command and
word and be led to understand them by God himself. Otherwise, you will remain deceived with the rest of the world.[26]

So confronted with a perverted and persecuting Christendom,
Hut proposes to set forth "God's order" (*die ordnung gottes*)
exactly "as Christ instituted and commanded it and the Apostles
maintained it." [27] He will counter aberration with the perfect
original. Hut sees God's covenantal arrangement ideally sum-

---

25. Although Luther is nowhere mentioned by name, Hut does explicitly censure
the notions being dispensed in Wittenberg and Paris: "Dan es mag die gehaimnus
göttlicher weisheit niemant lernen in der spellunken oder mördergrueben aller
büeberei, wie man vermaint zu Wittenburg, noch zu Paris." Müller, p. 14.
26. Müller, p. 13.
27. Ibid., p. 15.

marized in the threefold formula of Mark 16 : 15–16, which he
divides in the following fashion: "[1] Go into the world and preach
the gospel of every creature [*evangelion aller creatur*]. [2] He who
believes [3] and is baptized will be saved." Where this order is in
force there is a true Christendom (*ein rechte christenhait*); where
it is ignored we have only the "Devil's congregation." [28]

Taking up the first part of this order—the clarification of the
"gospel of every creature"—Hut makes two polemical comments
by way of basic definition. First, this is a "gospel of Christ the
crucified . . . ; not of Christ the head alone but of the whole
Christ which all creatures preach and teach." [29] Hut's qualification
is no doubt directed against the Lutheran insistence on the sole
sufficiency for salvation of Christ's historical sacrifice (*solus
Christus*), the christological correlate of the *sola fides*. "The entire
Christ must suffer in all his members and not, as our learned
theologians preach [when they tell us] . . . that Christ as the head
has borne and executed absolutely all [the necessary suffering]." [30]

For the dissenter it is essential that Christ be, as it were, de-
historicized or existentialized, a truly democratic experience in the
depths of the heart rather than an object of the past monopolized
by a theological aristocracy. Those to whom the historical media of
authority (Scripture and tradition) are closed cannot otherwise
lay claim to him in an authoritative way. Their chances are
greatly enhanced, however, when, as Hut pointedly puts it, it is
clear that "the gospel is not a sermon, but the power of God." [31]
This is the concern behind Hut's plea for a participatory Christianity.

The second polemical comment appears in Hut's insistence that
the gospel is not only recorded in Holy Scripture but also preached
and taught by the whole of creation. One misses, I think, the
central point of this "gospel of all creatures," if one interprets it

28. Ibid. Hut does not mistakenly read a genitive for a dative in this rendering
of "evangelion aller creatur." Grammatically it could be either, as Hut well knew.
His subsequent interpretation of Mark 16 : 15–16 through Romans 1 : 20–21 is a
conscious choice for the genitive. As I will point out in the text, it is a choice of
major importance for his dissent ideology.

29. Ibid., p. 16.

30. Ibid. Note Müntzer's similar criticism of the Lutherans: "They pretend that
Christ is one who fulfills the law, so that by citing his cross they can avoid suffering the work of God." Franz, 404. 10–11.

31. Müller, p. 21.

along the lines of a "natural theology." [32] By making the *biblical covenant* a gospel equally proclaimed by the whole of creation, Hut has done two things. First, he has ridiculed established Christendom for failing to discern and proclaim the obvious. Secondly, he has made possible an alternative route and test of God's revealed truth. The "gospel of all creatures" is indicative of one of the most important ingredients in effective dissent, viz. the successful creation of a persuasively competing objective authority. It is certainly not coincidental that, under interrogation, Hut's own followers confessed that he employed Mark 16 : 15–16 to illustrate how the pastors and priests acted "against the order of God." [33] Hut defines the gospel of all creatures by first turning to Romans 1 : 20–21.

> Here (Mark 16 : 15–16) it is not meant that the gospel is to be preached to creatures, as if to dogs and cats, cows and calves, leaves and grass. Rather, as Paul says [in Rom. 1 : 20–21], it is "the gospel which is preached to you in all creatures." Paul points out that the eternal Power and Deity is seen and

32. Despite possible Thomist parallels and his careful qualifications, Rupp's effort so to interpret this motif obfuscates its primary polemical purpose. *Bulletin of the John Rylands Library* 43 (1961): 492 ff. Herbert Klassen passes its intent altogether with his conclusion that it is "not thought of as a substitute for the written Word of God, but merely a means for explaining the Gospel message to seeking people." *MQR* 33 (1959): 193. Williams is only a bit more helpful: "Far from being either a matter of rational observation unaided by revelation or a matter of written observation and creedal formulation, 'the gospel of all creation' was for the South German Anabaptists an inspired vision and propaedeutic insight into the nature of the world as it is" (*Radical Reformation*, p. 305). Walter Klaassen is on the verge of discovery when he concludes: "The true significance and force of this conviction [viz. that a man could actually see the truths of the gospel of Christ in the creatures of the world] is seen when we remember that in the sixteenth century there were many illiterate folk who could not read the Scriptures, but who *could* read from the created world about them the 'Gospel of all the creatures.' " *The Baptist Quarterly* 19 (1962): 217.

33. Thomas Spiegel of Ostheim is recorded to have confessed: "Die pfaffen [according to Hut's teaching] fahen mit der tauf an, das sei unrecht, dan Christus habe gesagt: 'Welcher glaube und werde getauft, der werde selig'; doch solle die predig vorgeen, dann die kinde sinde nit verstendig, die tauf zuempfahen; derohalben sei es wider die ordnung Gottes durch die priester furgenommen mit der tauf der kinder, vor und ehe sie die verstentnus haben." Document in Wappler 1913, p. 230. Viet Weischenvelder, who associates Hut with Müntzer, identifies his teaching in the same breath with Mark 16 : 15–16, the gospel of all creatures, as do also the advisors of the Bishop of Bamberg. Ibid., pp. 241, 247. To the princes of Christendom the gospel of all creatures bulwarked a seditious challenge of established authority.

perceived in the creatures or works [of God] from the creation of the world. And here I say and confess that, still in our time, the gospel, as Christ commanded it and as he and his Apostles preached it, is still not known; even those who want to be the best [theologians] still do not know what the gospel of all creatures is.[34]

The ignorance of the establishment theologian is attributed by Hut to his preoccupation with his own belly and position in the world. In larger perspective, however, he also scores the theologian's traditional approach to the communication of God's truth: formal appeal to the mind of the hearer. In order to discern God's presence in the works of creation, Hut, anticipating Franck and Castellio, chides,

one must observe how Christ always announced to the common man the kingdom of heaven and the power of the Father in created things through parables, i.e. through the handwork [of God] in every work with which men are associated. He did not direct the poor man to books, as our learned theologians now unknowingly do, but rather taught and proclaimed the gospel [to them] at their work.[35]

One sees in the creatures of the world not only the power and deity of God the Father. One also learns there the lesson of suffering, that there is no realization of one's natural end, no achievement of one's true goal, save through the way of suffering.

From such parables one should diligently perceive how all the things of creation must suffer the work of man and come to the end for which they were created through suffering; how no man can be blessed save through the suffering and sorrow that God works in him; and how the whole of Scripture and creation points to nothing else than the suffering of Christ in all his members.[36]

34. Müller, p. 16.
35. Ibid., pp. 16–17. Cf. below, pp. 148 ff., 193–94.
36. Müller, p. 17. Hut's focus on achieving one's natural end could suggest Aristotelian entelechy and the influence of a Thomistic natural theology. Cf. Rupp, *The Bulletin of the John Rylands Library* 43 (1961). In my opinion Hut is much less sophisticated; he here pursues in commonsense fashion his own experience and the synoptic gospels. Note how crudely he illustrates his point by saying that, should man bring a domestic animal to its proper end (viz. to be eaten by man), then one must first inflict suffering on it (kill and cook it). So too, he concludes, must God deal with man if he is to make use of and enjoy him. Müller, p. 18.

Hut maintains, then, that, every bit as much as Holy Scripture, the world in which men live and work is a proclamation of the gospel. The everyday world teaches God's power and preaches (the existential) Christ who lives and suffers in his members. Indeed, there is nothing in the written book of Scripture which is not also to be learned from the "book of all creatures."

> The entire world with all creatures is a book, in the workmanship of which one sees everything that is read in the written book. All the elect from the beginning of the world until Moses have taken their lessons from the book of all creatures and have silently partaken of the understanding which is written in them by nature through the Spirit of God in the heart, for the entire law is written into the works of creation. And all men work daily with creatures, even (as the law shows) the heathen, who do not have the written law but still do the same as those who have it.[37]

Hut concludes by pointing out that Christ had need of a Bible only to communicate with the learned scribes. "He did not go through the Bible chapter and verse as our learned theologians do. For everything that one can point out through the creation is documented in the Scripture, and Christ needed Scripture only to prove his points with the refined scribes." [38]

Before moving on to the second and third parts of Hut's depiction of "God's order," a short excursus on his hermeneutics is in order. Hut's method of interpreting Scripture is of one piece with his definition of the Christian gospel, and it is compactly set forth in his second treatise, *A Christian Instruction on How Divine Scripture Should Be Compared and Judged*. The basic concern throughout is to demonstrate that the personal experience of the individual, taught directly by God, and not the imposed decisions of so-called experts is the only authoritative criterion of Scripture's meaning.

With a deceptively conservative gesture, Hut advances a hermeneutical principle modeled on the trinitarian nature of God.

---

37. Müller, p. 19. Compare Denck's appeal to "the Master, who takes all teachers to school": "Wer nit leesen kan, der gee mit gantzer übergebung seyn selbs zu dem mayster, der alle doctores zu schul fürt, welcher auch allain den schüssel hat zu disem buch, darin alle schetz der weysshait begryffen seind." *Wer die Wahrheit wahrlich lieb hat, Schriften* 2: 74.

38. Müller, p. 19.

"As we recognize God according to three parts [*nach dreien teilen*]," he writes, "so must we also recognize the Scripture. First, God is known through his omnipotence and power in all creatures. Secondly, through the severity [*ernst*] and righteousness of the Son. And, finally, through the goodness and mercy of the Holy Spirit." [39] Hut asserts—and those who would convict him of a "natural theology" might take note—that recognition of God according to the first part, i.e. according to his omnipotence and power in all creatures, is absolutely insufficient. One must discern all three parts if any one part is to be meaningful. "If man does not find, recognize, and suffer all three parts in himself, then he knows no more of God than a Turk or heathen." [40] "Where man has the first, but not the second and third parts, it is much too little and remains vain folly and darkness; and no matter what they may think [those who have come only so far] are still silly fools." [41]

God, to be truly known, must be known through the severity and righteousness of the Son and the goodness and mercy of the Spirit, as well as through his power in all creatures. Hermeneutically applied, this model teaches that Scripture is not truly known through detailed scholarly contact—a point Hut attempts to drive home by citing Denck's list of contradictory scriptural statements[42]—but through the understanding that suffering produces.[43] The trinitarian parallel in this application can be dis-

39. Ibid., p. 28, cf. p. 32.

40. Ibid., p. 28.

41. Ibid., p. 33.

42. Some indication of the arbitrary (and in my judgment absolutely polemical) nature of the "gegenschrifften" is evident in the very first three: (1) "Who knows the mind of the Lord?" (Rom. 11 : 34) vis à vis "He has revealed the mystery of his will to us" (Eph. 1 : 9); (2) "Without Him is nothing made" (John 1 : 3) vis à vis "Pride is not created in men" (Eccles. 10 : 22); (3) "God has not created death" (Song of Sol. 1 : 13) vis à vis "Fire, hail, hunger, and death are all created in wrath" (Eccles. 39 : 35). Some are not only arbitrary but downright silly: e.g. (14) "Preach the gospel to all creatures" (Mark 16 : 15) vis à vis "Do not throw pearls before swine" (Matt. 7 : 6). According to Denck, he who has been taught by the Spirit can relate these contradictory passages so that the one embraces the other and hence overcomes the apparent contradiction. *Schriften* 2: 68–70; Hut's version in Müller, pp. 29–31.

43. In terms of the *existentialized*, not the historical, Christ, one can say that, for Hut, one knows God only "through Christ." "Wer die fueszstapfen und weeg nit wandlet und das creiz Christi nit tragen will, der hat und erkennt den sun nit. Und wer den sun nit hat und erkennt, der erkennt und hat den vater nit, kan auch durch die güete des heiligen geists, welcher in uns wonet, nit erleuchtet werden." Müller, p. 34.

cerned: the Son/suffering brings the Spirit/understanding in and through which God/Scripture is known and judged. With introductory polemic, Hut summarizes thus:

> Yes, the scribes and pharisees knew the Bible in masterly fashion backwards and forwards. Nevertheless, their teaching and understanding were false, as they are now in our time, although they preach and teach Scripture handsomely to all. They still preach one against the other, and no improvement [of life] results from their teaching. Nor do they exhibit self-improvement. The cause of all this is that they lack the judgment which one receives in suffering and poverty, through which one leaves the world and becomes solitary[44] and is incorporated into the body of Christ, where all things are understood. . . . It is in such misery and poverty that man learns the true judgments of God.[45]

Once personal experience and/or morality becomes the hermeneutical norm, and transactions in the depths of one's heart more authoritative than the disputations of the learned, the objective correlates of faith can become quite promiscuous. A case in point in Hut's circle of friends is the German translation of selected Apocryphal writings published in 1528 in Worms by a casual acquaintance of Hut and close colleague of Hans Denck, Louis Haetzer.[46] Haetzer's preface to this work demonstrates the lengths to which the dissenter found himself forced to go in quest of authorization when the accepted historical media of authority were closed to him.

Haetzer had originally planned to translate the whole of the Apocryphal literature, but having been caught up in the tumult and persecutions of what he calls "these last days," he was unable to complete the work. In his preface he assesses the forced abridgment of the project by concluding that books are not the most

44. "Dardurch man der welt ledig und gelassen wirt." This is the mystical language of *Gelassenheit* and *Abgeschiedenheit*.
45. Müller, pp. 31–32.
46. *Baruch der Prophet. Die Histori Susannah. Die histori Bel zu Babel. Alles newlich auss der Bybli verteutscht* (MS in Landesbibliothek Darmstadt). Hut confesses having seen Haetzer only very seldom ("sei lutzel bei den bruedern alhie gewesen"). Meyer, pp. 226, 229. Denck and Haetzer combined to translate the Old Testament prophets in 1527.

important thing and that God has an alternative platform for the proclamation of his truth.

> I am content even though it has not succeeded. And should it not be completed in the future, no one should be angry. [What we need] must not be acquired in letters or in words, but in the power of God. Satan presumes to close off every refuge so that neither I nor others may have a place to answer or write anything. God can overcome this treachery. Even if our work should simply remain incomplete, every student of Christ, contrary to the works of God's enemies, will receive and enjoy the sermon of the Lamb of God, of the divine seed [*götlichs samens*], which is inserted into the hearts of all men at their conception, and [proclaimed] in all creatures, even though from now into eternity not a single letter is written or printed.[47]

Why, if this is the case, should Haetzer desire to translate and disseminate the Apocryphal literature at all? As he is well aware, any authoritative use of it is forbidden by the power-brokers of Christendom. On the face of it, Haetzer publishes this literature to defend God's freedom to speak to men wherever and whenever he wishes. With his polemic in full control, he writes:

> All the learned say that the books I have mentioned [the various Apocryphal writings] are not in the canon, i.e. they are not rightly and truly biblical, the church has not accepted them, they are not [a part of the] Hebrew [Scriptures], and therefore one may not execute, confirm, or maintain anything with them. And so I say: whether in or out of the canon, the books have no fault and give as true an account of how one may come again into Unity [*in das Eynig*][48] as do other books, although they do not everywhere agree with one another, as is also the case often in the biblical books. And therefore, my dear learned theologians, it is not right that, for this reason [of canonicity], the Holy Spirit is forced to reveal or not to reveal.[49]

---

47. *Baruch der Prophet,* p. ij b.
48. Compare the use of "das Einig" in Denck's *Etliche Hauptreden,* appended to Haetzer's 1528 edition of the *Theologia Deutsch. Schriften* 2: 111 ff.
49. *Baruch der Prophet,* pp. iij a-b.

The most sincere motives notwithstanding, Haetzer has in effect simply replaced the judgments of ecclesiastical councils with the conclusions of individual experience. He is fully prepared to let the heart create anew the canon. "The sum of the matter is that every student of Christ who does not want to be deceived should neither accept nor reject any writing which is not previously excluded through the revelation of Jesus Christ, regardless of the canon or any language." [50] Haetzer can draw such a conclusion because he has in fact recourse to only one authoritative teacher —God himself[51]—and accepts only one definitive locus of his presence—the depths of his own soul.[52] It was not possible in the sixteenth century, to repeat Haetzer's own description, for the "learned Magistri" to adjudge this teaching other than "fanatical, gangsterish, seditious, heretical, and Anabaptist." [53]

Hut's concluding definition of "God's order," set forth now in his interpretation of the second and third parts of Mark 16 : 15–16 —"He who believes [the gospel] and is baptized will be saved"— relegates the contemporary institutions of Christendom to a secondary if not altogether superfluous role. The occasion of his comments is the sacrament of baptism. For the sixteenth-century dissenter, no ecclesiastical ceremony symbolized the presumption and tyranny of the church so perfectly as the baptism of infants. There was, to be sure, scant biblical justification for it,[54] but beyond that it was, on the face of it, a staggering affront to the intelligence and freedom of the individual. A weak, passive, uncomprehending infant is pronounced afflicted with Original Sin, a state of bondage to the Devil, which the priests of Christendom graciously counter by pouring water over its head and collecting a fee from its parents.[55]

50. Ibid., pp. iij b–iiij a.

51. "Dann das ist eyn warhafftige warheyt in Gott dem HERREN/das Gott von nichts mag erkant noch erlent werden/weder alleyn von Gott/das ist/durch Gottes krafft/die man den heyligen geyst nent/und ist war/Wer Gott nit bei Gott und mit Gott suchet/der wirt allweg suchen/unnd doch nichts finden." Ibid., p. iiij b.

52. "Darauff sag ich frei dise warheyt imm Herren Gott/das keyn mensch/er sei wie gelert er immer wölle/eynige schrifft verstehen mag/er hab sie dann zuvor selbst in der warheyt mit der that/imm abgrundt seiner seelen erlernet." Ibid., p. iiij b.

53. "Schwermerisch, rottish, auffrürisch, ketzerisch und widertaufferisch." Ibid., p. iiij a.

54. As Hut is keen to underscore, Meyer, p. 227; Müller, p. 27.

55. A follower of Hut insisted to his judges that Hut maintained it was not the infant but the priest who was possessed by the Devil. Confession of Hans Hübner of Zeegendorf (March, 1527), Wappler 1913, p. 244.

Hut repeatedly insists that becoming a Christian is, rather, a matter of understanding and earnest resolve: "No man should be accepted and bound to a [Christian] community unless he has previously heard and been taught the gospel, believes singularly what he has heard, and has made a decision for it." [56]

To be baptized, therefore, is a process quite other than Christendom would have people think. Just as the gospel is something other than words in a holy book, so baptism is far different than a ceremonial act with water and priestly vestments. There is a living gospel behind the written gospel and a baptism of the Spirit behind baptism with water. And, in both instances, it is always the former to which the Christian pledges himself when he acknowledges and uses the latter.

> The baptism which follows preaching and faith is not the true essence [of the baptism] through which one becomes devout; it is only a sign, a covenant, a likeness and memorial to one's resolve to be prepared for the true baptism of which Christ speaks [Matt. 20 : 17 ff.], viz. [baptism with] the water of every sorrow [*das wasser aller trüebsal*], in which the Lord makes one clean, washes and justifies one from all fleshly lusts, sins, and unclean deeds and acts.[57]

> The water of every sorrow is the true essence and power of baptism in which man sinks into the death of Christ. This baptism did not first appear in the time of Christ, but has been from the beginning. In it have all the elect friends of God from Adam on been baptized, as Paul points out [1 Cor. 10 : 1 ff.]. . . . Therefore the sign and the essence of baptism must be sharply distinguished. The Christian community extends the sign or covenant of baptism [to one] through a true servant, as Christ received [baptism] from John. The true baptism [*recht tauf*] is given thereafter by God through the water of every sorrow and, further, in the consolation of the Holy Spirit.[58]

56. Müller, p. 20.
57. Ibid.
58. Ibid., p. 21. Hut also speaks of this as the "tauf der widergeburt" (ibid., p. 24). During his trial, he summarized his teaching on true baptism with the following compact statement: "The first [baptism], that of the Spirit, is the assurance and pledge to God's word that one wishes to live as God's word would have one live. This is the covenant of God (*der bundt gottes*), which God makes with men

Hut milks polemic from these statements not only against the *sola fides* of Luther ("a thoroughly wicked gospel, which . . . does not better man"),[59] but also against the Lutheran concept of vocation (*Beruf*). In opposition to monasticism, Luther had sanctioned the given social occupations as the arena of Christian perfection. To the dissenter, the Lutheran embracing of worldly vocations simply traded evils; it undid monasticism only by condoning the sociopolitical status quo. Hut's logic is as striking as it is simple. As there is a more perfect gospel behind the readable, audible gospel and a more perfect baptism behind visible, ceremonial baptism, so there is a vocation more perfect than those into which men are born.

> The entire world now speaks of freedom and still remains in physical servitude. It will forsake nothing and wants always to have more. O, how masterly can the world conceal its true intent! For this reason one says that every man should remain in his profession [*Beruf*]. But if that is so, then why did Peter not remain a fisherman, and Matthew a publican? And why did Christ tell the rich young man to sell what he had and give it to the poor?[60]

Hut died in September, 1527, while in prison, the victim of an accidental fire in his cell. While his dependence on Müntzer and Denck limits his originality, it also highlights his significance. He is the most important contemporary witness to both the tensions and the points of continuity between the revolutionary dissent of Müntzer and the first generation of Anabaptists. Although still far from Weigel's constructive fraud,[61] Hut's life illustrates the tactical adjustments forced on dissent by the swift exercise

---

through his Spirit in their hearts. Beyond this he has given water as a sign of this previous covenant, so that one may show and confess that he wishes to live in true obedience to God and all Christians and lead an irreproachable life. . . . The third [baptism] is that of blood. This is the baptism which Christ pointed out to his disciples when he said: 'May you be baptized with the baptism with which I am baptized,' i.e. the baptism which gives a witness to the entire world when the blood [of a disciple] is poured forth." Meyer, p. 227.

59. Müller, p. 22. Hut borrows Müntzer's phrase "feigned faith" (ibid., p. 23).

60. Ibid., p. 22. At the conclusion of his attack on the *sola fide*, Denck points out how 1 Cor. 7 : 20—"Every one should remain in the state in which he was called"—is used to justify unethical conduct. *Was geredt sei . . . , Schriften* 2: 43. 20–28.

61. Cf. below, pp. 243 ff.

of the royal sword. In the wake of the debacle in the city of Münster in 1534–35, the necessity of this adjustment was to be fully driven home to all nonconformists.[62] Thereafter dissent would be wiser, more prudent and subtle, packaged to survive and to persuade gradually. In this sense, Hut is a forerunner of the future form of dissent.

62. See the "Confession" of Obbe Philips in *Spiritual and Anabaptist Writers,* pp. 204–25.

5

Hans Denck

The manuscript of Thomas Müntzer's *Special Exposé,* which the
fleeing Müntzer delivered to Hans Hut in Bibra, was subsequently
directed by Hut to Nürnberg. There assistants of the publisher
Johann Hergot saw to the printing of five hundred copies in the
early fall of 1524. Müntzer himself apparently made a personal
visit to Nürnberg around this time (October) to deliver for publication his last tract against Luther—the vitriolic yet poignant
swansong, *A Highly Provoked Defense and Answer to the Spirit-
less, Soft-Living Flesh at Wittenberg*—which was published before
December 17, 1524, by Hieronymus Hölzel.[1]

Not only were the last and strongest of Müntzer's polemical
writings in circulation in Nürnberg, but the city also knew the
recent (1524) blistering sacramental treatises of Andreas Bodenstein von Karlstadt against Luther.[2] Karlstadt argued that it was

1. Franz, pp. 265–66, 321–22. Four hundred copies of the *Special Exposé* were
confiscated on October 29, one hundred copies having earlier been shipped off to
Augsburg. Documents detailing their publication and the subsequent punishment
(by fine) of those responsible are presented and discussed by Theodor Kolde, who,
however, confuses the *Special Exposé* with the *Highly Provoked Defense.* "Hans
Denck und die gottlosen Maler von Nürnberg," *Beiträge zur Bayerischen Kirchengeschichte* (Erlangen, 1902) [hereafter cited as Kolde 1902], 8: 9–10. Cf. G. Baring,
"Hans Denck und Thomas Müntzer in Nürnberg 1524," *ARG* 50 (1959): 145–81,
152–53. The *Highly Provoked Defense* was confiscated on December 17, and very
few copies have survived. Hans Hillerbrand has translated it: "Thomas Müntzer's
Last Tract Against Martin Luther: A Translation and Commentary," *MQR* 38
(1964): 20–36.

2. *Ob man mit heiliger Schrift erweisen möge dass Christus mit Leib, Blut und
Seele im Sakrament sei* (Basel, 1524); *Auslegung dieser Worte: Das ist mein Leib*
(n.p., 1524); *Dialogus oder ein Gesprechbüchlin: Von dem grewlichen unnd
abgöttischen Misbrauch des hochwridigsten sacraments Jesu Christi* (Basel, Nov.,
1524); and *Von dem widerchristlichen Misbrauch des Herrn Brot und Kelch* (n.p.,
1524). This last-named treatise was reprinted in Nürnberg by Hölzel. Cf. Hermann
Barge, *Andreas Bodenstein von Karlstadt,* (Leipzig, 1905), 2: 151–52.

inconsistent to deny the repetition of Christ's sacrifice in the Mass and still maintain, as Luther was doing, the real presence of Christ's crucified body in the Eucharist. For Karlstadt, Christ's words, "This is my body," referred to the body given over to the Jews and crucified fifteen hundred years ago, not to sacramental bread and wine. One therefore feeds spiritually on the risen Christ, not physically on a sacramentally embodied Christ. As Karlstadt has the layman Peter instruct the learned theologians in the *Dialogus:* "Personally I don't need the external witness [i.e. bread and wine]. I wish to have my witness from the internally present Spirit [*vom Geist in meiner Inwendigkeit*], as Christ promised." [3]

Karlstadt's theological views, like those of Müntzer, bore patent anti-institutional consequences. Karlstadt himself had earlier drawn some of these consequences, not, to be sure, as Müntzer was to do, by military undertakings, but by renouncing his professorship and privileges at the University of Wittenberg and becoming a "new layman," whose profession was to live among and lead the peasants of Orlamünde.[4] In Nürnberg Karlstadt's writings penetrated the intelligentsia and were especially popular among the younger generation of painters in the city, who, alienated and cynical because of their economic straits, were in a position to appreciate attacks on the ignorance of contemporary society.[5]

3. Cited by Barge, 2: 161; larger discussion, ibid., pp. 157 ff. The *Dialogus* is in the modern edition of Erich Hertzsch, *Karlstadts Schriften aus den Jahren 1523–25* (Halle, 1956), 2: 7–49. Cf. the (strongly Lutheran) view of the matter by F. Kriechbaum, *Grundzüge der Theologie Karlstadts* (Hamburg, 1967), pp. 102 ff. In a letter to Müntzer (Dec. 21, 1522), Karlstadt writes: "Deus cordis mei potens est, cujus potentiam et fortem manum experiencia didici. Hic plus de visionibus et somniis dixi quam aliquis professorum." Franz, 387. 13–15.

4. Barge, 2: 12–13. Among the characteristics of Karlstadt's new "an der spätmittelalterlichen Mystik orientierten Theologie," Barge lists "eine auf höchste potenzierte Verinnerlichung des Heilsvorganges, der gegenüber alle äusseren Heilsinstitutionen als wertlos erscheinen." Ibid., pp. 21, 4. On the important differences with Müntzer, see Rupp, *Patterns of Reformation*, pp. 120, 257. Müntzer's efforts to enlist Karlstadt were quite unsuccessful. Barge 2: 14 ff., 112 ff.; Hinrichs, *Luther und Müntzer*, p. 90.

5. Kolde (1902), p. 19. Already before the case of the "godless painters" (cf. below), a painter named Hans Greiffenberger, who authored seven tracts with mystical leanings, publicly denied Christ's real presence in the Eucharist, and painted satirical theological pictures, escaped severe penalty only through the friendship of the powerful Osiander (ibid., pp. 12–15). So acute did this discussion over the Eucharist become in Nürnberg, that the humanist Willibald Pirckheimer felt compelled in 1525 to take a strongly Lutheran position against Oecolampadius's Zwinglian leanings, which Pirckheimer interpreted as pointed in the direction of

Through the patronage of the reformer Johann Oecolampadius, whose lectures on Isaiah he attended in Basel, the young linguist Hans Denck had entered Nürnberg and the company of its intelligentsia already in September, 1523, as rector of the prestigious school of St. Sebald.[6] In this position Denck was well aware of the new intellectual currents sweeping Nürnberg. Whether he had direct contact with Müntzer during the latter's brief visit to the city is not clear,[7] although it is incontestable that Denck read deeply in Müntzer's writings and found there major building blocks for his own thoughts.[8] Denck certainly knew about the ac-

---

Müntzer and Karlstadt. Lewis W. Spitz, *The Religious Renaissance of the German Humanists* (Cambridge/Mass., 1963), pp. 189 ff.; Ernst Stähelin, *Das theologische Lebenswerk Johann Oekolampads* (Leipzig, 1939), p. 248.

6. I have chosen to begin with Denck's catalytic years in Nürnberg. There are a number of biographical studies which fill in the earlier years. Foundational are the works of Ludwig Keller: *Ein Apostel der Wiedertäufer* (Leipzig, 1882) and *Johann von Staupitz und die Anfänge der Reformation* (Leipzig, 1888). In line with Keller are the works of A. M. Schwindt, *Hans Denck: Ein Vorkämpfer undogmatischen Christentums 1495–1527* (Habertshof, 1924); F. L. Weis, *The Life, Teachings and Works of Johannes Denck 1495–1527* (Strasbourg, 1924); and the homiletical effort of A. Coutts, *Hans Denck 1495–1527: Humanist and Heretic* (Edinburgh, 1927). There is a pregnant sketch by Christian Neff in the *Mennonitisches Lexikon* 1: 401–14. Not always dependable are the articles by Jan J. Kiwiet, "The Life of Hans Denck (ca. 1500–1527)," *MQR* 31 (1957): 227–59; "The Theology of Hans Denck," *MQR* 32 (1958). Recent German studies are the Tübingen dissertation of Albrecht Hege, *Hans Denck 1495–1527* (1939) and the brief but solid synthesis by Walter Fellmann, *Hans Denck. Schriften*, 2: 8–19. In addition to Schwindt and Neff, E. Teufel's *Forschungsbericht* also looks at the role Denck plays in the studies by Stähelin, *Lebenswerk Johann Oekolampads*, and R. Stadelmann, *Vom Geist des ausgehenden Mittelalters* (Halle, 1929). "Täufertum und Quäkertum im Lichte der neueren Forschung III," *Theologische Rundschau* 13 (1941): 183–97.

7. Denck's apparent visit to Mühlhausen after his exile from Nürnberg has led some to argue for direct contact in 1524 (Kolde 1902, p. 23). Want of historical evidence for such a conclusion is stressed especially by Neff, *Mennonitisches Lexikon*, p. 404.

8. The Fellmann edition refers some twenty-four statements by Denck to "Müntzer's mysticism," which leads Baring to conclude that Müntzer was Denck's most important source, although Denck's pacifism placed him closer to Tauler than to Müntzer. *ARG* 50 (1959): 162–63; 173–74. Fellmann, not discounting Müntzer's important mediatorial role, still sees the *Theologia Deutsch* as Denck's most influential source. *Hans Denck. Schriften*, 2: 6; "Der theologische Gehalt der Schriften Dencks" in *Die Leibhaftigkeit des Wortes . . . Festgabe für A. Köberle*, ed. O. Michel and Ulrich Mann (Hamburg, 1958), pp. 157–65; 159. Cf. Neff, p. 402. Keller maintained in 1882 that Denck was more the student of Tauler than of either Oecolampadius or Erasmus (*Ein Apostel der Wiedertäufer*, p. 32). Schwindt saw the mediation of medieval mystical ideas through Müntzer and Haetzer as setting Denck on the path to his own teaching. *Hans Denck*, pp. 5–6, 14. Kiwiet,

tivities of Müntzer's more aggressive comrade, Heinrich Pfeiffer, whose preaching led to his official dismissal from the city on October 29.[9] And Hans Hut claims to have lodged with Denck during a visit to Nürnberg.[10] There was, to be sure, no lack of personal contacts and publications conducive to the "radicalization" of a young intellectual like Denck.

The increase of radical literature and activities brought a corresponding increase in the vigilance of the authorities. The situation was made even more tense by the apparent outbreak in the city of a rash of "bigamies."[11] In early January, 1525, with the arrest of the so-called godless painters, Sebald and Barthel Beheim and Jorg Pentz, for making insulting remarks about the Eucharist, the events which would lead to Denck's first defense of his beliefs and subsequent exile from the city were set in motion. At their trial the painters were asked the following set of questions, which instructively reveal the intimate connection in the mind of established authority between theological deviation and political sedition: (1) whether they believed in God; (2) what they thought of Christ; (3) whether they believed that the holy gospel and Word of God was contained in Scripture; (4) what they thought of the Eucharist and (5) of baptism; (6) whether they believed in worldly government and recognized the rulers of Nürnberg as lords over their bodies and external goods.[12]

Sebald Beheim, the more moderate of the trio, had doubts only about the fourth and fifth articles. He confessed that he could not believe that the body and blood of Christ were in the form of bread and wine, but was certainly "willing to be patient until God convinced him otherwise." Regarding baptism, he doubted that there was any religious significance in water ("es lig am wasser

---

however, has questioned (quite unconvincingly) the centrality of mystical influence on Denck, and considers the parallels with Müntzer coincidental. *MQR* 31 (1957): 236–41.

9. Kolde 1902, p. 12. Kolde also makes much of a writing "out of Müntzer's circle" by the Allstedt preacher, Simon Haferitz—*Ein Sermon vom Fest der heiligen drey konig*—which blends Müntzerian ideas with (Anabaptist) pacifism. Ibid., pp. 23–27.

10. Meyer, p. 229.

11. Kolde 1902, pp. 51–52.

12. Documents are assembled by Theodor Kolde, "Zum Process des Johann Denck und der 'drei gottlosen Maler' von Nürnberg," *Kirchengeschichtliche Studien. Hermann Reuter zum 70. Geburtstag gewidmet* (Leipzig, 1888) [hereafter cited as Kolde 1888], p. 244.

nichts"). His brother Barthel, however, interpreted the Eucharist and baptism as "sheer human trifling" (*einen plosen menschen dant*), said he could not believe Scripture, and confessed to believing in only one "Ober," "God the almighty." And, finally, Jorg Pentz could answer only the first question in the affirmative, responding with a blunt "I have no thoughts on the matter" or "no" to the others.[13] According to the further incriminating testimony of Veyt Wirsperger, which was hardly needed for conviction, the brothers Beheim "preoccupy themselves with the books of Müntzer and Karlstadt." [14]

At the conclusion of his testimony, Sebald Beheim had listed among the "company" with whom he discussed his views "the schoolmaster of St. Sebald," Hans Denck.[15] Summoned to give an account of his beliefs, Denck's theological abstractions so confused his judges that he was requested to submit a written confession of faith on the points in question.[16] His *Confession for the Authorities in Nürnberg*, which was formally submitted on January 14, 1525, is a subtle and uncompromising statement of the sovereignty of his own instincts in religious matters, and it is foundational in every respect for his subsequent challenge of the Lutherans.

Without denying responsibility, Denck confesses disillusionment with the faith into which he was born and has since tried to live.

> From childhood I learned the faith from my parents and took it onto my lips. Thereafter I read through the books of men and boasted often of the singularity of my faith. But I have never truly recognized the opposition which is inborn in me by nature, although it has been thrown before me many times. This inborn unhappiness . . . certainly punishes [my] false faith. For I truly see that all this time my inborn sickness or unhappiness declines in no significant way. The more I punish and redress myself, the more urgently does it advance.[17]

Denck will no longer feign the faith of his fathers; his judges desire to know whether he now considers the faith of his fathers

13. Kolde 1888, pp. 244–45; Kolde 1902, pp. 49–50.
14. Kolde 1888, p. 246.
15. Ibid., p. 244; Kolde 1902, p. 65.
16. "Bei der mystischen Redeweise Dencks konnte man sich nicht verständigen." Kolde 1902, p. 52.
17. *Hans Denck. Schriften* 2: 20. 15–24.

feigned. To what extent is he guided by the judgments of established ecclesiastical authority? Where, if not in the faith of his fathers, does he seek the power to cure his inborn sickness? "I still detect something within myself [*ettwas in mir*]," Denck writes, "that powerfully resists my inborn wantonness and points me to a life and happiness which seems as impossible for my soul to reach as for my body to climb into the visible heaven." [18] This innate orientation to superabundant life and happiness, also related by Denck as the *synteresis* or *füncklin*, "seed," "image," and "light" of God in the soul,[19] will be his guide to an effective moral remedy and a true religious authority. He tells his judges:

> I do wish that I had faith, i.e. life. But as long as it does not appear deep within me [*gründtlich in mir*], I can deceive neither myself nor others [with pretending]. Indeed, should I say today that I believe, I might punish myself tomorrow for lying. But it would not be me [who punishes myself], but the truth which I find, in part, within myself. I know without doubt that it is the truth, and therefore I will listen, as God wills, to what it wants to tell me, and I will resist anyone who would take it from me.[20]

Only to the extent that external authority agrees with this internal truth can Denck be in agreement with external authority. "Where I find that [i.e. the truth that speaks within me] present in a creature, whether high or low, I will listen to it. Wherever it directs me, I will go, according to its will; and where it prevents me, I will flee." [21] This rule applies also to Holy Scripture. The latter's authority is contingent upon its confirmation and clarifica-

18. Ibid., 20. 9–12.
19. *Von der waren Lieb* (1527), *Schriften*, 2: 77. 6 ff.; *Ordnung Gottes und die creaturen werck* (1527), ibid., 90. 14–21; *Etliche Hauptreden* (appended to the 1528 Worms edition of the *Theologia Deutsch*), wherein the "etwas in mir" is interpreted anthropologically ("der Som Gottes oder Gottes bildnuss, welche der freiheyt on underlass begeret") and Christologically ("Jesus Christus von Nazareth"), ibid., 112. 15–16, 26–27. Keller already pointed out that Denck's inner voice was "ein Funke des göttlichen Geistes selbst"; "ein guter Keim . . . im Menschen vorhanden" is the "Grundlage" of his theology. *Ein Apostel der Wiedertäufer*, pp. 50, 60. Dobratz's argument that Denck, like Müntzer, "spekuliert nirgends über die Seelenkräfte oder den Seelengrund" is in serious need of amendment. *Der Einfluss der deutschen Mystik auf Müntzer und Denck*, p. 71.
20. *Schriften*, 2: 21. 2–9.
21. Ibid., p. 21. 10–12.

tion of what is experienced within. Denck writes that the "something within" moves him to accept Scripture as a "witness," which, in turn, gives a name to this inner drive.

> By nature I cannot believe Scripture. But that within me, which is not mine yet drives me without my willing and doing, also moves me to read Scripture as a witness. So I read Scripture and there I find in part a witness which powerfully testifies that that which is so driving me is indeed Christ, whom Scripture witnesses to be the son of the Almighty.[22]

Scripture, Denck would have his judges understand, is not the province of a learned group of experts, nor is it capable of interpreting itself. With a line of argumentation that anticipates more explicit criticism of Luther's principle of "Scripture alone," Denck describes Scripture as a lantern shining in darkness, yet, "as something written with human hands, spoken by human lips, seen with human eyes, and heard with human ears, it cannot by itself completely overcome the darkness." [23] Hermeneutically and existentially, something more basic and authoritative than Scripture is necessary:

> Hence Peter says further [2 Pet. 1 : 20–21] that Scripture is not its own interpreter, but rather interpretation belongs to the Holy Spirit, who first gave Scripture. One must have the interpretation of the Spirit [*auszlegung des geysts*] before one can be certain. Where this interpretation is not present, what one knows is false and nothing.[24]

Denck's judgment of the disputed questions on baptism and the Eucharist follows to the letter the formula set forth for determining the authority of Scripture. As there is a Spirit who precedes and is more authoritative than written Scripture, so there is a baptism into and a feeding upon Christ more basic than the visible sacramental acts. Only the "almighty word of God" can penetrate the abyss of human filth; hence "external baptism is not necessary for salvation . . . but inner baptism is." [25] Keeping the "covenant of a good conscience with God," maintaining the commitment to live a godly life, is the meaning of baptism.

22. Ibid., p. 21. 16–21.
23. Ibid., p. 21. 28–31. Cf. Luther, *WA* 4: 356. 7 ff. (*Scholion* to Ps. 118 : 105).
24. *Schriften*, 2: 22. 18–22.
25. Ibid., p. 23. 19–20; 24. 25 ff.

Water or baptism saves according to 1 Pet. 3[: 21] not because it removes dirt from the body, but because [it witnesses] the covenant of a good conscience with God [*von des bunds wegen eins guten gewissens mitt Gott*]. This is the covenant: that one who lets himself be baptized do so on the basis of Christ's death, in that, as Christ has died, so also does he die to Adam, and, as Christ is risen, so also does he enter into a new way of life in Christ, according to Rom. 6[: 4]. Where this covenant is present the spirit of Christ comes and kindles the fire of love which utterly consumes the remaining defects and completes the work of Christ.[26]

When he comes to the Eucharist, Denck highlights the centrality of an "invisible" bread, cup, and wine, which have existed "from the beginning of time." The appeal to the goal of deification highlights the extent of mystical influence on Denck already at this time.

Although (the killing of Adam) is not completed as long as I live in my body, it is still begun while I am in my body. And it is suffered in part for the sake of the covenant [which I make] with God when I place my will with his through Christ the mediator, as I said above in regard to baptism. He who is of such a mind and eats the living, invisible bread will always be strengthened to live a good life. He who is of such a mind and drinks from the invisible cup the invisible wine, which God, through his Son, through the Word, has mixed from the beginning of time, becomes inebriated and no longer reproaches himself; through the love of God he is completely deified, and God is made man in him [*durch die liebe Gottes gantz vergottet und Gott in im vermenscht*]. That is what it means to have eaten the body and drunk the blood of Christ. John 6.[27]

26. Ibid., p. 24. 14–20. In his first defense of his faith, Peter Ridemann also defined water baptism in strong ethical terms as a sign of a preexisting "pundt eines gueten gwissen mit Got." The superior "baptism of the heart and conscience" is exalted with sharp words for the practitioners of infant baptism: "Darumb ist der kindertauff kain tauff, sunder ein unnütze waschung. Dan das ist nit ein tauf, der auswendig gschicht, sunder der im hertz und gwissen gschicht in verneuerung des menschen." *Ein Rechenschafft und Bekanndtnus des Glaubens* (1529–32) in *Glaubenszeugnisse oberdeutscher Taufgesinnter*, ed. R. Friedmann (Gütersloh/Heidelberg, 1967), 2: 18.
27. *Schriften*, 2 : 25. 9–20.

Denck understandably concludes, in exact parallel with his comments on baptism, that one can live through the power of God without "external bread," but not without the inner.[28]

While imprisoned in Gmunden in Upper Austria from 1529–32, the later Hutterite leader Peter Ridemann employed even more striking mystical imagery to shift the focus from God's supposed presence in sacramental bread and wine to his identification with the heart of the believer in love. He told his judges that, just as individual grains of corn when ground to meal and baked are indistinguishable in the resulting loaf, and just as grapes when crushed to make wine are no longer individually identifiable, so is the Son one with the Father and we with the Son in the union of love.[29] The polemical context is highlighted when Ridemann goes on to score the blindness of contemporary ecclesiastical leaders who make bread, rather than the heart of the believer, God's "house." [30] Like Denck, Ridemann employs mystical imagery in order to support a relationship with God more direct, intimate, and ultimate than that mediated through traditional sacramental acts.

The preachers of Nürnberg, led by Andreas Osiander, were given Denck's confession on January 16, and, after four days of study, delivered their assessment to the authorities. The report exalts historical and linguistic study as the sine qua non for understanding Scripture and makes the reception of faith absolutely dependent upon *physically* hearing or reading the "word of God." It also leaves little doubt that, in the eyes of these experts, Denck's theological notions are his own concoction and have no persuasive objective authorization.

> Scripture is understandable enough if one approaches it with knowledge of the language in which it is written and the historical period it describes [*wann man zuvor die sprach kan und dy hystorien waysz, darauff sie sich zeuchet*]. But human wickedness discovers that it has neither desire nor love for what Scripture says and teaches, and so it creates for itself

28. Ibid., p. 26. 16–18.

29. *Rechenschafft*, pp. 33–34. Bridal and essentialistic mystical imagery of union with God abounds in Melchior Hofmann's chiliastic *Ordinance of God* (1530). See *Spiritual and Anabaptist Writers*, pp. 182–203, esp. pp. 193–94.

30. "O wee der grossen blindtheit, die ietz in der gantzen welt umbgeth und dem, der im selb ainen lebendigen tempel erbauen hat, nemlich das hertz der glaubigen, darinen zu wonen, sy erst ain brot zum hauss zuerichten." *Rechenschafft*, p. 35.

another meaning and interpretation, which neither the Spirit of God, the language of Scripture, nor one's own conscience can bear.[31]

Hence:

> When Denck says that God alone gives faith and that one who has faith from Scripture has it from himself and not from God, he speaks with cunning and deceit, as is the accustomed practice of these prophets. It is certainly true that God gives faith, but he gives it through the means of hearing [*durch mittel des gehors*]. . . . That hearing comes either from sermons or books [*aus predigen oder schreyben*]. God remains the master and Scripture or pulpit the tool; and just as little as a master could perfect something without using a tool, just so little will God give faith to those who despise his Scripture or preaching.[32]

On January 21, Denck was exiled from Nürnberg and forbidden ever to return within ten miles of the city on pain of death.[33]

THE ASSAULT ON THE LUTHERAN *Solae*

Following his exile Denck conceivably made his way to Müntzer's Mühlhausen and then to St. Gallen, where we find him in the summer of 1525. In September he settled in Augsburg with employment as a language instructor. Here he was to remain a little over a year, until his departure was pressured by the Lutheran preacher Urbanus Rhegius. While in Augsburg, Denck wrote his two major indictments of Luther's view of human destiny: *What Scripture Means When it Says that God is the Cause of Good and Evil* and *On the Law of God: How the Law is Abolished and Yet Still Must be Fulfilled.*[34] Together these treatises form a frontal assault on the three Lutheran *solae: sola scriptura* as authoritative revelation; *solus Christus incarnatus* as the agent of salvation; and *sola fides ex auditu verbi* as the narrow gate to Chris-

---

31. *Schriften,* 3 : 137. 34–138. 1. Regarding the Eucharist, the preachers accuse Denck of offering a view not grounded in Scripture, but "fabricated out of his own head" (*aus seinem aigen kopff erdicht*). Ibid., p. 141. 7 ff.

32. Ibid., p. 138. 13–20.

33. Document reproduced in Kolde 1902, p. 62, n. 1.

34. Denck also wrote in Augsburg the hermeneutical treatise used by Hut, *Wer die Wahrheit wahrlich lieb hat.* Cf. above, pp. 103, 109.

tian life. Denck's manifest concern, as we will see, is to dehistori-
cize and deinstitutionalize "Truth" absolutely.

In the first treatise, Denck uses the (quite secondary) issue of
God's guilt or innocence for evil in the world—a version of the
traditional problem of predestination and the bondage of the will
—to mount his attack on Luther. After some traditional homiletical comments on this topic,[35] he shifts to his primary concern,
namely, to counter Luther's views on Scripture and Christ, and
thereby his authority, by making God's unique habitation the
human soul rather than books and history.

> It is a fabrication when false Christians say that they can do
> nothing but what God works in them. . . . Such persons
> steal from God the will which he has created good and
> free. . . . Yes, the mouth and the heart steal from God his
> highest and greatest honor that they can conceive, and say:
> God has made a temple in which he does not wish to dwell.[36]

> Salvation is *in* us although not *of* us. . . . And if God is in
> me, then in fact everything is in me that belongs to God—
> omnipotence, righteousness, mercy. If I do not believe this,
> I am a liar, for it is true what God has declared: he fills the
> heaven and the earth, that is, all creatures.[37]

For Denck, the testimony and mediation of the discarnate Christ
(the omnipresent eternal Lamb or Word) in one's own heart takes
precedence over the testimony of Scripture about the mediation
of the historical Christ in the church.

> This testimony [about how God deals with men] is in all peo-
> ple, and it preaches to every single one, especially according
> to how one listens to it. . . . Whoever wants to exhaust him-
> self saying he does not hear it is a liar. . . . For this Lamb has
> been from the beginning of the world and remains to the
> end a mediator between God and man.[38]

35. *Schriften*, 2 : 28. 15 ff. English translation, "Whether God is the Cause of Evil,"
in *Spiritual and Anabaptist Writers*, LCC 25, p. 89. Henceforth I will give reference
to Williams's translation under LCC 25. I have followed this translation, with some
stylistic and occasional content adjustments, in my citations.
36. Ibid., 2: 31. 17 ff. in LCC 25, pp. 92–93.
37. Ibid., 32. 14–21, in LCC 25, pp. 93–94.
38. Ibid., 33. 24–28, in LCC 25, p. 95.

God sets forth a means, which has been prepared from eternity, in which men will be saved just as they have been created therein; that is, his Word. In this Word is hidden alike the mercy and the righteousness of God. . . . This means is so near to all persons (however much they have wanted to reject God) that they can easily receive it by turning to God. . . . The Word of God addresses everyone clearly: the dumb, the deaf, the blind; yes, unreasoning animals, indeed, leaf and grass, stone and wood, heaven and earth, and all that is therein, in order that they might hear and do his will.[39]

Christ is not to be understood primarily as a historical figure but in terms of that existential state the mystics call "resignation" or "tranquillity" (*Gelassenheit*). "Scripture speaks of a tranquillity, which is the means of coming to God, that is, Christ himself, not to be regarded physically, but rather spiritually [*nit flaischlich . . . sonder gaistlich*], as he himself also proclaimed before he came in the flesh." [40] As an incarnate, historical figure, Christ's importance lies in his being the visible precedent and example of the deification (*Vergottung*) men should seek:

You may ask: If then the Word is thus in all people, what need had it of the humanity of Jesus of Nazareth? . . . Answer: The Word was in men for this purpose, viz. that it might divinize them, as happens to all the elect. . . . The Word, however, had to become man in Jesus for this reason, viz. that people both in spirit and in the flesh, from within and without, behind and before, and in all places might have testimony [of this goal of divinization].[41]

Those who pay heed more to the "witness" (the historical Christ of Scripture) than to the "Truth itself" (the discarnate, omnipres-

39. Ibid., 38. 10–32, in LCC 25, pp. 100–01.
40. Ibid., 35. 29–31, in LCC 25, p. 97. See note 41.
41. Ibid., 39. 5–12, in LCC 25, p. 101. Elsewhere: "All Christians are in some sense like Christ, for, as he offered himself up to the Father, so they are ready to offer themselves. Not . . . that they are so perfect as Christ was, but rather that they seek exactly the perfection which Christ never lost" (Ibid., p. 37. 15 ff., in LCC 25, p. 99). Cf. Otto E. Vittali, *Die Theologie des Wiedertäufers Hans Denck* (Offenburg, 1932), p. 35. Generally, for Denck historical "externals" may have their (secondary) significance insofar as they pass muster before what the Spirit teaches in the heart: "[Do] not arbitrarily throw out all external testimony, but rather hear and test all and make, in fear of the Spirit, comparisons." *Schriften*, 2: 36. 36–37. 2, in LCC 25, p. 99.

ent Christ of the heart) pervert Christian faith. In the following passage Denck brings together and dismisses Luther's *sola scriptura* and *solus Christus incarnatus* as profane errors.

> This [i.e. confusing the witness with the Truth itself] is what all perverse Jews do and have done, who denied the law which God has written with his finger in their hearts and sought it [instead] in the book written by human hands. . . . This same thing all perverse Christians do today who deny Christ preaching in their hearts. . . . For they do not wish for Christ from above, but rather they seek him only in the [historical] flesh, all in the expectation that it is enough that the work of God be manifested in him [the incarnate Christ], and need not be made manifest in all.[42]

Having so shelved the *sola scriptura* and the *solus Christus incarnatus,* Denck turns now to the *sola fides ex auditu verbi.* As he has subordinated the historical Christ of Scripture to the living Christ of the heart, so he moves against Luther's "faith alone" in God's preached and written word with the criterion of what is present and living. The reader senses Denck's own excitement over the consistency of his argument.

> Clearly, all who truly fear God must renounce the world. . . . For the Lord is coming. He will come at night, when none will take note of him. . . . Then it will help no one to cry: Lord, I have preached the gospel! Lord, I have heard it [preached] . . . ! O, dear brethren, he will not need a long reckoning with us. The words which he declared from the beginning and which we have heard will convict us. He always says: "Blessed is he who hears the Word of God and keeps it" (Luke 11 : 28); "Whoever hears it and does it not is like unto a fool" (Matt. 7 : 26). . . . For they who hear the law of God and do not fulfill it in practice [*mit der that erfüllen*] are not righteous before God. If now someone wishes to come before God without the righteousness which holds before God, he kicks out of the way the means.[43]

42. Ibid., 36. 20–32, in LCC 25, p. 98.
43. Ibid., p. 42. 31–43. 18, in LCC 25, p. 106. Denck intertwines ethics and Christology; the "practiced Christ" is the "means" for coming to God: "this means is Christ, whom none may truly know unless he follow after him with his life" (Ibid., p. 45. 6–7, in LCC 25, p. 108). Note the attack on those who approach Christ shouting "Frid, frid, glaubet nur!" Ibid., p. 102. 10–13.

In a historical sense the fulfillment of the law demanded by Denck is as objectless as faith in the eternal Christ of the heart. Especially in his second Augsburg treatise, *On the Law of God,* is it made clear that the law fulfilled by Christ and, contrary to the Lutherans,[44] still to be fulfilled by every individual member of his body, is not the law written by Moses, but "that spoken and written [by Christ] from the beginning until the end of the world in the hearts [of his own]." [45] We are dealing with a spiritual law of love, a law beyond the law, as it were, evident to all who would simply read their hearts.[46] This must be borne in mind when Denck, on the one hand, sounding like a Free Spirit, exalts the extralegal status of the true Christian ("he fulfills God's law in the highest way even when he breaks it"; "he is a law unto himself"),[47] and, on the other hand, appearing to be an absolute legalist, urges the most abject obedience to all written laws. In both instances he is consistent in defining Christian faith in terms of

44. Denck bemoans those who twist Matthew 5 : 17—"I am come not to abolish but to fulfill the law"—to mean that Christ has fulfilled the law in such a way that we need not, and, indeed, should not try lest we imply that Christ did not sufficiently fulfill it. "If this understanding were true, it would be a matter of indifference how a man lives after his conversion." Ibid., p. 52. 8–17; cf. p. 53. 8–9.

45. Ibid., p. 53. 18 ff.

46. Denck, in Müntzerian fashion, turns this forcefully against the learned theologians: "He who has received the new covenant of God, i.e. the one in whose heart the law is written by the Holy Spirit, is truly righteous. But one who thinks that he can keep the law by simply believing a book ascribes to the dead letter what belongs to the living Spirit. He who does not have the Spirit and thinks he can find it in Scripture seeks light and finds darkness, seeks life and finds but death, not only in the Old Testament, but also in the New. And that is why the most learned in every age are the most angered by the truth. They think that their understanding [of truth], which they have in a clever and refined manner derived from Holy Scripture, cannot fail them. Should the son of a carpenter, who had not gone to school, come and censure them for falsehood, what could he have learned from them? Because he [Christ] would not affirm the ignorance which they derived from the letter [of Scripture] [*ires buchstabischen unverstands*], they thought he rejected the law. O Brother, such happens still today. Blessed is he who does not take offense at Christ. *He who has the truth in the truth can say what the truth is without any Scripture whatsoever.* But the learned theologians could never do that because they do not receive the truth from the truth, but steal it from the witnesses to truth." Ibid., p. 59. 5–21 (emphasis mine).

47. "Glauben ist, dem wort Gottes gehorchen, es sei zum todt oder zum leben, mit gwisser zuversicht, dass es zum besten weise, Hebr. 11. Welcher das thut, dem ist nit müglich, dass er irre, wenn er schon irret. Er erfüllet das gsatz Gottes auffs höchst, wenn er es schon bricht. Er sucht aller ding frommen in himel und auff erden, ime gescheh selbs wol oder weh, darumb hat er auch keyn gesatz mer, 1 Timot. 1, sonder er selb ist im selb eyn gsatz, Rom. 2 [14!] . . . ist mit Christo so gar wol eynss, wie Christus mit dem vatter, Johannis 17." Ibid., pp. 97. 17–24.

a living posture of "obedience" (*gehorsam*). In terms of dissent, his purpose is to displace Luther's Scripture and sermon-oriented faith with a universal ethical criterion.

A particularly striking statement is the following, which is deceptively reminiscent of Luther's classical definition of the Christian man as "a perfectly free lord of all, subject to none . . . [and] a perfectly dutiful servant of all, subject to all:" [48]

> To the extent that one is united with God, to that extent is one free from every time and place and its laws. But he may enjoy such freedom only as he is gladly willing to be subject to all laws. For he who is not a servant of all creatures for God's sake can never inherit the Kingdom of God with his Son.[49]

In his treatise on *The Freedom of a Christian,* Luther concluded by subordinating ethics to faith in the definition of the religious man: "As a man is, whether believer or unbeliever, so also is his work." [50] Denck stresses the very reverse: as the work is, whether good or bad, so is the man and his faith. "If we are still living in the old life, then we do not in truth and with certainty believe, nor do we desire to be beautiful and guiltless." [51] "Faith is obedience to God and trust in his promise [to us] through Jesus Christ. Where this obedience is not present, the trust is false and deceitful." [52]

By making an ethical criterion (vis-à-vis Luther's *sola fides*) primary in the definition of the religious man, Denck not only set forth what can be called a "Protestant" version of the medieval *fides charitate formata,*[53] but also, and this is the primary conse-

48. *The Freedom of a Christian,* in *Three Treatises: Martin Luther* (Philadelphia, 1960), p. 277.

49. *Schriften,* 2: 64. 36–65. 2.

50. *The Freedom of a Christian,* p. 297.

51. *Widerruf* (1528) in *Schriften,* 2: 106. 28–29. "Anstelle der Rechtfertigung aus Glauben durch Gnade—Rechtfertigung durch Tat auf Grund eigener Leistung." "Die Rechtfertigung ist für Denk ein durch und durch sittliches Geschehen." Hege, *Hans Denk,* pp. 113, 119; cf. p. 123.

52. *Schriften,* 2: 107. 3–5. Denck brings his treatise *On the Law of God* to a conclusion with the curse: "Let him who does not truly love God and keep his commandment be cursed. Let him who, with prideful hand, transgresses even the smallest commandment of God be cursed." *Schriften,* 2: 66. 17 ff.

53. Vittali maintains that Denck created a new, Reformation version of "works-righteousness," fundamentally different from the medieval version against which the Reformation protested because "die Werke sind *Folge den geschehenen Recht-*

quence, he put himself in the position to argue that ethical short-comings indicate false authority. Subsequent to his expulsion from Strasbourg in December, 1526, Denck dedicated an entire treatise to that very proposition: *The Order of God and the Work of Creatures: [Written] to Overturn the Feigned Hypocritical Pretence of the False and Lazy Elected Ones so that the Truth May Have Room to Manifest the Eternal Unchangeable Will of God* (1527). In a statement of the purpose of this treatise, Denck wrote:

> We wish very briefly to compare the order of God [*ordnung Gottes*] and the work of creatures since the beginning of the world so that we can show fully how far the men fall who, without the command of God, Ps. 50[: 16–17],[54] open their mouths to speak of the covenant and sacrament of God which they themselves have never understood, 1 Cor. 13, and to teach the true way to salvation which they themselves have never walked and indeed lack the will to walk, Phil. 3[: 18–19]. They say they believe. How they believe they also say. But they have never forsaken the old life and taken up a new one, as is certainly fitting for scribes and pharisees.[55]

In his very last letter, written in the month of his death (October, 1527), a flight-weary and plague-ridden Denck unsuccessfully petitioned his old teacher Oecolampadius to assist in his receiving a modest refuge in Basel. Denck also made available at this time a final statement of his beliefs, which Oecolampadius published after his death under the questionable title "Recantation" (*Widerruf*). In the letter, Denck offered the following assessment of his life and work, which has led to some debate over whether

---

fertigung, nicht das 'meritum de congruens' [sic] . . . Das unterscheidet diese neue Werkgerechtigkeit grundlegend von aller mittelalterlichen und drückt ihr den Stempel der Reformation auf." *Die Theologie des Wiedertäufers Hans Denck,* p. 41. It would be more correct to characterize Denck's position as a version of the medieval *fides charitate formata* with which the Reformation, as Luther understood it, was in fundamental disagreement. As a matter of fact, Denck develops a *facere quod in se est*—the correlate of the *meritum de congruo*—along the lines of both the scholastic *non ponit obicem* (2: 32. 29–35, in LCC 25, p. 94) and the mystical "still halten" (2: 33. 15, in LCC 25, p. 95). Cf. also 2: 92. 22–26.

54. This verse, a favorite among dissenters, reads: "But to the wicked, God says: 'What right have you to recite my statutes, or take my covenant on your lips? For you hate discipline, and you cast my words behind you.' "

55. *Schriften,* 2: 89. 23–31.

or not he approached his death in despair over all historical forms of religious life.[56]

> Exile is bitter and hard for me, but still more difficult to bear
> is the fact that the success and fruit [of my life] does not cor-
> respond to my zeal. I seek no other fruit (God knows) than
> that as many as possible glorify God the father of our lord
> Jesus Christ with one heart and voice, whether they be cir-
> cumcized or baptized or neither. I am far from agreed with
> those, whoever they may be, who bind the kingdom of God
> too much to ceremonies and elements, although I cannot deny
> that I, for a while, adhered to such.[57]

In the so-called Recantation a full section, "Von Ceremonien," appears as a formal statement on this matter.

> In nothing so much as in their earnest quarreling over exter-
> nal things do men prove themselves to be human. Those who
> insult (external things) excessively are persecuted by ignorant
> men, and those who value them too highly take away the
> honor of God. Ceremonies in themselves are no sin, but he
> who thinks he will reach his goal through a ceremony, be it
> baptism or the Eucharist, is plagued by superstition. The
> faithful man is free in external things, yet he will diligently
> see to it that God's honor is not lessened by them, nor love
> of the neighbor wantonly scorned. He who puts time and
> effort into ceremonies gains very little. Indeed, should one
> forfeit all ceremonies no great harm would be incurred, and
> it would certainly be much better to be without them than
> to misuse them.[58]

56. Sebastian Franck twice cites Denck's *Widderuf* as an example of the foolish zeal of the *Täufer*, which the better among them (as Franck thinks Denck is) later renounce: "Etlich zweiflen an jrem berüff/und hat sy der unweiss eyfer umb des Herrn hauss gerawen/walten sy hetten nye einichen geteufft/wie Joh. Denck." *Chronica, Zeytbüch und Geschichtbibel* (Strasbourg, 1531), ccccxlvi b; cf. ccccxlvii b. Ernst Stähelin sees the latter as a reflection of Denck's retreat from Anabaptism to "Spiritualism." "Er war [im Herbst 1527] nicht mehr der Täuferapostel, sondern war unterdessen am Täufertum irre geworden und hatte sich auf seinen Spiritualismus zurückgezogen." *Das theologische Lebenswerk Johannes Oekolampads*, p. 393. Mennonite historiography maintains, correctly I think, the consistency of Denck's thought. Cf. Neff, *Mennonitisches Lexikon*, p. 409. As Albrecht Hege puts it, the *Widderuf* is at most a "Gemilderung," not a recantation. *Hans Denck*, p. 59.

57. *Schriften*, 3: 134. 30–135. 2.

58. Ibid., 2: 108. 31–109. 9.

In an earlier treatise Denck had dismissed ceremonies as "an external arrangement (*ordnung*) given for the betterment of the coarse people of Israel, to whom all spiritual talk was alien." [59] That now, at the end of his life, he should so relativize traditional historical forms is fully consistent with the direction of his thought since the confession to the authorities in Nürnberg.[60] It is the essence of effective dissent to undercut the traditional symbols of power and authority. In his embracing of mystical axioms and his theological assault on the Lutheran *solae,* as here in the relativizing of ceremonies, Denck consistently followed this course, reaching for that which was primordial to all historical forms.

POSTSCRIPT: PILGRAM MARBECK'S NEW COVENANT

Denck, like Hut before him, relativized the historical forms of the Lutherans by appealing to something more primordial and universal: a Word behind their preached word, a Bread and Baptism behind their physical bread and baptism. Another early Anabaptist leader reached the same polemical goal by pursuing a different and, for the future of Anabaptism in Oberdeutschland, very fateful route. From mid-December, 1531 to early January, 1532, Pilgram Marbeck composed a confession of faith for the authorities in Strasbourg. This confession climaxed at least a half year of running controversy with Martin Bucer and was soon followed by Marbeck's expulsion from the city. The modern editors of the confession have printed Bucer's point-by-point rebuttal in parallel with Marbeck's detailed defense of his beliefs, thus making it possible to locate precisely the hinge on which the controversy turned.

Marbeck, like Hut and Denck before him, defines true baptism as "the covenant of a good conscience with God," a circumcision of the heart which infant baptism cannot begin to effect and sacramental (adult) baptism can only attest.[61] Marbeck, however, does

59. Ibid., p. 54. 14–15.

60. Vittali draws the conclusion: "War—wie uns Dencks Leben und Lehre ersehen liess—die ursprüngliche Absicht *nicht aller* Täuferführer die Bildung einer eigenen Sondergemeinschaft und eines eigenen dogmatischen Bekenntnisse, sondern eine über dogmatische Gegensätze hinaus führende religiöse Gestaltung des Lebens unter Auflösung staatlicher wie kirchlicher Ordnungen, so führt die historische Entwicklung zur Aufgabe dieses Standpunktes." *Die Theologie des Wiedertäufers Hans Denck,* pp. 45–46.

61. *Pilgram Marbecks Gleubensbekenntnis* in *Quellen zur Geschichte der Täufer,* vol. 7, *Elsass I* (Strasbourg *1522–1532*), ed. M. Krebs and H. G. Rott (Gütersloh, 1959), p. 423. 1–6; 432. 3 ff. There is an earlier edition and discussion of the confession by John C. Wenger in *MQR* 12 (1938): 137–202.

not polemically turn this covenant of conscience against externals as something more primordial and universal. He takes a different tack. Appealing to Jeremiah 31 : 31 ff., he exalts it as the new *historical* covenant inaugurated by Christ's advent in the flesh and having no continuity whatsoever with the past.

> Christ came first after the promise to Abraham as the very covenant itself [*als der punt selbs*], and this does not concern the covenant of Abraham. Otherwise the prophet Jeremiah (31 [: 31 ff.]) must have had a different understanding of the matter [for he writes]: "I will make a covenant not as I made before with your fathers. Rather I will write my law into your heart." [62]

The historical novelty of this covenant is fully matched by its new existential benefits. It gives true believers the very keys to heaven (in accordance with Matthew 18 : 18).[63] Marbeck summarizes the new freedom so: "In the new covenant, which is reached through the Holy Spirit (through Christ), there is another being (*wesen*). We are no longer born to servitude but are brave, free children, uncoerced and without guardians, ourselves lords over all things." [64]

The nature of the disagreement between Marbeck and Bucer is not difficult to surmise. Bucer saw very close continuity between the Old and New Testaments; the faith and love of the latter are "more perfect," not radically different, forms of that known in the Old Testament.[65] The transition from the historically old to the historically new is gradual and modest. To Bucer, Marbeck not only miscalculated the degree of grace possessed by the Old Testament faithful, but he also inflated quite unrealistically the spiritual power and independence accorded New Testament Christians. Marbeck, on the other hand, saw in Bucer's refusal to distinguish absolutely between the old and the new the reason for his failure to enact radical reforms in Strasbourg. To Marbeck, Bucer was a man more of the old than of the new covenant. The following exchanges are representative.

---

62. *Pilgram Marbecks Glaubensbekenntnis*, pp. 431. 6–432. 2. Cf. Klassen, *Covenant and Community*, pp. 124–27, 145, 154, 181 ("borders on Marcionitism").
63. *Pilgram Marbecks Glaubensbekenntnis*, p. 424. 1 ff.
64. Ibid., p. 439. 4–8.
65. Ibid., pp. 435. 26–28; 437. 36–37; 439. 27–30; 444. 35 ff.; 465. 20 ff.

Marbeck: Now and henceforth faith in Christ can do God's will. Sickness and death are no more. Life and wholeness have come. The salvation of all men is now upon us. Ignorance is excused. The kingdom of God is given to children and all who are truly pure.

Bucer: Nevertheless, no one is yet finished, Phil. 2[: 12], and all the saints pray for forgiveness of sins, Ps. 32 [6].[66]

Marbeck: The [written] law, together with John (the Baptist), is past. . . .

Bucer: Why then does the Lord say, "I am come to fulfill, not to destroy the law" [Matt. 5 : 17]? And Paul: "We uphold the law" [Rom. 3 : 31]?[67]

Marbeck: All ceremonies have passed away since Christ, the Son of God, has himself come as the true consolation and redeemer.

Bucer: Not all. Baptism, Eucharist, ordination, time, place, common prayer, fasting, and preaching are also ceremonies.[68]

Marbeck: No external force can be used, rule, or reign within the kingdom of Christ.

Bucer: The kingdom of Christ consists of the faithful who, while they are in this body, must have external order and government.[69]

Marbeck: Worldly government [*gewallt*] with all its activities is of no use in the kingdom of Christ, which is a kingdom not of this world. . . .[70]

Bucer: But the kingdom of Christ lives within the world. It therefore truly demands those things which are necessary to live in this world, the chief among them being government [*oberkeit*].[71]

66. Ibid., p. 420. 8–12, 26–27; cf. p. 442. 12–16, 32–34.

67. Ibid., p. 448. 6–8, 21–22.

68. Ibid., p. 472. 8–9, 20–22; cf. p. 507. 12–16, for a general defense of externals.

69. Ibid., p. 425. 1–2, 3–4; cf. p. 424. 10–12, 32–34.

70. Ibid., p. 511. 10–11; cf. p. 507. 1–2.

71, Ibid., p. 511. 32–33. Elsewhere Bucer argues that government is to be called Christian and given a role in the *ecclesia militans;* tyranny, not government per se, is what Christians oppose and what Marbeck, if he understood the matter correctly, would condemn. Ibid., pp. 507. 31 ff., 510. 33 ff.; cf. p. 525. 26 ff.

Bucer finally dismissed Marbeck and his followers as self-righteous rascals who fled their civic duties (*sie sich alles burgerlichen wesens abgethon*) and harbored a desire to be martyred.[72]

Save for a certain utopian strain, Marbeck's thought hardly seems to differ significantly from that of Denck, whom Bucer had also sent packing from Strasbourg. Yet Marbeck's peculiar "new covenant" concept, hammered out against Bucer in 1531–32, built into his theology a practicality and flexibility not evident in Denck's. As is well known, Marbeck later came to the defense of externals in the famous showdown with Caspar Schwenckfeld in 1542.[73] Because he worked with two absolutely different *historical* orders, rather than with a spirit-history (or inner-outer) contrast, Marbeck could later support concrete religious forms and organizations without feeling that he had fallen into the snare of his enemies. There are externals and there are externals. The outer forms of the New Testament are not those of the Old Testament and contemporary Christendom. Although keeping them theologically at arm's length, Marbeck's "new covenant" concept of Christianity permitted Anabaptism that degree of appreciation for mundane externals which is necessary even for the members of a new order historically to survive. Not faced with the decision either to reform the world altogether or to abandon it entirely, Marbeck could assemble a particularized and withdrawn, yet perfect, community within it.

72. Ibid., p. 521. 31 ff. Cf. Miriam U. Chrisman, *Strasbourg and the Reform* (New Haven, 1967), pp. 177–200.

73. Cf. T. Bergsten, "Pilgrim Marbeck und seine Auseinandersetzung mit Caspar Schwenckfeld," *Kyrkohistorisk Arsskrift* 57 (1957): 39–100, esp. 95 ff.; 58 (1958): 53–87; Williams, *Radical Reformation*, pp. 472–76.

6

Sebastian Franck

The Bruised Idealist

In 1528, Sebastian Franck was a fledgling, twenty-nine-year-old Lutheran preacher in the village of Gustenfelden. Gustenfelden, 1528 is an appropriate time and place to begin his intellectual biography.[1] It marks not only his intriguing marriage to Ottilie Beheim, the allegedly conservative sister of the "godless painters" of Nürnberg, but also the publication of his first independent work, the treatise *On the Detestable Vice of Drunkenness*.[2] This work, which is dedicated to the magistrate of Colmburg, Wolff von Hesberg, was published in the hope of converting the intemperate nobility to an abstemious life.[3] Franck writes in the expectation that "the spark of divine love [*das füncklin gotlicher lieb*] will at some time blaze up and become fire." [4] Beneath the traditional homiletics of this idealistic effort, the reader can detect an already seriously disillusioned young man, who has learned by the

1. On Franck's biography prior to 1528, see especially Eberhard Teufel, *"Landräumig": Sebastian Franck, ein Wanderer an Donau, Rhein und Neckar* (Neustadt an der Aisch, 1954). A larger biography, not always as precise in details, is the volume by W.-E. Peuckert, *Sebastian Franck: Ein Deutscher Sucher* (München, 1943). A popular short sketch is Paul Joachimsen, "Zur inneren Entwicklung Sebastian Francks," *Blätter für deutsche Philosophie* 2 (1928): 1–28. Hans J. Hillerbrand gives a thumbnail sketch in his *A Fellowship of Discontent* (New York, 1967). For the bibliographer, Lotte Blaschke discusses literature on Franck from 1892–1925, *Blätter für deutsche Philosophie* 2 (1928): 73–77.

2. Franck's very first work was a German translation of Andreas Althamer's *Dialloge, hoc est Conciliatio locorum scripturae, qui prima facie inter se pugnare videntur* (1527), a strongly Lutheran tract against Anabaptism, especially Denck's *Wer die Wahrheit wahrlich lieb hat*. See above, p. 103. It is discussed by Teufel, *"Landräumig,"* pp. 23–27. On Franck's marriage, cf. Teufel, pp. 20–21, and Kolde 1902, p. 72.

3. Franck is at this time convinced of the pedagogical value of good magisterial example: "Richt der Fürst mer mit seinem Exempel als/dann mit ir mandaten." *Von dem grewlichen laster der trunckenheit* (n.p., 1531), p. D iiij b.

4. Ibid., p. A iij a.

shock of firsthand experience that men, as he puts it, prefer "Bacchus und der bauch" to God's truth.[5] "The world has never been worse," he moans. "We are truly on the threshold of the last day. All things have reached their end. We probably spill as much wine today as has [ever] been drunk." [6]

The constructive theme of the treatise, which has been influenced by Luther's[7] as well as mystical writings, is that the singular way to God is suffering (*leiden, trübsal*). One must go through the "Klaghaus," not through the "Weinhaus." [8] Unlike Luther, however, Franck's way of suffering does not culminate theologically and existentially in sheer, patient faith in God's eventual consummation of his promises, but rather in a visibly changed moral life here and now. One does not grasp the gospel by faith, he maintains, but "by a deed" (*mit der that*).[9]

It has been argued to the point of commonplace that Franck's final departure from the Reformation was the result of what he considered to be the sparse ethical fruits of Wittenberg theology.[10] Yet already in this his first writing, Franck's view of religious life is so intensely ethical in nature that it could be adjusted to the inevitable imperfections of an institutionalized religion only with great difficulty. Where there are no visible fruits of faith, he tells us, a heathen hides under Christ's name. And "when the lightning strikes, the name Christian will not help." Then one must

5. Ibid., p. A iij b; B iiij b.

6. Ibid., p. D ij b. The concluding chapter of the treatise is entitled: "Wie das züsauffen/fressen und trinken/ein gewisse zeychen sey vor dem jungsten Tag" (p. H iij a). Portions of the treatise have understandably found their way into English translation in "Classics of Alcohol Literature," ed. E. M. Jellinek, *Quarterly Journal of Studies on Alcohol* 2, no. 2 (Sept., 1941).

7. The dedication paraphrases Luther's *Freiheit eines Christenmenschen. Von dem grewlichen laster der trunckenheit*, p. A iij a. Teufel sees Luther's 1519 *Sermon von dem hl. hochwürdigen Sakrament der Taufe* so much in evidence that he concludes: "die stärksten Stellen sind hier nicht *täuferisch*, sondern *gut lutherisch*," "Landräumig," p. 30. (Those who insist that Franck departed from the Reformation because of the sparse ethical fruits of Luther's theology might take note.) Franck also cites the Lutheran Johannes Brenz twice. *Von dem grewlichen laster der trunckenheit*, pp. A iiij b; F i a.

8. Ibid., p. A iiij a.

9. Ibid., p. B iij a.

10. See especially the discussions by Alfred Hegler, *Geist und Schrift bei Sebastian Franck*, pp. 22–27; Rudolf Kommoss, *Sebastian Franck und Erasmus von Rotterdam* (Berlin, 1934), pp. 12–14. Franck's historical judgment of Luther and Lutheranism is documented by Eberhard Teufel, "Luther und Luthertum im Urteil Sebastian Francks," *Festgabe für Karl Müller* (Tübingen, 1922), pp. 132–44.

have recourse to the true armor of the Christian, which is "temperance, knowing when to stop [*abbruch*], fasting, hunger, thirst, work, alertness, prayer, keeping God's word, and remembrance of Christ's suffering." [11] Franck defends "pure doctrine," as a good Lutheran should, but it is clearly the doctrine of pure life on which he hinges everything. "Although," he writes, "no Christian is ever so perfect that he can forget himself in this life, still his imperfection must not go uncensored, lest the pure doctrine of the gospel lose its free concourse among the people, and the community gain a bad reputation." [12]

The treatise culminates in the threatening demand for the exercise of the ban (i.e. the forced expulsion from the community of those whose conduct is unbecoming to a Christian).

> Preachers should punish public vice with the word [of God] and the ban, and princes with the sword and the law. For where the ban is not enforced, I can speak of no gospel or Christian community.[13]

HISTORY AS EXPOSÉ

In 1529, Franck, apparently fulfilling his threat, surrendered his position in Gustenfelden and moved to Nürnberg. There, having put the priesthood behind him, he continued to labor as a translator and author. His major work was the translation of a fifteenth-century account of the Turks.[14] This account, recently published in Wittenberg with a preface by Luther under the title *Libellus de situ et moribus Turcorum,* was written by a Western observer who had been in mild servitude to Turkish masters from 1436 to 1458. Franck's translation is important, not only because it gives us an accurate measure of the extent of his alienation, but also because the treatise itself sets forth value judgments about religious truth which were to become Franck's own. The chapter on Turkish religion makes disunity a discredit of authority,[15]

11. *Von dem grewlichen laster der trunckenheit,* p. B iiij a.
12. Ibid., p. G ii a.
13. Ibid., p. C j a. See Teufel's discussion, *"Landräumig,"* p. 32.
14. *Cronica-Abconterfarung und entwerffund der Türckey* (Augsburg, 1530). Cf. Teufel, *"Landräumig,"* p. 33.
15. In a chapter entitled "Von der Türcken unreingkeit/Secten und zwytrache yhn yhrem glaubenn," the author concludes: "diese zertrennung und zerteilung der gemüt/einem jeden gnügsam zeugnus geben solt/das dise seckt nit von Got sonder von Teuffel sey/und jren anfang hab." *Cronica . . . Türckey,* p. H iij b.

exalts spiritual over historical religion,[16] and cites ethics as a
final court of appeal.[17]

Franck exposes himself only briefly, once in his preface and
again in a famous statement on the contemporary ascendency of
spiritual over historical religion, which he appends to chapter 30.[18]
The prefatory remarks measure fully the shattering personal effect
of his ministry in Gustenfelden.

> Surely God helps when the world becomes so desolate and
> savage! Who should not rightly groan because he lives in
> this darkened world? Everything works so absurdly against
> everything, and of nothing are we so sure than that we do
> not know. For the first time I experience and understand
> that the world is not only dark but darkness itself, as John
> 1[: 3] says, and that the Devil is its god and prince. When we
> read through the chronicles and perceive there the work of
> God, we discover nothing else than that the world is God's
> carnival, a fable in his eyes. Hence he always plays the op-
> posite and makes the world, which wants to go another way,
> work against itself. . . . [19] Behold now how many beliefs,

16. The author defends the "geistlichen" among the Turks, who give religious
laws, customs, and ceremonies a spiritual or allegorical interpretation. They are
opposed by the priests who reject their allegory and "bleiben bey dem büchstaben
des Alkorans," maintaining that those who interpret the Koran spiritually "es also
haben ausgelegt/selbs nit habenn gewist/was sie sagen/weyl sye in verzuckung on
vernunfft und witz ausserhalb ynen selbs gewesen seind/do sie diss sagten." Ibid.,
p. G iiij a.

17. Chapter 24 bears the title: "Von dero münich frücht und bübenstuck/dabey
man yren geyst erkent," and the conclusion is drawn that "wöllen wir nun jre
frücht besehen/die yren geyst verratten/und dabey man sie/wye Christus lert
erkennen sol." Ibid., p. G iiij b.

18. "Weytter seind zu unsern zwyten drey fürnemlich glauben auffgestanden/die
grossen anhang haben/als Lutherisch/Zwinglisch/und Taufferisch/der vierdt ist
schon auf dem ban das man alle eusserlich predig/Ceremoni/Sacrament/ban/berüff/
als unnötig/wyl auss dem weg raumen/und glat ein unsichtpar geystlich kirchen in
einigkeit des geysts und glaubens versamlet/under allen völckern/und allein durchs
ewig unsichtbar wort/von Got on eynich eusserlich mitel regiert wil anrichten/als
sey die Apostolisch kirch bald nach der Apostel abgang/durch den greüel verwüst/
gefallen/und seyndt zümal geferlich zeyt/Got helff uns allen/unnd geb uns/das wir
in seiner forcht ergreyffen das recht ist/und den rechten weg in diser finsternuss
wandeln." Ibid., pp. K iiij b–L i a. Cf. Weigel, below, p. 237.

19. Luther also assessed history as God's game or masquerade, a conflict-ridden
working out of a concealed *sapientia Dei*. See T. E. Pederson, "Schöpfung und
Geschichte bei Luther," *Studia Theologia* 3 (1949): 22–24; H. Fausel, "Luther und
Melanchthon während des Augsburger Reichstag," *Theologische Aufsätze: Karl Barth
zum 50. Geburtstag (München, 1936)*, p. 407; Heinz Zahrnt, *Luther deutet Geschichte*

sects, and parties exist only among those who are Christians. I pass over the subdivision of the sects into further sects and the way the parts of the various churches have nothing to do with one another. It is impossible that one God . . . baptism, Supper, and gospel can exist in so many repugnant churches.[20]

Franck concludes that, unpleasant as it is, such an experience of the confusion and desolation of the world is ultimately salutary for the man who truly seeks God. Repelled by what he hears and sees, this man learns to look to and trust only God. Indeed, it is through just such an experience that God "tears us away from the school of men and pulls us into his school, so that we may sit at his feet and hear his word . . . no longer surrendering ourselves to men and looking to them as our masters." [21]

What was begun philosophically as well as historically in the *Chronicle of the Turks* is brought to completion in Franck's 1531 *Chronicle of World History,* which was composed in Nürnberg and published in Strasbourg in September, 1531.[22] If the 1530 chronicle was to Franck a revelation of the folly of the Eastern world, the 1531 chronicle is an exposé of human perversion from the very beginning of the world until the present (which, as we have seen, was very near the end for Franck). This second chronicle not only marks a significant stage in his intellectual biography, but it also introduces a potent new weapon into the arsenal of sixteenth-century dissent: the historical chronicle joins satire, the learned treatise, and the polemical pamphlet as an instrument of protest.

As a form of dissent, the 1531 chronicle has two patent purposes. It is first of all an exposé, revealing in depth the imperfection and ever penultimate nature of established authority, whether political or ecclesiastical. In the preface Franck appeals to the *Magnificat,*

(München, 1952), p. 21; and H. W. Beyer, "Gott und die Geschichte nach Luthers Auslegung des Magnificat," *Luther Jahrbuch* 21 (1939), pp. 110–33. On the admonitory and unmasking roles of historical study for Luther, see John Headley, *Luther's View of Church History* (New Haven, 1963), pp. 46–51; H.-W. Krumwiede, *Glaube und Geschichte in der Theologie Luthers* (Göttingen, 1952), p. 76; M. Schmidt, "Luthers Schau der Geschichte," *Luther Jahrbuch* (1963), p. 64; Zahrnt, *Luther deutet Geschichte,* p. 82.

20. *Cronica . . . Türckey,* p. A ii a.
21. Ibid., p. A ii a-b.
22. *Chronica, Zeytbüch und Geschichtbibel von anbegin biss inn diss gegenwertig A.D. xxxj. jar* (Strasbourg, 1531).

also Thomas Müntzer's text for his own *Special Exposé.*[23] The second purpose is to provide the basic building blocks for an alternative interpretation of the *potentia Dei ordinata,* which will make possible new value judgments on human nature and destiny.

When he makes the transition from Book 2, the history of kings and political events,[24] to Book 3, the history of the church and spiritual events,[25] Franck summarizes history's message:

> Until now [i.e. through Book 2] we God-fearing readers have heard the dealings, events, and tragedies of the external world. There [we have seen] nothing but warring, wrangling, blood-letting, hacking, stabbing, ruling, misery, and every conceivable external calamity, military force, and kingdom. Now let us turn with God to the world of spiritual fraud [*an die geistlich doppel welt*], to the Devil who prowls around at high noon, to the pestilence and shafts which fly and kill in broad daylight. Yes, let us look to the lost masses who imagine they are clean and pure and still remain filthy and unwashed. And [let us spy out] the Christians who are there as a few kernels amidst a mountain of chaff, as a Lot in Sodom, a Daniel in Babylon, a Moses in Egypt, a rose among thorns.[26]

The biting preface to the history of kings, which was to brand Franck as a subversive in the eyes of many and provide an occasion to challenge his right to citizenship in Strasbourg and Ulm, is a dissertation, heavily influenced by Erasmus, on why rulers have chosen the eagle as their symbol. The purpose, Franck tells the reader, is to describe "the nature and character of the eagle and thereby portray the life, habitat, servants, and governance of emperors, princes, and lords." [27] Writing no doubt with the recent

23. "Demnach sihe doch durch gott hie in diser Chronick/wunder von dem wunderparlichen got/und lerne die art seiner werck erkennen/Da findstu nicht dann das Maria Luc j. singt." Ibid., A i. Cf. above, pp. 79 ff.

24. Entitled "Der Keyser Jarbuch" or "Chronick und historien der Keyser."

25. Entitled "Die drit chronica der Bäbst unnd Geistlichen Händel/von Petro biss auff Clementem . . ." with some eight separate sections.

26. *Chronica, Zeytbüch und Geschichtbibel,* p. cclv a.

27. Ibid., p. cxix b. The preface largely repeats Erasmus's *adagia:* "Scarabeus aquilam quaerit" and "Aut regem aut fatuum nasci oportet." Cf. Kommoss, *Sebastian Franck und Erasmus,* p. 31. As a young man Franck read extensively in the writings of Erasmus, and, according to Kommoss, the latter's influence was basically "destruktiver, raumschaffender" (ibid., p. 37). Kommoss views Franck's mature thought as a blending of medieval mysticism and Erasmian *philosophia Christi,*

slaughter of the peasants and such rulers as his own Markgraf Casimir of Brandenburg, who blinded Anabaptists before exiling them from his land)[28] in mind, Franck depicts the eagle as absolutely untamable,[29] born to kill and plunder,[30] feared, hated, and befriended by neither man nor beast.[31] In a wry summary, which ridicules the wise as it exposes the powerful, Franck concludes:

> Only the eagle, which signifies the life of kings, and which is neither beautiful, well-formed, useful, nor edible, but, on the contrary, is ravenous, thievish, solitary, useless, warlike, factious, hostile, a handicap and a plague to all men, capable of inflicting harm on many yet eager to inflict harm on still more and expand its power—only the eagle has been esteemed by the wise.[32]

An equally severe exposé of the spiritual rulers of Christendom follows in Book 3. In the preface to his history of heretics, a subsection within the history of the church, Franck points out that he would canonize many whom Rome has anathematized, for "they have more of the Spirit in one of their fingers than Antichrist in all his sects." [33] He accuses the papacy of being as fully in discord with the ecclesiastical tradition of which it boasts as

---

with the former providing the clearly constructive impulses (ibid., pp. 17–18, 48–49). On this problem, cf. Alexandre Koyré, who considers "humanist" a more substantial characterization of Franck than "mystic." "Sebastian Franck" in *Mystiques, spirituels, alchimistes: Schwenckfeld, Seb. Franck, Weigel, Paracelse* (Paris, 1955), pp. 21–43. Reprinted here from *Cahiers de la revue d'histoire et de philosophie religieuses* 24 (1932).

28. Cf. Teufel, *"Landräumig,"* pp. 18 ff., 39. Franck, however, is clearly opposed to redress of legitimate grievances by revolution. The Peasants' Revolt, he concludes, "sey zum Exempel und abschreckung von aller auffrhür gnüg/das wir sollen wissen/ das Gott kein auffrhur ye gefallen hat/und das Evangelium gwalt leiden und nit auffrhüren lert." *Chronica, Zeytbüch und Geschichtbibel,* p. ccxxxviii a.

29. "Ist zu einicher zucht nicht tüchtig/mag auch mit keiner übung gezämpt oder heymlich gemacht werden." Ibid., p. cxix b.

30. "Des frids hässig und feindselig/gleichsam zu rauben/mörden/streiten geporn ist . . . er von der andern vögel blüt und fleisch lebt." Ibid.

31. "Liebet der Adler nimandt/würt auch von nyemant gehertzt/sunder alles was sich von hym bucket unnd förcht/das thüt es mer auss forcht genötigt dann auss lieb selbs willig." ". . . hatt nitt allein mitt allen thieren feindschafft/sunden auch mitt allen menschen." Ibid., p. cxxii a.

32. Ibid., p. cxxii b.

33. Ibid., p. cccxxxv a.

it is with Holy Scripture.[34] And, although the description of Luther and organized Protestant sects proceeds with noteworthy objectivity—an objectivity assessed by Teufel as the "historical relativism of mystical spiritualism" [35]—Franck does not manage to conceal his discontent with the organized critics of Rome. He opposes the "many who today make an idol out of Scripture," [36] and his avowed "neutrality" vis-à-vis Luther is expressed in the words: "Inasmuch as I can neither believe, grasp, nor understand his theology, I will not judge it." [37] Müntzer, whose *Special Exposé* Franck has obviously read closely, is censured for "sounding too rebellious." [38] And the Anabaptists, whom Franck describes as the most divided and disunited of all the sects,[39] are lectured for not understanding sufficiently that God wants men gathered together "more in heart, spirit, and faith than in body, time, and place in external ceremonies." [40]

Franck's aloofness and criticism notwithstanding, the Anabaptists remained his closest ideological kin. By his own account they shared with him the *synteresis* anthropology of medieval mysti-

34. "Hie wirstu augenscheinlich sehen und mit verwunderung hören/das yr ding eben so wenig auff den alten decreten der heiligen vätter/concilien/und bäptsten steet/als auff der schrift." Ibid., p. cccxxxvii a.

35. Teufel, *"Landräumig,"* p. 48: "Der mystische Spiritualismus klingt hier in historischem Relativismus aus." Franck depicts himself as being above and beyond all the competing ideologies of the world: "Ich kan gott hab lob als ein unparteischer ungefangner/ein yeden lesen/und bin keiner sect oder menschen auff erden also gefangen/das mir nit zügleich alle frumme von hertzen gefallen . . . dann Christi meines gottes und mitlers in des gehorsam ich mein vernunfft allein gefangen nymm" (*Chronica, Zeytbüch und Geschichtbibel,* p. A ii a). It is interesting, however, that, simultaneous with this boast, Franck informs the reader that he has deleted "was zu wissen unnötig ist/das nitt ein besunder geheimnüs nutz oder wunderwerck gottes auff ihm hatt" and highlighted what best promotes knowledge of God: "Das am meisten getriben und angezogen/das die art der weissheit gottes aussdruckt und die gotseligkeit fürnemlich fürdert und antrifft." Ibid., p. A i.

36. Ibid., p. cccxxxvii b.

37. Ibid., p. ccccxviii a.

38. "Lauten sein Episteln zuvil auffrürisch" (ibid., p. ccccxl a). Franck reports that Anabaptists have defended Müntzer, although many of his followers in Thuringia are not Anabaptists.

39. "Wiewol alle Secten in jnen selbs zerspalten seind/so seind doch sunderlich die Teuffer also under einander uneynig und zerrissen/dass ich nichts gewiss und endtlichs von jnen zu schreiben weiss." Ibid., p. ccccxlv b; cf. cccclij a. Franck considers Hubmaier, Melchoir Rinck, Hut, Denck, and Haetzer to be the "vorsteher and bischoff" of Anabaptism (ibid., p. ccccxlv a). On this matter, cf. R. Weiss, "Die Herkunft der osthessischen Täufer," *ARG* 50 (1959): 1–16, 182–99; John S. Oyer, "Anabaptism in Central Germany," *MQR* 34 (1960): 219–48; *MQR* 35 (1961): 5–37.

40. *Chronica, Zeytbüch und Geschichtbibel,* p. cccclii a.

cism,[41] and, usually in more modest form, they adopted from this important foundation much the same critical posture toward Rome and Wittenberg.[42] If we can assume that Franck's private letter to his friend John Campanus was written in the same year as the *Chronicle of World History*,[43] then we have a highly partisan summary of Franck's sincerest feelings about contemporary religious movements and institutions at this early date. This en-

41. Franck writes of the Anabaptists: "Der merer teyl helt/Got/Christus/sein wort/und geist sey in allen menschen. Dann der heylig geist strafft die welt umb die sünd in aller menschen gewissen. So sey das nagendt würmlin und fincklin/das Gottes wort entpfach fähig sey und uns allzeit über sich zeucht/Gottes reich und geist in uns" (ibid., p. cccxlviii a). On the *synteresis* anthropology among the magisterial Anabaptists, see in regard to Denck, above, p. 121; in regard to Hubmaier, David C. Steinmetz, "Scholasticism and Radical Reform: Nominalist Motifs in the Theology of Balthasar Hubmaier," *MQR* 45, no. 2 (1971); and in regard to Pilgram Marbeck, Horst Quiring, "The Anthropology of Pilgram Marbeck," *MQR* 9 (1935): 155–64. Horst Weigelt argues that it is precisely at the point of the *scintilla* concept that the Anabaptist and spiritualist, Caspar Schwenckfeld, differs from Franck. "Für den Donauwörther war nämlich die Wiedergeburt, die ihren Anknüpfungspunkt in der scintilla hat, konstitutiv für das Heil des Menschen, für den schlesischen Edelmann hingegen der immerwährende spirituelle Genuss des deifizierten Fleisches des erhöhten Christus." "Sebastian Franck und Caspar Schwenckfeld in ihren Beziehungen zueinander," *Zeitschrift für Bayerische Kirchengeschichte* 39 (1970): 3–19, 15. Cf. E. Hirsch, "Zum Verständnis Schwenckfelds," *Festgabe für Karl Müller* (Tübingen, 1922), pp. 145–70, 155–56.

42. Franck, for example, points out that some Anabaptists are inclined to mystical ecstasy, dreams, and visions and eschew externals: "Etlichen kumpt dise verzuckung [2 Cor. 11] oft/etlichen selten/vilen gar nit. Vil under yhnen halten gross bede auff gesicht und treüm/ettlich gar nichts." Further, "etlich halten weder auff predig noch auff bücher." And some argue that "weil wir bücher haben so sey noch kein Christus vorhanden. Dise halten auch nit vil auff alle eüsser predigt und schrifft/ meynen wir müssen all on mittel von got geleert werden. Auch das die schrifft Gots wort sey/und man on dise wol gleubig und selig werden mög. Sihe J. Denck articel. Item Ludwig Hetzers/Thome mintzers. etc." *Chronica, Zeytbüch und Geschichtbibel*, p. cccxlvii a; cf. cccli b. Wilhelm Wiswedel's defense of the central importance of the Bible for the Anabaptists is weakened not only by Franck's contemporary report, but also by the fact that the sources he cites in support are really appealing to the Bible *against* the Bible, at least as established Christendom in the sixteenth century would view the latter. "Zum 'Problem inneres und äusseres Wort' bei den Täufern des 16. Jahrhunderts," *ARG* 46 (1955), esp. p. 19.

43. The surviving Dutch translation of this letter dates it in February, 1541, the surviving German translation, 1531. See G. H. Williams (who opts for the earlier date), *Spiritual and Anabaptist Writers*, p. 147, n. 4. It seems to me that the important appendix to chapter 30 of the *Chronicle of the Turks* argues in favor of the earlier date. Here we find the first statement of the themes of the fall of the church and the superiority of spiritual to Lutheran, Zwinglian, and Anabaptist external religion. See above, n. 18. These are also the central themes of the letter and reflect accurately the philosophical concerns of the 1531 *Chronicle of World History*.

gaging letter harvests the fruits of the two chronicles. Here Franck
maintains (as he also does in the *Chronicle of the Turks*)[44] that
the church fell with the death of the original apostles and disciples,
and he goes on to dismiss the magisterial church fathers as simply
"wolves, doctors of unwisdom, apes of the apostles, and antichrists." [45] The letter closes with a blunt conclusion, which, significantly and surely not accidentally, excludes only the Anabaptists from blanket judgment: "In brief, all that we have learned
since childhood from the papists, we must all of a sudden unlearn.
Again, the same for what we have received from Luther and
Zwingli—all must be abandoned and altered." [46]

Before concluding this consideration of Franck's historical work
as an exposé of human corruption, especially in circles of highest
power, it is instructive to take account of a work he proudly entitled, *Four Regal Little Books*.[47] The first of the four is Franck's
German translation of Erasmus's *Praise of Folly*. Then follows his
translation of Agrippa of Nettisheim's *On the Wretchedness,
Vanity and Uncertainty of All Human Arts and Wisdom,* to which
is appended a translation of Agrippa's *Praise of the Donkey*. The
final two works are, at least in part, Franck's own contributions:
On the Tree of the Knowledge of Good and Evil[48] and *A Praise
of the Foolish Word of God*. Each book is a specialized, basically
satirical exposé of human folly. Franck comments in his brief
preface:

> Kind reader, I have wanted to bring these four regal little
> books together in one volume because they all have one argu-
> ment and purpose, namely [to show] that, before God, the
> course, nature, piety, and wisdom of the whole world is noth-
> ing but vanity, stupidity, sin, fable, and horror. And hence
> that God's word is to the world a cross, foolishness, and thorn
> in the eye, because it censures and attacks the vanity which
> the world is even when it is at its best. Therefore, these books

44. Above, n. 18.
45. *A Letter to John Campanus* in *Spiritual and Anabaptist Writers*, p. 150.
46. Ibid., p. 160.
47. *Die vier Kronbüchlin* (Ulm, 1534). Often listed under the title of the first
selection: *Das Theür und künftlich Buchlin Morie Encomion/das ist/Ein Lob der
Thorheit/von Erasmo Roterodamo. . . .*
48. A London, 1642, translation under the title, *The Forbidden Fruit or A
Treatise on the Tree of Knowledge of Good and Evil*, exists.

mock all human wisdom and piety and press everything toward a new birth.[49]

Erasmus's *Praise of Folly* is familiar enough. The selections from Agrippa, much more sharply than the other works, bring the traditional Christian exaltation of love (will) over knowledge (intellect) to the brink of aggressive anti-intellectualism and anti-institutionalism. The injustice and evil of "learned" governments is documented,[50] and the conclusion is drawn that human arts are the gift of the Serpent, which the converted faithful "let fall, unlearn, and forget as an obstacle to grace and faith." [51] The selection from Agrippa's *Praise of the Donkey*—the donkey being honored here as the prototype of the true Christian[52]—pursues somewhat more jocularly the same basic theme. Balaam's ass appears among the surprisingly numerous distinguished donkeys in biblical and secular history to prompt the observation by Agrippa: "Often a wretched, coarse idiot . . . sees what the great schoolteachers and doctors, ruined and corrupted by human arts, cannot see." [53]

In the first of what are apparently his own offerings, *On the Tree of the Knowledge of Good and Evil,* Franck develops the theme that the tree forbidden Adam was human wisdom, reason, and arts, which prevent men from "becoming as fools and children." [54] "All knowledge and every art," Franck maintains, "which God himself does not plant and teach in man by his holy finger, spirit, and word, i.e. all knowledge and every art which are taken in from without, from the teaching and lessons of men, are death,

---

49. *Die vier Kronbüchlin,* p. A ii a.

50. Ibid., 91 b ff.

51. "Die Gottgläubigen haben all jr vorigen künst/als ein obstackel der gnad und des glaubens lassen fallen/entlernet und vergessen." Ibid., p. 85 b. Cf. p. 79 b for a more cautious statement.

52. Agrippa summarizes: "Auss disem nu/so itzt gesagt ist clärer dann die Sonn/das kein Thier der Gotheit so vähig ist/als Esel/in welchen wo jr mit bekert werdet/so köndt jr zwar das hailigthumb/das ist/die Gottliche gehaimnus/nit tragen noch vernemen/Wie Christus zu den Aposteln sagt/ehe sie recht zu Eseln worden/Ich hab euch vil zu sagen/aber jr mögt es itzt nit tragen etc. Christus müst sie erst zu rechten Eseln machen/und der hailig Gaist allein in jn wissen/weyss und clüg sein/sie Esel/Kinder und Narren bleiben/on alle annemung einicher witz/kunst/willens/namens/etc." Ibid., p. 89 a.

53. Ibid., p. 85 b.

54. "Der baum ist nun in unser hertz versetzt/und ist nu nichts anders dann unser weyssheit vernunft/und des flaisch kunst/und wil/weil wir daran hangen/und nit zu narren und kindern werden." Ibid., p. 138 b.

truly an idol." [55] The last of the regal books, *A Praise of the Foolish Word of God,* belabors the distinction between God's external and internal word and concludes that ultimately only one art need be mastered: "The true magic and theology, which is to know God and his word in God and to be taught by God himself, is the single art needed for happiness." [56]

Humanists and Protestant reformers had already unmasked the sophistry of scholastics with satire and biting polemic. Franck's attack on the learned may be of another order. Hegler, for example, points out that, while fighting from the same corner as humanists and Protestants, Franck "battles generally against the learned world's claim to be of independent significance," whether it be the learned world of mossback scholastics or that of young Protestant divines.[57] Perhaps we could go still further and suggest that, rather than humanist satire or Protestant polemic, Franck's publication of the *Four Regal Little Books* is best classified as part and parcel of his historical exposé. It seeks not only to unmask abuse but also to expose sub specie aeternitatis the totally insubstantial character of human arts per se.

The second purpose of the 1531 chronicle as a form of dissent is constructive. It provides material for an alternative source and definition of the rules by which man's destiny is supposedly fixed. The critical exposé of human folly and corruption goes hand in hand with the revelation of the truth. Franck will find truth not in the writings of the contemporary experts who command tradition but in the free field of world history. It is not accidental that his *Chronicle of World History* is entitled a "Geschichtbibel." "The whole world and all creatures," he writes in the preface, "will be to you nothing else than an open book and a living Bible, in which you may study, without any previous introduction, the science of God [*gottes kunst*] and learn his will." [58] The written

55. Ibid., p. 141 a. Franck elsewhere cites Tauler (p. 129 a) and the *Theologia Deutsch* (p. 130 a), and mentions Agrippa's first treatise when he censures human arts (p. 153 a).

56. "Die recht Magia/und Theologei/das ist Gott und sein Wort/in Gott kennen/und das selbig von Gott gelert wissen/ist allein die einige kunst/zur seeligkeit von nöten." Ibid., p. 155 b. The clearly anti-Lutheran conclusion that salvation can occur without Scripture and preaching—*as a rule,* not as an exception —follows as a logical consequence. Ibid., p. 176 b.

57. Hegler, *Geist und Schrift bei Sebastian Franck,* p. 113.

58. *Chronica, Zeytbüch und Geschichtbibel,* p. A iiij a. Compare Hut's "gospel of all creatures," above, pp. 105 ff.

Bible itself cedes to this living Bible. David teaches in the Psalms that all creatures preach to the man who is taught by God, and Christ never spoke to the people without parables and examples taken from God's creatures and works in the world.[59]

Not only is history a "living Bible" where one can learn immediately the nature of God, but it is also a definitive "key" to the meaning of the written Bible itself. What the Holy Spirit is subjectively and proleptically to Scripture, history is objectively and retrospectively: the final interpreter of the will of God. As Franck puts it:

> Because the [historical] event, example, experience, and fulfillment of things straightway elucidates prophecy, events and examples are esteemed by many as a key to the teaching [of Scripture] [*ein schlüssel der leer*]. The event or experience informs and enlivens the sheer letter of Scripture as a spirit, soul, and living understanding. Often one finds [clearly] in an event what is only darkly taught by the words of Scripture and sees before his eyes and actually experiences what he has heard there. That is why, for those who understand them, the Holy Spirit is and remains the divine key to all prophecies until they are fulfilled by an event.[60]

For Franck, history truly "lives." Albeit recorded, it is still actual experience, and, more than any other textbook, it can speak with lasting effect about human nature and destiny.

> Because so much lies in experience and we are not inclined to believe before we see, I esteem and value histories before all textbooks because histories live [*die historien lebt*], and doctrine alone is a dead letter. Had Adam been able to see an example of his fall before his eyes and had not been forced to rely on sheer doctrine and an [abstract] commandment, perhaps he and we would all still be in paradise today.[61]

The practical consequence of these comments is that, vis-à-vis the oppressive masters of Scripture and tradition, one can now con-

---

59. Ibid., p. A iiij a. Psalm 19 and Matthew 13 are cited as documentation.

60. Ibid., p. A iiij b. Arnold Reimann summarizes: "Die Geschichte ist ihm [Franck] Fleisch gewordener Geist Gottes." *Sebastian Franck als Geschichtsphilosoph: Ein moderner Denker im 16. Jahrhundert* (Berlin, 1921), p. 56.

61. *Chronica, Zeytbüch und Geschichtbibel*, p. A v a.

struct an authoritative view of life from experience—both recorded and personal. What history is as the manifest past working
of God, the Holy Spirit is now in one's own present experience.
Every individual life becomes for Franck a kind of "chronicle"
of God's work, an explication of the nature of God, truly a "living
Bible." Present personal experience—what can also be called the
voice of conscience or reason or feeling—like recorded historical
experience, is a key to the divine secrets. It is not too much to say
that the study of history and the observation of oneself are the
final science of God. Franck puts it so:

> The living histories and experiences, especially those which
> God himself brings about in every man, [as] he directs [each]
> by experience from one [thing] to another, teach us every-
> thing. He who attends to his own life, observes what God is
> doing with him, and sees how God leads him in and out of
> all things from his youth, will become aware of a great deal
> and have a personal chronicle to write of his own life. . . .
> Living faith must also be learned and received in experience.
> . . . The inner man believes only what he has learned, heard,
> seen, and experienced of God in accordance with his own
> nature [*glaubt . . . der inner mensch allein was er nach
> seiner art innerlich von Gott gelert/gehort/gesehen/und
> erfaren hat*]. . . . For this reason experience is like a key to
> Scripture.[62]

Later, in his controversial treatise, *The Golden Ark* (*Die güldene
Arch,* 1538), Franck proclaims: "The heart of the believer is a
living office of the Holy Spirit and a basic library, bookstore, and
Bible, out of which all the books of truth are written and cer-
tified." [63]

Franck's concluding words to the reader in the preface to the
Chronicle of World History bring together in personal address the
two purposes of the chronicle as a form of dissent. Dire pessimism
(the conclusion to be drawn from the chronicle as an exposé) is
balanced once again by hope in a "spark of God's light" in the

62. Ibid. In the *Paradoxa* Franck attacks the "inexperienced" priesthood, and
speaks of "das lebendige Wort," which is proclaimed to everyone already "aus der
Kanzlei und lebendigen Bibel ihres Herzens." *Sebastian Franck Paradoxa,* ed. S.
Wollgast (Berlin, 1966), p. 287.
63. Cited by Hegler, *Geist und Schrift bei Sebastian Franck,* p. 103.

heart of the reader (a conclusion which can be drawn from the chronicle as a source of a new version of the *potentia Dei ordinata*).

> I worry that the world is now and forever neither to be advised nor helped with writing, crying, preaching, etc. . . . But if something living and a spark of God's light is still present within one, I hope he will better himself in all things and find many witnesses to what is in his own heart from my work.[64]

PARLEY WITH THE LUTHERANS IN ULM

Due largely to the zeal of his former schoolmate in Heidelberg and present guardian of the Reformation in Strasbourg, Martin Bucer, and, to a lesser degree, to complaints from such dignitaries as Erasmus (who was not complimented by his inclusion in Franck's list of noble heretics), Franck's *Chronicle of World History* brought the kind of notoriety which led to his imprisonment and subsequent dismissal from Strasbourg. After an unsuccessful attempt to return to the city, Franck moved on to Kehl and, by the autumn of 1532, Esslingen where, although pursued by Bucer's disapproval, he received citizenship and took up the unprofitable but noncontroversial occupation of soap-making. In the late summer of 1533 Franck presented himself to the mayor of Ulm, Georg Besserer, and requested admission either to nearby Geislingen or to Ulm. Besserer, impressed by Franck, passed on the request with a favorable recommendation to his father and former mayor of Ulm, Bernhard Besserer in Augsburg.[65] With the backing of the powerful Besserers, Franck, together with his wife and two children, was accepted into the city without a decision by the town council. In October, 1534, the right of citizenship was granted, however with the ominous condition that it could be withdrawn should his writings bring imperial threat or other harm to the city.[66]

Franck was not only successful in obtaining citizenship in Ulm. He also returned to his true profession of writing and publishing. He assisted the Ulm printer, Hans Varnier, in the publication of his *Four Regal Little Books* and the *Paradoxa* (1534). And,

64. *Chronica, Zeytbüch und Geschichtbibel,* p. A vi b.
65. Teufel, *"Landräumig,"* pp. 35–36, 54–55. The letter of the younger Besserer is in Julius Endriss, *Sebastian Francks Ulmer Kämpfe* (Ulm, 1935), pp. 34–35.
66. Teufel, *"Landräumig,"* p. 55.

thanks to the patronage of a former Donauwörth Anabaptist now
resident in Augsburg, Georg Regel, he was in the process of
establishing his own printing press, which was to include a rare
and lucrative set of Hebrew type.[67] But this good fortune was
overshadowed before it could be realized by a letter of warning to
the city (dated December 31, 1534) from Landgraf Philip of Hesse,
the last link in an apparently conspiratorial chain that began with
the Ulm preacher Martin Frecht (also a former schoolmate of
Franck's in Heidelberg) and ran through Bucer and Philip
Melanchthon, who was the person most immediate to Landgraf
Philip. In his letter, Landgraf Philip stated that Franck was to be
considered an "obvious revolutionary and Anabaptist" and suggested that the city spare itself suspicion by turning him away.[68]

So threatened, the city council passed a resolution on January
25, 1535, ordering Franck to depart within a month. But exercising
his right as a citizen to a hearing, Franck received a temporary
suspension of this order. Then, on March 3, two resolutions were
passed by the council, the first demanding only that Franck neither
write nor publish anything without imperial permission, the
second, however, ordering him to depart the city by June 24 and
forbidding publication of his works in the intervening time.[69]

This decision prompted a second supplication by Franck. In an
eloquent statement he offered to answer orally or in writing all the
charges directed against him. He disavowed any connection with
heretics and Anabaptists ("nie angehangen bin"), mocked his
accusers ("they will perhaps soon call me *Münsterisch*"),[70] and in-

67. Ibid., pp. 57–58; Endriss, *Francks Ulmer Kämpfe,* pp. 36–37; Weigelt, *JbKG* 39
(1970): 10 ff.

68. "Man ine offentlich fur ainen aufrurischen und widerteufer erkennen und
vernemen möge." Document in Alfred Hegler, *Beiträge zur Geschichte der Mystik
in der Reformationszeit,* ed. Walther Köhler, *Archiv für Reformationsgeschichte:
Texte und Untersuchungen,* Ergänzungsband 1 (Berlin, 1906) [hereafter cited as
Hegler-Köhler], p. 114. Cf. Teufel, *"Landräumig,"* p. 58.

69. Hegler-Köhler, p. 115; Endriss, p. 14; Teufel, *"Landräumig,"* p. 59; Peuckert,
Sebastian Franck, pp. 266–67.

70. Hegler-Köhler, p. 117. The reference is of course to events in the city of
Münster in 1534–35. Radical Anabaptists under the leadership of John Matthys and
John of Leiden gained control of the city and proceeded to restructure life on the
model of an Old Testament theocracy. See Fritz Blanke, "Das Reich der Wiedertäufer zu Münster 1534/35," *ARG* 37 (1940): 13–37, and Norman Cohn, *The Pursuit
of the Millenium,* 2d ed. (New York, 1961), pp. 283 ff. Further bibliography on
Münster in G. H. Williams, "Studies in the Radical Reformation (1517–1618): A
Bibliographical Survey of Research Since (1939)," *Church History* 27, no. 2 (1958):
129.

sisted on the neutrality and wholesomeness of his writings: "My books have assisted no sect or rebellion, nor is there now to be found anything in them which would discredit any particular person or realm." [71] With uncharacteristic but understandable capitulation, Franck pledged:

> I am more than happy to lay down the pen, and I wish, with the help and favor of God and devout people, to establish and operate here in your sovereign realm a worthy and distinguished printing press (for which I already have several hundred gulden). There I shall publish solid and noteworthy books in every language and tongue, and with the condition that I will not only not publish what is forbidden but, further, I will let not one letter be printed which does not serve to edify and unite. Thereby the city of Ulm, my city, my child's city, our common city, shall benefit, receive honor, prosper and increase.[72]

The eloquent pledge culminates in the poignant plea:

> Should your grace take away my citizenship [*mich . . . burgerlich tödten*] and without farewell expel me from your realm and land, I would never again be able to return, and hence I would be an outlaw and a man without a place [*landröumig und geächt*], who must die many times each day rather than just once someday.[73]

A hearing having been granted, a committee under the leadership of Franck's chief adversary, Martin Frecht, was appointed. In the report of the Frecht committee, paradoxes 124/25, 163, 44, and 171 from Franck's recently published *Two Hundred and Eighty Paradoxes* (the *Paradoxa*) were cited as needing clarification if Franck were to avoid classification among "those spirits who . . . write and babble about nothing but the inner word, spirit, calling, sacraments, church, and their own revelations, visions, and dreams." [74] It is further pointed out that such statements in Franck's writings

> make him suspect and distrusted not only among Lutheran, but also among what one calls "Zwinglian" preachers. [For

71. Hegler-Köhler, p. 118.
72. Ibid., pp. 118–19.
73. Ibid., p. 120.
74. Ibid., p. 124.

they make it appear] that Franck desires to diminish or destroy the true art, practice, and custom of the external service of the word [of God] in the church, and thereby possibly create unspeakable error and unrest.[75]

A brief look at the indicated paradoxes helps one to understand Frecht's confusion and concern about Franck's true intentions.[76] Paradoxes 124/25 deal with Scripture or the written word of God as an image and shadow of the living, inner word of God.[77] "One should assign happiness only to the inner, living word of God," Franck writes, "which Christ was to the ancients [before there was a written word], and not bind it to the external word or Scripture, however effective Scripture may always be for those who have received from God an understanding of it." [78] Paradox 163—"The Languages and Arts of the Godless are Unclean"—seems to accuse the learned of intellectual Pelagianism while approvingly urging a kind of spiritual Donatism. "Those who now want to be learned about God through much reading and writing and many books, arts, and languages do precisely the same thing as those who want to be righteous through good works." [79] Franck argues that "God needs no external means to perform his inner work," and he brings forth half a page of quotations from Tauler as proof.[80] Paradox 44 again marshals support from Tauler to maintain that God "teaches (one who is *gelassen*) more in a flashing moment than all external words, sermons, and Scripture until the end of time." [81] Paradox 171—"Without a Calling No One Can Be a Pastor"—seems to skirt the borders of Donatism, as it demands an experienced and morally

75. Ibid., p. 125.

76. Teufel, it seems to me, is excessively partisan when he concludes: "Man darf vielleicht neben dem Glaubensfanatismus als zweites Motiv bei Frecht eine gewisse Eifersucht auf Franck als Geschichtsschreiber vermuten" (*"Landräumig,"* p. 56). Peuckert is no more impartial with his overall conclusion of the entire investigation of Franck: "Es geht nicht um die Sache, denn die Sache wird im innersten Grunde kaum verstanden, und wo man sie versteht, da ist sie diesen Menschen sicher nicht entscheidend—es geht nur [*sic*] um die Auseinandersetzung zwischen dem freien, nur dem Geiste Unterworfenen, und denen, die man am besten, als den ewigen Kleinbürger charakterisieren wird." *Sebastian Franck*, p. 281.

77. Franck also refers the reader to his *Praise of the Foolish Word of God*, which, as we saw, made mastery of the inner word the only necessary art. Cf. above, p. 148.

78. *Paradoxa*, p. 206.

79. Ibid., p. 267.

80. Ibid., pp. 267–68.

81. Ibid., p. 88.

upright (i.e. "called") rather than merely learned and duly appointed ministry: "Although one [who is not called] may be able to take a Bible in hand and, without a single error, explicate its contents, he still does it in vain and preaches absolutely nothing. For God is not in what he says." [82] The anti-intellectualism behind this requirement comes to the surface as Franck berates the learned theologians with a favorite paradox: "the more learned, the more perverted." [83]

Still more expressive of establishment anxiety is the case against Franck which the Ulm School Board, also under Frecht's direction, assembled. This report goes beyond the first Frecht committee's findings by documenting Franck's alleged misdealings and heterodoxy. He is accused of engineering the publication of two works of the spiritualist friend of Caspar Schwenckfeld, Valentin Crautwaldt, in which the necessity of the external means of grace is denied.[84] Evidence is brought forth from the *Paradoxa* and the 1531 chronicle to link Franck with the teaching of Anabaptists and spiritualists. He is accused, together with Denck and Haetzer, of exalting the "book of the heart"—God's "word and seed" in the hearts of all men—over historical authority (i.e. Scripture and tradition).

> (Franck) has written publicly at the end of the last paradox (where one normally expects to find the best) that Scripture and every book which testifies to God should be read, not for doctrine [*zür leer*], but only as a witness [*züm zeugnusz*], and that everyone should above all learn of God by reading the book of his own heart and listening to the voice of the Lamb and Word within himself. Denck and Haetzer have taught and written the same thing, viz. that God's word and seed

82. Ibid., p. 285; cf. p. 289.

83. Ibid., p. 286. Earlier cited as paradox 65, where the stinging judgment of the learned occurs: "Wer hat (Christum) und seine Boten töten lassen . . . als die Gelehrtesten, Weisesten und Frömmsten im Volk?" (ibid., p. 108). It also appears in the preface to Franck's *Weltbuch: Spiegel und Bildtnisz des ganzen Erdbodens* (Tübingen, 1534), the first geography in the German language, which was written in 1531 and originally intended for publication as Book 4 of the *Chronicle of World History*. It was subsequently published separately in 1534 in Tübingen. Cf. Peuckert, *Sebastian Franck*, p. 157. The statement is also to be found in Franck's last writing, the Latin paraphrase of the *Theologia Deutsch*. Cf. above, p. 35, n. 65.

84. Hegler-Köhler, p. 130; Weigelt *ZbKG* 39 (1970): 11–12. Paradoxes 163 and 226 are cited as confirmation of Franck's independent support of this position.

is placed in the hearts of all men, and hence each must be taught by the preaching of the Lamb from his birth on.[85]

The school board's authorities in these matters were Luther, Bucer, and the conservative Lutheran theologian, Nicholas of Amsdorf. The latter, in the wake of the revolutionary events in the city of Münster, had written a treatise against "Anabaptists and Sacramentarians [i.e. Zwinglians]," in which Franck was censured as a "coarse and unlearned fellow" because of an alleged misinterpretation of Luther's views on the Eucharist in the 1531 chronicle.[86] Exaggerated or not, the school board harbored apparently sincere fears that Franck's teaching could bring a version of the Münster affair to Ulm. The report culminated in the suggestion that Franck and Schwenckfeld, who, probably by coincidence, seemed constantly to be trailing Franck from town to town,[87] were in league to create a new church.

> We are told that there is now no true calling, service, pulpit, administration, or reception of the sacraments in the Lutheran and Zwinglian churches. Rather, one awaits the appearance of the *ministerium spiritus,* the true office of the Holy Spirit, which will perhaps come from the Silesian [i.e. Schwenckfeldian] and Franckian churches, although Franck, in the preface to the *Paradoxa,* vigorously denies that he awaits a new church. The two above-mentioned books which have been published here in Ulm [viz. the two Crautwald volumes] indicate otherwise.[88]

Franck had said earlier that his accusers would perhaps soon call him "Münsterisch." It is more a measure of establishment panic at the revolutionary events in the city of Münster than of Franck's prophetic powers that precisely this accusation was now made. Continued attacks on "externals" and the imperfections of

---

85. Hegler-Köhler, p. 131. The 1531 chronicle, wherein Franck places Denck, Haetzer, and Müntzer together as exponents of the sovereignty of the internal word, is cited. Cf. above, n. 42.

86. Hegler-Köhler, pp. 135–36. On Amsdorf's treatise see Teufel, *"Landräumig,"* p. 51.

87. Teufel's assessment is probably correct: "Von Nürnberg nach Strassburg, von da nach Esslingen, von dort nach Ulm ist Schwenckfeld unsrem Franck wie sein Schatten gefolgt. Man darf daraus keine Schlüsse auf enge Gesinnungsgemeinschaft ziehen. Franck war und blieb durchaus Einzelgänger." Ibid., p. 53. Cf. Weigelt *ZbKG* 39 (1970).

88. Hegler-Köhler, p. 136.

the established clergy, the school board warned, could eventually lead to anarchy: "In time there could come in place of the external pulpit nothing but spiritual speculations about the inner word, visions, and revelation, as one now unfortunately beholds in the affair at Münster." [89]

Finally, the issue between Franck and the city fathers of Ulm—indeed, the issue between every sixteenth-century dissenter and established authority generally—was succinctly brought to a head as the school board lectured Franck on the distinction between God's absolute and ordained powers. The medieval theologian had prevented (theoretically if not always practically) the absolutizing of the political and ecclesiastical status quo by distinguishing between God's absolute and ordained (or covenanted) powers. A truly omnipotent God could, it was argued, conduct the affairs of the world without secondary causes and external means, ignoring the princes and laws, priests and sacraments he himself had ordained for the regular execution of his bidding. The most popular example of this divine freedom to work extraordinarily was the conversion of Paul on the road to Damascus—an example of salvation executed directly without external mediation of any kind.[90] Franck drew on this medieval tradition when he argued in the censured 118th paradox that, for 3,684 years (i.e. from Adam to Moses, according to the calculations of Eusebius and Philo), no Scripture or other externals existed and "still there was abundant knowledge of God." [91]

In opposition to Franck and all who would attempt to collapse the *potentia Dei ordinata* into the *potentia Dei absoluta*—which would theoretically remove the divine mandate from all vested authority—the school board moved to absorb the *potentia Dei absoluta* into the *potentia Dei ordinata,* which would theoretically absolutize vested authority:

> Sebastian Franck should not have written what he announces in paradox 44: "The Master (God) teaches us more in one

89. Ibid., p. 136. The German has "in der Müntzeriche sach," indicating Thomas Müntzer rather than the city of Münster. The editors suggest that the reference to "now" (i.e. 1535) indicates, rather, that the latter is intended. It seems quite plausible in fact that Müntzer and Münster could be used interchangeably by a Lutheran establishment like Ulm. Earlier in the report, reference is made to "Müntzeriche gaister" who separate the internal and external word as Franck does in paradox 174. Ibid., p. 131.

90. Cf. Oberman, *The Harvest of Medieval Theology,* pp. 30–56; esp. 45–46.

91. *Paradoxa,* pp. 196–97.

flashing moment than all external words, sermons, and Scripture until the end of time." It is true that, *potentia absoluta*, by his completely perfect omnipotence, God can do absolutely anything. He can, as one says, make an ax under a bench crow. But one should speak *de potentia dei ordinata*, of God's orderly [use of his] power, as he has employed it in his word and works. [Then one sees] that he . . . gives his grace through the means of his word and sacraments [as these are set forth through] servants chosen by him. He also dealt with the [old Testament] fathers *by word of mouth* before the law was given. And Christ converted Paul from heaven by *word of mouth*.[92]

There is and always has been only one true medium of God's power and truth—the spoken, audible word, heard by the patriarchs, the apostle Paul on the road to Damascus, and all who are obediently attendant upon the service of worship in the local Lutheran church. That is the board's final word to Franck.

In conclusion, the school board challenged Franck either to renounce or to clarify the following motifs from his writings: (1) that God's grace is given without external means; (2) that Scripture is not God's word; (3) that he teaches differently than do the church-fathers (who were quite learned about God) on such subjects as external and internal word, letter and spirit, Old and New Testament, and the ministry; (4) that scripture is to be read not for doctrine but only as a witness, contrary to the expressed words of Paul in 2 Timothy 3[: 16]; and (5) that the godless do not preach the gospel of Christ and have neither calling nor office as priests. Finally, Franck is asked to comment on how peace and unity may best be achieved in the church.[93]

As his earlier supplication to the council made clear, Franck considered exile perpetual death. He wished intensely to remain with his family in the city, and he knew that he must now argue his case as he had never argued it before.

His extended response to the charges brought against him is

---

92. Hegler-Köhler, p. 137 (emphasis mine).

93. The earlier Frecht committee also asked for clarification of these themes together with the following: what Agrippa says about Scripture in the work translated by Franck; how the liberal arts can be from the Devil and still remain God's gifts; and Franck's description of Ulm and Augsburg in the *Chronicle of World History*. Hegler-Köhler, p. 129.

as precise an illustration of mystical theology in the service of dissent as one will find in the sixteenth century.[94] Here Franck's presuppositions about human nature and destiny, and thereby the final justification for his critique of contemporary institutions, are made fully explicit. Slowly but deliberately, with logic and carefully elicited traditional support, Franck brings into focus a deceptively simple theological correlation, the ultimate inspiration of which, as we will see, is Tauler and Eckhart. What Franck finally must conclude about the disputed issues is dependent upon his fidelity to the obvious logical consequences of this fateful correlation.

Basically it is this. Over against the external word visibly and audibly communicated through established institutions, Franck critically places a more primal internal word, spiritually communicated through established psychological structures in the depths of the soul. There is an eternal word, free from and sovereign over all written words, and, correlatively, an eternal soul, free from and sovereign over the life of the body. Together they always have and always will compose the essential terms of the true covenant between God and man. Franck's appeal in the following passage to the eighth chapter of Deuteronomy, which recalls the covenants God made with the patriarchs and with Moses, is hardly accidental. He makes this key locus for God's *historical* covenant subserve his invisible, eternal covenant.

> The inner, truly living, natural [*natürlich* (!)], and almighty word of the Father, which in recent times has become flesh, and is taken to be the seed of Abraham and named "Christ" in the New Testament, is that which goes forth directly from the mouth of God, Deuteronomy 8, through which everything is created, sustained, nourished, and preserved, Hebrews 1[: 2]. This word is eternal; indeed, it is God himself, John

94. Teufel is to the point: "In diesem umfassenden Bekenntnis von 40 Druckseiten steigen wir mit Franck in den tiefsten Brunnenschacht der deutschen Mystik hinunter und hören die Quellen rauschen, aus denen er schöpft. . . . Auf eine kurze Formel gebracht ist ihre Bedeutung folgende: Sie zeigt die deutsche Mystik, die für *Luther* nur ein *Durchgangspunkt* war, als den *Endpunkt* von *Francks* religiöser Entwicklung, und sie zeigt die endgültige Theologie Luthers als ein von Franck 1525 überwundenes Entwicklungsstadium" ("*Landräumig,*" p. 65). Teufel also points out that, save by Hegler, this pregnant work has been practically ignored (ibid.). Regarding Luther, Franck, and mysticism, cf. Joachimsen, *Blätter für deutsche Philosophie* 2 (1928/29): 16–17.

1[: 1], free from all created things [*elementen*], and incapable
of being spoken or written. God must himself utter it in our
soul and heart so that the word may also become flesh and
Christ be born in us.[95]

Franck marshals, with exact references, an impressive list of
witnesses to this word "indwelling and implanted within us": the
Old and New Testaments, Cyril of Alexandria, Augustine, Jerome,
Ambrose, Fulgentius, Thomas Aquinas, Tauler, the *German
Theology*, and John Staupitz.[96] He contrasts it critically with the
written and spoken word of God, which he says is but its "image,
shadow . . . and echo," and with its ministers, who are "only
a witness and a voice crying in the wilderness." [97] The matter
comes to rest on a heightened version of the traditional anthropological dualism between the inner and outer man.

> The outer word, like the visible outer man, is only a figure
> and image of the true inner word. And as much as the inner
> man, who is conceived by the seed of the living God and
> born from God himself through the Holy Spirit, John 1[: 13],
> 1 Peter 1[: 23], excels the outer, so much does the inner the
> outer word, just as the thing itself excels its shadow, the
> essence the figure, the man the image, and the spirit the
> flesh.[98]

Given these basic definitions, Franck is ready for a critical application of the principle of likeness, the crucial rule of medieval
epistemology and soteriology that only like can truly know and
relate to like. In epistemology this principle supported the thesis,
challenged only by the Ockhamists, that knowledge was always and
only of the universal. An immortal and immaterial soul could not
know directly something as different as transient finite particulars.
In soteriology this principle bulwarked the sacramental system of
the church. Only a soul purified of its sin and thereby "likened"
to God could expect to enter lasting union with him who is purity
itself.[99] Choosing no less a *locus classicus* of Lutheran theology than

---

95. Hegler-Köhler, p. 144; cf. p. 152.

96. Ibid., pp. 145–46. Franck also cites Schwenkfeld and Zwingli on the secondary
importance of the external word. Ibid., p. 146.

97. Ibid., p. 146.

98. Ibid.

99. Cf. my article "Homo Viator: Luther and Late Medieval Theology" in
Reformation in Medieval Perspective, pp. 142–54.

the *fides ex auditu* of Romans 10 : 17 to support his version of this highly un-Lutheran principle, Franck comments:

> Paul speaks to the matter when he says that "faith comes from hearing." Now as God is a spirit, he deals with our spirit only through the like spiritual means of his Word or Spirit [*alein durch ein gleich geistlich mittel seins worts oder geists*], just as he maintains and teaches our outer man through a like outer physical bread and word.[100]

The practical consequence, which Franck leaves for the reader to draw, is that the outer word (i.e. the books and sermons of established theologians and clergy) can make neither contact with nor claim upon the inner man (i.e. what the heart and conscience conclude about divine truth). "God alone is and remains the father, teacher, and preacher of the inner man through his like inner word [*durch sein gleich inner wort*]." [101]

Franck concedes very little to the servants of the outer man, and even that seems finally to be only coincidentally effectual. If the inner teacher sleeps, the outer labors in vain.[102] He writes tellingly of St. Paul:

> The letter [of Scripture] is also no teaching or light for the outer man, because God means and seeks something quite different from what the [bare] letter can show and do. Paul was a teacher of Scripture before his conversion. But after he turned to God, the curtain of this letter, which had shielded his eyes, was taken away, 2 Corinthians 3[: 6 ff., 14 ff.], and the seven seals of this closed book were broken. Then he could see and understand what God had meant with Moses.[103]

Luther, then, may be Franck's friend and colleague but never his way to final truth and salvation. As Hegler has memorably put it (speaking in regard to Franck's criticism of the *sola scriptura*): "As little as the reformers would accept, in the sense of the Roman church, the statement, 'extra ecclesiam nulla salus,' so little will

---

100. Hegler-Köhler, p. 147.

101. Ibid., p. 148.

102. "Soll aber der euszer zeug und diener Christi etwz schaffen und sein wort frucht pringen, so müsz alweg der inner prediger mit predigen dem hertzen und innern menschen" (ibid., p. 148). This is, of course, a very traditional truth, which Franck now employs polemically.

103. Ibid., p. 152.

Franck accept the [reformers' principle] 'sine scriptura nulla salus.' " [104] Every historical authority is absolutely penultimate.

It is in pursuit of the logic of this principle of likeness that Franck is led to conclude that faith and theology are "more an experience than a science." For how can one learn from another something for which the singular medium is personal experience of the thing itself?[105] On this point Franck can and does muster considerable support from Erasmus. When he comments on how one can best achieve unity in the church, he cedes to a nostalgic passage from Erasmus's preface to his edition of Hilary (Basel, 1523; 2d ed., 1535). This preface, censured by the Inquisition in Rome and the theological faculty of the University of Paris, argued theologically that "faith consists more in life than in the confession of articles." Historically, it maintained that this was the clue to unity in the primitive church before heresy forced a "literal reading of Scripture" and the unfortunate rise of conciliar authority.

> Then it was that faith began to exist more in writings than in the heart, and there were as many beliefs as there were men. Then articles [of faith] increased while the purity of the heart diminished. Quarreling got the upper hand, and love expired. The teaching of Christ, which knows no quarreling, then began to depend on the guidance of philosophy.[106]

It is also in pursuit of the same principle of likeness that Franck appears to skirt again the fringes of Donatism. "God," he tells us, "gives and works his light, kindness, Holy Spirit, life, etc. only through similarly illumined, kind, living, spiritual people. The Holy Spirit will not grace anyone through the Devil, but will rather work like through like [*sondern Gleiches durch das Gleich wirken will*]." [107] With the kind of disbelieving commonsense rationality that was to be Sebastian Castellio's hallmark,[108] Franck asked his inquisitors:

104. Hegler, *Geist und Schrift bei Sebastian Franck*, p. 79.
105. *Paradoxa*, no. 223, pp. 349–50.
106. Cited by Hegler-Köhler, p. 175.
107. *Paradoxa*, nos. 171–74, pp. 286–87.
108. Hegler, who left little unanticipated, called attention to the movement of the mystical toward the rational in Franck. "Neben dem mystischen Element, das durchaus das herrschende ist bei Franck wie bei den allermeisten der protestantischen Dissenters—erst im Sozinianismus ist das rationalistische massgebend und hat das mystische verdrängt—regt sich doch leise ein *rationalistischer* Zug." *Geist und Schrift bei Sebastian Franck*, p. 16. On Castellio, cf, below, pp. 191 ff.

How can one who is not in God's house build something within God's house? How can one who is blind preach about colors and talk about light which he does not see? How can a minister who is the Devil's slave, graceless and standing in disgrace, be an instrument of grace? How can one who does not have the Holy Spirit preach the Holy Spirit?[109]

The issue raised by Franck finally transcends the heresy of Donatism (or perhaps drives it to its most extreme conclusion). While his critique of the imperfection of social institutions suggests Donatism to his judges, his metaphysical presuppositions suggest a kind of theological nihilism. Ultimately, the problem is not the imperfection of institutions but institutions themselves.

In this regard it is perhaps not coincidental that Franck finally credits Tauler,[110] "whom Luther somewhere praises so highly," and Eckhart for the position he has set forth:

Tauler, whom I have followed (and whom Luther somewhere praises so highly . . .), sees the matter this way, for he writes in so many places that God works in our soul without visible means [*on mittel und bild*]. He teaches further that the more our soul is separated from visible things [*von bilden*] the more it is prepared to receive God's word [*seins einsprechens empfälicher*]. He who wishes can read about this in Tauler's other sermon on folio page 3,[111] and one can also read the third doctrine of Dr. Eckhart, which is appended to the sermons of Tauler as a summary and conclusion of all Tauler's sermons.[112] Time after time Tauler testifies that God uses no external means for his inner working.[113]

Franck brings this line of argument to a conclusion by returning to the covenant concept that initiated it. His comments now are

---

109. Hegler-Köhler, p. 159.

110. For a kind of theological nihilism in Tauler, cf. my *Homo Spiritualis*, p. 46.

111. The reader is referred to the 1508, 1521, and 1522 editions and pp. 106 ff. of the 1826 Frankfurt a/M edition. Hegler-Köhler, p. 148, n. 2.

112. Cf. ibid., p. 148, n. 3.

113. Ibid., p. 148. Franck also brings forward Luther and Staupitz in support of this teaching of Tauler (ibid., p. 149). For a now hackneyed, but still basically correct statement of the important differences between Franck and Luther on this score, see Heinrich Bornkamm, "Aeusserer und innerer Mensch bei Luther und den Spiritualisten," *Imago Dei: Beiträge zur theologischen Anthropologie. Festgabe für Gustav Krüger* (Giessen, 1932), pp. 85–109. Cf. below, p. 244, n. 191.

doubly instructive. On the one hand, they reveal the integration of this concept with the principle of likeness and, on the other hand, they indicate the close (and, in the sixteenth century at least, perhaps necessary) connection between the advocacy of toleration and anti-institutionalism.[114] Not institutions and their servants but the heart and conscience of the individual is God's exclusive domain.

> Let no one, therefore, presume either to kill, teach, judge, or give life to the human spirit or soul. Rather, let external instruments and teachers stick to the external man and not try to reach into God's region [*nit got in sein gebiet greifen*], and rule, teach, and master the conscience and heart or instruct and enlighten the soul. Rather, let this inner work be left completely to God's management, so that everything may remain in its own order [*damit alles in seiner ordnung gee*].[115]

In conclusion, Franck would have his judges understand that precisely this, viz. putting everything in its proper place and keeping like paired with like, has been his singular and consistent concern.

> My desire has been to meet this error [of confusing internal with external word and inner with outer man] and to show what each in its own order is and does. Let everyone grasp this matter clearly. As little as the inner man can be fed with external bread . . . , so little can he be taught by the external word. Rather, the inner man is taught and made faithful by the inner word and the outer man is taught and made faithful by the outer word, Romans 10[: 8]. Hence each is paired with its own order, and like is joined with like [*also ein yedes in seiner ordnung gleichs auf gleichs gattet*], as Paul says: "Spiritualia spiritualibus comparantes," let one compare

---

114. Meinulf Barbers concludes: "Franck lehnt jede—christliche oder ausserchristliche—sichtbare, zur Kirche verfestigte, Religionsgemeinschaft als widergöttlich ab. Der kirchlichen *Institution* tritt er—bei formaler Toleranz—inhaltlich intolerant entgegen." *Toleranz bei Sebastian Franck* (Bonn, 1964), p. 169. Cf. Weigel, *Dialogus de Christianismo Sämtliche Schriften* 4: 71.

115. Hegler-Köhler, p. 150. There is, of course, extensive support for the integrity of the individual conscience even among Franck's foes. He cites the position of his friend Schwenckfeld, for example, which had been—to be sure in better days—directly praised by his adversary Martin Bucer and indirectly lauded by Oecolampadius. Ibid., pp. 150–51.

what is spiritual with the spiritual, 1 Corinthians 2[: 13].
God maintains order and measure. He does not create the
inner through the outer, but rather like through like.[116]

All things considered, Franck's response was an impressive document. It mustered support from the most prestigious past and
present authorities (including his very adversaries) and, while con-
ceding nothing, it was tactfully soft and sensible as well as highly
intelligent in its approach. However, when Frecht had finished
reading this supposed clarification of Franck's thought, he fumed
in a letter that it was an obscure and slippery document, which
itself needed a special clarification.[117] Frecht then set about with
the school board to engineer a foolproof plan to pin Franck down
once and for all. A special confession of faith, based on a ten-
article creed composed by Martin Bucer for the city of Augsburg
in 1530, was prepared for Franck. Special stress was laid on the
importance of God's "order," meaning thereby not Franck's
eternal Word and internal man correlation, but the concrete,
visible means of grace (physical churches, priests, and sacraments),
which God freely but "regularly" (*ordenlich*) employs to communicate his holy gifts.[118]

Confronted with the possibility of a special confession, Franck
issued a special pledge and plea. "I will not write against or oppose our accepted faith and religion or those who preach and teach
it," he promised. "I will in every way conform to the common
religion and policy of the city, as I have previously done, and, to
the extent of my ability, I will help promote good law and order."
Then, not as a condition for submission, but as solace for his own
conscience, he begged that he not be subjected to a "special oath,"
but permitted rather to live "as do my fellow citizens with a free
and uncoerced faith, heart, and conscience." [119]

Franck was rescued from Frecht's prickly oath by the only one
truly powerful enough to do so, the old *Bürgermeister*, Bernhard
Besserer. Besserer pointed out to those eager to convict Franck

116. Hegler-Köhler, pp. 153–54.
117. Endriss, *Francks Ulmer Kämpfe,* p. 19.
118. Hegler-Köhler, pp. 181–85. Note especially article 4, with the pointed comment on the outer word: "Dasz der hailig gaist ordentlich zu reden niemants
solchen glauben oder seine gabe gibt on vorgeend predig oder mündtlich wort
oder evangelion Christi, sonder durch und mit solichen mündtlichen wort wirckt
er und schafft den glauben, wo und in welchen er will." Ibid., p. 182.
119. Ibid., p. 185.

that he himself had sworn no allegiance to Bucer's articles for the city of Augsburg, but only to the rules and regulations of Ulm. He proposed an alternative set of conditions for Franck, which were much more concerned with his political support of the Ulm magistracy than with his fidelity to Lutheran theology.[120] On November 5, 1535, Franck was granted a conditional tenure, the major requirement being that he not write nor publish anything without the foreknowledge and permission of the Ulm magistracy and school board.[121]

The victorious Franck resided in Ulm without incident for three years. Then, in the summer of 1538, a decision dismissing him from the city was issued on the grounds that he had failed to maintain the conditions of his tenure.[122] The publication of his book *The Golden Ark (Die güldene Arch)* in Augsburg and three additional small writings in Ulm "behind the back" of the school board were cited as the immediate reason for reopening Franck's case.[123] The writings indicated to the board that Franck had altered his old errors not one whit, "but let everything remain irritating." [124]

In late 1538 Franck's relentless enemy, Martin Frecht, now belatedly sensing victory over Franck, presented a new "short and thorough excerpt of several provocative points" that was to underlie the inflexible January 4, 1539 decision to turn Franck out of the city.[125] With neither hesitation nor qualification, Frecht classified Franck with Thomas Müntzer, Louis Haetzer, Hans Denck, and the Donatists.

> [Franck has taught that] (1) The world has been better ruled where there was no law, Scripture, and external word than where such were present. (2) All human arts are useless, harmful, and invented by the Devil. (3) God's grace is given without external means. (4) Holy Scripture is not God's word. (5) The inner word of God dwells in the hearts of all men.

120. For details see Endriss, pp. 19–21.
121. Hegler-Köhler, p. 190.
122. Ibid.
123. Franck's immediate response was to cry "foul" ("das man mich nit, wie andere burger, auch gegen meinen misgunstigen verhört, schriftlich oder mundtlich"), and he writes of the publication of *Die güldene Arch:* "Ich kan je nit gedencken, das ich damit wider mein zusagen gefrävelt hab." Ibid., p. 192.
124. Ibid., p. 204.
125. Ibid., p. 215.

Here one ought bear in mind that Franck writes other than Scripture and past and present theologians on the subjects of the inner and outer word of God, letter and spirit, and the Old and New Testaments and their ministers. On these and other points he rather copies from Thomas Müntzer, Haetzer, and Denck. (6) Holy Scripture is given only as a witness, not as a source of doctrine. (7) The wicked man does not preach the gospel of Christ, and has no calling or office as a minister of God, which was also maintained by the heretical Donatists. (8) In his *Weltbuch* he writes shameful, slanderous things about the women of Bayern and Windisch.[126]

Franck and his family departed Ulm in July, 1539. Exclusion from the city did not make him the "outlaw and man without a place" he had feared it might. The journey from Ulm to his new home in Basel did cost him his wife, who was pregnant with their sixth child. But he soon remarried and spent two productive years composing a book of proverbs and writing the great paraphrase of the *German Theology* before his death in October, 1542. The parley with the Lutherans in Ulm reveals in as lucid and sophisticated a form as one will find it in the sixteenth century the antithetical concerns and tactics of dissenters and the authorities they opposed. Franck sought to enlarge as much as possible the contingency of established authority (and thereby his own sphere of freedom) by drawing the *potentia Dei ordinata* into the *potentia Dei absoluta:* all historical forms are only of accidental and momentary significance. His judges, on the other hand, sought to maximize the temporal legitimacy of their positions by drawing the *potentia Dei absoluta* into the *potentia Dei ordinata:* the given historical forms of power have final divine sanction. In such situations, where God argues with God, the temporal victors must finally be those who hold the greatest earthly power.

126. Ibid., pp. 208–09. On the last point, Franck had been censured already in the earlier report of the school board for writing that the women of Windisch, when stricken with illness, boarded with local priests as a remedy. See ibid., p. 140, n. 1.

7

Sebastian Castellio

In the Shadow of Calvin

The persecution of Protestants in France in the late 1530s provided the stimulus for many sensitive young humanists to join the French Reformation. Not only was a profound moral crisis created by the repulsive persecution; an eloquent charter of the new faith was set forth by one of their very own—the first edition of John Calvin's *Institutes of the Christian Religion* (1536).[1] In the spring of 1540, Castellio, a scant twenty-five years of age and fresh from his studies in Lyon, moved to Martin Bucer's Strasbourg, where the temporarily exiled Calvin was awaiting reentry into Geneva. There Castellio became a candidate for the Protestant ministry, a witness of Jean Sturm's educational system, and—most fatefully—a member of Calvin's circle.[2]

When Calvin returned to Geneva in September, 1541, the appointment of a rector for the *collége,* which had languished during his absence, was high on the list of priorities. Calvin hoped to secure the return of his old teacher and fiery friend, Mathurin Cordier. Cordier, however, could not obtain release from the authorities in Neuchâtel. After abortive efforts to secure Charles de Sainte-Marche and Claude Budin (whom Cordier had recommended), the suggestion of Calvin's colleague, William Farel, was followed and the invitation tendered to Castellio. Despite his appointment, Calvin doubted the youthful Castellio (who was, in truth, only six years Calvin's junior) and continued to work for

---

1. "L'*Institution chretienne* devait être pour Castellion et ses semblables un *sursum corda* decisif." Buisson 1: 100; cf. p. 93. On Calvin's own difficult transition from his commentary on Seneca's *De Clementia,* which epitomizes the humanist ideal of reform, to the surrender of his benefices in Noyon (1534) and alignment with the Reformation, see Quirinus Breen, *John Calvin: A Study in French Humanism* (1931; 2d ed., 1968).

2. Buisson 1: 102–09.

the eventual acquisition of Cordier. When Cordier was released by Neuchâtel, only to take a post in Lausanne, Calvin and the Genevan council acted ceremonially to install Castellio (April, 1542), and even then with the retention of the provision that he could be removed should Cordier be secured in the future.[3] Already, from the very beginning, Calvin placed Castellio at arm's length.

With the implementation of his own *Dialogi Sacri*—didactic biblical dramas in classical Latin and proper French translation —as the basic manual of instruction, Castellio made an auspicious beginning as a pedagogue.[4] It was not, however, so to continue. The years 1542–44 witnessed several confrontations with Calvin and the Genevan Church, which were finally to force the termination of Castellio's tenure in Geneva.

The first crisis highlights the paternalistic and, no doubt for Castellio, highly abrasive arrogance with which Calvin could treat his talented underlings. Castellio desired to publish a French translation of the New Testament and to this end submitted a manuscript to Calvin. In a letter to Pierre Viret (September 11, 1542), Calvin reported how he sharply opposed the project because "numerous corrections were needed," offering the following example as a summary of the problems in the translation.

> Where (the New Testament) says "The Spirit of God dwells in us," he (Castellio) has changed it to read *"haunts* in us." In French, however, *hauter* does not mean *habiter*, but *frequenter*. One such schoolboyish error would alone suffice to discredit the entire book. There you see the foolishness I must pore over in silence.[5]

Calvin confided to Viret that Castellio left the meeting "visiblement peine." [6]

A second, less serious confrontation, which nonetheless reveals

3. Ibid., 135–42.

4. Ibid., 152–79. "Les *Dialogues sacres* sont le véritable manuel d'instruction morale et civique d'une petite republique protestant a l'age heroique." Ibid., 173. Cf. Helena W. F. Stellweg, "Castellio Paedagogus" in *Autour de Michel Servet et de Sébastian Castellion*, ed. B. Becker (Haarlem, 1953) [hereafter cited as Becker 1953], pp. 181–94.

5. Letter in Buisson 1: 183–84. There is an English translation in *Letters of John Calvin*, ed. Jules Bonnet, (Philadelphia, 1858), 1: 350–51.

6. Buisson 1: 183.

the circumscription of Castellio's activity, came during the plague that visited Geneva in the winter of 1542–43. Castellio offered to serve the stricken as hospital chaplain, a task for which there was understandably not an overabundance of volunteers. Permission was, after much debate, denied, the reason given being that Castellio was not a full-fledged minister in the city. The decision no doubt reflected as much the city's desire to keep him in his place as rector of the school as it did the ecclesiastical concern to put him in his place as an unauthorized minister.[7]

The final and decisive confrontation came on the heels of the famine that hit the city in the winter of 1543–44. The school suffered greatly, and, after serious illness, Castellio made public his desire to retire as rector and to enter the financially more rewarding ministry of the city.[8] After a thorough but routine examination, Calvin, who had already launched a search for his successor as rector, stoutly resisted Castellio's admission. This was not for lack of high intellectual and ethical qualifications or for divergences from the capital points of the faith,[9] but because of discordant theological opinions. Specifically, Calvin found unacceptable Castellio's opposition to the creedal confession of Christ's descent into hell, and much more seriously—"our principal argument," as Calvin puts it—his conviction that the Song of Solomon was an "obscene and lascivious poem."[10]

Refused admittance into the ministry for candor about what to him seemed highly questionable if not trivial matters,[11] Castellio soon vented his anger publicly against the ministers of Geneva. Calvin wrote Farel on May 31, 1544, that "our Sebastian" recently launched an "attaque sanglante," charging that there was "in every respect opposition between Christ and us [the ministers of Geneva]." Calvin frankly admitted his personal animosity and repressive countermeasures: "As for myself, I have wanted to re-

7. Cf. Buisson 1: 186–87; Etienne Giran, *Sébastian Castellion et la Réforme calviniste: Les deux Réformes* (Haarlem/Paris, 1914), pp. 56–59.

8. Buisson 1: 195 ff.; Giran, *Sébastian Castellion*, pp. 60 ff.

9. In his concluding report on the matter, Calvin wrote: "Though he has not been admitted, it is not because of any blemish whatever in his life, nor of any impious doctrine upon a capital point of the faith or in contradiction to it." Cited by F. Wendel, *Calvin: The Origins and Development of His Religious Thought* (French: Paris, 1950; English: New York, 1963), p. 83.

10. Full text of Calvin's statement in Buisson 1: 198–99.

11. "Voilà tout la débat, il n'y a pas là d'autre hérésie, il y a une question de probité." Buisson 1: 200.

press the intemperance of this man not only because I have found the impropriety of his behavior and the violence of his language revolting, but also because he has insulted us with the most perverse slanders." [12]

In June, 1544, Castellio was sharply censured for this outbreak by the ministers of Geneva. Convinced of Calvin's permanent enmity and conscious of its ultimate consequences, he anticipated the inevitable by resigning his post as rector and departing Geneva.[13] He was soon in Basel, there to lick his considerable wounds and struggle to make ends meet as a corrector in the employ of the printer, Johann Oporinus.[14] The first round with Calvin was over.

THE CRITIQUE OF CALVINISM

Acting as the willing and even eager executor of a truly ecumenical conspiracy, Calvin engineered the capture and trial of his bête noire, the Spanish physician and amateur theologian, Michael Servetus. On October 27, 1553, Servetus, recalcitrant to the very end, died at the stake in Geneva for alleged "blasphemies against the Holy Trinity." [15] The outrage that followed the execution was as great as the clamor that had promoted it, and Calvin was obliged quickly to defend the use of capital punishment against heretics. His *Defense of the Orthodox Faith in the Holy Trinity Against the Monstrous Errors of Michael Servetus of Spain,* which he himself called a "libellus brevis . . . et tumultarie scriptus," appeared in both Latin and French versions in February, 1554.[16] The very next month saw Castellio's response to the execution: the publication in Latin and French editions of an anonymous anthology of writings on religious toleration (including a laudable excerpt from none other than John Calvin himself), bearing the title *On Heretics: Whether They Should Be Punished by the Sword of the Magistrate.* This work was introduced and edited by

12. Full text in Buisson 1: 209–11. English translation in Bonnet, *Letters,* 1: 416–22.

13. Buisson 1: 211–15.

14. Castellio's tenure and production in Basel from 1545 to 1552 is discussed by Buisson 1: 230–92.

15. Roland H. Bainton, *Hunted Heretic: The Life and Death of Michael Servetus 1511–1553,* 2d ed. (Boston, 1960), esp. pp. 202 ff. There is an English translation of Servetus's *On the Errors of the Trinity* by E. M. Wilbur in *Harvard Theological Studies* 16 (Cambridge, Mass., 1932).

16. Buisson 1: 350–51.

Castellio, who also contributed selections under his own and two pseudonymous names.[17]

Although it was not to see publication until 1612, Castellio at this time also authored and circulated privately a devastating response to Calvin's hasty defense of the execution of Servetus entitled *Against Calvin's Book in Which He Tries to Show That Heretics Are to Be Restrained by the Law of the Sword.* Together with but far more systematically than the anthology on tolerance, this work introduces Castellio's exposé of Calvin and Calvinism. It is the first in a series of three major critiques, being followed by the *Four Dialogues* (on predestination, election, free will, and faith), first published by the Italian reformer Faustus Socinus in 1578,[18] and Castellio's last work, *On the Art of Doubting and Believing,* which was written in 1563 and published posthumously.

Against Calvin's Book consists of 154 excerpts, the bulk of which come either from Calvin's defense of his execution of Servetus or from the *Institutes.*[19] Each statement is analyzed by one Vaticanus (i.e. Castellio) who is quick to catch logical contradictions, willful distortions, and staggering arrogance on Calvin's part. The book is a calculated exposé of established religious authority as it is represented by the character and teaching of John Calvin. The opening words of the preface pine for the day when "good men will possess great authority and evil men none at all." It is the way of the world, we are told, to curse and kill good men during their lifetime but to praise them after their death, and, conversely, to

17. A photo-reprint of the Basel original has recently appeared with an introduction by Sape van der Woude (Geneva, 1954). The third edition of Roland Bainton's 1935 translation has also recently appeared (New York, 1965). This work has been exhaustively analyzed. See especially the essays by Bainton, Becker, Marius Valkhoff, and van der Woude collected under the title *Castellioniana: Quatre études sur Sébastian Castellion et l'idée de la tolerance* (Leiden, 1951). Cf. also Buisson 1: 360–413; 2: 1–28. Buisson's treatment of the question of authorship has been brought up to date by Becker's contribution to *Castellioniana*.

18. Castellio's immense impact on Socinians and Arminians as well as later developments in so-called rational religion is documented by Hans R. Guggisberg, *Sebastian Castellio im Urteil seiner Nachwelt vom Späthumanismus bis zur Aufklärung* (Basel, 1956). J. Lindeboom sees Castellio as anticipating eighteenth-century rationalism. "La Place de Castellion dans l'histoire de l'esprit" in Becker 1953, pp. 158–80. In this connection, Becker documents Castellio's influence on the English Deist Thomas Chubb (d. 1746): "Sur quelques documents manuscrits concernant Castellion" in ibid., pp. 280–88.

19. A few excerpts are apparently also taken from the Reformed *Consensus Tigurinus* (1549), the unitive document of the Zwinglian and Calvinist churches.

praise evil men while they live and curse them only after they have passed from the scene. "John Calvin," Castellio adds pointedly, "is today a man of highest authority." [20] And he makes it clear that he is writing not to defend the teaching of Servetus, whose disciple Calvin accused him of being, but "to expose the false teaching of Calvin." [21] Later, in the preface to the *Four Dialogues,* he states that Calvin's teaching must be challenged, not only because it is false, but also because it is a peril to man's very salvation.[22]

In Castellio's view, Servetus was not "impious" (i.e. a willful blasphemer and apostate) but, at most, simply one "in error" about matters of universal dispute.[23] Servetus died for his views "about the trinity, fate, free will, and the like, even though the whole world puzzles over and argues about these matters." [24] Further, according to Christian tradition, it is the function of the magistrate to protect worldly goods, not to execute those who disagree theologically with Calvin or anyone else.[25] The fact that Servetus was faithful to his convictions even unto death suggested to Castellio that he was not a hypocrite. That Calvin, however, an ordained Christian minister, would put a man to death for errors in matters of universal doubt suggested that he, rather than Servetus, was the wolf in sheep's skin.[26] It was not, as Calvin charged, Servetus's allegedly heretical opinions but Calvin's un-Christian execution of him for holding them that had thrown all of Europe into tumult.[27]

The pattern of argument employed throughout by Castellio was to turn Calvin's accusations against Servetus back onto Calvin

---

20. *Contra libellum Calvini in quo ostendere conatur Haereticos jure gladij coercendos esse* (1562 [1612]), pp. A 1 b–A 2 a–b. On date of publication, see Buisson 2: 365.

21. "Calvini falsum doctrinam ostendo." Ibid., p. A 3 a.

22. "Sed postquam a curiosis hominibus invectae sunt opiniones non solum falsae sed etiam perniciosae, refellendae videntur, ne errent homines periculo suae salutis." *Sebastiani Castellionis Dialogi IV. De Praedestinatione. Electione. Libero Arbitrio. Fide* (Gouda, 1613), p. 2 a.

23. On the distinction between "impiety" and "error," see *Contra libellum Calvini,* §35, C 3 b–C 4 a; §2, A 3 b–A 4 a; §62, D 4 b; §147, L 4 b ff., which points out that doubting Thomas was not executed for his mistaken conviction.

24. Ibid., §49, D 1 b.

25. Ibid., §63–64, D 5 a–b.

26. Ibid., §4, B 2 a–b; §91, F 3 b. Castellio writes with patent bitterness: "Hijpocritis non licet interficere quenquam, quippe ovina pelle tectis." Ibid., §90, F 2 b.

27. Ibid., §31, B 8 b.

himself. It was Calvin, not Servetus, who transgressed the boundary
of divine majesty and mystery:

> *Calvin:* What of today? The majority of people have lost all
> sense of shame and openly mock God. They burst as boldly
> into God's awesome mysteries as pigs poke their snouts into
> costly storehouses.
>
> *Vaticanus:* Calvin appears to be criticizing himself. For truly
> the awesome mysteries of God are the trinity, predestination,
> and election. But this man speaks so assuredly about these
> matters that one would think he was in Paradise. So thorny
> is his own teaching about the trinity in this book [sc. the
> *Institutes*] that by his own curiosity he only weakens and
> makes doubtful the consciences of the simple. And he has
> taught so crudely about predestination that innumerable men
> have been seduced into a security as great as that which
> existed before the Flood.[28]

Castellio's basic strategy was to present Calvin's theology as a
transgression of man's most basic logical processes and cherished
ethical convictions. It is highly persuasive dissent. How can something that is patently illogical and ethically repugnant in the most
fundamental sense claim authority? Hence, it is not Servetus but
Calvin who has plagued Christendom with "sophismata" and
"absurdissima." [29] "O Calvin, Calvin!", Vaticanus exclaims, "do
you really think God is so like man that he permits himself to
be deceived by those Sorbonnist sophistries [of yours]?" [30]

Before turning to Castellio's ethical critique of Calvinist teaching, we must spend some time with its twin sister, the appeal to the
canons of commonsense judgment. It will be noted throughout
that Calvin's supralapsarian doctrine of predestination is the
focal point of Castellio's critique. It is hardly accidental that
Castellio chose to concentrate on this particular point. For although this doctrine may be no more prominent in Calvin's
theology[31] than infant baptism was in Luther's, it is, like infant
baptism, a teaching most vulnerable to a commonsense logical and

28. Ibid., §4, A 4 a–b.
29. Ibid., §112, G 5 a; §71, D 7 b.
30. Ibid., §129, L 1 a.
31. Cf. Wilhelm Niesel, *Die Theologie Calvins,* 2d ed. (Munich, 1957), pp. 161–62,
167–68.

ethical critique. And, again like infant baptism, it highlights, from the dissenter's point of view, the monstrous presumption of established religious authority.

In the preface to the *Four Dialogues,* Castellio declares the experience of the common man, who is uncorrupted by formal education, a much surer guide in the matter of predestination and free will than the judgment of certain learned theologians.

> In the first three matters—predestination, election, and free will—the common man (assuming he has not been corrupted by learning) is a better and more wholesome judge than certain of the learned. For uneducated men follow the judgment of reason and experience [*rationis et sensuum judicium*], which, in these matters that fall under reason and experience, is sound. If only the judgment of nature [*naturae judicium*] were in part granted to men in these matters, we would have no reason to write. But since certain of the learned are working very hard to convince men that there experience is false, i.e. to tear out their eyes, we will labor to refute this error.[32]

The critical use of the appeal to common sense can be overwhelming, as in the following short exchange in *Against Calvin's Book,* where logical and ethical canons of judgment coalesce perfectly:

Calvin: Kings are duty bound to defend the doctrine of piety.

Vaticanus: To kill a man is not to defend doctrine, but to kill a man.[33]

In the first of the *Four Dialogues,* "On Predestination," scholastic logic is taken over and given a commonsense twist to produce a kind of "mock scholasticism" by which Castellio's opponent is finally reduced to a self-confession of foolishness. Scholastic logical rigor and axioms are made to subserve the evident facts of daily experience (often with tongue-in-cheek) rather than the cogency of theoretical possibilities. The players in the dialogue are Federicus (Castellio) and Ludovicus (a Calvinist catechumen), and the argument runs like this:

Fed: Tell me, in brief, what you think about predestination.

Lud: I have been taught the following about predestination.

32. *Dialogi IV,* p. 2 b.
33. *Contra libellum Calvini,* §77, E 2 a.

All men are not created in an equal state. Rather, in eternity, God, by inevitable decree, determined in advance those whom he would save and those whom he would damn to destruction. Those whom he has deemed worthy of salvation have been chosen by his gratuitous mercy with no consideration of their worthiness. And those whom he has given over to damnation, he shuts off from life by his just and irreprehensible, albeit incomprehensible, judgment.

Fed: So you maintain that certain men are created by God already marked for damnation so that they cannot be saved?

Lud: Precisely.

Fed: What if they should obey God? Would they not then be saved?

Lud: They would then be saved. But they are not able to obey God, because God so excludes them from knowledge of his name and the spirit of his justification that they can will and do only evil and are inclined toward every kind of sin.

Fed: Hence they have that inclination [to sin] from God's creation and predestination?

Lud: They have it so, just as surely as God has created the wolf with the inclination to eat sheep.

Fed: Therefore they have been damned and rejected by God even before they are?

Lud: Exactly.

Fed: But are they not damned for their sins?

Lud: Indeed so. Those who were destined to that [damned] lot were worthy of it.

Fed: When were they worthy of it?

Lud: When they were destined to it.

Fed: Then they have been before they are. Do you see what you are saying?

Lud: I don't understand what you are driving at.

Fed: If they were worthy, then they were. For to be worthy is to be. And if you concede that they have been damned before they are, then they have been before they were.[34]

34. *De praedestinatione* in *Dialogi IV*, pp. 2–3.

Later Federicus returns to Ludovicus's statement that men are born to sinning as wolves to devouring sheep, and the exchange continues:

> *Fed:* If man is created to sin, then he does not degenerate when he sins whether he do so passively by simply following his nature or actively by earnest endeavor. It is the same as when he grows a beard. He does not degenerate although he grows a beard in dead earnest. For he is created earnestly to grow a beard. If, however, he degenerates when he sins, then he is not created to sin. Creation is the production of a [definite] species. And if man remains what he was created to be, then he maintains his species.
>
> *Lud:* You always lead me into absurdities.
>
> *Fed:* Indeed, it is you who lead yourself into absurdities when you set out to defend what is false. Your false thesis was prescribed in advance, yet at the same time you have been forced to concede that when one defends something false one slips straightway from absurdities into absurdities. And if you still rush ahead, you will fall into even greater absurdities.[35]

Ludovicus had also maintained that, although God chooses to save all men by his "manifest will," by his "hidden will" he chooses to damn many and save but a few. This prompts the following exchange, in which the most basic of logical axioms, the law of contradiction, forces Ludovicus into rapid retreat.

> *Fed:* You have again taken an absurd position. Do you not believe that two contrary things or (as the dialecticians call them) two contradictory things cannot simultaneously be present in the same subject?
>
> *Lud:* I do indeed believe [this axiom].
>
> *Fed:* But to will and not to will sin are absolutely contrary. Would you attribute to God that than which nothing is more contrary to nature? And behold still another absurdity. You say that the will by which God damns certain men is a "hidden" will. If it is hidden, why then do you speak about it as if it were something fully disclosed to you? And if it is so disclosed, why do you call it "hidden"?[36]

35. Ibid., p. 9.
36. Ibid., p. 10.

There is a peculiar anti-intellectualism at work in Castellio's commonsense use of scholastic logic to convict Calvin of sophistry. He views the learnedness of Calvin much as Luther had viewed that of medieval scholasticism. As Luther found it necessary to rid the university of Aristotle and canon law in order to restore theology to its true task, Castellio now entertains the idea of suppressing the "human and profane sciences" for the sake of the "simple, rustic truth" of the gospel.[37] Castellio's novel attack on Calvin at this point not only ties into the common dissent theme of the post-Apostolic fall of the church, but also evinces the class conflicts of the sixteenth century.

> *Calvin:* God elects the foolish things of the world to confound the wise. But he who began with fishermen afterwards delegated other ministers who were not so coarse and possessed a rather refined learning.
>
> *Vaticanus:* Calvin and his kind reject the foolish things of the world so that they may exalt the wise. Hence they admit hardly anyone into [the office of] teaching and their circle who is not accomplished in the sciences and languages, especially Latin. If Christ himself came to them, he would certainly be turned away if he spoke no Latin. . . . The church of Christ boasts because it does not have many who are wise and of noble birth, but they [the Calvinists] boast only of the wise and noble. . . . [Calvin] talks about those Doctors who began to destroy the church after the fishermen had built it. For when these Doctors began to mix the human arts into theology, everything came to a halt and started to deteriorate. They introduced (contrary to Paul [2 Tim. 2 : 16]) vain and useless questions, which encircled and obscured—I could almost say smothered out—the pure truth [of the gospel], so that it cannot be restored unless we return again to those same unlearned fishermen and make that saying true: "ex ore infantium et lactantium perfecisti laudem." [38]

This particular exchange climaxes in the accusation that, when he came to Geneva for the first time, Calvin undermined the

---

37. *Contra libellum Calvini*, §74, D 8 b. It is argued that the "simple rustic truth" of Christianity deteriorates in direct proportion to the increase of the "human and profane sciences." Cf. ibid., §74, E 1 a.

38. Ibid., §72, D 8 a–b.

evangelical work of Farel by mixing the profane with the sacred sciences. Things have since gone downhill to the point that "Farel himself (alas!) now Calvinizes [*calvinizet*]." [39]

Castellio's "anti-intellectualism" is really an appeal beyond technical reason to something much more basic and incontrovertible: commonsense experience and judgment. Citing several of Christ's parables, Federicus tells Ludovicus that Christ based his appeal to men squarely on their commonsense experience and judgment.

> Behold, Ludovicus, how Christ wishes to be judged by common sense [*communi sensu*] and refers the matters of the gospel to human judgment [*ad humanum judicium*]. Hence so many analogies from agriculture, planting, fishing, the household, poultry, military service, plant life, etc. He would never have employed such analogies had he wished to deprive us of our common sense. And, indeed, who would ever have believed him had he taught things repugnant to nature and in contradiction with human experience [*sensus hominis*]? Who would not rightfully have ridiculed him, had he denied movement to the walking, ears to the hearing, and life to the living? What kind of master would he have been, had he said to the woman who cried out to him and washed his feet with her hair: "O woman, whatever your sin, it was done by God's decree. You can in no way abstain from such sins, even if you had the will to do so! . . ." If God wants to teach us, it is necessary that he teach us according to nature [*secundum naturam*], leading us from the knowledge of natural things (most of which everyone knows) to that of heavenly things.[40]

The absurdity of Calvinist doctrine is documented by Calvinist deeds. As Roland Bainton has put it, with his customary grace: "Castellio would say not merely that deeds are more important than creeds, but that deeds must be the test of creeds." [41] When Castellio comes to itemize the "mala" of Calvin's doctrine of predestination, which doctrine epitomizes for him the entire Calvinist system, the alleged ethical shortcomings are quite prominent. Whereas Calvin considered this doctrine to promote hu-

---

39. "Postquam Calvinus introductus profanas scientias sacris admiscuit." Ibid., D 8 b.

40. *De libero arbitrio* in *Dialogi IV*, pp. 157–58.

41. "Sebastian Castellio: Champion of Religious Liberty" in *Castellioniana*, pp. 25–76, 67.

mility and confidence among the faithful,[42] Castellio finds it only destroys "sure faith" and gives the prideful a further excuse to persecute the humble.[43] Experience will testify that it encourages those who think themselves elect to live "laxly" and leads those convinced of rejection to despair altogether.[44]

When commonsense logic and ethics form the criteria of religious authority, some important hermeneutical consequences result for the disenfranchised dissenter. Piety and obedience—moral criteria—now replace professional rank and technical skill —so-called scientific criteria—as the sine quibus non for understanding Holy Scripture. In the preface to his 1551 Latin translation of the Bible, Castellio laments the way his age, so pregnant with scholarship and excelled by no other in learning (*eruditius*), still knows not the least about the gospel and deteriorates daily. On authority of the prophets he concludes that "impiety" has made understanding impossible.[45] And he admonishes his reader:

> The mind of Holy Scripture can be deciphered by no arts and sciences, no human industry, memory or skill. It is a divine matter, which the one who wrote it, the Spirit of God, understands and teaches. He teaches it to those who are of all men the most uneducated, infirm, demeaned, impoverished, and despised, lest we arrogate anything to our own erudition and mighty arts.[46]

In *Against Calvin's Book,* authority is ceded to those who are experts in the art of living well, not in the arts and sciences:

> It is written in the New Testament that Christ spoke to his audiences only in parables, i.e. with ambiguity, but privately explained everything clearly to his disciples [Mark 4 : 33–34]. This shows that sacred Scripture can only truly be understood by disciples of Christ. And who are his disciples? Those who obey him and exhibit love. . . . For the others, even if they are experts in all the sciences, the Scriptures are but a snare.[47]

42. See *Institutes of the Christian Religion,* Bk. 3, chap. 21/1.

43. *De praedestinatione,* pp. 62–63; *De libero arbitrio,* p. 191.

44. "Ita fiet: ut nemo salutem suam procuret cum timore et tremore: sed aut dissolute vivant, si credant electos esse se: aut desperent, si rejectos." *De praedestinatione,* p. 61.

45. *Biblia, Interprete Sebastino Castalione* (Basel, 1551), p. A 3 a.

46. Ibid., p. A 6 b.

47. *Contra libellum Calvini,* §29, B 7 b.

It is perhaps indicative of the vicious circle of sixteenth-century theological polemics that Calvin and his colleague Theodore Beza charged that Castellio's free translations of the Bible[48] were "indocta" and "impia." They found that such changes as "lavare" for "baptizare" and "genius" for "angelus" altered the traditional meaning as well as wording. Baptism became a mere washing, and man was presumed angelic.[49] Castellio responded with a *Defense of His Translations of the Bible* (written May, 1557, and expanded in December, 1561, before publication was permitted in January, 1562).[50] The charge of "impietas," it is revealing to note, was answered by an appeal to "conscience, which is worth a thousand witnesses." [51]

Castellio's commonsense logical and ethical criteria do not permit difficulties with words to obscure the true intention of the Bible.

> I think one must direct attention to the subject matter and not to the words [*rem, non verba*]. The word of God is neither Hebrew, Greek, nor Latin, only spiritual. And Christ redeems men of all races and tongues, who have put on the white robe [cf. Apoc. 7] and preach and praise God. A German who has the Spirit is no less able to preach the praises of God and untangle the heavenly secrets than a Hebrew in his native tongue.[52]

In his last work, *On the Art of Doubting*, Castellio's mature formulation of this matter centers on the concept of the "tenor"

48. Concrete examples follow. Here I wish to call attention to Castellio's openness to emendation by his reader: "Sed Lectorem prius admonitum volo, me non omnia in quibus a me dissentit, velle persequi (debet enim ipsi quoque liberum esse, interpretari pro cognitione aut opinione sua, non minus quam mihi)." *Sebastiani Castellionis Defensio suarum translationum Bibliorum* (Basel, 1562), p. 21. Elsewhere he typically confesses: "Scio me hominem esse, hoc est erroribus obnoxium. Itaque errores meos libenter agnosco atque corrigo: tanti est apud me veritas." Ibid., p. 232.

49. Ibid., pp. 3, 28–30.

50. Ibid., p. 233. Editions of the Latin Bible appeared in 1551, 1554, and 1556. The French translation was published in 1555. In 1557 came Beza's critically annotated New Testament, which severely criticized Castellio's translations, although without mentioning his name. On the difficulties Castellio had in publishing his reply, see van der Woude, "Censured Passages from Castellio's *Defensio suarum translationum*" in Becker 1953, pp. 259–79.

51. *Defensio suarum translationum Bibliorum*, p. 4.

52. Ibid., p. 19.

of Scripture, i.e. the overall point or thrust of the words.[53] "Tenor" in practical terms, however, is really what reason finally decides the meaning of Scripture must be. It was customary hermeneutical practice when one came upon an obscure passage of Scripture to resolve its meaning by comparison with other passages that dealt with the same issue. Castellio views this as a hopeless procedure. What one side will consider clear and definitive, the other side will consider obscure, and no concord will ever result.[54] One must, then, simply focus on and follow what commonsense judgment teaches is consistent with a good and merciful God and an ideal Christian life. We must do as the ancients did when they hit upon insoluble problems: follow reason.[55] Hence Castellio can confidently reject the canonical authority of the Song of Songs, as he rejects Calvin's doctrine of predestination, because it is "morally offensive." [56]

The point of Castellio's ethical critique of Calvinism is missed if it is seen simply as a visceral reaction to the execution of Servetus. It was surely this in its inception. As it developed, however, the critique was a calculated effort to simplify and democratize the criteria of religious authority. The major achievement of *Against Calvin's Book* is precisely the programmatic shift from doctrinal to ethical standards of authority.

For John Calvin the issue was absolutely clear: if there was no sure doctrine, uniform confession, and enforced discipline, there could be no church.[57] "There are many trouble-makers afoot today," Calvin warned, "and if they are free to babble whatever comes into their heads, they will destroy everything for the sake of their unrestrained impudence." In their case, "impunity is but the mother of license." [58] Realistically concerned with visible structures, Calvin pled: "If the doctrine of piety is uncertain and in suspense, how will religion identify itself? By what signs will

53. "Non esse scriptorum authoritatem in paucis quibusdam verbis, quae vitiari detrahive potuerunt, sed in perpetuo orationis tenore, qui mansit incorruptus, positam." *De Arte dubitandi et confidendi, ignorandi et sciendi*, ed. Elizabeth Feist in *Per la Storia degli Eretici Italiani del Secolo XVI in Europa* (Rome, 1937), p. 334.

54. Ibid., p. 354.

55. Ibid., pp. 365–66.

56. Cf. Heinz Liebing, *Die Schriftauslegung Sebastian Castellios* (Dissertation, Tübingen, 1953), pp. 45–46; 62–66. See my discussion, below, pp. 184 ff.

57. *Contra libellum Calvini*, §96, F 4 b.

58. Ibid., §22, B 4 b. Cf. §23, B 5 b; §29, B 7 a.

the true church be known? And what will Christ himself be?" In response, Castellio took dead aim at the reader's heart:

> Religion will be founded in certain faith in things which are hoped for but not seen, as it was with Abraham who, when ordered to go forth, obeyed without knowing where he was going. . . . [The true church will be known] by love which proceeds from a faith with a sure precept: "By this shall all men know that you are my disciples if you love one another." [John 13 : 35] [Christ will be] the rock of offense to those who believe only what they comprehend . . . [John 20 : 29]. The doctrine of piety [will be identified as follows]: love your enemies, do good to those who persecute you . . . [Matt. 5]. These and like precepts are certain even if those obscure questions about the trinity, predestination, election, etc., for which men are held as heretics even though many pious men have known nothing about them, remain unknown.[59]

Castellio considered Calvin so to have perverted the order of Christian priorities that he not only executed men for errors in confused and penultimate matters but would tend even to excuse men for the faults God most forbids.

> Calvin does not view as great faults those things which God holds to be the greatest of faults, as is obvious in the laws he wrote for the administration of the church [of Geneva]. There he classifies two types of faults. One group contains those things which are absolutely intolerable for a minister. The first of these is heresy, and among the other things we find games and dances forbidden by the laws [of the city]. The second group contains the tolerable faults. Here Calvin places scurrility, lying, slander, avarice, excessive anger, and quarrels. These faults are tolerable for him, although sacred Scripture knows nothing worse than those who are scurrilous . . . and avaricious.[60]

Elsewhere Castellio accused Calvinists (and, by implication, contemporary religious leaders generally) of viewing "rebaptism

---

59. Ibid., §28, B 6 b–B 7 a.

60. Ibid., §82, E 7 b; cf. §129, I 5 a. See Calvin's *Draft Ecclesiastical Ordinances* (September and October, 1541) in *Calvin: Theological Treatises* (Philadelphia, 1954), pp. 60–61.

as a far more deadly vice than adultery, envy, cursing, and gambling." [61] "The Calvinists want men to be judged not on the basis of their morals but according to their beliefs [*non ex moribus, sed ex Doctrina*]." [62] But, Castellio warned, "Come Judgment Day, Christ will repudiate their doctrines and ask about their morals. . . . In vain will one put forth doctrine, if there is no moral conduct corresponding to it [*nisi adsint mores Doctrinae congruentes*]." [63] In sum, theologians and their doctrines must be judged like physicians and their medicine, i.e. by their ability to produce successful results.

> If the common man finds that he cannot judge the disputes of the masters, the best and most expeditious solution would be to decide on the basis of their fruits [*ex fructu judicare*], to consider those best who best heal the sickness (i.e. faults) of souls.[64]

Castellio's critique of Calvinism operates with certain unshakable presuppositions. One is the necessity of divine equity. For Castellio, the majesty of God depends far more on absolute fairness than on unqualified omnipotence. God's power must be regulated by goodness. The very first "malum" of Calvin's doctrine of predestination is the transgression of this truth. This doctrine "does not square with the nature of God. Nothing could be more contrary to God than the creation of sons . . . for the purpose of punishing them. Not even wolves and tigers do that. This opinion [of Calvin's] destroys the teaching which exhorts us to imitate God's goodness to men." [65] Who, indeed, would imitate a God whose moral standards not only fail to meet man's, but even fall beneath those of wolves and tigers?

The concept of the fair God is systematized by Castellio in terms of three types of "impossibilia"—things God either cannot do or does not do even though it is conceivable that he could. The first

61. *Contra libellum Calvini*, §82, E 8 b. Heresy and rebaptism, of course, were a challenge to established authority in a way these other vices were not.

62. Ibid., §129, K 2 a.

63. Ibid., I 6 a.

64. Ibid., K 1 a–b. Cf. p. I 5 a for the same sentiment from the perspective of *doctrina*, and *De electione* in *Dialogi IV*, p. 87: "Qualis enim fructus est, talis est etiam arbor." One recalls that when Luther and Calvin employed this proverb "fructus" and "arbor" were reversed!

65. *De praedestinatione*, p. 59; cf. p. 52.

group contains the logically impossible. God cannot make what has been not to have been, or twice ten not twenty, or justice identical with injustice, or light the same as darkness. One ought no more to entertain the possibility of God's doing these things than to ask whether colors can be heard or voices seen.

The second group of impossibles embraces the religiously absurd, which Castellio illustrates by citing four biblical verses: "Without faith it is impossible to please God"; "How can you give a good account, when you practice evil?"; "No one can serve two masters"; "Father, if it is possible, let this cup pass from me." That God is pleased without faith, that goodness dwells with evil, that allegiance to God is divided, that the children of God escape suffering—these are religiously absurd things which are not willed by God.

The third and final group of impossibles concerns things "contrary to nature" that God, as the "author of nature," refuses to do. He could make a cat stronger than an elephant, but since such disparity between physical members and powers does violence to nature, he does not do it. He could make the best wine come from the highest Alps, Ireland as hot as Africa, grapes thrive among thorns, and figs grow in thistles; but he refuses. "Since nature herself does not do these things, God refuses to act against nature." [66]

There are, then, very definite logical, religious, and natural boundaries that God simply either can not or will not transgress. "Whenever we deal with God's power, I say that God can do everything he wills to do, only he does not will to do anything which is either impossible or absurd." [67]

A second firm presupposition of Castellio's critique is the abiding dignity of human nature. In the *Four Dialogues* Federicus tells Ludovicus (with considerable foreshortening of Calvin's position) that the point of the whole disputation with Calvin over predestination is the meaning of man's creation. Is man created a son of God and destined for perfection, or is he made for sin

---

66. Ibid., pp. 27–28. Ludovicus protests that God made a serpent out of Moses's rod, turned water into blood, and made Balaam's ass speak. Federicus points out that these things are not "contra naturam." For when he makes Balaam's ass speak, he employs his mouth, not his foot or ear, which is to proceed nature's way (!). Ibid.

67. Ibid., p. 28.

and destined to death and damnation? [68] For Castellio there is no doubt about the answer.

> What if God were to say to Adam: "I created you for sinning, and you can no more abstain from it than you can abstain from getting hungry. But take care that you do not sin. For if you sin, you will die." Could a more absurd thing be thought? [69]

> If man has been created in the image of God, then he has certainly been created for righteousness and not for sin. Is it [a sign that he was created for sin] when God gives him dominion over the earth and [other] creatures? [70]

Castellio intertwines these two motifs—divine fairness and human dignity—to justify considerable human initiative within the process of religious salvation, and only seemingly with immunity from the accusation of Pelagianism. For Castellio, a fair God simply does not create man for salvation without giving him all that he needs to reach it.

> *Fed:* To will salvation is also to will everything necessary for its attainment. If a doctor who alone could save you from a fever told you that, although he wanted to save you he would not give you all the things necessary to overcome the fever, what would you think?

> *Lud:* Either that he was a liar or was making fun of me.[71]

The traditional predestination image of the potter and the clay is handled by Castellio in a novel way,[72] which, again, highlights

68. "*Fed:* Age igitur perpendamus hominis creationem, a qua pendet haec tota disputatio. Credisne Adamum fuisse creatum filium Dei? *Lud:* Credo . . . *Fed:* Iam ego tuum ipsius animum, atque sensum testem advocabo. Vellesne filium gignere ad patibulum? *Lud:* Absit. Quin ne bestiam quidem ullam tam immanem esse arbitror, quae pullum gignere velit ad mortem. *Fed:* Quae igitur audacia est, id Deo tribuere, quod ne de fera quidem bestia dici fas est? Si tu qui malus es, tamen filium ad mortem procreare nolis, tanto minus credendum est Deum procreasse homines ad cruciatum sempiternum." Ibid., p. 13. Cf. *De electione*, p. 87.

69. *De praedestinatione*, p. 32.

70. Ibid., p. 15.

71. *De libero arbitrio*, p. 180.

72. The general conclusion—that man cannot be compared with clay—is reminiscent of Robert Holcot's treatment of this passage. See "Lectures on the Wisdom of Solomon" in H. A. Oberman, *Forerunners of the Reformation* (New York, 1966), pp. 148–50.

divine fairness and human dignity. Arguing that God desires to save men "as men," he maintains that

> the likeness here is not between God and the potter . . . but between God and the material of the potter. For [in the matter of religious salvation] God's material is man, who is capable of receiving and being formed by words and commands. The material of the potter, however, is clay, which is deaf and dumb, and hence to be shaped not by words but only by [the strength of] the hands.[73]

With spiritual as with corporeal diseases, contraries are the remedies of contraries. "If the disease contracted by Adam and his posterity was disobedience, then it is obedience which cures it. Hence God set forth for man's restoration, precepts, the obedience of which will be his salvation." [74] But "God commands nothing either visible or invisible, which man cannot do, or which he does not grant man the power to do [once it is commanded]." [75] Hence, after man's Fall, God began immediately and universally to restore the basic Adamic power to choose good or evil, i.e. to give all men the same chance as Adam had.

> God created man with the power of willing [*libera voluntas*] and endowed him with the power to do what he wills [*arbitrio*].[76] By his sin, man lost the latter, the power to do well [*potestatem benefaciendi*]. The former (the power of willing) he retained. Because he was wounded by sin, he either chose evil, or was unable to do the good he willed. God, however, who is rich in mercy toward all, decided to restore man by his Spirit to [his lost] integrity. As man perished by choosing evil, so should he also be saved by choosing good. Although it will not be perfected by Christ until the Last Day, that restoration [to Adamic freedom] was begun immediately after Adam's sin.[77]

God implements the restoration by working through man's normal rational and volitional processes. The Spirit of God func-

---

73. *De electione*, pp. 107–08.
74. *De libero arbitrio*, pp. 130–31.
75. Ibid., pp. 139.
76. Our translation implements Castellio's definition of these terms: "Est enim libera voluntas potestas volendi quidvis: Liberum vero arbitrium, potestas faciendi quidvis." Ibid., p. 127.
77. Ibid., p. 184.

tions vis-à-vis man's soul, as man's soul functions vis-à-vis his body.[78] In the language of medieval scholasticism, this would not be an *auxilium Dei speciale* but the *concursus Dei generalis,* a *gratia gratis data,* not a *gratia gratum faciens.* Castellio, however, phrases the matter in a striking and historically transitional formulation (which anticipates the famous "hymn to reason" in the *De Arte dubitandi*): "Just as reason aids the infirmity of the senses and is, as it were, the sense of the senses, or the eye of the eyes, so the Spirit [of God] aids the infirmity of reason, and is, as it were, the reason of reason (*quasi rationis ratio*)." [79] When the Spirit of God is the "ratio rationis," one better understands the superior authority of commonsense experience and judgment for Castellio.[80]

While man *post peccatum Adae* and *ex puris naturalibus* is far from achieving a perfect love of God,[81] he is capable of choosing effectively between good and evil. "It is evident . . . that man has the will to turn in two directions; without any special impulse from the Spirit [*sine novo spiritus instinctu*], he can choose good or evil. Yet he does not have that will from himself, but from God who created him as he is." [82] So equipped, man stands over against his salvation as the farmer over against his crops. "If the farmer fails to cultivate and till the soil, he will reap no harvest, but is it therefore his merit and by his power that the corn grows? Are not all good things the work of the Good, i.e. of God?" [83] Taking up a stock predestination proof-text, Castellio comments: "The reward is not to him who wills and runs, but to the mercy of God; yet there must be willing and running." [84] The formulation he finally latches onto as a "general and inviolable rule" is that, while man cannot "earn" his salvation, he can clearly "lose" it.[85] Adam was not placed in Paradise because of his merit, but he

---

78. Ibid., p. 186.
79. Ibid., pp. 186–87.
80. Cf. below, p. 191 f.
81. *De libero arbitrio,* p. 164.
82. Ibid., p. 171.
83. Ibid., p. 194.
84. Ibid., p. 193.
85. "*Fed:* Ex his opinor, generalem inviolabilemque regulam statuimus, quae est apud Prophetam. 'Pernicies tua a te est Israel: Salus autem a me': dicemusque omnes qui servantur, gratis servari, omnes vero qui pereunt, merito suo perire" (*De electione,* p. 88). "Perpetua, et inviolabilis est haec regula naturae, ut in quem cadit lux, in eundem cadant et tenebrae, et in quem cadit virtus, in eundem cadat et

was surely cast out by his just desert.[86] And, although committed to the salvation of all men, God cannot save one who chooses not to believe and follow Christ.[87]

To no small extent, Castellio thinks he has checked the Pelagian charge simply by extending God's grace to every wholesome human occurrence: universally, what is and is good is the product of God's grace.[88] Still, by any other name, the conveyance to man of the ability to initiate his salvation without special assistance from God is Pelegianism. To the extent that one would reproach Castellio for it, however, one must be prepared to contend with a God more sovereign than fair and a human nature more disposed to evil than to good. One must join the Calvinists.

THE SOVEREIGNTY OF REASON

Castellio's last work bears the title *On the Art of Doubting and Believing, of Not-Knowing and Knowing*. The views on reason in Book 1 and on religious justification in Book 2 bring to a climax the logical and ethical critiques of Calvinism, as Castellio now summarizes his constructive alternative. The final conclusions, as we shall see, are significantly influenced by the major themes of medieval mysticism.

The very title of the work catches the reader's eye. Castellio himself points to its relative novelty and warns against taking the ability to doubt and question for granted. Men do not do it naturally. It is an "art"—something they must be taught.

> Often men sin stubbornly simply because they believe where doubt is called for and doubt where belief is called for. They do not know things they should, and they desire or even presume to know what is not only unknown, but also quite

---

vitium. Contra hanc legem nihil vult Deus." God cannot violate the neutrality of human nature. *De praedestinatione*, pp. 35–36.

86. *De libero arbitrio*, pp. 194–95.

87. "Semper erimus peccati capaces, semperque periculum erit ne peccemus. . . . Vult omnes Deus salvos fieri: sed cum ad salutem non nisi per fidem veniri possit, servari nemo potest, nisi qui credat; credere autem non potest, nisi qui paratus sit relinquere omnia, et sequi Christum." *De praedestinatione*, p. 37. Cf. *De electione*, p. 109.

88. "Iam quicquid boni habet homo, sive a natura, sive a patre, sive a filio, id totum Dei muneris est, qui efficit omnia in omnibus, omnisque boni doni dator est." *De libero arbitrio*, p. 188.

capable of remaining unknown with no harm to their salvation.[89]

Deep pessimism over present religious authority underlies Castellio's promotion of an art of doubting. Christ had prophesied that so many false Christians and false teachers would appear in the last days that even the elect would be deceived (Matt. 24 : 24). Castellio's very first words inform the reader that this prophecy is now being fulfilled. Even good men doubt the very truth of the Christian religion. Castellio muses:

> Very often I have wondered whether there was anyone anywhere who could remedy the situation. If today (as was customary in ancient times) some prophet could arise in the land who was able to bring the quarreling parties together and with divine authority point the way clearly for those who are searching and eradicate the errors, then nothing would be better and more expeditious for us than to take refuge in his word, which would be presented from God, and follow it without any doubt or hesitation.[90]

But, Castellio laments, there are no prophets living today. One must therefore do as a military general is said to have done when faced with the apparently insoluble problem of transporting his army across a swollen river. Short-circuiting the usual chain of command, the general offered a reward to any common soldier in the ranks who could present a workable plan. Although he believes that in religious matters, as in no other, men in leadership are particularly immune to good counsel, Castellio, like a common soldier, will now step forth from the ranks with a solution to the present crisis.[91]

Castellio's modesty notwithstanding, the common soldier from the ranks looks very much like the prophet from God, or, at least, he steps forth as one privy to the present disguise of God's prophet. In the midst of the quarrels and errors of the established priests, there is one who exercises the prophetic function of discerning righteousness. This one is reason.

> Righteousness is learned and known as much by nature [*natura*] as by teaching [*doctrina*]. Nature endowed man with

89. *De Arte dubitandi*, p. 309; cf. pp. 346–47.
90. Ibid., p. 307.
91. Ibid., pp. 307–09.

reason, by which he can discern the true from the false, the good from the evil, the just from the unjust. And teaching, which is guided by reason [*ratione duce*], confirms nature and teaches that man is to live according to nature, pronouncing those who do so "just" and those who do not "unjust." [92]

The essentials of religious life have already been carved deep into the hearts of all men.

As regards (Christian) knowledge [*scientia*], I say man's duty [*officium*] is to know God and his commandments. If he knows this and acts accordingly, then he is blessed, even if there are many other things which he knows nothing about. To know this [his duty] is easy. For the world (which is God's creation) is unknown to no man anywhere, and the precepts of love, in which the teaching of Christ and the prophets culminates, are so clearly and naturally known to man that even the impious who refuse to follow them still know them, whether they want to or not. For they are inscribed, as it were, by the finger of God into the hearts of all men, and they can no more be erased than other universal human ideas. That is why I confidently dare to say that the things necessary for man to know [about the Christian religion] are very easily known.[93]

It is not surprising that Castellio finds no ambiguity whatsoever in Holy Scripture when it is searched on the really essential matters such as the existence and nature of God, the duty of love and worship, flight from sin, and the pursuit of virtue. In obscure and disputed matters, however, like baptism, the Lord's Supper, justification, predestination, and the like, Scripture is unclear.[94] In such cases as these, what is one to do? One is to adhere to the prophet, to the surest guide, to what Castellio alternately refers to either as sensory experience and commonsense judgment or, simply, reason.

Because sacred writings are obscure in controversial matters and often give probable support to both sides, it has not been possible down through the ages to end many controversies

92. Ibid., p. 314.
93. Ibid., pp. 351–52.
94. Ibid., p. 355.

simply by appealing to the words of Scripture. Hence it is
necessary to seek something in which truth is so manifest and
universally acknowledged that it cannot be controverted by
any force or probability to the contrary. When this [agent
of truth] is discovered, one will then know which side in
controversies may defend itself with the words of Scripture
and, further, which agrees with this manifest and firm [agent
of] truth and can claim its support. There is no doubt that
the side which has the support of both is more certain than the
alternative. And what is this [agent of truth] about which I
am speaking? It is [our] sensory experience and commonsense
judgment [*sensus et intellectum*]. Since these are the instru-
ments of judging [*instrumenta iudicandi*], one ought have no
doubt that they can exercise judgment.[95]

Although the senses and understanding are prone to natural
and self-inflicted "impediments"—blindness and insanity would
be examples of the former, obstinacy and related "carnal affections" examples of the latter—they are nonetheless, in themselves,
pure and uncorrupted.[96] That they have survived the Fall is already evident to Castellio in the fact that Adam and Eve immediately saw and judged themselves naked; the Fall is the birth of
moral judgment.[97]

The senses and understanding still have very definite natural
limitations, which must be borne in mind when the disputed
issues of Scripture are pondered. Castellio distinguishes things
"above" and things "contrary to" the senses in order to define the
perimeters of their authority. By sensory experience men evidently
cannot know the essence of God, whether, how, or when he created
the world, or whether souls lie dormant in their bodies after death
until the resurrection. Such matters are simply "supra sensus."
Some things are beyond human judgment, according to Castellio,
not because the senses are incapable of making a certain determina-
tion about them, but because they remain inaccessible to the

95. Ibid., p. 357.

96. Ibid., pp. 369 ff. "Sic statuimus, hominis sensus et intellectum non fuisse Adami
peccato vitiatum" (Ibid., p. 368). It is interesting in light of Castellio's experiences
with Calvin that he makes *pertinacia* the chief of all carnal affections: "Nam hoc
vitium non unius sed omnium rerum iudicium impedit." The obstinate man loves
only his own and cannot entertain the views of another. Ibid., pp. 376–77.

97. Cf. ibid., pp. 367–68.

senses. Who, for example, during his lifetime is in a position to say whether stars are solid bodies, whether the center of the earth contains empty places, or whether the pious will inhabit heaven or earth after the resurrection? With these and similar matters "supra sensus," the following rule holds:

> If they are clearly present in the sacred authors, they ought to be believed; if they are only ambiguously present, they ought to be doubted; and if they are not present even ambiguously, they ought to be ignored.[98]

The tolerance accorded to things "above" the senses and understanding is strictly to be denied to things "contrary to" the senses and understanding. If someone says that fire is cold when touch judges it hot, snow black when the eyes judge it white, or wormwood sweet when the tongue judges it bitter, he obviously deserves to be repudiated.

> For (human) nature is such that if you take this [viz. the judgment of sensory experience] away from man, you remove his ability to make any judgment whatsoever—unless you can cite another instrument with which man is naturally endowed for judging other than his senses and understanding.[99]

For Castellio, man's very humanity depends upon fidelity to his most basic experiences. He who denies what his senses and understanding communicate denies himself. Castellio cites once again Jesus's use, praise, and appeals to sensory verification and common sense—what one might call natural logic (John 4 : 35; Matt. 21 : 19; 27 : 34; Luke 7 : 22; 24 : 39; 7 : 41—and draws the conclusion:

> When I look at everything Christ did and said, I find nothing that was contrary to the senses and understanding, and for good reason. Since the senses and understanding are the works of the Father, and Christ came to destroy the works of Satan and not those of the Father, it is no surprise that he did not suspend men's senses and understanding. To the contrary, he did as all good teachers do and led men into his teaching by way of sensory experience and understanding. If he found the senses and understanding impaired in any to whom he spoke, he healed them. And he never tried to teach anyone who

98. Ibid., p. 360.
99. Ibid.

lacked senses and understanding. This was only right, for who would have believed him then and who would believe him now, had he spoken to men as if they lacked senses and understanding, teaching what contradicted their most basic experiences? If he had called stone bread or black white or fire cold and said that avarice and treachery were praiseworthy or that a student was greater than his teacher, who would have believed him? [100]

Against this background Castellio is ready to measure John Calvin by the authority of reason. This is undertaken in the twenty-fifth chapter, which culminates in the so-called hymn to reason. Castellio introduces the discussion:

I come now to those who want us to believe, as it were, with our eyes closed, and put our trust in things which contradict our experience. I would like first to know whether they also instruct us with closed eyes (i.e. without judgment, understanding, and reason), or if they have exercised prior judgment. For if they speak without judgment, we correctly reject their counsel. If they speak with judgment and reason, however, they are impertinent to try to persuade us to put aside our judgment of the matter and accept their own, as if we were blind and they seers whom we should follow regardless of the pits of absurdity into which they stumble.[101]

With this initial rebuke, Castellio now takes the crucial step toward justifying the sovereignty of reason in essential and disputed religious matters. Even the established religious authorities, when one examines closely their practice, adjust Scripture to the lessons of reason. Reason is and always has been the de facto arbiter of Scripture and religious truth, *even* among those who would tyrannize men with their own opinions. Castellio brings forth concrete examples.

---

100. Ibid., pp. 361–62. Castellio even argues that the pregnancy of Sara in her old age, an event which brought a howl of laughter from Sara herself, was not absurd, but a completely rational expectation. "Ratio enim iudicat deum, qui mundum creavit, posse etiam ex sterili foemina fertilem facere" (Ibid., p. 375). Such "miracles" as this are not impossible things repugnant to reason, but sensible possibilities above reason. "Longe aliud est credere rem impossibilem et credere rem miraculosam. Miracula multa credunt pii, sed impossibile nihil. Supra sensus item multa credunt, sed contra sensus nihil." Ibid., pp. 375–76.

101. Ibid., p. 362.

I would like for them to tell me why they themselves use reason against the manifest words of God . . . in so many matters. Is it not clear what was meant when Christ said that some have become eunuchs for the kingdom of God? [Matt. 19 : 12]. Yet they condemn Origen for castrating himself and argue that he was deceived by error when he drew such a conclusion from Christ's words. Further, are not the words of Christ clear when he says: "Call no man father or teacher on earth, for your father and teacher is in heaven" [Matt. 23 : 9]? And yet they do not hesitate to call themselves fathers and teachers, and to interpret the words of Christ other than they clearly are. There is no doubt about what is meant by the words: "If any man strike you on the right, turn to him your left, and give to everyone who asks of you, etc." [Matt. 5 : 39 ff.]. Yet, they do not follow these words; indeed, the Anabaptists, who do follow them, are gravely accused and condemned. The same is done with Christ's words forbidding swearing [Matt. 5 : 34]. Indeed, I can cite six hundred places where they judge and dispute against the words [of Scripture]. Why do they do it? No doubt because in other places they find these words contradicted. But why do they twist those particular statements which are so manifest and accommodate them to their own judgment of the matter, rather than twisting and accommodating their judgment to those statements? For example, Christ says that evil is not to be resisted [Matt. 5 : 39]. Why do they then approve the magistrate who resists evil against the Anabaptists [who do not resist evil]? Why do they not rather twist and interpret those statements which applaud the magistrate according to the manifest words of Christ which forbid resistance to evil? They can give but one answer, and I see no other response than this in their writings: reason judges [*iudicet ratio*] and draws a directive [*sententia*] which is to be followed against these words of Scripture, lest something absurd be embraced. This is a correct procedure. And if they can conclude that the judgment of reason is to be preferred to the words and followed in these and other places where the matter dealt with is deemed to fall under the judgment of reason, the same right ought to be extended to us in other places, if we can show that these are matters which fall under the judgment of reason or experience. Otherwise, they deny us, who are also endowed with reason, what they arrogate to themselves as rational men.[102]

It is on the heels of these trenchant comments that Castellio lifts his pen in praise of reason. The eternal and subjective voice of reason is lauded as more authoritative than "writings and ceremonies," i.e. historical tradition. Being the "more ancient and certain," reason claims absolute precedence, the very Son of God bowing to it.

> Reason is, so to speak, the daughter of God. She was before all writings and ceremonies and before the creation of the world, and she will always be after all writings and ceremonies have passed away and the present world is changed and renewed. She can no more be abolished than God himself. Reason, I say, is a certain eternal word of God, far more ancient and certain than writings and ceremonies, according to which God taught his own before there were any ceremonies and writings, and according to which he will teach when ceremonies and writings no longer exist, so that men may truly be taught by God. Abel, Enoch, Noah, Abraham, and many others lived piously according to this reason before the writings of Moses. Many of the ancients so lived, and many will continue to do so. It was according to this reason that Jesus Christ, the son of the living God, lived and taught others and refuted the Jews, who attributed more to writings and ceremonies than to reason. Christ is called in Greek *logos,* i.e. reason or word, which are the same. For reason is, as it were, a certain interior and eternal prayer or word, which always speaks the truth.[103]

While students of Castellio are agreed that this is no scholastic concept of reason, an identification of its sources, and therewith its precise definition, is still awaited. Roland Bainton finds it to be

102. Ibid., p. 363. Paracelsus's rebuke of sixteenth-century medical authorities makes a striking parallel to Castellio's rebuke of the Calvinists. Paracelsus exhorts those who would be "good and worthy physicians" to abandon "phantasei" and blind obeisance to tradition and proceed according to "kunst," that is, according to "alle vernunft, weisheit und sinnlikeit." This is to act in accordance with truth based on "erfarenheit." *Volumen medicinae Paramirum de medica industria* in *Theophrast von Hohenheim, gen. Paracelsus: Sämtliche Werke,* ed. Karl Sudhoff (Munich and Berlin, 1929), 1: 234.

103. *De Arte dubitandi,* p. 363.

a generally unclear concept, although unquestionably pointing to the Enlightenment definition of reason, which bases the truth of ideas on their clarity and universality.[104] Elizabeth Feist Hirsch, the editor of the *De Arte dubitandi,* has suggested that it finds its lineage in the Stoic concept of universal reason.[105] And Heinz Liebing, in a highly insightful yet unpublished work, has argued that the French "bon sens," the English "common sense," and the German "gesunder Menschenverstand" best communicate what Castellio is after.[106] More clearly than others, Liebing has isolated the dual dimensions of Castellio's concept of reason. On the one hand, it is something external, standing outside and over against man as an eternal light. Yet, on the other hand, it is an inborn capacity or organ, an inner light or word.[107]

I think the discussion can be carried to a more definite conclusion. The conjunction of eternal word and internal witness to truth, which marks this concept of reason, suggests the *synteresis* or *Seelengrund* of medieval mystical theology, that created organ of the uncreated in the depths of the human heart. As was seen in an earlier chapter, these anthropological categories deal with what transcends or is deeper than technical reason. They describe an inalienable and incorruptible divine standard, which can function in the stead, as well as judge the corruptible historical media, of God's truth. That Castellio's concept of reason finds its lineage in this mystical tradition is further indicated when he concludes chapter 25 of *On the Art of Doubting* with an appeal to Romans 2 : 14–16—a *locus classicus* for the *synteresis* concept of medieval theology. Harking back to his introductory quest for a present-day prophet to judge good and evil decisively, Castellio maintains that reason creates conscience, which is a present judge identical with the final Judge.

> This is the reason which will accuse those who have done evil and excuse those who have done good in the Last Judgment, as Paul wrote to the Romans: "When Gentiles who

104. "Sebastian Castellio: Champion of Religious Liberty," in *Castellioniana,* pp. 61–62.

105. 'Castellio's *De Arte dubitandi* and the Problem of Religious Liberty," in Becker 1953, pp. 244–58.

106. *Die Schriftauslegung Sebastian Castellios,* p. 83. The thrust of the work is embodied in Liebing's "Die Frage nach einem hermeneutischen Prinzip bei Sebastian Castellio" in Becker 1953, pp. 206–24.

107. *Die Schriftauslegung Sebastian Castellios,* p. 83.

have not the law do by nature what the law requires, they are
a law to themselves, even though they do not have the law.
They show that what the law requires is written on their
hearts, while their conscience also bears witness and their
conflicting thoughts accuse or perhaps excuse them on that
day when, according to my gospel, God judges the secrets of
men by Christ Jesus" [Rom. 2 : 14–16]. Paul speaks here
about his own conscience, a kind of natural self-knowledge
which proceeds from reason and tells him whether what he
has done is good or evil. Reason teaches what is good and
what is evil, and this instruction gives birth to conscience.
. . . Finally, the reason of which we speak searches, finds, and
interprets truth. If something in either profane or sacred writings is obscure or twisted by the passage of time, reason either
corrects it or places it in doubt for the present until the truth
is manifest.[108]

Preoccupation with mystical writings had been an understandable intellectual retreat for Castellio during the painful clashes
with the Calvinists. He was exposed to the medieval mystical
traditions, not only through his work on the *German Theology*
and the *Imitation of Christ,* but also by way of personal contacts.
Jean Bauhin, a man of marked mystical interests, whom Farel
suspected of being Castellio's collaborator on the 1557 edition of
the *German Theology*,[109] was a close friend. Castellio also knew
the radical Anabaptist, David Joris, who resided under a pseudonym in Basel from 1544 to 1556.[110] Joris was quite literate in the
German mystical tradition, and a letter from him to Castellio on
the topic of *Gelassenheit* exists.[111] Joris was also influenced by the

108. *De Arte dubitandi,* p. 364. An earlier parallel to this passage, centering on
Romans 2 : 14–16, is found in Castellio's discussion of the eternal *lex naturae* in the
notes on Exodus 20 in his 1546 Latin translation of the Pentateuch. *Moses Latinus*
(Basel, 1546), p. 486. Here Castellio is commenting on the question of whether or
not Christ abrogated the Mosaic law. The conclusion is drawn that the ceremonial
and national laws of the Jews—i.e. the peculiarly historical—have been abrogated
by Christ. The Mosaic law, however, because it is in agreement with this primal
unwritten law, to which even Christ bows, cannot be abrogated (Ibid., pp. 485–86).
This unwritten law is also described as "ratio divina," having originated simultaneously with the "mens divina." Ibid., pp. 482–83. Cf. Hut, above, p. 106.

109. Buisson 2: 96, n. 7.

110. Roland Bainton, *David Joris: Wiedertäufer und Kämpfer für Toleranz im
16. Jahrhundert* (Leipzig, 1937), esp. pp. 62–63, 74–76, 105–06.

111. Buisson 2: 137–38; 161–62. According to Buisson, Castellio considered trans-
lating a work by Joris—an indication that he may have read closely his writings

writings of Melchior Hofmann and by Joachite motifs. In fact, his spiritualized version of the Joachite vision of history—Joris speaks of three stages of growth in the Spirit modeled on the progression from boyhood through adolescence to manhood—appears almost verbatim in Castellio's discussion of the working of the Spirit in the faithful.[112]

If, as I have argued, a mystically influenced concept of rational autonomy climaxes Castellio's logical critique of Calvinism, then a no less mystically informed view of religious life can be said to conclude his ethical critique. Already in the nineteenth century, Buisson, albeit in bits and snatches, had maintained that Castellio's mature thought was a "new form of mysticism." [113] It was "new" for Buisson because it was strictly "moral"—a sense of self-denial oriented to family and society rather than to a withdrawn contemplative life, and based on the "moral conscience" rather than on priestly or scriptural mediation.[114]

The close connection between the rational, ethical, and mystical in Castellio's mature thought is manifest in his final views on religious justification. Foundational is a traditional insistence that man is "truly cleansed" (*vere sanatus*), "actually made pure" (*vere et reipsa mundum esse*), and is not righteous only by *belief* in an objective pardon (*venia peccatorum*).[115] Castellio—let those who

---

as well as communicated personally with Joris (Ibid., p. 162. Cf. Eugénie Droz, "Sur quelques traductions françaises d'ecrits de David Joris," *Het Boek* 37: 152–62). The "mystical motif" in Joris is treated by Johannes Kühn, *Toleranz und Offenbarung* (Leipzig, 1923), pp. 271–301. Cf. Bainton, *David Joris,* pp. 34–36.

112. Cf. below p. 201. On Joris, see Bainton, *David Joris,* pp. 36–37; Kühn, *Toleranz und Offenbarung,* pp. 288–89.

113. He sees it already emerging in the *Contra libellum Calvini.* Buisson 2: 37–38. Buisson cites as a possible source Bernhardino Ochino, an Italian refugee who entered Geneva in October, 1542, and whose *30 Dialogues* Castellio translated. Ochino placed great stress on clear and simple theological ideas, and supported "un moraliste mystique," i.e. true faith as *sentiment* rather than acquired knowledge. Buisson 1: 227–28. Cf. also Delio Cantimori, "Note su alcuni Aspetti del Misticismo del Castellione e della sua Fortuna" in Becker 1953, pp. 239–43.

114. Buisson 2: 213. Kühn's limited definition of mysticism leads him perhaps to underestimate the close connection, so well recognized by Buisson, between the rational, ethical, and mystical impulses in Castellio's thought. Cf. *Toleranz und Offenbarung,* p. 344.

115. *Tractatus de justificatione* in *Dialogi IV* (Gouda, 1613), pp. 12–14, 17. This treatise composes chapters 7–29 of Book 2 of the *De Arte dubitandi.* It has been deleted from the Feist edition of the latter work, however; hence the use here of the Gouda edition. Castellio summarizes the orthodox position he is opposing as follows: " 'Gratis nos esse justos propter Christum, quem solum invocet fides in omni invocatione, etiamsi nos injusti atque indigni simus. Hominem non in se ipso

incautiously tout his "modernity" take note—even embraces the scholastic categories of "fides inhaerens" and "fides charitate formata" [116] as accurate descriptions. His identification with tradition here is fully contingent upon his concern to define true faith in terms of the ethical ability to execute the commandments of God.[117] A "real change" in man is required to promote the moral life ("mores"). The orthodox Protestant theory of "alien" righteousness only encourages immodesty and bad morals,[118] and is as absurd as saying that health is not in the man who is healthy, but "outside" him in his doctor.[119]

The ethical criterion of religious life drives Castellio not only to exploit congenial scholastic concepts but also to embrace the presuppositions and imagery of mystical union with God. This is initially highlighted by the appearance in the treatise on justification of a special subsection, "De Moribus." Here Castellio lectures the reader on, of all things, horticulture, and with pictorial drawings no less. The purpose soon becomes evident. Castellio wishes to draw an analogy between the grafting of cultured shoots onto wild trees and the insertion of the Spirit of God into the hearts of the faithful. The new, superior growth, which is grafted onto the tree, gradually becomes one with and finally transforms the very nature of its wild host, which henceforth produces new and better fruit. By analogy, the Spirit of God, like a "divine seed" (*semen Dei*),[120] is inserted into the heart of man, gradually transforming his nature. A new man with a new "habitus" emerges.[121] He is a true "participant in divine nature," for whom all things are possible.[122]

---

justum esse, sed quia Christi justitia imputatione cum illis communicetur.'" Ibid., p. 32.

116. *Tractatus de justificatione*, p. 35; *De fide* in *Dialogi IV*, p. 207.

117. Well summarized in the statements: "Parum est credere, posse obediri Deo, nisi insuper viam teneas, qua possit obediri, sine qua obedientia nemo servari potest" (*De fide*, p. 197; cf. p. 206). "Regnum Dei verba non sunt, sed ejus praeceptorum executio." *An Possit homo per Spiritum Sanctum perfecte obedire legi Dei* in *Dialogi IV* (Gouda, 1613), p. 243.

118. *Tractatus de justificatione*, p. 33.

119. Ibid., p. 60.

120. Ibid., p. 88. On the reform significance and mystical sources of the concept of the *semen Dei*, see my article, "The University and the Church: Patterns of Reform in Jean Gerson," *Medievalia et Humanistica* n.s. 1 (1970): 111–26.

121. *Tractatus de justificatione*, pp. 82–83.

122. "Ego de vera justificaque fide loquor, quae hominem reddat participem divinae naturae, efficiatque ut ei sint omnia possibilia." *De fide*, p. 208.

In the dialogue on free will, religious justification is analyzed in terms of the Joachite vision of history. It is pointed out that man does not love God perfectly nor his neighbor as himself overnight. A gradual growth to this point is necessary, and Castellio schematizes it according to three ages of the Spirit within the believer. The first is the age of the Father or the Law, the "boyhood" of the Spirit in man, which is characterized by "faith" or knowledge of God only at a distance and inconsistent obedience. The second age is that of the Son or the Gospel, the "adolescence" of the Spirit in man, which is characterized by "hope" or greater but not perfect knowledge of God and consistent but not perfect obedience. The final age is that of the Spirit or full Truth, the "manhood" or the Spirit in man, which is characterized by "love" or perfect knowledge of God and perfect obedience.[123]

The final age is a realistic possibility even in this life. In February, 1562, Castellio completed a little treatise entitled: "Can Man, Through the Holy Spirit, Perfectly Obey the Law of God?" His answer to that question was a resounding yes. The possibilities open to Adam at his original creation are fully restored to the faithful in their "recreation."

> If God created man perfect and absolutely good, then one must agree that when he recreates him (through the Holy Spirit in Christ), he makes him perfect and absolutely good. God will be no less a perfect artisan when he recreates than he was when he first created.[124]

It is on this basis and in this very practical sense that Castellio maintains that "all things are possible for the faithful," that true faith is "omnipotent power." [125] This was also the central message he found in the *German Theology*. Man must be taught that he can fully conquer sin.[126]

---

123. *De libero arbitrio*, pp. 143–44. Some interesting hermeneutical consequences result from this scheme. E.g. when Scripture mentions the failure of all men to obey the law, it is to be borne in mind that this normally occurs during the age of the Father. Scripture, therefore, does not make a blanket judgment on all men at all times, but only describes the first age of the Spirit in man. Ibid., pp. 145–46.

124. *Questio, An Possit homo per Spiritum Sanctum perfecte obedire legi Dei* in *Dialogi IV,* p. 229.

125. Ibid.; *De fide,* pp. 223–25.

126. "Quis enim id conetur, quod fieri non posse credat? Quis peccata oppugnet, quae expugnari non posse vobis magistris sibi persuaserit? Itaque deest conatus, quia spes deest; neque quisquam unquam strenue peccata oppugnabit, nisi qui expugnari posse credit." *Tractatus de justificatione,* p. 72. Cf. above, pp. 44–45.

If Castellio's view of reason lends itself to interpretation within the *synteresis* tradition of medieval mystical theology, his views on religious justification appear well allied with the presuppositions and imagery of the mystical union with God. The consequences, to be sure, are more forward- than backward-looking, although consistent with the thrust of the medieval mystical tradition. Reason and conscience become the authoritative spokesmen for the divine will in this life, usurping the place of Scripture and the learned *doctores ecclesiae*. And man is granted the power, not only to recapture Adam's perfection, but even to grasp its unrealized possibilities.

8

Valentin Weigel

Dissent in Disguise

Unlike the other figures dealt with in this volume, Valentin Weigel remained an externally orthodox and respected member of the very establishment against which he wrote. In a practical sense this was made possible by the fact that his writings did not begin to see publication until some twenty-one years after his death in 1588.[1] The second half of the sixteenth century was an intense period of enforced doctrinal conformity, and Weigel would hardly have escaped censure had he been in print then. Later, in fact, during the visitation of 1598 when his coworker and deacon for eighteen years, Benedict Biedermann, was discovered to be a devotee of certain "Schwenckfeldian errors" (in truth the views of his mentor), swift measures were taken to harness heterodoxy in Zschopau.[2] When the authorities finally had a full look at Weigel's works in the seventeenth century, to a man they saw in them Thomas Müntzer *redivivus*.[3]

Weigel's only serious encounter with his superiors came very early in his career. Having earned B.A. and M.A. degrees in Leipzig, where he resided from 1554 to 1563, and having soaked up Lutheran school theology for four years in Wittenberg (1563–67),

1. Winfried Zeller, *Die Schriften Valentin Weigels* (Berlin, 1940) [hereafter cited as Zeller 1940], p. 68.

2. Julius Otto Opel, *Valentin Weigel: Ein Beitrag zur Literatur- und Culturgeschichte Deutschlands in 17. Jahrhundert* (Leipzig, 1864), p. 31; Israel, M. *Valentin Weigels Leben und Schriften*, pp. 24–25.

3. Opel, *Valentin Weigel*, pp. 201–23. In a posthumously published critique of Weigelian teaching, Theodor Thumm, Tübingen professor and church superintendent in the Stuttgart district, summarized the reaction with a statement by Luther: "Verum esse illud B. Lutheri: 'der Müntzer ist Todt/aber sein Geist ist noch nicht aussgerottet.'" *Impietas Wigeliana h.e. necessaria admonitio de centum et viginti erroribus novorum prophetarum coelestium, quos a Valentino Wigelio nostra haec aetas dicere coepit Wigelianos . . .* (Tübingen, 1650), p. 1.

the thirty-four-year old Weigel received ordination as a Lutheran pastor (November, 1567) and moved immediately into the parish house in Zschopau in Meissen.[4] No sermons from these important beginning years are extant to give us an independent judgment of Weigel's preaching. Critical reports of it, however, apparently from dissidents within his own congregation, reached the ears of his superintendent in Chemnitz, Georg Langevoith. Weigel found himself compelled, in 1572, to write what amounted to a tract in his own defense: *A Treatise on True Saving Faith or How Adam Must Perish and Die in Us and Christ Arise and Live.*

In the treatise, Weigel time and again wrapped himself in the writings of Luther, especially his sermons. This apparent embracing of orthodoxy once contributed to suspicions about the authenticity of the work. August Israel, a pioneer in text-critical work on Weigel's corpus, viewed it as "watered-down Weigel" and classified it, accordingly, among writings that were only "based on Weigel." [5] Hans Maier accepted the work as fully genuine. In so doing, he was aided by his conviction that Weigel himself was a composite of two quite irreconcilable persons: a mystic/spiritualist and a Lutheran pastor.[6] Maier saw in the defense a clear, if in the long run inconclusive, victory of the latter over the former—a "masterful accommodation" to church doctrine, which fully suspended Weigel's "ahistorical Spiritualism." [7] Recently Winfried Zeller, the modern coeditor of Weigel's works, has suggested that the defense may be an even more subtle matter. Weigel, he argues, does not simply appropriate Lutheran orthodoxy when he takes up citations from Luther. Rather, the latter are "carefully chosen proofs for genuinely mystical points of view." [8] Weigel, in other words, searches out and speaks through a very congenial Luther. In this regard, it is noteworthy that the subtitle of the defense is also that of the *German Theology*, to which Weigel dedicated a treatise in the previous year.[9]

4. Normally, pastors of this church served as apprentices for ten years or longer in surrounding village churches. Weigel, so to speak, went directly to the top.

5. Israel, *Weigels Leben und Schriften*, p. 147.

6. "Ein Doppelleben hat Weigel geführt." "Wir haben zwischen Weigel dem Mystiker und Spiritualisten und Weigel dem lutherischen Pfarrer zu unterscheiden wie zwischen zwei zusammenhangslosen Sonderexistenzen." Maier, *Der mystische Spiritualismus Valentin Weigels*, pp. 25, 31.

7. Ibid., p. 28.

8. *Valentin Weigel. Sämtliche Schriften* (Stuttgart-Bad Cannstatt, 1969), 4: 88; cf. 90–91, 93.

9. Cf. above, pp. 45 ff.

As we look at the defense itself, we might well ask whether the matter is even more subtle than Zeller depicts it. For if Weigel was "hiding" behind carefully chosen statements of Luther (which simultaneously supported his own theological predilections and sheltered him from orthodox criticism), he also covertly criticized the very orthodoxy he appeared to embrace when he turned Luther's words against the "external religion" of the "Maulchristen." To be sure, the latter were "Roman" by name, but by implication they also inhabited the universities and bishoprics of Lutheranism.

In the preface to the defense, Weigel offers the following assessment of the occasion for writing it and the purpose he intends it to serve.

> To the best of my ability, I try to keep two things in view in all my sermons—the knowledge of sin through the law and the grace (of God) in Christ. My sermons seek especially to plant true faith, from which uncoerced good works come forth as certain signs and fruits of a good tree. I always preach so that Adam may daily be sacrificed and killed, crucified and buried with Christ, and the new man arise from the old sinful way of life. Now I do not preach these things in words of my own devising nor with embellished speech, skimming around on the surface. Rather I plunge straightway into the inner core with the pure and unpretentious formulas and address of the Apostles. Because I do this some have spoken ill of me behind my back and given me a bad name. They judge with unseasoned understanding and betray their true selves by the very things they approve and disapprove. Hence, I am now forced, with God's help, to set forth a short summary of the content of all my sermons past and present and to offer and dedicate it to your grace, my dear superintendent and inspector.[10]

The defense proceeds to excoriate the "Maulchristen" who look only to "external history," "skimming around on the surface," as Weigel would have it.[11] The descriptions of these "men who are

10. *Ein Büchlein vom wahren seligmachenden Glauben, wie Adam in uns untergehen und sterben müsse und Christus dargegen in uns solle auferstehen und leben,* ed. W. Zeller, in *Sämtliche Schriften* (Stuttgart-Bad Cannstatt, 1969), 5: 9–10.
11. Ibid., pp. 28, 30, 52.

Christian in mouth only" draw upon polemical rhetoric and caricature already well intrenched in sixteenth-century circles of dissent, reaching all the way back to Müntzer's pioneer efforts against Luther. Representative is the statement:

> As the worldly man is absolutely oblivious to Adam and is yet fully Adamic in nature, so would the man who is Christian in mouth only now be like Christ. He tells us: "Christ has saved me. He has died for me. He has fulfilled the law. Let him hang on the cross, suffer, die, and render satisfaction for the sin of the world!" This man has his faith on his tongue and not in his heart, and he can very skillfully lecture and chatter about faith and Scripture. But true faith demands that Christ be taken up not only as a gift of grace, but also as an example and model for our own lives. He must be known in such a way that we put on the new man, Jesus Christ, and try "to live just as he lived," to let him dwell in our hearts by faith and begin "to purify us even as he was pure." 1 John 3 : 1, John 2.[12]

A historical Christ "outside me" is absolutely useless. "The merit of Christ is beneficial to me in direct proportion to my faith in him, i.e. to the extent to which I change and better myself in true faith." [13] "In short, where man does not fight against flesh and blood, and repent and improve himself, there I say without qualification that not a spark of faith is present, but only a dead feigned illusion [of faith] [*ein todter erdicter Wahn*]." [14] Weigel, as Müntzer had also done, censures those who think it sufficient simply to appeal to the faith of their fathers: "Parents save no one . . . Should the holiness and piety of parents make children faithful and blessed, then Lucifer and Adam would never have been unfaithful, for they had the holiest Father of all." [15]

Over against the Christ who lives "in the ears, on the tongue, and on paper" and "floats outside us like froth on beer," [16] Weigel exalts, in the vibrant language of German mysticism, the Christ who dwells in the "best part of man," in the "ground of the heart."

12. Ibid., p. 17.
13. Ibid., p. 27; cf. pp. 19–20.
14. Ibid., p. 29.
15. Ibid., p. 56.
16. Ibid., pp. 39–40.

True faith does not remain outside man, but is a living, active thing in the inner ground of the heart, i.e. in the core of man. For the heart or the inner man is the center of man where Christ dwells through faith. This tenant, Christ, chooses the best part, viz. the spirit or heart.[17]

Hence, so long as the external Christ, with all his history and accomplishments, remains on paper, sounds in the ears, and hovers on the tongue, and does not come into the inner ground of the heart through faith, he will not save you. For true faith does not spring from the mouth or the ear but from the inner ground of the heart.[18]

That, in a nutshell, is what Weigel had been preaching to his congregation. No doubt one source of official concern with it was that it seemed to question the necessity of a prominent institutional role in the religious life. Practically speaking, books, mouths, and ears are the sine quibus non of ecclesiastical routine. Had not Luther himself said that the "ears alone" are the organs of the Christian man? [19] Weigel courts his own suspicion when he writes of priestly absolution:

Everything hinges on true faith. Where that is present there is true absolution and forgiveness of sins, although you may not have a priest by your side. As often as you pray, "forgive us our sins . . . ," and then also forgive your neighbor from your heart, so long will you have true absolution. And as often as you bemoan your sins with a penitent heart, be-

17. Ibid., p. 34.
18. Ibid., p. 52.
19. This passage illustrates the ambivalent uses to which Luther's pronouncements lend themselves. On the one hand, the "ears alone" are defended as the organs of the Christian, but on the other hand, this is said in opposition to external ceremonial religion. "In the new law all those endless ceremonial burdens, which are merely occasions for sin, have been taken away. God no longer requires feet, hands, or any other member, only the ears. To this extent everything is restored to a simple rule of life. For if you ask a Christian what the work is by which he is made worthy of the name Christian, he can give no other answer than hearing the word of God, which is faith. Thus the ears alone are the organs of a Christian man, because not by the works of any other member but by faith is he justified and judged a Christian." *Lectures on the Epistle to the Hebrews,* ed. and trans. James Atkinson, in *Luther: Early Theological Works,* The Library of Christian Classics (Philadelphia, 1962), 16: 194–95.

lieving in Christ, you have the true priest, Jesus Christ, at your side, who absolves and forgives all your sins.[20]

Weigel meets his critics head on. Does this teaching threaten the external offices and ordinances of the church? On the contrary, he argues, it guarantees and even increases their importance!

> If one has true faith, one does not despise the office of preaching, as now unfortunately happens, nor does one neglect the holy sacraments. Rather, faith drives the believer to them so that he may hear, read, exercise, and use them with thanksgiving according to the will of Christ in genuine invocation of the Holy Spirit. For, by God's truth, if we have faith, we are truly driven and led to the right use and exercise of all external things and do not despise them.[21]

As those who would judge him know, the subtlety of the matter in the New Testament and Luther, as well as with Weigel, cannot be gainsaid. The defense was successful, and no action was taken against Weigel in 1572. As we look at it in larger perspective, it suggests that the posthumous publication of his writings was not the only factor in his ability to survive his own nonconformist views. He was not, it appears, above disguising his dissent and practicing what might be called constructive fraud.[22] Given the spirit of the times, a certain duplicity was the most effective, as well as the most prudent, course for the reform-minded dissenter. It permitted the retention of at least half a loaf in an age not loath to remove the whole.

IN DEFENSE OF SUBJECTIVITY

Zeller has distinguished three periods in Weigel's development. The first is a mystical early period (1570–71) in which the concepts of Eckhart, Tauler, and the *German Theology* (especially the key notion of *Gelassenheit*) were uncritically taken up in order to pose a solution to contemporary Lutheran battles over the nature of religious justification.[23] Zeller argues that it is only with his first epistemological treatise, *Know Thyself* (*Gnothi seauton*) in 1571,

20. *Ein Büchlein vom wahren seligmachenden Glauben*, p. 72.

21. Ibid., p. 57.

22. See below p. 243.

23. "Meister Eckhart bei Valentin Weigel," *ZKG* 57 (1938): 320–21, 313–14; cf. Zeller 1940, pp. 7–8. See our discussion above, pp. 45 ff.

the last writing before the defense of 1572, that Weigel began to emerge as his own man.[24] The second period in Zeller's scheme is one filled with didactic and sermonic literature and dated 1572–76. The *Informatorium* of 1576, cited as the terminus of this period, is said to consolidate the lessons of the mystical period and to mark the beginning of the transition into the final, mature period.[25] In this last period, dated 1578–84 and introduced by the great *Postille* of 1578–79, Zeller sees Weigel as breaking with the spiritualizing tendencies of German mysticism and turning to the more involved and forward-looking tenets of Paracelsist natural philosophy. "In place of a simple mysticism come a point of view schooled in the natural philosophy of Paracelsus and a sharp critique of the church." [26] The transition, according to Zeller, is marked by the closely interrelated concepts of the "heavenly flesh of Christ" (i.e. the teaching that Christ's human nature is not from Adam, but, like his divine nature, from God) and the necessity of man's "bodily" renewal or new birth in Christ.[27] These motifs are latent in Weigel's thought from the beginning, but they do, as Zeller argues, come into prominence only in the later writings.[28]

Without challenging the broader outlines of Zeller's development thesis, we will want to concentrate on the possibility that Weigel's manifest later concern for "bodily" renewal, not only individually but also sociopolitically, agrees as much with his mystical sources as with the natural philosophy of Paracelsus. In Weigel medieval mysticism and Paracelsist natural philosophy meet more in an alliance than in a break or transition. In this

24. "Die erste wirklich selbständige Leistung Weigels." Zeller 1940, p. 7; *ZKG* 57 (1938): 334–55.

25. Zeller 1940, pp. 7, 39.

26. Ibid., p. 52.

27. "In dieser Zeit bricht Weigel mit der Spiritualisierung, der Vergeistigung der Mystik, und an ihre Stelle tritt eine an der Naturphilosophie des Paracelsus geschulte Mystik der 'Verleiblichung'" (Zeller 1940, pp. 7–8). Cf. *Valentin Weigel. Sämtliche Schriften* (Stuttgart-Bad Cannstatt, 1964), 2: 114.

28. They also form the major point of divergence between Weigel and his deacon Biedermann, who not only coauthored and in strong partisan fashion expanded several of Weigel's works, but is also to be regarded as the author of several writings once ascribed either to Weigel or to unknown disciples. Fritz Lieb, *Valentin Weigels Kommentar zur Schöpfungsgeschichte und das Schrifttum seines Schülers Benedikt Biedermann* (Zürich, 1962), pp. 11, 27. A history of the concept of the heavenly flesh of Christ is Hans J. Schoeps, *Vom himmlischen Fleisch Christi* (Tübingen, 1951).

section, however, we want to look at background still more basic
to Weigel's thought, especially at one recurrent theme that is as
prominent an assumption in the defense of 1572 as it is in the
offense he launched in his last literary period: the subjective
character of knowledge.[29]

The elaboration of this theme is the purpose of the two epistemological treatises, *Know Thyself* and *The Golden Grasp* (*Der
güldene Griff*) (1578).[30] Although in some ways two sides of the
same coin, the motif assumes two distinct basic forms. The first
is more philosophical and concerns the epistemological primacy of
the individual mind over against so-called objective reality. The
title of chapter 11 in Book 1 of *Know Thyself* states it succinctly:
"All natural knowledge or conceptualization comes from the
[inner, knowing] eye itself, and not from the [external, known]
object." [31] "As the eye is, so is the knowledge." [32] Or, in its most
popular form: "Knowledge is in the one who knows, not in the
thing known; judgment is in the one who judges, not in the thing
judged." [33]

Weigel, a Lutheran pastor in hypertense times, was not concerned simply to theorize about the foundations and mechanics
of human knowledge. Hence a more theological (and increasingly
polemical) version of the motif is also present, which exalts the
soteriological primacy of the depths of the soul over against the
institutional loci of divine knowledge and presence (Scripture,
creeds, and sacraments). This is the form in which the motif, fully
controlled, appears in the defense of 1572. It is well summarized

29. Zeller deals with this motif under the description "immanence of supernatural knowledge" (*ZKG* 57 [1938]: 335, 347). Koyré treats it at length in his
chapter on Weigel in *Mystiques, spirituels, alchimistes* (Paris, 1955), esp. pp. 94 ff.
This chapter previously appeared in *Cahiers de la revue d'histoire et de philosophie
religieuses* 22 (1930). It is now subject to qualification in light of the fact that the
Studium universale, a basic document in Koyré's interpretation, is not an authentic
writing of Weigel's. Cf. Lieb, *Valentin Weigels Kommentar*, p. 58; Zeller 1940, p. 69.

30. Certain chapters from *Gnothi seauton* appear only in the published version
and are absent from the original manuscripts. These are: Book 1, chaps. 12–14, 19–
21 and Book 2, chaps. 2, 6–10, 18–21 (Zeller 1940, pp. 22–23). *Der güldene Griff*
repeats material from Book 1 of *Gnothi seauton*, chaps. 10, 11, 14, and 15 (ibid., pp.
42–45). According to Zeller, it must be read with critical caution since numerous
points have been "tendenziös korrigiert" in order to tone down Weigel's sharp
statements. Ibid., p. 42.

31. *Gnothi seauton. Nosce Teipsum. Erkenne dich selbst* (Newenstadt, 1615), p.
29.

32. Ibid., p. 30.

33. Ibid., pp. 32–33.

(without baring its polemical teeth) in the title of chapter 14 of Book 2 of *Know Thyself*: "That we are sufficiently persuaded by the image of God within us of what Christ or the unchangeable will of God is and that we come to the Father in heaven only through Christ." [34] Weigel summarizes simply in *The Golden Grasp*: "Man is before all books." [35]

> All knowledge of divine things comes from man himself and not from books. . . . If only the universities and wise men of the world could grasp this "handle" and brief rule, they would not work so hard to gather wisdom from books and, in the presence of God, lead themselves and others into such great darkness and error.[36]

Here the polemical concern emerges. Weigel, in fact, maintains in conclusion that he has written *The Golden Grasp* precisely so that the simple man of faith can learn to stand strong like David before Goliath, i.e. before "the clever, worldly-wise theologians and *doctores*." [37]

His defense of the subjective character of knowledge earned Weigel the reputation of being, not only among the first to pose the "basic problem of modern philosophy," but also of materially anticipating the critical philosophy of Immanuel Kant.[38] Quite apart from the issue of Weigel's modernity, however, this motif, in both forms, can be interpreted well within the theological and philosophical traditions of his earliest and most basic sources, the writings of German mysticism.[39]

The early writings evidence the larger metaphysical presuppositions we associate with Augustinian theology and Neoplatonic philosophy, and they are conveyed to Weigel primarily through

34. Ibid., Bk. 2, p. 102. Or: "Nun ist Christus der aussdrückliche Wille Gottes/ und das unwandelbare Göttliche Gesetze in unser Hertz geschrieben." Ibid.

35. *Der güldene Griff/Das ist: Alle Dinge ohne Irrthum zu erkennen/vielen Hochgelehrten unbekannt/und doch allen Menschen nothwendig zu wissen*, in *Theologia Weigelii* (Frankfurt, 1699), p. A 6 b.

36. Ibid., p. A 6 a.

37. Ibid., p. J 5 b.

38. Längin, *ZGPh* 41 (1932): 435, 439. Maier states: "Kant ist die Uebersetzung Weigels ins Rationalistische. Die mystisch-transzendenten Züge Weigels sind bei Kant exproprиiert." *Der mystische Spiritualismus Valentin Weigels*, p. 109.

39. Zeller already relates Book 1, chap. 13 of *Know Thyself* to the teaching of Eckhart that man is a dwelling-place and temple of God. *ZKG* 57 (1938): 335. Koyré described the motif as "un Augustinisme paracelsiste," a wedding of Augustinian epistemology and Paracelsist cosmology. *Mystiques, Spirituels, Alchimistes*, p. 98.

his mystical sources (Eckhart, Tauler, and the *German Theology*).[40] In the *Scholasterium christianum* of 1571, for example, eternity (which is equated with *Deus, quies, stabilitas, nunc indivisibile*) and time are contrasted in terms of cause and effect, the simple and the composite, being and image, and the one and the many.[41] A parallel contrast between *spiritualitas* and *corporalitas* also appears and culminates in the lavish praise: "Our soul is spirit and God is spirit; hence the soul is in God and God in the soul, for they are of the same nature." [42] A little treatise written in the same year, *God Cannot Deny Himself (2 Timothy 2)* (dated July 17, 1571), sets forth the correlative disparagement of temporal being. The theme of this treatise centers on how appropriate it is for man, as created being, to deny himself, whereas God, as uncreated unity and goodness, could hardly do so.[43] Weigel summarizes:

> Everything that has come into being at the creation was previously nothing. Hence, all created being is properly and in itself [*proprie et per se*] nothing, having being only accidentally [*per accidens*]. This is what it means to be created: to be nothing *per se* and something only *per accidens*.[44]

As created being, man is himself the forbidden tree in the garden of Eden.[45] Understandably, the constructive moment in this trea-

40. It is also to be noted that as *magister artium* Weigel held responsibility for seminars in natural philosophy at the University in Leipzig. The philosophy in question was Aristotelian and included the study of astronomy (Opel, *Valentin Weigel*, p. 13). This background no doubt contributes to the cosmological speculation of *Gnothi seauton*, as does also a beginning acquaintance with the writings of Paracelsus, whose name already appears in this early period. Book 1, chapter 18 of *Gnothi seauton* praises astronomy as the noblest of crafts after the study of Scripture and credits it with being the expert on the natural man. *Gnothi seauton*, pp. 47–48.

41. *Scholasterium christianum Seu Ludus credentium, quo taedium horarum seu temporis molestia abigitur et levatur*, in Paracelsus, *Philosophia mystica* (Newenstadt [Magdeburg?], 1618), pp. 158–60, 162. The *Scholasterium* alternates German and Latin chapters, the former being, according to Zeller, later interpolations. Zeller 1940, p. 16.

42. *Scholasterium christianum*, pp. 170–71.

43. *Deus non potest se ipsum negare. 2. Thimoth. 2*, in *Libellus theosophiae De veris reliquiis seu semine Dei in nobis post lapsum relicto* . . . (Newenstadt, 1618), pp. 20–22.

44. Ibid., p. 23; cf. pp. 24, 26, 28.

45. "So ist nun eine jede vernünftige creatur der verbotene baum selbst/das ist sie soll nicht ihr eigen sein/sie soll nicht zu ihr selbst sich neigen/sie soll allein des

tise concerns mystical *Gelassenheit:* he who is nothing should deny himself altogether and await the advent of divine being.[46]

Already in the *Scholasterium christianum* the polemical possibilities of this traditional dualism are being tested. Criticism is turned on the "extra nos": "The kingdom of God or God is not found in any place outside us [*extra nos*], only in the Spirit within ourselves." [47] And it is said of those who look to the historical Christ: "The Antichrist clings to the external merit, death, and passion of Christ." [48]

Much more detailed is the treatise *Know Thyself.* The stated purpose of this dense little work is to study microcosmic man first as he is "by nature" (*natürlich*) (Book 1) and then "according to the teaching of Christ" or supernaturally (*übernatürlich*) (Book 2), the latter referring to his rebirth in Christ.[49] Man, we learn, consists of body, spirit, and soul. The first two proceed from the physical creation. The body originates in the elements of the earth, the spirit in the firmament of the stars (hence its name "spiritus sydereus"). The latter is equivalent to imagination and reason and embraces all "earthly craft, understanding, and wisdom." [50] Since body and spirit are "from nature," which in turn is "from nothing," they are mortal. The soul, on the other hand, is a "spirit from God." It proceeds "ex spiraculo vitae," from the very mouth of God, and is absolutely indestructible.[51]

This threefold anthropology is also expressed in terms of man's having "two bodies" (visible and invisible) and "two spirits" (from nature and from God). The second "body" is but a comprehensive way of saying that spirit and soul comprise an (invisible) individual entity distinct from the body proper. This is fully consistent with the foregoing, as can be illustrated with the following diagram.

---

bleiben/in gantzer gelassenheit/von dem sie geschaffen ist. In Summa, sie soll die eigenschafft eines bildens oder eines schaffers wol behalten." Ibid., p. 25.

46. The mystical terminology in the treatise at this point is striking: "absterbung und verleugnung sein selbst"; "stille halten wie eine reine braut/und sich besamen oder beschlaffen lassen von Gott von ihme schwanger werden"; "es muss stracks das wort Gottes in uns vermenscht werden/Gott will alles in uns sein." Ibid., p. 25.

47. *Scholasterium christianum*, p. 176; cf. p. 178.

48. Ibid., p. 179.

49. *Gnothi seauton*, Bk. 1, pp. 3, 8.

50. Ibid., pp. 11–12, 22.

51. Ibid., pp. 11–12.

Created Man

2 bodies		2 spirits	
1. Visible (= "Body")		1. From nature	⎰ Imagination ⎱ (= "Spirit")
2. Invisible			⎱ Reason ⎰
		2. From God (= "Soul")[52]	

Weigel summarizes his reflection with a version of the traditional "three-eye" anthropology: the fleshly eye (*oculus carnis/sen-
suum*), which perceives the physical world; the eye of reason
(*oculus rationis*), which develops worldly knowledge and crafts;
and the eye of the mind (*oculus mentis/intellectus*), which can
reach even to God and has "knowledge not unlike that of the
angels."[53] The fleshly eye is described as both "outer" (the five
senses) and "inner" (imagination). Imagination is the inner light
that makes sense out of sensory data. Very important to Weigel is
the fact that it can, even without immediate external stimulation,
recreate and even elaborate upon the sensory experiences of the
external world. However, imagination still remains circumscribed
by the limitations of the corporeal world, since it cannot conceive
a matter other than in terms of space and time. It is bound by
nature to operate in corporeal forms and figures.

Not so reason. The superiority of reason to imagination lies
in the former's ability to abstract completely from time and
place.[54] And, as reason surpasses imagination, so the eye of the
mind transcends still further the eye of reason. For it not only
abstracts from time and place as does reason, but it can also
penetrate even to the eternal and rationally inconceivable God
and his angelic host. Indeed, when the eye of the mind is active,
"imagination and reason must cease their operations altogether."[55]
Weigel pulls all this together in the following diagram.[56] The

52. Ibid., pp. 19–22. The influence of Paracelsus is clear. Cf. W.-E. Peuckert,
Pansophie: Ein Versuch zur Geschichte der weissen und schwarzen Magie, 2d ed.
(Berlin, 1956), pp. 196–200, 297 ff.; Walter Pagel, *Das medizinische Weltbild des
Paracelsus: Seine Zusammenhänge mit Neuplatonismus und Gnosis* (Wiesbaden,
1962), pp. 46–66; esp. pp. 53 ff.

53. *Gnothi seauton*, Bk. 1, pp. 24–28; cf. *Der güldene Griff*, pp. C 1 a–C 3 b.
Compare Gerson, above, pp. 5–6.

54. "Die Vernunfft sihet wol ein Ding/in keiner Zeit nit Orte . . . Solches sihet
Ratio wol/aber die imaginatio mag es nicht erkennen/uber leibliche Dinge. Aber
die vernunfft uberhebet sich uber alle leibliche Dinge." *Gnothi seauton*, Bk. 1, p. 27.

55. Ibid., pp. 27–28.

56. *Der güldene Griff*, p. C 3 a.

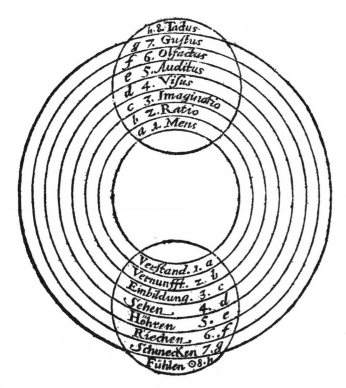

concentric circles indicate decreasing degrees of "inwardness, spirituality, and nobility." The eye of the mind abuts the very core of ultimate reality, and the sense of touch is considered the coarsest of all human functions.

It is against this theoretical background that Weigel maintains the primacy in knowledge and salvation of the individual mind and soul. His anthropology teaches that the "illumination" requisite to true knowledge, sacred and profane, exists within and proceeds from the soul. It is not imported from the outside world. As in classical Augustinian (Neoplatonic) epistemology, the soul's first orientation and alliance are vertical and not horizontal. Its first interaction is with the exemplary world of the divine mind, not with the physical and historical forms of the external world. Echoes of Augustine are quite perceptible in Weigel's summaries of this point. "All knowledge of truth and wisdom are preexistent (*zuvor . . . liege*) in man and are not brought into him from without, from the object." [57] "The inner eye of the heart or the

57. Ibid., p. D 2 b.

soul needs no external light or medium, for it has its own sight and light within." [58] "Supernatural knowledge can well be called divine knowledge, for it does not enter us from without but comes down to us from above, from God and the illumination of the Holy Spirit; there, above us, the object is already present within us, in the inner ground of the soul and heart, i.e. God, the Word, finds there his dwelling-place." [59]

Polemical application of these reflections is quickly forthcoming in the two epistemological treatises. Already in the 1571 sections of *Know Thyself* [60] Weigel attacks the external religion of those variously described as "learned theologians" (*Schrifftgelehrten*), the "worldly-pious" (*Weltfrommen*) and the "worldly-wise" (*Weltgelehrten*). These men, he tells us, are God's "worst enemies," more difficult to convert than whores and adulterers.[61] "They lead the people away from the kingdom of God to external things and bind Christ to external places, persons, and forms." [62] Against them Weigel argues that the kingdom of God is "placeless" (*illocale*) and closer to us than we are to ourselves. For, as Eckhart and Tauler teach, the purified soul is God's true dwelling-place and temple.[63] Indeed, the man who has Christ in his heart already has all the necessary "externals"; "for Christ is all these things—all laws, Scripture, books, and ceremonies are found perfectly in Christ." [64]

It must be borne in mind that the 1570s were the heyday of Protestant scholasticism in the sixteenth century. This was a period of intense intra- and inner-confessional quarreling and, as Weigel's defense of 1572 pointedly illustrates, of policing the faith. *The Golden Grasp* was written at a time when the *Formula of*

58. Ibid., p. B 2 a; cf. *Gnothi seauton*, Bk. 1, 30.

59. *Der güldene Griff*, E 4 a; cf. ibid., G 8 a.

60. In dealing with the polemical material in *Gnothi seauton*, I will also draw somewhat on chapters added after 1571. Although some of this later material may not be from Weigel's own hand but from that of a disciple (Biedermann?), it should be dealt with at this juncture for two reasons: (1) it illustrates in the appropriate context the polemical possibilities, if not necessary consequences, of Weigel's early philosophical reflections; (2) all of the material used conforms well with the later criticisms, indisputably Weigel's own, which we will encounter in the *Postille* of 1578–79 and his last writings. In fact, I find nothing here which is not only later affirmed but also stated even more strongly.

61. *Gnothi seauton*, Bk. 2, pp. 110–11.

62. Ibid., p. 99.

63. Ibid., pp. 99–101.

64. Ibid., pp. 108–09.

Concord was imposing the peace of doctrinal conformity upon Lutherans. This document, which Weigel, like every other Lutheran pastor who wished to remain in business, was obliged to ratify, set forth consensus formulae which, from Weigel's theological perspective, spelled out a thoroughgoing conservative victory.[65] The "golden grasp" of which the title speaks refers to that inner light and truth which every man can confidently hold to during the storms of worldly madness.[66]

The correlation between Weigel's preoccupation with the mechanics of knowledge and his polemical purposes is perhaps most instructively revealed by the fact that the very formulation of the principle of subjectivity cited by scholars (from Book 1, chapter 12 of *Know Thyself*) to highlight his modernity comes, not at the conclusion of prolonged philosophical reflection, but as the punchline in an argument with those who exalt the priority of Scripture.

> No one will understand the Bible, read it with profit or receive its true witness, if he is not first taught and illumined by God, so that he comes to the Bible with a pure eye. For all external things or visible objects only witness, admonish, awaken, guide, or introduce [us to something]. They cannot effect understanding or judgment. The latter must be present beforehand in the eye and is not first discovered in the object. For knowledge is in the one who knows, not in the thing known, and judgment is in the one who judges, not in the thing judged.[67]

Like the angels in heaven, man was originally created to live without externals altogether. In the beginning Adam "was inwardly and not outwardly oriented [*innerlich und nit eusserlich*], needing no external Scripture, laws, or ceremonies, since he lived in the law of the Spirit and of Light." [68] "God has not created man for the earth, although he must dwell upon the earth; rather he is created for heaven, and it is there that he finds his home and fatherland." [69] It was only with Adam's Fall, when he ceased

---

65. Cf. below, pp. 224–25. On the *Formula of Concord* see Seeberg, *Textbook*, 2: 378 ff.

66. Cf. above, pp. 57–58.

67. *Gnothi seauton*, Bk 1, 32–33.

68. *Ibid.*, Bk. 2, p. 121.

69. Ibid., p. 124. Weigel appeals to Colossians 3 and Philippians 3.

to be exclusively inner and heaven directed, that externals made their appearance.

> Then the law of the letter proceeded from the law of the Spirit, and Scripture, together with ceremonies, came forth from the Word, as an image or shadow of the true reality, in order to guide the outer man back into the inner man and to Christ.[70]

Since the Fall, the inner begets the outer, not for its own sake but in order to initiate the return to the inner.[71] Externals are both a testimony to human frailty and, if correctly employed, the means of returning man to his lost strength and glory.

> After the fall into sin, the law, together with ceremonies and books, appeared as an introduction to the [now forgotten] inner man, i.e. to the true, inner book of the law of the heart, from which all books have been written. Hence all ceremonies, scripture, and law are given as a memorial, witness, stimulus, and pointer to the inner ground [of the heart].[72]

The poverty of Scripture per se is evident to Weigel by the absence of agreement among its interpreters. "If understanding is imported into man from a book, i.e. if knowledge comes from the object, then it should follow that a hundred readers [of the same text] will reach the same understanding; our experience, however, is the very reverse." [73] Indeed, the more complete one's preoccupation with Scripture, the greater the likelihood that one's true self will be forgotten. Weigel censures the learned for lacking "Gelassenheit," that passive tranquillity and openness which gives God room to work. "They are far from the kingdom of God with their books, Scripture, and scholarship; they are so crammed with arts and sciences that God cannot find space the size of a pin's head to work within them." [74] The heathen masters, Hermes

70. Ibid., p. 121. Cf. ibid., p. 38, with citation of Erasmus's *Encomion moriae*.
71. *Der güldene Griff*, p. F 3 b.
72. Ibid., p. F 6 b.
73. Ibid., p. A 7 b; cf. ibid., p. H 1 a–b.
74. Ibid., p. J 2 a. The common man is also censured for lacking "Gelassenheit" —but because he is too preoccupied with physical labor or frivolous, carnal pursuits (ibid.). Weigel (citing Tauler) argues that the degree of divine illumination one receives is directly proportional to the degree of *Gelassenheit* one achieves: "nach der Maass der Gelassenheit oder Glaubens wird empfangen des Liechtes von dem ewigen Objecto, die Wohnung im Himmel sind ausgetheilet/einem jeden/nach dem

Trismegistos and Proclus, are credited with having better understood the matter of new birth than the "high theologians." [75]

If the primary hermeneutical horizon is God's spirit in the heart and not the written page of Scripture, then how does this teaching differ from the condemned doctrines of the fanatics ("Enthusiasta")? This question is raised on two occasions in Book 1 of *Know Thyself*. And, as in the defense of 1572, the shrewdly self-serving reply is that such teaching actually enhances the institutional role in the religious life. Indeed, it is the final justification for it.

> Because the Word of God is already present in us, it does not follow that one ought not preach, teach, and study it. And, conversely, because it is preached, taught, and heard in church, it does not follow that it is not previously present in us. Indeed, one should preach, read, hear, pray, and strive for the Word of God precisely because it is already there. For were it not, then there would be no book, no Scripture, and all writing, preaching, reading, and hearing would be in vain.[76]

COSMOLOGY AS EXPOSÉ

In 1575–76, Weigel composed *A Useful Little Treatise on the Place of the World*. This work, a sign of his intellectual expansion, combines a variety of geographical (notably Franck's chronicles), mystical (notably Boethius, Eckhart, and the *German Theology*) and hermetic (Hermes Trismegistos and Paracelsus) material.[77] It is distinguished by a somewhat novel attempt to place cosmology in the service of theological polemic. As the title only partially reveals, it is a study of the earth's place in the larger scheme of the universe and the appropriate didactic lessons to be drawn from it. In truth, the treatise is a kind of "scientific" monastic routine or exercise. In what approximates enraptured

---

er sich im Glauben Gott gelassen und ergeben hat" (ibid., p. E 7 b). On Tauler, cf. my *Homo Spiritualis*, pp. 30 ff.

75. *Gnothi seauton*, Bk. 2, p. 117.

76. Ibid., Bk. 1, p. 54. The second answer reiterates the Bible's role as "Warnung/Zeugnuss/Unterricht/Lehre/Memorial/etc." of the Spirit within. Ibid., Bk. 1, pp. 33–34.

77. Cf. *Valentin Weigel. Sämtliche Schriften* (Stuttgart-Bad Cannstatt, 1962), 1: 103–18.

meditation, Weigel contemplates the world and discovers that the
more its true nature and destiny are recognized, the more imperative and justified become one's retreat from and criticism of it.
"When, with my inward eye, I transcend myself and behold the
fullness of the cosmos, the world seems so small. And the more I
rise above it, the smaller it becomes, so that finally it is hardly the
size of a pea or a mustard seed. In fact, it is nothing." [78] In such
"flight," one sees that "the earth is but a small point, and the
entire world, viewed against the infinity in which it hangs suspended, is so very tiny, indeed, it is nothing at all." [79] One learns
that all corporeal things are but "the excrement or coagulated
smoke of invisible stars, consisting of [impermanent] sulphur, salt,
and mercury." [80] And so the exercise goes.

Full discovery of the perishable nature of *temporalia* occasions
an adjustment of one's posture in relation to the world in the most
practical way. Daily life becomes a less intimidating affair. One
sees that

> it is very foolish for men to labor anxiously over kingdoms,
> cities, fields, houses, meadows, gardens, money, and the like.
> For the earth is but one point in the firmament, and before
> eternal heaven the entire world is and will remain nothing.
> Everything that is external to us is not our own and cannot
> make us happy. The body itself is not our home, for it can be
> taken away by men and worms. Our fatherland is within us
> and embraces all things.[81]

Earthly potentates, secular and ecclesiastical, are rendered much
less awesome.

> From such observations many useful and necessary things are
> discovered about this mortal life. There you will see truly
> your earthly potentates and kings, and observe how small
> and weak your rulers are when compared with others, and how
> they are all nothing at all when compared with the eternal
> kingdom of Christ. The same will be seen in your theologians,
> who serve you wantonly for the sake of the Antichrist. You

78. *Ein nützliches Tractätlein: Vom Ort der Welt,* ed. W. E. Peuckert, in *Sämtliche Schriften* 1: 45; cf. p. 49.
79. Ibid., p. 10.
80. Ibid., p. 47.
81. Ibid., p. 57.

will recognize your error and see that the kingdom of heaven cannot be bound to place, person, tradition, or external ceremony, but stands free in the Spirit and in faith, bound neither here nor there. Luke 17.[82]

Normally the dissenter makes his case by critically juxtaposing to the present a past or future historical ideal. Weigel's exercise suggests an even more ambitious critique: the juxtaposition of eternal heaven itself! Heaven and infinity put the earth and its powers in manageable perspective. Thomas Müntzer had earlier accused the Lutherans of using eschatology as an excuse for leaving the world exactly as it is. Only at the end and not within history, they counsel, can one expect a definitive separation of good and evil.[83] Without taking up the sword as Müntzer had done, Weigel argues that the future situation is a critical norm which can now be applied to the present. In Müntzerian prose, he chides the dawdling theologians.

> The worldly-wise dare to tell us: "It is not to be pursued further now; it is too high a matter; it must be postponed *ad Academiam aeternam.*" O you poor theologians! Who will exegete the Scripture for you in heaven? For then there will be no Scripture. Have you learned nothing here? In heaven one will not look on you as privileged professors. There one will preach no sermons. There, within each, God alone will be preacher, teacher, and professor to high and low, learned and simple alike. . . . And this does not apply only to eternity, but even more to this life. I must be taught now in this world by God. And what I learn here from him will also serve me then. Were I to postpone this and wait as you say until the next life, I would join you in acting against Christ. . . . For Christ says in John 6[: 45] that we are to be taught by God and hear it directly from the Father.[84]

Accordingly, the learned in the universities are informed that the future life will be without language teachers and interpreters and will have no grammar, dialectic, astronomy, arithmetic, medicine, or jurisprudence, "for all such things deal only with the

82. Ibid., p. 8.
83. Cf. above, p. 93.
84. *Vom Ort der Welt*, p. 83.

temporal and mortal man." [85] Weigel points out to politicians, secular and ecclesiastical, that in heaven there will be no kaiser, pope, king, bishop, prince, or preacher, no commands, laws, and statutes to obey. There no one will possess his own lands, serfs, and fields, and monopolies on streams, game, and fish will not be permitted, since all will then be held in common. [86]

In the end, Weigel's cosmological exercise, not unlike monastic practices or the mystical *via salutis,* drove him away from the physical and historical forms of the world and into the world of possibilities latent within the self. There one discovers final power and authority; there one discovers the Self resident within oneself.

> It is not vain to study carefully why the world, although it stands on no place, does not fall. We have not done it simply for the world's sake, but for the sake of doctrine. From such study come things useful and necessary to Holy Scripture. From it I learn what heaven and hell, sin, damnation, and happiness are, and how heaven, the true fatherland, is not to be sought here or there but rather in ourselves, and that the kingdom of Christ on earth is not bound to particular authorities, places, persons, or traditions. [87]

In a poignant summary, Weigel concludes:

> Our fatherland is not this world or Europe or Germany. It is not this or that principality. It is not Leipzig or Worms. Our homeland and dwelling-place is not this or that house. It is no external place and certainly not our perishable body. For mortal men and that poisonous worm, death, can drive you from these. Our true home is God in us and we in God. He who lives in God and God in him is at home in his fatherland, and can be driven out by no one. Wherever he may be in the world, he cannot lose God's word, although the Eucharist, baptism, the sermon, books, and all ceremonies are taken away. He loses nothing thereby, for Christ is in him—the very Christ who is baptism, the Eucharist, and the Word itself. [88]

85. Ibid., pp. 80–81.
86. Ibid., pp. 84–85.
87. Ibid., p. 39.
88. Ibid., p. 52. Cf. conclusions no. 9 and no. 10, p. 57, and pp. 43, 51.

THE *Postille* OF 1578–79

The sermons written and preached between Easter 1578 and Palm Sunday 1579[89] introduce Weigel's final literary period and mark a watershed in his career. Here, for the first time in explicit detail, he turns upon his own profession (inclusive of founder Luther), scoring not only its training methods, doctrinal tenets, and ethical example, but especially its willing participation in a repressive ecclesiopolitical alliance. Weigel reaches the brink of outright misanthropy. But only the brink. The uncompromising criticism also fosters the formation of a societal alternative, a modest "new Jerusalem" no less, which Weigel bases in the now increasingly central doctrine of Christ's "heavenly flesh" and "bodily" presence in true believers.

THE ECCLESIOPOLITICAL COMPLEX

"The world believes, and yet, in truth, does not know what it believes," Weigel laments in a sermon on the story of doubting Thomas.

> The one consults and tries to please the other—the subjects their princes, the princes their scholars, the scholars their books, commentaries, *Postillen,* and old teachers. They speak then of faith much as a blind man speaks of colors. All are blind, the blind are leading the blind.[90]

Stated in even starker terms, an unknowing and malevolent ecclesiopolitical system has presently gotten the upper hand and holds the world in bondage.

> The learned come together in the universities and suppress the truth, smother the Spirit, and see to it that no pious man arises to preach faith or Christ. What they lack the power to do against Christ, they accomplish with the aid of the government, and what the government lacks the knowledge to do, it obtains from the universities.[91]

89. On dating and division into three parts, see Zeller 1940, pp. 46–47.

90. *Kirchen- oder Hauss-Postill oder die Sonntags- und fürnembste Fest-Evangelien durchs gantze Jahr/aus dem rechten Catholischen und Apostolischen Grunde und Brunnen Israelis vorgetragen und geprediget durch M. Valentinum Weigelium . . .* (n.p., 1700), Bk. 3, p. 18.

91. Ibid., Bk. 1, pp. 112–13.

Together church and state exploit the poor. "It is not right that
. . . the poor man alone bears the yoke. By his sweat he must
clothe, feed, and wait upon the secular and spiritual powers
alike." [92] Together they prevent a world-changing gospel from
being preached in the pulpits of the land.

> Many thousands . . . know nothing of the inner word, inner
> hearing, the signs of the Father's presence, or the indwelling
> Christ. Such blindness and ignorance come from the false
> teachers who wrongly interpret the Scripture and have the
> power, through the assistance of the government, to command
> that nothing be heard of God, lest it be "Schwenckfeldian,"
> "enthusiastic," or "Osiandrian." [93]

The compromise formula of the Peace of Augsburg (1555), which
permitted the ruler of a particular region to determine the religion of that region (*cuius regio, eius religio*), is especially singled
out as an obstacle to the realization of the kingdom of Christ:
"How many subjects are there in cities and villages, states and
kingdoms, who would like to accept the child Jesus but are not
permitted by the government, since every city and land must
abide by the religion of the ruler." [94] The predilection of preachers for politicizing religion, Weigel bitingly points out, is not
of recent vintage. Even Luther took a couple of princes with
him to the Diets of Worms and Augsburg, whereas Paul had gone
undefended into Athens and Corinth.[95]

No one should, under any circumstances, order another about
in matters of faith, and one certainly should not be put to death
because of what one believes.[96] The problem lies ultimately in
the fact that society's brain trust in these matters, the learned
theologians in the universities, are least attuned to the way in
which God intends the world to be run.

> No one knows of God's ever having taken a scholar out of
> the university and made him a pastor or prophet. Simple men,

---

92. Ibid., Bk. 2, p. 334.
93. Ibid., p. 173.
94. Ibid., Bk. 1, p. 111.
95. Ibid., Bk. 2, p. 355.
96. "Keiner habe uber den andern zu gebieten in Glaubens-Sachen/keiner soll
den andern tödten in Glaubens-Sachen/keiner soll den andern tödten um der Sünde
willen/denn wir sind alle gleich Sünder/Gott straffet alleine die Sünde/und nicht der
Mensch." Ibid., p. 157.

who think little of themselves, have always been chosen. Paul, to be sure, was a scholar, but he had to repudiate everything he had learned in the synagogue. . . . And if someone comes to the ministry today from the university, he must, with Paul, forget everything and start all over again. . . . As long as Herod and the learned theologians [*Schrifftgelehrten*] sit together on the throne of Moses and dispense ordination, no understanding of Christ will come into the world.[97]

Weigel protests a theological education which binds young pastors, from the beginning, to set theologies and creeds—the writings of Luther, Zwingli, and Calvin, the *Loci communes* of Melanchthon, the *Augustana confessio*, the *Corpus doctrinae*, the *Formula concordiae*. "Don't we have enough already in the twelve articles of our [i.e. the Apostles'] creed?" [98] Why is it, he asks, that the sermons of pastors are so universally unfruitful, improving society not one whit? Is it not because we are taught and appointed by men in universities, who, although they write the authoritative commentaries and glosses on Scripture, know less about Christ than the Jews? [99] "I say as truly as I am a man that in no university in the world is Christ to be found, for he would not let himself be caught among such arrogant and worldly-wise men who despise the truth." [100] Weigel puts the matter in intensely personal terms.

Preachers should be angels of the Lord, taught and sent by God and not by men. . . . Those who preach while uncalled [by God] are but mercenaries, as, alas, we now all are without exception. For who among us has been taught or called by God? Do we not all come from the university? Are we not all ordained by human favor and power? And are we not confined within our own knowledge? Indeed, should one among us really desire to preach from the Holy Bible, he would not be permitted to do so. He would be forced rather to take up

97. Ibid., p. 167.
98. Ibid., Bk. 1, p. 218.
99. Ibid., pp. 251–54.
100. Ibid., p. 221. Note the dated, personal confession: "Alle hohe Schulen biss auf diese Zeit/da ich jetzung rede meines Alters fünff und viertzig Jahr/welches ist Anno Christi 1578/noch niemahls Christum erkandt haben/dennoch muss man aus ihnen Prädicanten nehmen/Kirchen und Schulen bestellen/sie seind das Volck ohne Häupt/davon Daniel saget/die da Grosse und Kleine verführen." Ibid., Bk. 2, p. 292.

human books, and pick his sermons from the [approved]
Postillen.[101]

The bad example of the pastors contributes to their ineffective-
ness. The common man, seeing and imitating the "neglect and
laziness of those who go around reading the Scriptures," soon loses
sight of "the inner ground of his soul." [102] "The shiftlessness of
preachers and scholars is the reason why Christ remains unknown
to the common man." [103] But bad example roots in bad doctrine.
Lutheran theology teaches an imputed, alien righteousness (*iustitia
imputativa*), which permits and even encourages one to avoid
existential suffering with Christ.[104]

Weigel looks especially hard at the doctrinal slogans "verbum
vocale" and "fides ex auditu." Designed to enhance the sermon
as the unique medium of God's presence, the ultimate effect is
to alienate the people from the depths of their souls. "O, woe to
you teachers on that [last] day," warns Weigel, "because you did
not teach your poor, simple congregation to listen inwardly and
guide them to the inner word. Woe to you in eternity because
you condemned such talk from your pulpit as fanaticism and
enthusiasm [*Schwermerey und Enthusiasterei*]." [105] "The false
preachers will [on that last day] say: 'Lord, Lord, have we not
done many deeds in your name? Have we not prophesied, preached,
written books, made commentaries on the Psalter and composed
Postillen?' But the Lord will only answer: 'I know you not.'" [106]
And rulers who have failed to follow the inner light and practice
the golden rule, tempering the *processus iuris/Justiniani* with the
processus Christi, can expect the very same response.[107]

Weigel advises his people to ignore the so-called learned authorities and follow quietly their own instinctive reading of the
Scriptures. He preaches a very telling sermon on the three wise
men who followed the star in the East to find the Christ Child in
Bethlehem (Matt. 2). When these wise men entered Jerusalem and
inquired about the Messiah, King Herod and his theological ad-

101. Ibid., Bk. 1, p. 52.
102. Ibid., p. 113.
103. Ibid., p. 155.
104. Ibid., pp. 196, 198–99, 236.
105. Ibid., p. 185.
106. Ibid., Bk. 2, p. 193.
107. Ibid., pp. 196; 329–30.

visers—i.e. political and ecclesiastical authority—hardly knew what they were talking about. In fact, Weigel points out, the wise men momentarily lost the guiding star (i.e. the meaning of Scripture) among the powerful and learned in the city.

> The wise men did not find Jesus in the great city of Jerusalem among the learned. In fact, they lost there the star which was to lead them to him. So let no one think that he will find any understanding of Christ in the universities and great cities. Indeed, one loses there the very holy Scripture which should guide him, because it is there so falsely interpreted. He who diligently studies nature and marvels at God's creation will be led to him who is lord over nature, for the works lead to their maker and creatures to their creator, as we learn from the wise men from the East.[108]

The old issue, which has haunted Weigel from the beginning and will haunt him in the end, reappears, as he once again faces the nature and necessity of the external means of grace. It is now clear to him that, "although Christ has ordained and established preaching, the Eucharist, and baptism, false preachers misuse them and make them a hindrance, so that they are cut off from the inner man, where the soul finds peace and eats hidden manna." [109] If external structures are more harmful than beneficial, should they continue? Alluding to Luther as merely a "more recent pope" in this matter,[110] who shaded God's grace with clerical mediation, Weigel goes as far as he can, short of urging open revolt, to neutralize what he considers to be the detrimental influence of his own ecclesiastical system.

> The priest should not be placed between the believer and divine forgiveness as the pope and Luther do. For God estab-

---

108. Ibid., Bk. 1, p. 107. Weigel adds in commentary: "So bald des sich einer wenden wird von grossen Handelstädten/und von der hohen Schulen und ihren Schrifften/so wird ihm wiederumb erscheinen der Stern/das ist/die heilige Schrifft wird ihme hell und klar werden/und wird keiner menschlichen Auslegung bedürffen" (ibid., p. 110). In this same discussion, he also comments that the "Buch der Natur" can teach kings where to find Christ (ibid., p. 109). In a later sermon, Weigel, echoing Müntzer's kindred critique of the learned, maintains that when Christ entered Jerusalem on an ass, the learned theologians of the city could only exclaim in dismay: "He is neither rich nor princely, and he has not studied in the academy. Why he doesn't even have a doctor's degree!" Ibid., p. 269.

109. Ibid., Bk. 2, p. 306.

110. Ibid., p. 295.

lishes no representative [*Stadhalter*], and Christ needs no bishopric, no regent, to stand in his place and forgive sins. He remains alone the highest of priests over the faithful.[111]

The "office of the Holy Spirit" (*Amt des Geistes*) is pitted against the false preachers of established Christendom.[112] Ministers like himself are to use the external offices and ordinances, so to speak, against the external offices and ordinances, to enhance what is within rather than what is outside men.[113] And what does one do in the face of those who "preach for their bellies' sake" and "alone want to control the Holy Spirit and deny that it speaks in all believers, and tell their congregation that they cannot judge matters of the Spirit because they have not been to the university"? [114] One ignores these "stupid dogs" and retreats to the "inner preacher in conscience." [115]

We become, with David, more learned than all our teachers. . . . For after one hour with the Spirit a peasant graduates to doctor [of theology]. The Spirit teaches him languages and explains the meaning of Christ, so that he knows why Christ came, died, descended into hell, and ascended into heaven. Any man who gives the Spirit room to work in him learns perfectly all the articles of faith.[116]

A NEW JERUSALEM

Juxtaposed to Weigel's criticism of contemporary Christendom in the *Postille* is an alternative social vision fashioned from his

---

111. "Dass man aber auch den Priester unter die Göttliche Vergebung ziehen wolle/wie der Pabst und Luther thun/kann auch nicht sein/denn Gott setzet keinen Stadhalter/Christus bedarf keines Bissthums/keines Verwesers/der an seiner Statt sollte die Sünde vergeben/er bleibet allein der oberste Priester über seine Gläubigen" (ibid.). Caspar Schwenckfeld argued that Luther's dependence on "kreaturlicher Vermittlung" made him as "antichristisch" as Rome (Maron, *Individualismus und Gemeinschaft bei Caspar von Schwenckfeld*, p. 104). Maron argues that the "Unmittelbarkeit des Gottesverhältnisses" was the "Grundvoraussetzung all seines (Schwenckfelds) Denkens." Ibid., p. 83.

112. *Kirchen- oder Hauss-Postill*, Bk. 2, p. 298.

113. "Hie sehen wir/wie vonnöthen sey das Amt des Geistes/oder das Ministerium, nehmlich/es erwecke/ermahne/erinnere/bezeuge/bestätige und führe hinein in dasjenige/das zuvor in uns ist/wie denn die Aposteln nichts anders lehren noch schreiben denn eben das/das in uns ist." Ibid., p. 302.

114. Ibid., p. 47.

115. Ibid., p. 203; cf. p. 198.

116. Ibid., p. 64.

theological reflection on the notion of Christ's "heavenly flesh." This doctrine is as old as Christian theology itself, and its intention is twofold. First, it seeks to exempt divinity from the weaknesses and sinfulness of the humanity it assumes in Christ. How can a holy God be embodied in sinful human flesh? Secondly, it seeks to insure that the God who does take flesh and dwell among men is truly God. For how could men be saved by one as weak and sinful as they themselves? [117] The indirect social relevance of the doctrine lies in its basic problem: how to maintain the perfect in the midst of what is imperfect.

Two versions of the doctrine were in circulation in the sixteenth century, one more extreme and associated with the radical Melchior Hofmann (d. 1543)[118] and another more moderate and associated with Caspar Schwenckfeld (d. 1561). According to Hofmann, Christ in effect possessed only one nature, having brought his own body with him from heaven. He received nothing from his earthly mother Mary, but rather passed through her "as water through a pipe." [119] Schwenckfeld, on the other hand, recognized the initial integrity of Christ's two natures. The human nature, however, was not human according to the old sinful order of Adam. Christ, rather, was born of a "reborn" and thereby sinless virgin.[120] According to his human nature, he was an uncreaturely creature. The Holy Spirit conceived "pure uncreaturely flesh" in a pure, reborn virgin. Christ's body belonged therefore to "the new order of recreation or rebirth." [121] During his lifetime on earth this new flesh was progressively deified, so that by the time of his glorification and session in heaven it was virtually identical with divine nature. It is upon this "heavenly flesh" that the believer now feeds in faith.

117. The prominence of the Greek-mystical principle of likeness in this doctrine is evident in the following statement by Hofmann: "Wer mag van eynem Unreinem gereinigt werden oder die worheitt van einem ligner verhoffen? So der Grund bestan solt, das cristus fleisch Maria(e) nathurlich Fleisch und blut wer, so wurd folgen, das wir alle auff eynen andern Erlösser wartten müsten, dan in einem solchen wer kein Gerechtigkeit zu bekommen" (cited by Schoeps, *Vom himmlischen Fleisch Christi*, pp. 43–44). See Schwenckfeld's appeal to Tauler on this same point. Maron, *Individualismus und Gemeinschaft bei Schwenckfeld*, p. 85.

118. Hofmann is "der reinste Valentiner des Reformationszeitalter." Schoeps, *Vom himmlischen Fleisch Christi*, p. 45.

119. Williams, *Radical Reformation*, p. 329; Schoeps, *Vom himmlischen Fleisch Christi*, pp. 37 ff.

120. Schoeps, pp. 29–30.

121. Williams, pp. 332–33.

Weigel's Christology exhibits the broader outlines of Schwenck-feld's doctrine.[122] The flesh and blood of Christ is said to be not from the earth, from the seed of man, but from heaven.[123] He is a true *natural* son of God. "Christ does not come in the flesh of Adam, but in that of a virgin, having been conceived by the Holy Spirit. His birth is not from the blood or race of earthly men. He did not take his flesh from Joseph, David, Abraham, or Jacob, but from the Holy Spirit." [124] The virgin from whom he was born was just as immaculately conceived as he, having received from her mother "nothing more than human customs." [125] As with Schwenckfeld, Weigel views Christ as new flesh from new flesh.[126] And he rejects the *communicatio idiomatum* Christology of Lutheran theology as a deadly compromise:

> All the universities know about as much about Christ as the Jews who said that he was the natural son of Joseph. Although they also say that he was not of the earth but of heaven, they say this only in the sense that his divine nature could bear human properties and his human nature divine properties

122. Schoeps (following Ernst Benz against Zeller) suggests that Schwenckfeld (together with Osiander) is as important a source for Weigel's "Mystik der Ver-leiblichung" as Paracelsus (*Vom himmlischen Fleisch Christi*, p. 57). Schoeps had for his discussion two works that were not at my disposal: Weigel's *Vom Leben Christi*, written the same year as the *Postille*, and the unpublished dissertation of Gerhard Krodel, "Die Anthropologie Valentin Weigels."

123. *Kirchen- oder Hauss-Postill*, Bk. 1, p. 46.

124. Ibid., p. 66.

125. "Wie sichs nun mit Christo hält/dass er ist ein Sohn Gottes nach dem Fleische und Blute/dann das Wort ward Fleisch; also hält sichs auch mit der Geburth der Frauen/sie ist incarnirt von heiligen Geiste/und nicht von Joachim/ sonst wäre sie nicht Jungfrau und könte nicht eine Mutter Gottes sein/sie hat von Anna nichts mehr/denn Menschliche Sitten/Geberden/aber nicht Fleisch und Blut/Menschliche Natur hat sie an sich genommen/wie ihr Sohn Christus." Ibid., Bk. 2, p. 287.

126. The puzzling statement is elsewhere made that Christ had "two bodies": "a divine, heavenly body from the Holy Spirit" and "an earthly, visible body from the Virgin." Ibid., Bk. 1, p. 242. The latter apparently refers to the accidental form in which Christ appeared during his tenure on earth; the former to his true substantial form. Weigel goes on here to say that the divine and heavenly body is the one which is significant for the believer and "becomes flesh and blood in us and infuses itself into our flesh and blood" (ibid. Cf. Schoeps, *Vom himmlischen Fleisch Christi*, p. 59). Weigel elsewhere states that an "invisible, eternal body" is sown within the "visible, perishable" body of man, and that the former must necessarily (*notwendig*) spring forth in the resurrection (*Kirchen- oder Hauss-Postill*, Bk. 2, pp. 6–7). Apparently it is this resurrection body which the heavenly flesh of Christ is to nourish.

[*communicatione idiomatum*], so that, while according to his divinity Christ is from heaven, his flesh is still from Adam, from the earth.[127]

It is of crucial importance for the direction of his religious and social alternatives to established Christendom that Weigel separates Christ's nature and destiny absolutely from Adamic humanity. "Christ does not come to help the flesh of Adam," he writes, "for it is totally worthless [*nirgends zu gut*]; rather he comes to save the soul and clothe it with heavenly flesh and blood." [128] Weigel does not look to a reform of the old Adam. The old must perish altogether and the new replace it absolutely. The goal is not a recapitulation even of integral Adamic man, but deification, essential union with the "heavenly flesh" of Christ.[129]

In Weigel's soteriology, man's Fall had a double consequence: the withdrawal of the special presence of God's Spirit and the loss of the earthly body, which became irretrievably mortal and was, as Weigel puts it, "forfeited to the worms." [130] Since spirit and soul are retained intact, redemption or rebirth becomes an affair of the "body." "God creates no new soul or spirit, and hence rebirth does not involve the spirit or the soul, but rather the body." [131] Already in the *Informatorium* of 1575/76, Weigel argued that God is in men and men in him by virtue of their souls, whereas Christ is in men "bodily and essentially [*leiblich und wesentlich*] with his spirit, flesh, and blood" only by rebirth in faith.[132]

The close parallel that Weigel draws between human rebirth and the uncreaturely conception of Christ is striking. In our re-

---

127. *Kirchen- oder Hauss-Postill,* Bk. 1, p. 155.

128. Ibid., p. 141. Cf. p. 47: "Die erste Schöpffung umsonst wäre gewesen/umb des Falls willen/und es alles gelegen an der Schöpfung von Himmel."

129. Compare Tauler's notions about the mystical union in my *Homo Spiritualis,* pp. 36 ff.

130. *Kirchen- oder Hauss-Postill,* Bk. 2, p. 109.

131. Ibid., p. 114.

132. "Auss dem Mund Gottes ist unsere Seele gangen/so ist Gott in uns/und wir seind in Gott. Aber das seind wir in Christo durch den Glauben new geboren. Also ist Christus in uns mit seinem Geist und Fleisch und Blut leiblich/wesentlich" (*Informatorium oder kurtzer Unterricht/welcher Gestalt man durch drei Mittel den schmalen Weg zu Christo sich führen kan lassen* [Newenstatt, 1616], p. B 3 a). Cf. p. G 6 a, where the rational creature is described as not only the *imago Dei,* but also the serpent which tempts himself to eat of the forbidden fruit, which he himself also is. Compare Franck, above, p. 147.

birth, he tells us, we too are born of God and are not his adopted sons. We are "corporally" in Christ as he was "corporally" in God. There is an "essential indwelling" (*wesentliche Einwohnung*).[133] "As Christ, so are we all in this world, according to 1 John 4, born of God himself, and that means being [*Wesen*] and not shadow, for we are natural children of God [*natürliche Kinder Gottes*] by the grace of Christ, and that is the new birth." [134] Indeed, "we are joined with Christ *somatikos, leibhafftig,* for we have his flesh and blood in us. . . . Christ, God and man, is in us." [135]

Weigel universalizes this process. The Spirit of God is graciously at work to sanctify all men already at their conception in the womb! For this reason, Weigel, who never questioned the practice of infant baptism, now pleads for the baptism of all infants, whether of heathen or of Christian parents.[136] Infant baptism attests the inchoate intrinsic spiritual power of the individual. Its practice becomes as much a protest of the tyranny of externals to Weigel as its denial was to Hut and Denck. It is even argued (by inexact analogy) that the water of baptism is to the infant what Mary's womb was to the Christ Child, a physical medium for the Holy Spirit's conception of a "new heavenly flesh and blood."

> The water is the mother, and the Spirit is the father. Just as Christ was conceived by the Holy Spirit in flesh and blood in the virgin Mary and born a child of God, so are all the faithful born from the Holy Spirit in water with a new, heavenly flesh and blood, and because they are born of God they can never again die.[137]

The argument for real union with God takes advantage, not only of certain Paracelsist notions and the contemporary theologies

---

133. "Aus Gott seind wir gebohren/nicht wie der falsche adoptivische Theologus schreibet/sondern gantz wie Christus selber/Johan. am 14." *Kirchen- oder Hauss-Postill,* Bk. 2, p. 301.

134. Ibid., p. 287.

135. Ibid., Bk. 1, p. 232. Cf. the defense of Osiander and Schwenckfeld, ibid., Bk. 2, p. 234, and the larger summary of this point, focused on the sacrament of the Eucharist, ibid., pp. 115; 181.

136. "Muss man all Kinder täuffen/anzuzeigen/dass sie durch den heiligen Geist in Mutterleibe in die neue Geburt getaufft sein aus Gnaden/denn so gross ist Gottes Güte/Gnade und Barmhertzigkeit/dass er keinen versäumet/erkommet allen zuvor ohne ihr Wissen. . . . Derhalben wie alle Kinder aller Christen Heiden empfangen und gebohren werden von Natur/also alle Kinder aller Menschen werden durch den heiligen Geist getaufft aus Gnaden/und sein gläubig durch den heiligen Geist." Ibid. Bk. 1, p. 67; cf. p. 38.

137. Ibid., Bk. 2, pp. 111–12.

of Schwenckfeld and Andreas Osiander (d. 1552), but also of Luther's defense of the ubiquity of Christ's risen body and real presence in the Eucharist.[138] But Weigel's most accessible precedent in this matter is the milk on which he was weaned, medieval mysticism. He adopts the more commonplace mystical imagery of union,[139] and points to the fact that Pseudo-Dionysius and Tauler wrote much about the way the believer, although still dwelling in the body, passes over with Christ into the Father and becomes one with the Spirit of God.[140] While his mystical sources may not have operated with an involved "heavenly flesh" Christology, they certainly introduced Weigel as early as in his youth to the notion of essential union with God.

This teaching of Christ's real presence in the faithful is Weigel's soteriological alternative to what he calls the "fictitious imputed righteousness" and "*Christus extra nos*" of the learned theologians. "The [theologians in the] universities with their imputed righteousness . . . absolutely refuse to be essentially [*wesentlich*] one with Christ." [141] But "imputed righteousness will not cover their sins; only an essential indwelling and rebirth will truly [*wesentlich*] cover them." [142] "If the suffering, death, and merit of Christ is to be of any use to us, then it must not remain outside us and be only attributed to us as a fictitious imputed righteousness [*erdichteten imputativae justitiae*]. *Christus extra nos non salvat.*" [143] Weigel rests his case with a crescendo of Latin infinitives:

> *Christus inhabitans, non ab extra manens,* now brings true
> faith, which is the *vita Christi* within us. . . . *Conbaptizari,*
> *compati, concruci, figi, commori, consepeliri* and *consurgere*
> *—unio essentialis—*this must effect Christ's spiritual and cor-

138. "Der einige Luther unter allen hat gründlich gelehret vom Fleische Christi/da er im Buche/dass diese Wort Christi/das ist mein Leib/noch feste stehen/über die fünffmahl und öffter bekennet/Christi Fleisch sei nicht aus Adams Saamen/sondern vom heiligen Geiste vom Himmel." Ibid., p. 210; cf. Bk. 3, p. 61.

139. "Sein Wort . . . durchdringet in den Geist/wie ein Eisen lange liegt in den Kohlen in der Esse wird feurig gantz einig/also ein guter Mensche wird mit Christo vereiniget durch das nachdencken nachsinnen und wird aus Gott gebohren." Ibid., Bk. 1, pp. 256–57.

140. "Es können auch die Gläubigen in dieser Zeit noch im Leibe wohnende durchs Gebet eingehen durch Christum zum Vater . . . denn so sich die Seele abscheidet von allen sündlichen Dingen/so mag sie mit dem Geiste Gottes vereiniget werden. Davon Dionysius und Taulerus auch viel handeln." Ibid., Bk. 2, p. 106.

141. Ibid., p. 349.

142. Ibid., p. 308.

143. Ibid., Bk. 3, p. 57.

poreal presence in us. Where do you now remain with your
imagined imputed righteousness? [144]

H.-J. Schoeps has argued that Weigel's concept of the heavenly
flesh of Christ "discharges into a highly subjective, ahistorical,
and idealized intellectualistic mysticism." [145] In regard to the
Postille of 1578–79, such an assessment may be only partially correct. For, although it is modest in scope and finally forsaken,
Weigel does here entertain an alternative form of community to
that engineered by the ecclesiopolitical complex of established
Christendom. He does so by wedding the concept of Christ's
heavenly flesh and bodily presence in believers with diluted
(pseudo-)Joachite ideas.[146]

The point of departure is the prophecy of a "new covenant"
in Jeremiah 31 : 31 ff.,[147] wherein three ages of the world are distinguished. Weigel comments:

> Here the prophet embraces all three ages of the world. First,
> the age of the Father according to the Old Testament or
> covenant, when he says: "Not like the old covenant with the
> paschal lamb after the flight from Egypt, when I had to use
> laws and force." Then he speaks of the age of the Son in ac-
> cordance with the New Testament, when he says: "But a
> new covenant, wherein I will write my law in their hearts,
> and they will freely, out of love and without coercion, be
> my people and I their God." And he speaks finally of the age
> of the Holy Spirit, when he says: "One shall no longer teach
> the other, but they will all know me, and the city of the

144. Ibid., p. 17; cf. p. 19.

145. Schoeps, *Vom himmlischen Fleisch Christi*, p. 62. Cf. Kurt Goldammer,
"Friedensidee und Toleranzgedanke bei Paracelsus und den Spiritualisten, II.
Franck und Weigel," *ARG* 47 (1956): 210.

146. In addition to certain parallels with the pseudo-Weigel tract *Astrologia
Theologizata* in the first book of the *Postille*, Zeller questions the authenticity of
the apocalyptic passages which appear in all three books (Zeller 1940, p. 51). The
apocalyptic material on which I draw in this section is not only quite modest in
scope, but also consistent with the development of Weigel's thought in the *Postille*.
In light of Zeller's hesitation, however, the very cautious reader may prefer to read
these comments as "Weigelian" rather than as Weigel.

147. It does not seem outside reasonable expectation that Weigel knew the pseudo-
Joachite commentary on Jeremiah, which was published three times in the sixteenth
century prior to the *Postille* and was known to Thomas Müntzer. Cf. above, p. 71,
nn. 38 and 39.

Lord shall be built with gates that shall never again be broken down." [148]

Just as he had virtually combined the bodily presence of the risen Son and the Holy Spirit within the individual believer, so Weigel now seems to merge the "age of the Son" and the "age of the Spirit" in the life of the world. When he moves from the old to the new covenant, he already makes that transition from external and institutionalized to internal and universalized religion, which Joachim of Fiore delayed, at least on a wide scale, until the implementation of the age of the Spirit. The ambivalence can be seen in the following passages, the first of which deals with the movement from the old to the new covenant, the second with the transition from the new covenant to the "time of the Spirit":

> The external Jerusalem is internalized, i.e. our heart becomes a Jerusalem, a dwelling-place and temple of God in accordance with the nature of the new covenant, and we need not run here and there seeking places where God is present as in the old covenant.[149]

> Then all monasteries, cloisters, temples are to be torn down, so that not one stone stands upon another. Then the false prophet of Satan will withdraw and the new Jerusalem, the holy city of God, arise. The outer will be brought into the inner. Man himself will be Jerusalem and the temple in which God dwells. Then one will have no need for ordained preachers or other teachers, for each will be taught by God. Christ will dwell in his temple and be the teacher, and all people will go to him alone. That will be the time of the Holy Spirit, the revelation of Jesus Christ, still in this world in the new Jerusalem on earth.[150]

This tendency to overlap the two ages is not surprising given Weigel's concept of Christ's bodily presence in believers. This notion contributes to a much more intense sense of divine immediacy within a community of true believers than does the tra-

148. *Kirchen- oder Hauss-Postill*, Bk. 1, pp. 262–63. In his later critique of the "impietas Wigeliana," Theodor Thumm accused the Weigelians of teaching four ages—those of the Father, Son, Spirit, and Devil! *Impietas Wigeliana*, Index, 2 b.
149. *Kirchen- oder Hauss-Postill*, Bk. 1, p. 265.
150. Ibid., p. 271.

ditional affirmation of only a spiritual presence. On the level of individual salvation, the concept, as we have seen, is highly anticipatory of man's final end. When Weigel entertains its social extension, the vision of the "new Jerusalem" proleptically appears. The interconnections are manifest in the statement:

> The new Jerusalem must dwell on earth, and Christ must still come to pass [*ereignen*] on earth—not that he must come physically and visibly in person as before, but rather that he dwell bodily [*leibhafftig*] in his own in the house of Jacob, so that we all, under him, are taught by God, needing no longer preachers and prophets, for Christ is everything in us.[151]

Commenting on the first chapter of Luke's gospel, which was Thomas Müntzer's text for the *Special Exposé,* Weigel criticizes the learned for making Christ's kingdom only a "spiritual" and not also a physical reality on earth.

> Although, according to the inner, spiritual man or nature, the holy church has only one head and is invisible, to be seen neither here nor there, still it must come together. The new Jerusalem must take flesh [*muss leiblich sein*] just as Christ went bodily [*leiblich*] upon the earth and was not only spiritually among us. All the worldly-wise in the universities are against that, calling it "Anabaptist," "Schwermerisch," and "Müntzerite" for one to teach the apocalypse of Daniel. They say that Christ does not rule here and now.[152]

Weigel is no advocate of revolution, and he seems in the end to desire only a kind of pietistical *ecclesiola in ecclesia,* confining the "golden age" of love and the Spirit[153] to model communities of true believers. The secular impact of the new Jerusalem fades. In a sermon on John 13, he tells his congregation that the lesson of Jesus's washing the feet of his disciples is to teach us to

151. Ibid., Bk. 3, p. 41.
152. Ibid., p. 39. The Apocalypse is elsewhere described as the "Haupt-Buch der Schrifft" and those *doctores* who slight it, including Luther, are criticized. It is to be emphasized here that the Apocalypse is defended as a book which sets forth Christ as the crucified and true, embattled faith, not as a manual for Armageddon. Ibid., Bk. 2, p. 282.
153. Ibid., Bk. 3, p. 47.

move among one another in love and remain in the garden of this world under one father as children without property, holding our goods in common, using freely among ourselves the fruits, vegetables, and fish of the earth. . . . We are redeemed by the Son so that we may live together as brothers in the world without hatred . . . upholding one another . . . and killing no one because he has sinned. For that very reason have we been anointed by the Holy Spirit, viz. so that we shall live in the world in love and be changed into the new Jerusalem.[154]

An extension of the "new Jerusalem" into the centers of worldly power as well is not completely out of view, for Weigel also draws a lesson from this biblical story for the government, viz. "that we be jurists according to the New Testament and lay aside the entire kingdom of Justinian as heathen," henceforth administering justice according to the golden rule.[155]

In more traditional language, one could say that in the *Postille* Weigel's "new Jerusalem" is finally a modest approximation of that select *ecclesia praedestinatorum* in the midst of the penultimate *ecclesia militans*. This is suggested by his descriptions of the "holy universal catholic church," which stands over against and can count its members among the truly pious within the "sectarian" religions of the pope, Luther, Zwingli, and Mohammed.[156] Such a position is also supported by the ethical criterion of true

---

154. Ibid., pp. 46–47.
155. Ibid., p. 50, with reference to Matthew 7, 15, and 18.
156. Weigel's most comprehensive statement of this theme is: "Es seind zwo Kirchen auf Erden/als die heilige allgemeine Catholische Kirche Gottes/die da ist eine unsichtbare Versammlung aller Gläubigen und Neugebohrnen/aus dem heiligen Geist gezeuget/auf den einigen Eckstein J. Christum gesasset/einig im Glauben/im Geiste/ohne alle Spaltung und Trennung/nicht gebunden an äusserliche Geberden/Ort/Stadt/Menschen/Ceremonien/da Christus allein das Haupt ist und bleibet. Dieser Kirche Gliedmassen seind Felsen/fürchten sich für keiner Secten oder Ketzerei/sie sehen sich nur für/und prüfen die Geister/sie verfolgen/noch tödten/noch injuriren keinen in Glaubens-Sachen. Die falsche Kirche aber ist eine sichtbare Versammlung der Menschen/nicht aus Gott/sondern aus der Natur gebohren/gebunden an gewisse Oerter/Personen/Ceremonien/ac. In viel Partheien/ Secten/Rotten/zurissen und zertheilet/da nicht Christus das Häupt ist/sondern etliche Lehrer und Menschen: Als Pabst uber die Päbstlichen/und Luther über die Lutherischen/der Zwinglius über die Zwinglischen/der Mahomet über die Türcken." Ibid., Bk. 2, pp. 209–10. Cf. pp. 206, 102–03, and below, pp. 241–42. Franck's influence is patent.

faith in his last writings.[157] And it is quite consistent with the dissent pattern of protesting the *potentia Dei ordinata* by appeal to the *potentia Dei absoluta.*

THE RELIGIOUS SOVEREIGNTY OF THE INDIVIDUAL: THE LAST WRITINGS

"ES LIGET ALLES IM INWENDIGEN GRUNDE" [158]

On the surface there are three combatants in Weigel's last writing, the *Dialogue on the Nature of Christianity* (1584): an auditor who speaks for the lay congregation and Weigel himself; a preacher who represents the ecclesiastical establishment; and death who, because dying to oneself is the key to understanding Christ, speaks in Christ's place. Inasmuch, however, as death consistently champions the cause of the auditor, there are, in fact, but two participants.

The auditor is described as

> not only the lay or common man, but everyone who lets himself be taught, led, and directed by the pulpit, writings, books, and comments of the spiritual office, inclusive of the kaiser, kings, princes, lords, earls, knights, nobility, commonality, citizens, peasants, learned and unlearned, young and old, man and wife, etc. These are all embraced and understood by the word *idiota, auditor,* or listener.[159]

The preacher is likewise conceived in the broadest terms, embracing

> pope, cardinal, bishops, prelates, doctors high and low, all interpreters of Scripture in the universities, consistories, seminaries, cloisters, etc. and all public teaching, oral and written, which interprets the law of God, inclusive of the jurists, the whole chair of Moses and Peter.[160]

So defined, the auditor and the preacher represent respectively the well-being of the public at large and the self-interest of the ecclesiastical establishment. The doctrine on which the auditor's

---

157. Below, p. 241.
158. *Dialogus de Christianismo,* ed. Alfred Ehrentreich, in *Valentin Weigel. Sämtliche Schriften* (Stuttgart-Bad Cannstatt, 1967), 4:70.
159. Ibid., p. 5.
160. Ibid., pp. 5–6.

every argument hangs is that of essential union between Christ and the believer, a teaching which makes the believer religiously self-sufficient. The fundamental doctrine of the preacher, on the other hand, is justification by the imputation to the believer of an alien righteousness, a teaching which makes the mediation of the ecclesiastical establishment a sine qua non of salvation. The auditor maintains that the very "doctrine of Christ" is "the prophetic and apostolic axiom that God indwells essentially in man." [161] The preacher, on the other hand, limits the "essential indwelling" of God to the second person of the trinity, and insists that there is only a "divine attendance or presence" (*Beiwohnung oder Gegenwart*) among men,[162] mediated through the offices of the church.

The doctrine of essential union remains basically unchanged from the *Postille* of 1578–79,[163] although some stronger formulations now appear. Weigel, for example, describes the mutual indwelling of God and the believer as an "essential *Verbündtnis*," an "eternal *Verknüpfung* and *Verbindung*" [164]—terms which highlight the transference of God's covenantal presence from visible historical forms to the hidden depths of the soul.[165] Another noteworthy change is the disappearance of the social dimension. The end of creation and redemption is now described much more individualistically than in the *Postille*.[166] But what is most significant in the *Dialogue* is the use of the doctrine of essential union to divest the ecclesiastical establishment of religious authority.

While the teaching of the believer's essential union with Christ abounds in the prophetic and apostolic writings, the auditor says he hears nothing of it from the pulpits of the land, nor can he find any mention of it in the recent confessional documents of the church (viz. the *Augustana confessio, Loci communes, Corpus doctrinae, Formula concordiae*). "In fact, I find there the very op-

161. Ibid., p. 93; cf. p. 8.
162. Ibid., pp. 28–29; cf. pp. 9–10.
163. Cf. ibid., pp. 16–18. There is a parallel with Castellio in the use of the simile of grafting: "Dieweil nu der himlische Vater ist der Weingertner und Christus der Weinstock und wir Christen die Reben, so kan ich anders nicht gleuben denn wie die Schrifft zeiget, das wir müssen inn Gotte wonen und Gotte in uns." Ibid., p. 25. See above, p. 200.
164. Ibid., pp. 96–97; cf. p. 91.
165. Cf. my discussion of "natural covenant" in Tauler. *Homo Spiritualis*, pp. 13 ff.
166. See especially *Dialogus*, pp. 23–24.

posite . . . and I am astonished that your grace should be so completely ignorant of holy Scripture." [167] He goes on to argue that one best ignores ecclesiastical tradition and follows his own instinctive reading of the Bible:

> Dear sir, hear me out kindly. I believe that it is more useful for a good and pure heart to read the Bible one year than to read all the church fathers for fifty years. In fact, if one spent his entire life reading the writings of men, he would not discover as much as the Bible can teach him in one day or week.[168]

Given the fact of essential union, the believer becomes, religiously speaking, absolutely self-sufficient. External guidance is secondary to the point of being useless, even when it is correctly administered. Hence the auditor can boast in his own self-defense:

> I have not learned my teaching from any preacher or books of men. Rather the unction [of the Holy Spirit], which is in me and in all men, has led me to holy Scripture, wherein I find many witnesses to my teaching. . . . I hold firmly . . . to the law or word of God implanted within us, inscribed in our hearts by the finger of God, the living law, which also finds an external witness in the writings of the prophets and apostles. For without the inner, the outer is completely dead and in vain.[169]

The auditor insists that this is not subjectivism, since he has not learned these things from himself, but from the Self that dwells within himself [170]—a distinction which must necessarily prove in practice to be more nominal than real.

The full implications of the auditor's case are still more pointedly revealed in a small treatise written shortly before and in preparation for the *Dialogue*. The very title of this work focuses the issue of ecclesiastical authority: *On the Forgiveness of Sins or the Keys of the Church* (ca. 1582).[171] The basic premise of the treatise is that the power of binding and loosing (i.e. the forgive-

167. Ibid., pp. 19–20.

168. Ibid., p. 20; cf. p. 23.

169. Ibid., pp. 38–39.

170. "Nicht von mir selber lerne ich diese Dinge, sondern von deme, der in mir ist, nemlich von Gotte höre und lerne ich diese göttliche Dinge." Ibid., p. 42.

171. Cf. Zeller's discussion of the circumstances and probable date of the treatise, *Sämtliche Schriften* 2: 114, 118; Zeller 1940, pp. 56–61, 112–13.

ness of sins) is given to every individual believer and not to Peter or priests alone. "The faithful man in Christ is himself temple, sacrifice, and priest." [172] "Every faithful man is Peter and has the key to heaven within himself." [173] "The power of binding and loosing lies in my own conscience and not in someone else's mouth." [174] Everything hinges on the will to muster one's own internal strength, not the importation of power from without.

The logic of this argument leads to an individual ethical formula of salvation: "You have the key, the power is in your hand as to whether God will or will not forgive you. For as you act toward your brother on earth, just so does God act toward you in heaven." [175] One's ethical action or inaction initiates or delays the exercise of divine grace in one's regard. And since it is by God's grace that all men have this key within them, Weigel would have us understand that he is not being Pelagian when he argues that ethical activity controls salvation.[176] Indeed, an unconditional forgiveness of sins is hypocrisy too great for the conscience to bear.

> What kind of penance is it, and how can there be a good conscience, when, after you have been a public thief, whore, adulterer, and unjust servant, known to every child in the streets, you go to confession or summon the priest into your home and beg him to forgive your sins, console you, and give you the sacrament? [177]

As in the *Postille,* Weigel's case in the *Dialogue* comes to a halt with a proleptic dethronement of the imperfect, visible *ecclesia militans* by an ideal, invisible church of true believers.[178] The

172. *Von der Vergebung der Sünden oder vom Schlüssel der Kirchen,* ed. W. Zeller, in *Sämtliche Schriften* 2: 24.

173. Ibid., p. 36; cf. p. 38.

174. Ibid., p. 42; cf. pp. 18, 21.

175. Ibid., p. 10. In a larger summary, Weigel states: "zweyerley Vorgebung sey, eine menschliche auff Erden durch bruderliche Versununge und eine göttliche im Himel aus Gnaden durch den Todt Christi. Hie wirdt kein Priester begriffen noch kein Ohrenbeucht, sondern wie wir unttereinander uns versohnen, von Hertzen vergeben und durch Gottes Gnade dem Anfangt machen auff Erden, also vergiebet uns Gott auch durch den Todt Christi, und alle Sunde, die wir wieder ihn gethan haben. Wenn wir aber nicht unsern Nechsten vorgeben, ihme abbitten und mit ihme versöhnen, so will Gott im Himel auch alle Sunden uns vorbehaltten und nicht vorgeben, wie solches clerlich zu erkennen ist Math. 5.6.18." Ibid., pp. 14–15. Cf. also p. 23.

176. Ibid., pp. 28–29.

177. Ibid., p. 76; cf. p. 79.

178. *Dialogus,* pp. 66–67, 70–71.

spokesman for the ecclesiastical establishment is dismissed by death/Christ as "a doctor who has not studied with the Holy Spirit." [179]

In response, the preacher, whose doctrinal and practical concerns are fairly constructed by Weigel, turns immediately to the naked challenge of his authority. "Are you implying that the truth is not with me?", he asks. "Do you think I preach lies?" [180] It is not I, he argues, but the auditor himself who should reexamine his credentials.

> Here you are, an *idiota* who has not studied as we, and yet you presume to read holy Scripture. The power to interpret Scripture belongs to me. You have not been commissioned to do it. Your role is rather to listen to us, to look to us, to learn from us, and not set forth new doctrines.[181]

We hear the echoes of Franck's trial in Ulm as the preacher lectures the auditor on the meaning of the *potentia Dei ordinata.*

> The Holy Spirit will not come from heaven and teach you, as happened before the advent of Christ when he taught the prophets directly. Rather, God has ordained [*hat es verordnet*] that one man be the teacher of the others. Accordingly, God will let his word be preached by men and not by the Spirit. Anyone who spurns the office of preaching and looks directly to the Spirit is an enthusiast and *Schwermer.* . . . We have no other word than that which is embraced in the writings of the prophets and apostles.[182]

The auditor is quickly catalogued by the preacher with recent heresies and revolutionaries.

> You must in the end discard the holy *ministerium,* i.e. the office of preaching. Just as the Anabaptists, Schwenckfeldians, enthusiasts, *Schwermerey,* and other *phanatici spiritus* do, who reject the *verbum vocale* and lead the people to an inner illumination. As if one should retreat into a corner and look there for special revelations, inspiration, and rapture! [183]

179. Ibid., p. 109.
180. Ibid., p. 21.
181. Ibid., p. 31.
182. Ibid., pp. 40–41. Cf. *Von der Vergebung der Sünden,* p. 85.
183. *Dialogus,* pp. 44–45.

> Should I now direct the people to the inner word, hearing,
> and witness of the heart, or to their own experiences in the
> inner ground of their souls, I am certain they would look
> upon me as a Müntzerite spirit, a heavenly prophet! [184]

Weigel does not leave his man bested. Death/Christ enters to
settle the argument over authority, unmasking the preacher as
the true fanatic (*Schwermer*).[185] In a somewhat theatrical concluding scene, Weigel has the preacher, now dead and a shade
in outer darkness, return to admit his error to the auditor.[186] The
preacher begs release from the darkness in which he is now imprisoned and pledges to suffer the most awful purgations if death
will show him mercy. Death's answer is a revealing commentary
on the seething intolerance of those sixteenth-century advocates
of tolerance who knew it not. "Your wish is in vain," death tells
the preacher.[187] "You have not erred only in one, but in every
article of the whole of religion. You have darkened your own
heart and will not make room for the light. Therefore, go forth
to wander in your own darkness until the Judgment Day." [188]

CONSTRUCTIVE FRAUD

In what can be taken as an autobiographical comment, Weigel
has the auditor confess to the preacher that he too has signed
the confessional documents of the church and is legally bound
to them. However, the qualification is quickly added: "But I
have not thereby sworn an oath to the books of men. My signature
is rather a pledge to remain faithful and never deviate from the
writings of the prophets and apostles." [189] Weigel thus binds himself to the very creeds he ridicules in his writings. But it is only
an illusion of orthodoxy. In signing the documents, he really does
not underwrite the documents. He underwrites the documents
behind the documents. He acts fraudulently, yet with a salutary
deeper purpose in mind. Although his exposé of established Christendom is hardly less scathing than Müntzer's, he suppresses it
and will be no militant critic, certainly no revolutionary.

184. Ibid., p. 51.
185. Ibid., p. 95.
186. Ibid., pp. 141 ff.
187. Ibid., p. 146.
188. Ibid., p. 150.
189. Ibid., p. 58.

Aided by the hindsight of historical precedent, Weigel sees more keenly than Müntzer the practical futility and sad consequences of belligerent reform.[190] The bridge between the inner and outer worlds, which appeared momentarily in the *Postille* to support the possibility of a "new Jerusalem" in social as well as individual flesh, now collapses altogether as Weigel, faithful to his more consistent impulses, beats a retreat within. In a remarkable series of statements in the treatise *On the Forgiveness of Sins or the Keys of the Church,* he comments in detail on the reasoning behind his duplicity.

> Divine illumination shows me that priestly confession and absolution are but human laws and commands of the Antichrist. I know that God's commands are to be obeyed, and these I follow faithfully with the inner man and heart. For God looks only on the heart and commands us to love him and our neighbor. By this he means that I should also obey all human commands, and not argue or fight about them and try to introduce something new. So I let the outer man follow the statutes and laws. I obey them for Christ's sake, and, out of love for God, I bear the cross, placing the outer man under the yoke and in Babylonian captivity. But this in no way harms my faith and salvation. For the kingdom of God is not an external thing, but rather something in my heart that no devil can take away. I could break forth with the truth and say: "Confession and absolution are false, and I will no longer be party to them. Here and now I cast off the yoke of the outer man and no longer will I bear the cross patiently or fulfill Christ's law." But then I would begin a disputation, which would lead to quarreling and in turn to war and revolution, as I sought to create something special. And it would all be done in vain. For I would not be able to erect something better. It would be as it was with Luther. He broke loose against the pope, attacked the indulgence, and even smashed it to the ground, yet he brought nothing better in its place.[191]

190. Zeller writes of Weigel's pessimism after the triumph of the Formula of Concord: "Der Sieg der Konkordienformel von 1578 hat seine Sehnsucht nach einer Reformation der Innerlichkeit, in der lutherischer Glaube und mystischer Geist in eins gehen, endgültig zunichte gemacht." *Sämtliche Schriften* 2: 118. Cf. Israel, *Weigels Leben und Schriften,* p. 2.

191. *Von der Vergebung der Sünden,* pp. 50–52. Weigel continued to admire the

For the sake of external order, the outer man should perform the meaningless rites and in this way bear the cross, while the inner man, fully conscious of this "fraud and deception," looks only to God.

> There are some preachers (although very few) who understand such fraud and deception, and, while they are captive to this yoke, they bear the cross gladly and do not try to start a revolt. For they know that such would not better but only worsen the situation. . . . We are not commanded to start new sects. Therefore, out of love of neighbor and God, they let the outer man sit in the confessional and absolve the people with mouth and hand. But they preserve the inner man, allowing him to be neither confessor nor dispenser of absolution. In this way they fulfill in patience, obedience, and love the law of Christ according to the inner man, and they also keep the human laws against social division and new sects. They know that decorum is better than chaos, and order better than disorder. In this way each becomes with Paul all things to all men [1 Cor. 9 : 22] and yet wounds neither conscience nor faith.[192]

It would not be unfair to say that, in the end, Weigel despaired altogether of significant social reform. The "abomination of desolation," he laments, is that apparently incurable naïveté by which men complacently view the external rites of religion as the very thing itself.[193] Weigel could not be party to such gross caricature of the new Jerusalem. He was as completely immune to naïveté as he felt his contemporaries to be smitten by it. For him, prudence and pessimism closed the revolutionary door. In constructive fraud he tended his flock in Zschopau and wrote for a more receptive posterity.

---

young Luther and count him as an ally, despite this judgment on Luther's ultimate achievement. When in the *Dialogus* the preacher says he has found nothing in Luther, Melanchthon, or any traditional church teaching to support the auditor's position, the auditor replies: "Von Philippi und andern Büchern ists nicht wunder, dann ehr kein Theologus, sondern nur ein Grammaticus Graecus, aristotelischer Philosophus gewesen. Aber in den Büchern Lutheri suchet besser! Do findet ir eben solche Reden, wie itzt von mir gehöret, sonderlich in seinen ersten Schrifften." *Dialogus*, p. 47.

192. *Von der Vergebung der Sünden*, p. 54; cf. pp. 61–62, 56, 58.
193. Ibid., p. 63.

Epilogue

By pen and personal example our dissenters laid bare the penultimate character of their institutions, secular and divine. They planted, so to speak, a new tree of the knowledge of good and evil, and having eaten from it, would not be returned to medieval innocence. To a man they were beyond that naïveté and condescension which trustingly accept traditionally sanctioned norms and rituals. They faced the institutions of their day with a spectrum of rejections ranging from outright rebellion to barely feigned acceptance. The traditional symbols of authority from the baptism of infants to the display of the eagle, were challenged. God may live in the depths of the heart, they concluded, but he will not be found in the universities and churches of Christendom. Truth may appear in the natural instincts of the simple, but it is sought in vain among the learned and the powerful.

In itself such protest was hardly novel. Still, it would be difficult to find so historically compact and influential a group of nonconformists in any preceding period. They were incomparable, not only because they had new things to say, but also because they said them memorably and with a vengeance. Whether it be Müntzer's revolutionary interpretation of the *Magnificat,* Hut's quest for a gospel behind the gospel, Denck's weary despair of "ceremonies and elements," Franck's chronicles of societal stupidity, Castellio's praise of commonsense judgment, or Weigel's constructively fraudulent ministry in Zschopau, arguments are set forth in rhetoric as pungent, eloquence as earthy, and logic as convincing as any ever penned by Luther or Erasmus.

To their contemporaries these men were simply anarchists. In the perspective that has come to dominate modern historiography they were advocates of reform. These evaluations are not necessarily mutually exclusive. If one considers modern society morally superior to sixteenth-century society, then those who attacked the latter are understandably characterized as having been progressive. If, on the other hand, one thinks as their contemporaries doubtlessly thought, namely, that sixteenth-century society excelled that of the late Middle Ages, then those who challenged the former could only be saboteurs.

From a modern perspective sixteenth-century society deserved their criticism and, in many ways, even their contempt. But having said this one has simply said the obvious. No society has not justifiably had contemptuous critics. So long as the legitimacy of sixteenth-century dissent is the focus of assessment, its distinctiveness is not fully grasped. The full story is told only as the ideology of sixteenth-century dissent becomes paramount.

For our dissenters final authority lay in principle with the individual, the invisible, the ethically ideal, the perfect community—things no earthly society could ever be. When the values and goals of mystical theology were gathered into the arsenal of dissent, the institutional links with truth were severely weakened, if not severed altogether. A *translatio imperii* from institutional to anthropological structures, from official to experiential criteria, from traditional to ethical norms of authority was undertaken. Measured by standards it could only poorly approximate, sixteenth-century society was denuded of virtue. History failed the test of eternity. Were not princes ravenous predators, government the Devil, learned scholars sophists, priests mindless lackeys, the masses slaves of Bacchus, the written word a fleeting shadow, the traditional rite an affront to God, temporal things the excrement of stars?

It was brilliant and even necessary dissent, the kind that must in time topple tyrants. But could it also build cities short of the new Jerusalem? Could it foster that patience with the humdrum and the penultimate which is necessary to maintain a viable, if not to create the perfect, society? Or was it destined to spawn lonely individuals and artificially constructed ideal communities encamped only on the fringes of the "real" world?

The legacy of sixteenth-century dissent is not only tolerance of diversity but also rejection of bureaucracy, not only the integrity of the individual but also the depersonalization of social institutions, not only a firm sense of self but also scorn for imperfect community. The impulse to reform competes with a desire to abandon society altogether—truly to die to the world. It is not too much to say that in such dissent the seeds of social disintegration are as prominent as those of individual liberation.

Bibliography

1. PRIMARY SOURCES

Bonaventure. *Itinerarium mentis in Deum.* Edited by J. Kaup. Munich, 1961.

————. *Opera omnia.* Quaracchi, 1882–1902.

Calvin, John. *Letters of John Calvin.* Vols. 1–2, edited and translated by Jules Bonnet. Philadelphia, 1858.

————. *Calvin: Theological Treatises.* Translated by J. K. S. Reid. Philadelphia, 1954.

————. *Institutes of the Christian Religion.* Edited by J. T. McNeill and translated by F. L. Battles. Philadelphia, 1960.

Castellio, Sebastian. *Moses Latinus ex Hebraeo factus.* Basel, 1546.

————. *Biblia, Interprete Sebastino Castalione.* Basel, 1551.

————. *Sebastiani Castellionis Defensio suarum translationum Bibliorum.* Basel, 1562.

————. *Contra libellum Calvini in quo ostendere conatur Haereticos jure gladij coercendos esse.* N. p., 1562 (1612).

————. *Sebastiani Castellionis Dialogi IV. De Praedestinatione. Electione. Libero Arbitrio. Fide.* Gouda, 1613.

————. *Questio, An Possit homo per Spiritum Sanctum perfecte obedire legi Dei.* In *Dialogi IV.* Gouda, 1613.

————. *Tractatus de justificatione.* In *Dialogi IV.* Gouda, 1613.

————. *De Arte dubitandi et confidendi, ignorandi et sciendi.* Edited by Elizabeth Feist. In *Per la Storia degli Erectici Italiani del Secolo XVI in Europa,* edited by D. Cantimori and E. Feist. *Reale Accademia d'Italia: Studi e Documenti,* vol. 7. Rome, 1937.

Denck, Hans. *Hans Denck. Schriften.* Vol. 2. *Religiöse Schriften,* edited by Walter Fellman. *Quellen und Forschungen zur Reformationsgeschichte,* vol. 24. Gütersloh, 1956.

————. *Hans Denck. Schriften.* Vol. 3. *Exegetische Schriften, Gedichte und Briefe,* edited by Walter Fellmann. *Quellen und Forschungen zur Reformationsgeschichte,* vol. 24. Gütersloh, 1960.

Eckhart, Meister. *Das Buoch der götlichen Troestunge.* In Franz Pfeiffer, *Deutsche Mystiker des 14. Jahrhunderts.* Vol. 2. *Meister Eckhart.* Leipzig, 1857.

————. *Meister Eckhart: A Modern Translation.* Edited and translated by R. B. Blakney. New York, 1941.

————. *Meister Eckhart. Die deutschen Werke.* Edited by Josef Quint. I. Stuttgart, 1958.

Franck, Sebastian. *Cronica-Abconterfarung und entwerff und der Türckey.* Augsburg, 1530.

―――. *Chronica, Zeytbüch und Geschichtbibel von anbegin biss in diss gegenwertig A.D. xxxj. jar.* Strasbourg, 1531.

―――. *Von dem grewlichen laster der trunckenheit.* N.p., 1531.

―――. *Weltbuch: spiegel und bildtnisz des gantzen erdbodens.* Tübingen, 1534.

―――. *Die vier Kronbüchlin.* Ulm, 1534.

―――. Paraphrase of the *Theologia Deutsch.* In Alfred Hegler, *Sebastian Francks lateinische Paraphrase der Deutschen Theologie und seine holländisch erhaltenen Traktate.* Tübingen, 1901.

―――. Trial documents in Ulm. In Alfred Hegler, *Beiträge zur Geschichte der Mystik in der Reformationszeit,* edited by Walther Köhler. In *Archiv für Reformationsgeschichte: Texte und Untersuchungen,* Ergänzungsband 1. Berlin, 1906.

―――. *A Letter to John Campanus.* In *Spiritual and Anabaptist Writers,* edited by G. H. Williams and A. M. Mergel. Philadelphia, 1957.

―――. *Sebastian Franck Paradoxa.* Edited by S. Wollgast. Berlin, 1966.

Der Franckforter ('Eyn Deutsch Theologia'). Edited by Willo Uhl. Bonn, 1912.

Der Frankfurter: Eine Deutsche Theologie. Edited by Joseph Bernhart. 3d ed. Munich, 1946.

Gerson, Jean. *De mystica theologia speculativa.* In *Ioannis Carlerii de Gerson: De mystica theologia,* edited by André Combes. Lugano, 1958.

―――. *Jean Gerson: Oeuvres complètes.* Edited by P. Glorieux, III. Paris, 1962.

―――. *Jean Gerson: Selections from A Deo exivit, Contra curiositatem studentium and De mystica theologia speculativa.* Edited and translated by S. E. Ozment. Leiden, 1969.

Haetzer, Ludwig. *Baruch der Prophet. Die Histori Susannah. Die Histori Bel zu Babel. Alles newlich auss der Bybli verteutscht.* Worms, 1527.

Hubmaier, Balthasar. *Von der Freiheit des Willens.* In *Balthasar Hubmaier. Schriften,* edited by G. Westin and T. Bergsten. *Quellen und Forschungen zur Reformationsgeschichte,* vol. 29. Gütersloh, 1962.

Hut, Hans. Trial documents. In Christian Meyer, "Zur Geschichte der Wiedertäufer in Oberschwaben, Pt. 1: Die Anfänge des Wiedertäuferthums in Augsburg." *Zeitschrift des historischen Vereins für Schwaben und Neuburg* 1 (Augsburg, 1874): 207–53.

―――. *Von dem geheimnus der tauf, baide des zaichens und des wesens, ein anfang eines rechten warhaftigen christlichen lebens;*

Joan. 5. In *Glaubenszeugnisse oberdeutschen Taufgesinnter,* vol. 1, edited by Lydia Müller. *Quellen und Forschungen zur Reformationsgeschichte,* vol. 20 (Leipzig, 1938), pp. 12–28.

——. *Ein christlicher underricht, wie göttliche geschrift vergleicht und geurtailt solle werden. Aus kraft des heiligen geists und zeuknus der drei tail christlichens glaubens sambt irem verstand.* In *Quellen und Forschungen zur Reformationsgeschichte,* vol. 20 (Leipzig, 1938), pp. 28–37.

Karlstadt, Andreas Bodenstein von. *Karlstadts Schriften aus den Jahren 1523–25.* Edited by Erich Hertzsch. Vol. 2. Halle, 1956.

Luther, Martin. *D. Martin Luthers Werke. Kritische Gesamtausgabe.* Weimar, 1883–   .

——. *Luther's Works.* Philadelphia, 1957–   .

——. *Three Treatises: Martin Luther.* Philadelphia, 1960.

——. *Lectures on the Epistle to the Hebrews.* Edited and translated by James Atkinson in *Luther: Early Theological Works.* Library of Christian Classics, vol. 16. Philadelphia, 1962.

Marbeck, Pilgram. *Pilgram Marbecks Antwort auf Kaspar Schwenckfelds Beurteilung des Buches der Bundesbezeugung von 1542.* Edited by J. Loserth. Vienna, 1929.

——. *Pilgram Marbecks Glaubensbekenntnis.* In *Quellen zur Geschichte der Täufer.* Vol. 7. *Elsass I (Strassburg 1522–32),* edited by M. Krebs and H. G. Rott. Gütersloh, 1959.

Müntzer, Thomas. "Thomas Müntzer's Last Tract Against Martin Luther: A Translation and Commentary." Translated by Hans Hillerbrand. *MQR* 38 (1964): 20–36.

——. *Thomas Müntzer: Schriften und Briefe. Kritische Gesamtausgabe.* Edited by Günther Franz (and Paul Kirn). In *Quellen und Forschungen zur Reformationsgeschichte,* vol. 33. Gütersloh, 1968.

Paracelsus. *Theophrast von Hohenheim, gen. Paracelsus: Sämtliche Werke.* Edited by Karl Sudhoff I. Munich and Berlin, 1929.

Ridemann, Peter. *Ein Rechenschafft und Bekanndtnus des Glaubens (1529–32).* In *Glaubenszeugnisse oberdeutscher Taufgesinnter.* Vol. 2. Edited by R. Friedmann. Gütersloh/Heidelberg, 1967.

Servetus, Michael. *On the Errors of the Trinity.* Edited and translated by E. M. Wilbur. *Harvard Theological Studies* 16. Cambridge, Mass., 1932.

Tauler, Johannes. *Die Predigten Taulers.* Edited by Ferdinand Vetter. Berlin, 1910.

Theologia Deutsch. Edited by Hermann Mandel. Leipzig, 1908.

La théologie germanique: Chapîtres choisis. Edited by Marius Valkhoff, introduced by Sebastian Castellio, and translated by Pierre Poiret. Haarlem, 1960.

Vincent of Aggsbach. *Tractatus cuiusdam Carthusiensis de Mystica theologia.* In E. Vansteenberghe, *Autour de la docte ignorance: une controverse sur la théologie mystique au XVe siècle.* Münster i.W., 1915, pp. 188–201.

Weigel, Valentin. *Gnothi seauton. Nosce teipsum. Erkenne dich selbst.* Newenstadt, 1615.

———. *Informatorium oder kurtzer Unterricht/welcher Gestalt man durch drei Mittel den schmalen Weg zu Christo sich führen kan lassen.* Newenstadt, 1616.

———. *Scholasterium christianum Seu Ludus credentium, quo taedium horarum seu temporis molestia abigitur et levatur.* In Paracelsus, *Philosophia mystica.* Newenstadt, 1618.

———. *Deus non potest se ipsum negare. 2. Thimoth. 2.* In *Libellus theosophiae De Veris reliquiis seu semine Dei in nobis post lapsum relicto.* Newenstadt, 1618.

———. *Der güldene Griff/Das ist: alle Dinge ohne Irrthum zu erkennen/vielen Hochgelehrten unbekannt/und doch allen Menschen notwendig zu wissen.* In *Theologia Weigelii.* Frankfurt, 1699.

———. *Kirchen- oder Hauss-Postill oder die Sonntags- und fürnembste Fest-Evangelien durchs gantze Jahr/aus dem rechten Catholischen und Apostolischen Grunde und Brunnen Israelis vorgetragen und geprediget durch M. Valentinum Weigelium. . . . N. p.,* 1700.

———. *Valentin Weigel. Sämtliche Schriften.* Edited by W.-E. Peuckert und W. Zeller. Vols. 1–5. Stuttgart-Bad Cannstatt, 1962–69.

2. Secondary Works

Appel, Heinrich. *Die Lehre der Scholastiker von der Syntheresis.* Rostock, 1891.

———. "Die Syntheresis in der mittelalterliche Mystik." *ZKG* 13 (1892): 535 ff.

Bainton, Roland H. "Sebastian Castellio and the Toleration Controversy of the Sixteenth Century." In *Persecution and Liberty: Essays in Honor of George Lincoln Burr.* New York, 1931, pp. 183–209.

———. *David Joris: Wiedertäufer und Kämpfer für Toleranz im 16. Jahrhundert.* Leipzig, 1937.

———; Becker, B.; Valkhoff, M.; and van der Woude, S. *Castellioniana: Quatre études sur Sébastien Castellion et l'idée de la tolérance.* Leiden, 1951.

———. "Sebastian Castellio: Champion of Religious Liberty." In Bainton, Roland H.; Becker, B.; Valkhoff, M.; and van der Woude, S. *Castellioniana: Quatre études sur Sébastien Castellion et l'idée de la tolérance.* Pp. 25–79, Leiden, 1951.

————. *Hunted Heretic: The Life and Death of Michael Servetus 1511–1553.* 2d ed. Boston, 1960.

————. *Collected Papers in Church History.* Vol 2. *Studies on the Reformation.* Boston, 1963.

Barbers, Meinulf. *Toleranz bei Sebastian Franck.* Bonn, 1964.

Barge, Hermann. *Andreas Bodenstein von Karlstadt.* Vols. 1–2. Leipzig, 1905.

Baring, Georg. *Hans Denck. Schriften.* Vol. 1. *Bibliographie, Quellen und Forschungen zur Reformationsgeschichte,* Vol. 24. Gütersloh, 1955.

————. "Neues von der 'Theologia Deutsch,' und ihrer weltweiten Bedeutung." *ARG* 49 (1957): 1–11.

————. "Hans Denck und Thomas Müntzer in Nürnberg 1524." *ARG* 50 (1959): 145–81.

————. "Ludwig Haetzers Beareitung der 'Theologia Deutsch' Worms, 1528: Ihr Druck und ihre Handschrift von 1529, ihre Nachwirkung und ihr Verhältnis zu Luthers Ausgabe von 1518." *ZKG* (1959): 218–30.

————. "Die französischen Ausgaben der 'Theologia Deutsch.'" *Theologische Zeitschrift der theologischen Fakultät der Universität Basel* 16 (1960): 176–94.

————. *Bibliographie der Ausgaben der 'Theologia Deutsch' (1516–1961). Ein Beitrag zur Luther Bibliographie.* Baden-Baden, 1963.

Becker, Bruno, ed. *Autour de Michel Servet et de Sébastien Castellion.* Haarlem, 1953.

————. "Sur quelques documents manuscrits concernant Castellion." In *Autour de Michel Servet et de Sébastien Castellion,* edited by B. Becker, pp. 280–88. Haarlem, 1953.

Bender, Harold S., "The Zwickau Prophets, Thomas Müntzer and the Anabaptists." *MQR* 27 (1953): 3–16.

Bensing, Manfred. *Thomas Müntzer und der Thüringer Aufstand 1525.* Berlin, 1966.

Benz, Ernst. *Ecclesia Spiritualis: Kirchenidee und Geschichtstheologie der franziskanischen Reformation.* Stuttgart, 1934.

Bergsten, T. "Pilgram Marbeck und seine Auseinandersetzung mit Caspar Schwenckfeld." *Kyrkohistorisck Arsskrift* 57 (1957): 39–100; 58 (1958): 53–87.

Bernhart, Joseph. *Bernhardische und Eckhartische Mystik in ihren Beziehungen und Gegensätzen.* Kempton, 1912.

————. *Die philosophische Mystik des Mittelalters von ihren antiken Ursprüngen bis zur Renaissance.* Munich, 1922.

Beyer, H. W. "Gott und die Geschichte nach Luthers Auslegung des Magnificat." *Luther-Jahrbuch* 21 (1939), pp. 110–33.

Bizer, Ernst. *Fides ex auditu. Eine Untersuchung über die Entdeckung der Gerechtigkeit Gottes durch Martin Luther.* Neukirchen, 1961.

Blanke, Fritz. "Das Reich der Wiedertäufer zu Münster 1534/35." *ARG* 37 (1940): 13–37.

Blaschke, Lotte. "Neueres Schrifttum über Sebastian Franck." *Blätter für deutsche Philosophie* 2 (1928): 73–77.

Bloch, Ernst. *Thomas Müntzer als Theologe der Revolution* (1925). 3d ed. Berlin, 1963.

Bloomfield, Morton. "Joachim of Flora: A Critical Survey of His Canon, Teachings, Sources, Biography and Influence." *Traditio* 13 (1957): 248–309.

Boehmer, Heinrich. *Martin Luther: Road to Reformation.* 3d ed. New York, 1960.

Bornkamm, Heinrich. *Mystik, Spiritualismus und die Anfänge des Pietismus im Luthertum.* Giessen, 1926.

——. "Aeusserer und innerer Mensch bei Luther und den Spiritualisten." In *Imago Dei: Beiträge zur theologischen Anthropologie. Festgabe für Gustav Krüger.* Giessen, 1932, pp. 85–109.

Bräuer, S. "Zu Müntzers Geburtsjahr." *Luther-Jahrbuch* 36 (1969): 80–83.

Breen, Quirinus. *John Calvin: A Study in French Humanism* (1931). 2d ed. Hamden, Conn., 1968.

Buisson, Ferdinand. *Sébastien Castellion: Sa vie et son oeuvre (1515–63): Étude sur les origines du protestantisme libéral Français.* Vols. 1–2. Paris, 1892.

Butler, Cuthbert. *Western Mysticism.* 2d ed. London, 1966.

Cantimori, Delio. *Italienische Haeretiker der Spätrenaissance.* Basel, 1949.

——. "Note su alcuni Aspitti de Misticismo del Castellione e della sua Fortuna." In *Autour de Michel Servet et de Sébastien Castellion,* edited by B. Becker, pp. 239–43. Haarlem, 1953.

Chrisman, Miriam U. *Strasbourg and the Reform.* New Haven, 1967.

Clasen, Claus Peter. "Medieval Heresies in the Reformation." *Church History* 32 (1963): 392–414.

——. "The Sociology of Swabian Anabaptism." *Church History* 32 (1963): 150–80.

——. *Die Wiedertäufer im Herzogtum Württemberg und in benachbarten Herrschaften: Ausbreitung, Geisteswelt und Soziologie.* Stuttgart, 1965.

Cohn, Norman. *The Pursuit of the Millennium.* 2d ed. New York, 1961.

Combes, André. *La théologie mystique de Gerson: Profil de son evolution.* Vols. 1–2. Rome, 1963–64.

Coutts, A. *Hans Denck 1495–1527: Humanist and Heretic.* Edinburgh, 1927.

Denzinger, H. *Enchiridion symbolorum.* 32d ed. Freiburg i.B., 1963.

Dobratz, Felicitas. *Der Einfluss der deutschen Mystik auf Thomas Müntzer und Hans Denck.* Münster/Westfalen, 1960.

Dress, Walter. *Die Theologie Gersons: Eine Untersuchung zur Verbindung von Nominalismus und Mystik im Spätmittelalter.* Gütersloh, 1931.

Droz, Eugénie. "Sur quelques traductions françoises d'écrits de David Joris." *Het Boek* 37: 152–62.

Elliger, Walter. *Thomas Müntzer.* Berlin-Friedenau, 1960.

Endriss, Julius. *Sebastian Francks Ulmer Kämpfe.* Ulm, 1935.

Fast, Heinold. "Pilgram Marbeck und das oberdeutsche Täufertum: Ein neuer Handschriftenfund." *ARG* 47 (1956): 212–42.

———, ed. *Der linke Flügel der Reformation.* Bremen, 1962.

Fausel, H. "Luther und Melanchthon während des Augsburger Reichstag." In *Theologische Aufsätze: Karl Barth zum 50. Geburtstag.* Munich, 1936. Pp. 405–16.

Fellmann, Walter. "Der theologische Gehalt der Schriften Dencks." In *Die Leibhaftigkeit des Wortes. Festgabe für Adolf Köberle zum 60. Geburtstag,* edited by O. Michel and U. Mann. Hamburg, 1958. Pp. 157–65.

Forest, Aimé. "Das Erlebnis des consensus voluntatis beim hl. Bernhard." In *Bernhard von Clairvaux: Mönch und Mystiker. Internationaler Bernhardkongress Mainz 1953,* edited by Joseph Lortz. Wiesbaden, 1955. Pp. 120–27.

Franz, Günther. *Der deutsche Bauernkrieg.* 7th ed. Darmstadt, 1965.

Frei, W. "Was ist das Seelenfünklein beim Meister Eckhart?", *Theologische Zeitschrift* 14 (1958): 89–100.

Fremantle, Anne, ed. *The Protestant Mystics.* New York, 1965.

Friedmann, Robert. "Thomas Müntzer's Relation to Anabaptism." *MQR* 31 (1957): 75–87.

———. "Leonhard Schiemer und Hans Schlaffer: Two Anabaptist Martyr-Apostles of 1528." *MQR* 33 (1959): 31–41.

———, ed. *Glaubenszeugnisse oberdeutscher Taufgesinnter* 2. Gütersloh/Heidelberg, 1967.

Friesen, Abraham. "Thomas Müntzer in Marxist Thought." *Church History* 34 (1965): 306–27.

Gerdes, Hayo. *Luthers Streit mit den Schwärmern um das rechte Verständnis des Gesetzes Mose.* Göttingen, 1955.

Gieraths, Gundolf. "Johannes Tauler und die Frömmigkeitshaltung des 15. Jahrhunderts." In *Johannes Tauler: Ein Deutscher Mystiker.*

Gedenkschrift zum 600. Todestag, edited by E. M. Filthaut. Essen, 1961. Pp. 422–34.

Giran, Etienne. *Sébastian Castellion et la réforme Calviniste: Les deux réformes.* Haarlem/Paris, 1914.

Goebke, H. "Neue Forschungen über Thomas Müntzer bis zum Jahre 1520: Seine Abstammung und die Wurzeln seiner religiösen, politischen und sozialen Ziele." *Harz-Zeitschrift* 9 (1957): 1–30.

Goertz, H.-J. *Innere und äussere Ordnung in der Theologie Thomas Müntzers.* Leiden, 1967.

Goeters, J. E. Gerhard. *Ludwig Haetzer (ca. 1500 bis 1529): Spiritualist und Antitrinitarier. Eine Randfigur der frühen Täuferbewegung.* Gütersloh, 1957.

Goldammer, Kurt. "Friedensidee und Toleranzgedanke bei Paracelsus und den Spiritualisten, 2: Franck und Weigel." *ARG* 47 (1956): 180–211.

Grabmann, Martin. *Die Kulturwerte des deutschen Mystik des Mittelalters.* Augsburg, 1923.

———. *Mittelalterliches Geistesleben: Abhandlungen zur Geschichte der Scholastik und Mystik.* Vols. 1–3. Munich, 1926 ff.

Greschat, Martin. "Der Bundesgedanke in der Theologie des späten Mittelalters." *ZKG* 1 (1970): 44–63.

Gritsch, Eric. *Reformer Without a Church: The Life and Thought of Thomas Müntzer 1488[?]–1525.* Philadelphia, 1967.

Gröber, Conrad. *Der Mystiker Heinrich Seuse: Die Geschichte seines Lebens.* Freiburg i.B., 1941.

Grolman, A. von. "Das Wissen um das Verhältnismässige in der Paradoxie des Seins: Studie zur teutschen theologie des Sebastian Franck." *Blätter für deutsche Philosophie* 2 (1928): 57–72.

Grünewald, S. *Franziskanische Mystik: Versuch zu einer Darstellung mit besonderer Berücksichtigung des hl. Bonaventura.* Munich, 1932.

Grundmann, Herbert. *Religiöse Bewegungen im Mittelalter.* 2d ed. Darmstadt, 1961.

———. "Die geschichtliche Grundlagen der deutschen Mystik." In *Altdeutsche und altniederländische Mystik,* edited by Kurt Ruh. Darmstadt, 1964. Pp. 72–99.

Guggisberg, C. "Jean Calvin und Niklaus Zurkinden: Glaubensautorität und Gewissensfreiheit." *Zwingliana* 6 (1937): 374–409.

Guggisberg, Hans R. *Sebastian Castellio im Urteil seiner Nachwelt vom Späthumanismus bis zur Aufklärung.* Basel, 1956.

Headley, John. *Luther's View of Church History.* New Haven, 1963.

Hege, Albrecht. *Hans Denck 1495–1527.* Tübingen, 1939.

Hege, Christian. "Pilgram Marbeck und die oberdeutschen Taufgesinnten: Neuere Forschungsergebnisse." *ARG* 37 (1940): 249–57.

Hegler, Alfred. *Geist und Schrift bei Sebastian Franck: Eine Studie zur Geschichte des Spiritualismus in der Reformationszeit.* Freiburg i.B., 1892.

──────. *Sebastian Francks lateinische Paraphrase der Deutschen Theologie und seine holländisch erhaltenen Traktate.* Tübingen, 1901.

──────. *Beiträge zur Geschichte der Mystik in der Reformationszeit.* Edited by Walther Köhler. *ARG: Texte und Untersuchungen,* Ergänzungsband 1. Berlin, 1906.

Hermelink, Heinrich. "Text und Gedankengang der Theologia Deutsch." In *Aus Deutschlands kirchlicher Vergangenheit: Festschrift zum 70. Geburtstage von Theodor Brieger.* Leipzig, 1912. Pp. 1–19.

Hillerbrand, Hans J. "Anabaptism and the Reformation: Another Look." *Church History* 29 (1960): 404–23.

──────. *Die politische Ethik des oberdeutschen Täufertums.* Leiden, 1962.

──────. *A Fellowship of Discontent.* New York, 1967.

Hinrichs, Carl. *Luther und Müntzer: Ihre Auseinandersetzung über Obrigkeit und Widerstandsrecht.* Berlin, 1952.

Hirsch, Elizabeth Feist. "Castellio's 'De Arte dubitandi' and the Problem of Religious Liberty." In *Autour de Michel Servet et de Sébastien Castellion,* edited by B. Becker. Haarlem, 1953. Pp. 244–58.

Hirsch, Emmanuel. "Zum Verständnis Schwenckfelds." In *Festgabe für Karl Müller.* Tübingen, 1922. Pp. 145–70.

Hof, Hans. *Scintilla animae.* Lund, 1952.

Holl, Karl. *Gesammelte Aufsätze zur Kirchengeschichte.* Vol. 1. 7th ed. Tübingen, 1948.

Inge, W. R. *Christian Mysticism.* Bamptom Lectures, 1899.

Iserloh, Erwin. "Zur Gestalt und Biographie Thomas Müntzers." *Trierer Theologische Zeitschrift* 71 (1962): 248–53.

──────. *The Theses Were not Posted: Luther Between Reform and Reformation.* Boston, 1968.

──────. "Luther und die Mystik." In *Kirche, Mystik, Heiligung und das Natürliche bei Luther. Vorträge des III. Internationalen Kongresses für Lutherforschung.* Göttingen, 1968. Pp. 60–83.

Israel, August. *M. Valentin Weigels Leben und Schriften.* Zschopau, 1888.

Ivánka, Endre von. *Plato Christianus: Uebernahme und Umgestaltung des Platonismus durch die Väter.* Einsiedeln, 1964.

Joachimsen, Paul. "Zur inneren Entwicklung Sebastian Francks." *Blätter für deutsche Philosophie* 2 (1928): 1–28.

Jones, Rufus M. *Spiritual Reformers in the Sixteenth and Seventeenth Centuries.* 2d ed. Boston, 1959.

———. *Mysticism and Democracy in the English Commonwealth.* Cambridge, Mass., 1932.

Keller, Ludwig. *Ein Apostel der Wiedertäufer.* Leipzig, 1882.

———. *Die Reformation und die älteren Reformparteien.* Leipzig, 1885.

———. *Johann von Staupitz und die Anfänge der Reformation.* Leipzig, 1888.

———. "Die Gottesfreunde, die 'Deutsche Theologie' und die Rosenkreuzer." *Monatshefte der Comenius Gesellschaft* 11 (1902): 145–57.

Kintner, Philip L. "Sebastian Franck: An American Library Finding List." *ARG* 55 (1964): 48–55.

Kirchner, Hubert. *Johann Sylvius Egranus.* Berlin, 1961.

Kiwiet, Jan J. "The Life of Hans Denck (ca. 1500–1527)." *MQR* 31 (1957): 227–59.

———. "The Theology of Hans Denck." *MQR* 32 (1958): 3–27.

———. "Die *Theologia Deutsch* und ihre Bedeutung während der Zeit der Reformation." *Mennonitische Geschichtsblätter* 15 (1958): 29–35.

Klaassen, Walter. "Hans Hut und Thomas Müntzer." *The Baptist Quarterly* 19 (1962): 209–27.

Klassen, Herbert. "The Life and Teachings of Hans Hut." *MQR* 33 (1959): 171–205, 267–304.

Klassen, William, *Covenant and Community: The Life, Writings and Hermeneutics of Pilgram Marbeck.* Grand Rapids, Mich., 1969.

Knowles, David. *The English Mystical Tradition.* New York, 1961.

Koch, Josef. "Meister Eckharts Weiterwirken im Deutsch-Niederländischen Raum im 14. und 15. Jahrhundert." In *La mystique Rhénane: Colloque de Strasbourg 16–19 Mai 1961.* Paris, 1963. Pp. 133–56.

Kolde, Theodor. "Zum Process des Johann Denck und der 'drei gottlosen Maler' von Nürnberg." *Kirchengeschichtliche Studien: Hermann Reuter zum 70. Geburtstag gewidmet.* Leipzig, 1888. Pp. 228–50.

———. "Hans Denck und die gottlosen Maler von Nürnberg." *Beiträge zur Bayerischen Kirchengeschichte* 8 (1902): 1–72.

Kommoss, Rudolf. *Sebastian Franck und Erasmus von Rotterdam.* Berlin, 1934.

Koyré, Alexandre. *Mystiques, spirituels, alchimistes: Schwenckfeld, Séb. Franck, Weigel, Paracelse.* Paris, 1955.

Kriechbaum, F. *Grundzüge der Theologie Karlstadts.* Hamburg, 1967.

Krumwiede, H.-W. *Glaube und Geschichte in der Theologie Luthers.* Göttingen, 1952.

Kühn, Johannes. *Toleranz und Offenbarung.* Leipzig, 1923.

Kunisch, H. *Das Wort "Grund" in der Sprache der deutschen Mystik des 14. und 15. Jahrhundert.* Osnabrück, 1929.

Längin, Heinz. "Grundlinien der Erkenntnislehre Valentin Weigels." *Archiv für Geschichte der Philosophie* 41 (1932): 435–78.

Leclercq, J.; Vandenbroucke, F.; Bouyer, L. *La spiritualité du Moyen Âge*. Paris, 1961.

Lieb, Fritz. *Valentin Weigels Kommentar zur Schöpfungsgeschichte und das Schrifttum seines Schülers Benedikt Biedermann*. Zürich, 1951.

Liebing, Heinz. *Die Schriftauslegung Sebastian Castellios*. Dissertation, Tübingen, 1953.

———. "Die Frage nach einem hermeneutischen Prinzip bei Castellio." In *Autour de Michel Servet et de Sébastien Castellion*, edited by B. Becker. Haarlem, 1953. Pp. 206–24.

Lindeboom, J. "La place de Castellion dans l'histoire de l'esprit." In *Autour de Michel Servet et de Sébastien Castellion*, edited by B. Becker. Haarlem, 1953. Pp. 158–80.

Littell, Franklin H. *The Origins of Sectarian Protestantism: A Study of the Anabaptist View of the Church*. 3d ed. New York, 1964.

Lohmann, Annemarie. *Zur geistigen Entwicklung Müntzers*. Leipzig/Berlin, 1931.

Lücker, Maria A. *Meister Eckhart und die Devotio moderna*. Leiden, 1950.

Maier, Hans. *Der mystische Spiritualismus Valentin Weigels*. Gütersloh, 1926.

Maron, Gottfried. *Individualismus und Gemeinschaft bei Caspar von Schwenckfeld*. Stuttgart, 1961.

Mecenseffy, Grete. "Die Herkunft des oberösterreichischen Täufertums." *ARG* 47 (1956): 252–59.

Mellink, A. F. *De Wederdopers in de noordelijke Nederlanden 1531–1544*. Gronigen, 1953.

Mennonitisches Lexikon. Edited by C. Hege, et al. Vols. 1–3. 1913–56.

Meyer, Christian. "Zur Geschichte der Wiedertäufer in Oberschwaben, I: Die Anfänge des Wiedertäuferthums in Augsburg." *Zeitschrift des historischen Vereins für Schwaben und Neuburg* 1. Augsburg, 1874. Pp. 207–53.

Moeller, Bernd. "Tauler und Luther." In *La mystique Rhénane: Colloque de Strasbourg 16–19 Mai 1961*. Paris, 1963. Pp. 157 ff.

———. "Frömmigkeit im Deutschland um 1500." *ARG* 56 (1965): 5–30.

Müller, Georg. "Jugendrevolte und Linksopposition im Hochmittelalter." *ZRGG* 22 (1970): 113–30.

Müller, Lydia, ed. *Glaubenszeugnisse oberdeutschen Taufgesinnter I*.

Quellen und Forschungen zur Reformationsgeschichte, Vol. 2. Leipzig, 1938.

Neff, Christian. "Hans Denck." In *Mennonitisches Lexikon* 1 (1913 ff.): 401–04.

Neuser, Wilhelm. *Hans Hut: Leben und Wirken bis zum Nikolsburger Religionsgespräch.* Berlin, 1913.

Niesel, Wilhelm. *Die Theologie Calvins.* 2d ed. Munich, 1957.

Nigg, Walter. *Das Buch der Ketzer.* Zürich, 1949.

Nipperdey, Thomas. "Theologie und Revolution bei Thomas Müntzer." *ARG* 54 (1963): 145–81.

Nitzsch, F. "Der gegenwärtige Stand der Streitfrage über die Syntheresis." *ZKG* 19 (1898): 1–14.

Oberman, Heiko A. *The Harvest of Medieval Theology.* Cambridge, Mass., 1963.

———. *Forerunners of the Reformation: The Shape of Late Medieval Thought.* New York, 1966.

———. "Simul Gemitus et Raptus: Luther und die Mystik." In *Kirche, Mystik, Heiligung und das Natürliche bei Luther: Vorträge des III. Internationalen Kongresses für Lutherforschung.* Göttingen, 1968. Pp. 20–59.

O'Brien, E. *Varieties of Mystic Experience.* New York, 1964.

Oncken, Hermann. "Aus den letzten Jahren Sebastian Francks." *Monatshefte der Comenius-Gesellschaft* 11 (1902): 86–101.

Opel, Julius Otto. *Valentin Weigel: Ein Beitrag zur Literatur und Culturgeschichte Deutschlands in 17. Jahrhundert.* Leipzig, 1864.

Otto, Rudolf. *Mysticism East and West.* New York, 1932.

Oyer, John S. "Anabaptism in Central Germany." *MQR* 34 (1960): 219–48.

———. *Lutheran Reformers Against Anabaptists: Luther, Melanchthon and Menius and the Anabaptists of Central Germany.* The Hague, 1964.

Ozment, Steven E. *Homo Spiritualis: A Comparative Study of the Anthropology of Johannes Tauler, Jean Gerson and Martin Luther (1509–16).* Leiden, 1969.

———. "The University and the Church: Patterns of Reform in Jean Gerson." *Medievalia et Humanistica* n.s. 1 (1970): 111–26.

———, ed. *The Reformation in Medieval Perspective.* Chicago, 1971.

Pagel, Walter. *Das medizinische Weltbild des Paracelsus: Seine Zusammenhänge mit Neuplatonismus und Gnosis.* Wiesbaden, 1962.

Pahncke, Max. "Zur handschriftlichen Ueberlieferung des 'Frankfurters' ('Theologia Deutsch')." *Zeitschrift für deutsches Altertum und deutsche Literatur* 89 (1958/59): 275–80.

Peachey, Paul. "Social Background and Social Philosophy of the Swiss Anabaptists, 1525–1540." *MQR* 28 (1954): 102–27.

———. *Die soziale Herkunft der schweizer Täufer in der Reformationszeit.* Karlsruhe, 1954.

Pederson, T. E. "Schöpfung und Geschichte bei Luther." *Studia Theologia* 3 (1949): 1–30.

Pelikan, Jaroslav. "Luther's Attitude Toward John Huss." *Concordia Theological Monthly* 19 (1948): 747–63.

Petry, Ray. *Late Medieval Mysticism.* Philadelphia, 1957.

Peuckert, W.-E. *Sebastian Franck: Ein deutscher Sucher.* Munich, 1943.

———. *Pansophie: Ein Versuch zur Geschichte der weissen und schwarzen Magie.* 2d ed. Berlin, 1956.

Post, R. R. *The Modern Devotion: Confrontation with Reformation and Humanism.* Leiden, 1968.

Preger, Wilhelm. *Geschichte der deutschen Mystik im Mittelalter.* Vols. 1–3. Leipzig, 1874–93.

Quiring, Horst. "The Anthropology of Pilgram Marbeck." *MQR* 9 (1935): 155–64.

Reimann, Arnold. *Sebastian Franck als Geschichtsphilosoph: Ein moderner Denker im 16. Jahrhundert.* Berlin, 1921.

Roth, Fritz. "Zur Geschichte der Wiedertäufer in Oberschwaben, II: Zur Lebensgeschichte Eitelhans Langenmantels von Augsburg." *Zeitschrift des historischen Vereins für Schwaben und Neuburg* 28 (1902): 1–45.

Ruh, Kurt. *Bonaventura Deutsch: Ein Beitrag zur deutschen Franziskaner-Mystik und Scholastik.* Bern, 1956.

———. "Eine neue Handschrift des 'Frankfurters.'" *Zeitschrift für deutsches Altertum und deutsche Literatur* 89 (1959): 280–87.

———. "Zur Grundlegung einer Geschichte der Franziskanischen Mystik." In *Altdeutsche und altniederländische Mystik,* ed. Kurt Ruh. Darmstadt, 1964. Pp. 240–74.

Rupp, Gordon. "Word and Spirit in the First Years of the Reformation." *ARG* 49 (1958): 13–26.

———. "Thomas Müntzer, Hans Hut and the 'Gospel of all Creatures.'" *Bulletin of the John Rylands Library* 43 (1961): 492–519.

———. "Thomas Müntzer: Prophet of Radical Christianity." *Bulletin of the John Rylands Library* 48 (1966): 467–87.

———. *Patterns of Reformation.* Philadelphia, 1969.

Schiel, Hubert. "Heinrich von Bergen oder Johannes de Francfordia als Verfasser der 'Theologia Deutsch.'" *Archiv für mittelrheinische Kirchengeschichte* 22 (1970): 85–92.

Schmidt, Martin. "Das Selbstbewusstsein Thomas Müntzers und sein Verhältnis zu Luther. Ein Beitrag zu der Frage: War Thomas Müntzer Mystiker?" *Theologia Viatorum* 6 (1954/58): 25–41.

Schoeps, Hans J. *Vom himmlischen Fleisch Christi.* Tübingen, 1951.

Schraepler, Horst W. *Die rechtliche Behandlung der Täufer in der deutschen Schweiz, Südwestdeutschland und Hessen 1525–1618.* Tübingen, 1957.

Schwarz, Reinhard. "Luthers Erscheinen auf dem Wormser Reichstag in der Sicht Thomas Müntzers." In *Der Reichstag zu Worms von 1521: Reichspolitik und Luthersache,* ed. Fritz Reuter. Worms, 1971. Pp. 208–21.

Schwindt, A. M. *Hans Denck: Ein Vorkämpfer undogmatischen Christentums 1495–1527.* Habertshof, 1924.

Seeberg, Reinhold. *Text-Book of the History of Doctrines.* Vol. 2. Translated by C. E. Hay. Grand Rapids, Mich., 1968.

Siedel, Gottfried. "Nochmals zum Text der 'Theologia Deutsch.' " *ZKG* 55 (1936): 305–12.

Sigmund, Paul E. *Nicholas of Cusa and Medieval Political Thought.* Cambridge, Mass., 1963.

Smirin, M. M. "Thomas Münzer und die Lehre des Joachim von Fiore." *Sinn und Form* 4 (1952): 69–143.

———. *Die Volksreformation des Thomas Münzer und der grosse Bauernkrieg.* 2d ed. Berlin, 1956.

Spamer, Adolf, ed. *Texte aus der Deutschen Mystik des 14. und 15. Jahrhundert.* Jena, 1912.

Spiess, Bernhard. "Sebastian Castellio: Ein Vorkämpfer der Glaubensfreiheit im 16. Jahrhundert." *Monatshefte der Comenius-Gesellschaft* 5 (1896): 185-209.

Spitz, Lewis W. *The Religious Renaissance of the German Humanists.* Cambridge, Mass., 1963.

Stähelin, Ernst. *Das theologische Lebenswerk Johann Oekolampads.* Leipzig, 1939.

Steinmetz, David C. *Misericordia Dei: The Theology of Johannes von Staupitz in its Late Medieval Setting.* Leiden, 1968.

———. "Scholasticism and Radical Reform: Nominalist Motifs in the Theology of Balthasar Hubmaier." *MQR* 45 (1971): 123–43.

Steinmetz, Max. "Philipp Melanchthon über Thomas Müntzer und Nikolaus Storch: Beiträge zur Auffassung der Volksreformation in der Geschichtsschreibung des 16. Jahrhunderts." In *Philipp Melanchthon: Humanist, Reformator, Praeceptor Germaniae.* Berlin, 1963.

Stellweg, Helena W. F. "Castellio Paedagogus." In *Autour de Michel Servet et de Sébastien Castellion,* edited by B. Becker. Haarlem, 1953. Pp. 181–94.

Strauss, Gerald, ed. *Manifestations of Discontent in Germany on the Eve of the Reformation.* Bloomington, Ind., 1971.

Stroudt, John J., *Jacob Boehme: His Life and Thought.* 2d ed. New York, 1968.

Stupperich, Robert. *Das Münsterische Täufertum: Ergebnisse und Probleme der neueren Forschung.* Münster/Westf., 1958.

Teufel, Eberhard. "Luther und Luthertum im Urteil Sebastian Francks." *Festgabe für Karl Müller.* Tübingen, 1922. Pp. 132–44.

————. "Die 'Deutsche Theologie' und Sebastian Franck im Lichte der neueren Forschung." *Theologische Rundschau* 11 (1939), 304–15.

————. "Täufertum und Quäkertum im Lichte der neueren Forschung III." *Theologische Rundschau* 13 (1941): 183–97.

————. *"Landräumig": Sebastian Franck, ein Wanderer an Donau, Rhein und Neckar.* Neustadt an der Aisch, 1954.

Thimme, Wilhelm. "Die 'Deutsche Theologie' und Luthers 'Freiheit eines Christenmenschen': Ein Vergleich." *ZThK* 3 (1932): 193 ff.

Thudichum, F. "Die 'deutsche Theologie': Ein religiöses Glaubensbekenntnis aus dem 15. Jahrhundert." *Monatshefte der Comenius-Gesellschaft* 5 (1896): 44–62.

Thumm, Theodor. *Impietas Wigeliana, h.e. necessaria admonitio de centum et viginti erroribus novorum prophetarum coelestium, quos a Valentino Wigelio nostra haec aetas dicere coepit Wigelianos.* Tübingen, 1650.

Ueda, Schizuteru. "Ueber den Sprachgebrauch Meister Eckharts: 'Gott muss . . .': Ein Beispiel für die Gedankengänge der spekulativen Mystik." *Glaube, Geist, Geschichte: Festschrift für Ernst Benz,* ed. G. Müller and W. Zeller. Leiden, 1967. Pp. 266–77.

Underhill, Evelyn. *The Mystics of the Church.* London, 1925.

————. *Mysticism: A Study in the Nature and Development of Man's Spiritual Consciousness.* 12th ed. New York, 1961.

Valkhoff, Marius. "Chronique Castellionienne." *Neophilologus* 42 (1958): 277–88.

Van der Woude, Sape. "Censured Passages from Castellio's *Defensio suarum translationum.*" In *Autour de Michel Servet et de Sébastien Castellion,* edited by B. Becker. Haarlem, 1953. Pp. 259–79.

Vansteenberghe, E. *Autour de la docte ignorance: Une controverse sur la théologie mystique au XVe siècle.* Münster i.W., 1915.

Vittali, Otto E. *Die Theologie des Wiedertäufers Hans Denck.* Offenburg, 1932.

Walton, Robert C. "Was There a Turning Point of the Zwinglian Reformation?" *MQR* 42 (1968): 45–56.

————. *Zwingli's Theocracy.* Toronto, 1967.

Wappler, Paul. *Thomas Müntzer in Zwickau und die "Zwickauer Propheten."* 1908. 2d ed. Gütersloh, 1966.

————. *Die Täuferbewegung in Thüringen von 1526–84: Beiträge zur neueren Geschichte Thüringens* 2. Jena, 1913.

Weigelt, Horst. "Sebastian Franck und Caspar Schwenckfeld in ihren Beziehungen zueinander." *Zeitschrift für Bayerische Kirchengeschichte* 39 (1970): 3–19.

Weis, F. L. *The Life, Teachings and Works of Johannes Denck 1495–1527.* Strasbourg, 1924.

Weiss, R. "Die Herkunft der osthessischen Täufer." *ARG* 50 (1959): 1–16.

Wendel, François. *Calvin: The Origins and Development of His Religious Thought.* New York, 1963.

Wessendorft, K. "Ist der Verfasser der 'Theologia Deutsch' gefunden?" *Evangelische Theologie* 16 (1956): 188–92.

Wicks, Jared. *Man Yearning for Grace: Luther's Early Spiritual Teaching.* Washington, 1968.

Williams, G. H. and Mergal, A. M. (eds.) *Spiritual and Anabaptist Writers.* Philadelphia, 1957.

Williams, G. H. "Studies in the Radical Reformation (1517–1618): A Bibliographical Survey of Research Since 1939." *Church History* 27, no. 1 (1958): 46–69; 27, no. 2 (1958): 124–60.

———. *The Radical Reformation.* London, 1962.

———. "Popularized German Mysticism as a Factor in the Rise of Anabaptist Communism." In *Glaube, Geist, Geschichte: Festschrift für Ernst Benz,* edited by G. Mueller and W. Zeller. Leiden, 1967. Pp. 290–312.

———. "Sanctification in the Testimony of Several So-Called Schwärmer." In *Kirche, Mystik, Heiligung und das Natürliche bei Luther. Vorträge des III. Internationalen Kongresses für Lutherforschung.* Göttingen, 1968. Pp. 20–59.

Wilms, H. "Das Seelenfünklein in der deutschen Mystik." *Zeitschrift für Aszese und Mystik* 12 (1937): 157–66.

Wiswedel, W. *Bilder und Führergestalten aus dem Täufertum.* Vol. 1. Kassel, 1928.

———. "Zum 'Problem inneres und äusseres Wort' bei den Täufern des 16. Jahrhunderts." *ARG* 46 (1955): 1 ff.

Yoder, John H. "The Turning Point in the Zwinglian Reformation." *MQR* 32 (1958); 128–40.

———. "The Evolution of the Zwinglian Reformation." *MQR* 43 (1969): 95–112.

Zahrnt, Heinz. *Luther deutet Geschichte.* Munich, 1952.

Zeller, Winfried. *Die Schriften Valentin Weigels: Eine literarkritische Untersuchung.* Berlin, 1940.

Zumkeller, Adolar. "Thomas Müntzer—Augustiner?" *Augustiniana* 9 (1959): 380–85.

Index

Williams, George H., viii, 15, 59, 99, 101, 106, 126, 136, 145, 152, 229
Wilms, H., 5
Wirsperger, Veyt, 120
Wiswedel, Wilhelm, 145
Worms, Diet of (1521), 68, 224

Yoder, John H., 75

Zahrnt, Heinz, 140
Zeiss, Hans, 71, 74, 78

Zeller, Winfried, 15, 56, 203, 204, 205, 208, 210, 211, 212, 223, 230, 234, 240, 244
Zschäbitz, Gerhard, 72, 103
Zumkeller, Adolar, 61
Zurkinden, Nikolaus, 39–44, 52
Zwickau prophets, 64, 72–73
Zwingli, Ulrich, 74–75, 117, 153, 156, 160, 172, 225, 237
Zwinglianism. *See* Zwingli, Ulrich